Ceanothus

Ceanothus

David Fross

&

Dieter Wilken

TIMBER PRESS

Fontispiece: *Ceanothus* 'Julia Phelps', Royal Horticultural Society Garden Wisley, England

Photographs in Part 1 by David Fross, in Part 2 by Dieter Wilken except for leaf cross sections, which are by Sherwin Carlquist. Line drawings by Marjory DeJean, Edna Russell, and Emily Patterson Thompson adapted from Van Rensselaer and McMinn's *Ceanothus* (1942) except for those of *C. bolensis, C. cuneatus* var. *fascicularis, C. ophiochilus,* and *C. roderickii,* newly drawn by Janine Beckert. Unless otherwise specified, drawings are approximately life-size except for those of the fruits, which are approximately ×2.

Published in 2006 by

TIMBER PRESS, Inc.
The Haseltine Building
133 S.W. Second Avenue, Suite 450
Portland, Oregon 97204-3527, U.S.A.
www.timberpress.com

For contact information regarding editorial, marketing, sales, and distribution in the United Kingdom, see www.timberpress.co.uk.

Printed through Colorcraft Ltd., Hong Kong

Library of Congress Cataloging-in-Publication Data

Fross, David, 1946–
    Ceanothus / David Fross and Dieter Wilken.
        p. cm.
    Includes bibliographical references and index.
    ISBN-13: 978-0-88192-762-7
    ISBN-10: 0-88192-762-7
    1. Ceanothus. I. Wilken, Dieter, 1944– II. Title.
    SB413.C4F76 2006
    635.9'3386—dc22
                                                                2005017927
A catalog record for this book is also available from the British Library.

Contents

Preface

In the early 1970s, Dieter Wilken introduced the topic of hybridization to his plant taxonomy class at Occidental College using a population of *Ceanothus crassifolius* and *C. megacarpus* in the Verdugo Mountains of Los Angeles County, California, as an example of how to analyze hybridity under natural conditions. Laboratory exercises in estimating patterns of variation were supplemented by having students read the original literature, among them publications by Howard McMinn and Malcolm Nobs. The exercises and discussions were among the highlights of the class, at least from the perspective of the instructor, and served as a model for later ones taught at other institutions. Botanical forays in the Rocky Mountains and the Southwest brought further attention to geographical variation in other species of *Ceanothus*, most notably in what had been called *C. greggii* (included in *C. pauciflorus* here).

In the early 1990s, recollections of these and other problems in *Ceanothus* were shared with John Thomas Howell over occasional lunches and sometimes tea at the California Academy of Sciences in San Francisco. Tom Howell kindly shared his own observations, including questions and comments he had addressed in a series of papers published on *Ceanothus* in the journal *Leaflets of Western Botany.* His remarkable knowledge and memory of unresolved problems, combined with enthusiasm and a genuine interest in sharing ideas, served as a lasting inspiration.

In 1983, David Fross accompanied a group of botanists along the coastal terraces above Arroyo de la Cruz in northern San Luis Obispo County to view a center of localized California endemic plants found on the Hearst Ranch. Cliff Schmidt was working on a treatment of *Ceanothus* for the then forthcoming *Jepson Manual* and had asked Austin Griffiths, David Keil, Malcolm McCloud, and Dave to join him as he considered *C. maritimus* and *C. hearstiorum*. The conversation that February morning was captivating, the discussion ranging from the effects of cattle grazing on these low-growing species to the nature of speciation and plant migration.

Austin Griffiths and Dave collected cuttings from many individuals of *Ceanothus maritimus* and *C. hearstiorum*. They argued the horticultural merits of the different forms and compared the nuances of foliage and flower color as they moved slowly up the slope. Two cultivars resulted from these collections and were introduced into the nursery trade some years later as *C. maritimus* 'Frosty Dawn' and 'Point Sierra'. The experience among these species that day focused Dave's interest in the genus, and Native Sons nursery was soon growing a much wider selection. For a period of years in the 1980s, the best-selling plants at the nursery were *C. thyrsiflorus* var. *griseus* 'Yankee Point' and the hybrids 'Dark Star' and 'Ray Hartman'.

As the genus increased in economic significance for the business, Dave's curiosity about the origin of *Ceanothus* selections, cultivar development, and garden tolerance led to further investigation. He quickly was led to the seminal *Ceanothus* treatment by Maunsell Van Rensselaer and Howard McMinn. *Ceanothus,* the book published in 1942 by the Santa Barbara Botanic Garden, is a classic treatment of the genus and is the model for our own book. Much has been learned in the more than 60 years since it was published. As stated in the preface of the original book, "The purpose of this volume is to provide a working manual of ceanothus for both the botanist and horticulturist." We divide our book as Van Rensselaer and McMinn did, into two parts. Part 1, primarily Dave's responsibility, is a horticultural treatment of the genus intended for gardeners, nursery people, and landscape professionals, and it includes a horticultural evaluation of the species as well as a complete account of the numerous cultivars that have been developed and that play such an important role in the cultivation of ceanothus. Part 2, Dieter's responsibility, is intended for taxonomists and other students of plant biodiversity, and it provides a botanical perspective, benefiting from the more extensive collections and field observations made since the original book was published.

After submission of the manuscript to Timber Press, we found a report by Maunsell Van Rensselaer in the Santa Barbara Botanic Garden archives. It is a detailed account of his travels through the Monterey Peninsula, San Francisco Bay Region, and Yosemite National Park, April 20–29, 1938. His itinerary included wild populations of *Ceanothus* in the field and visits to nurseries, gardens, and herbaria. Along the way, he met and spoke with botanical luminaries such as Alice Eastwood, Herbert Mason, Howard McMinn, Carl Wolf, and John Thomas Howell about *Ceanothus.* The stated purpose of his trip was "to gather all possible data on the botany and culture of Ceanothus." Reading Van Rensselaer's report evoked fond memories of the travels and discussions that inform our book, and reminded us of the respect for and purpose of our joint effort: to advance the knowledge of *Ceanothus.*

Acknowledgments

We could not have completed this book without the generous support and counsel of a diverse group of friends and colleagues. We gratefully acknowledge and especially thank

Howard McMinn and Maunsell Van Rensselaer, and the standard they set by their work;

field and garden companions Michael Barry, Carol Bornstein, Cort Conley, Mike Curto, Greg Donovan, Tom Eltzroth, Dara Emery, Olivier Filippi, Blair Fross, Tim Fross, Austin Griffiths, I. S. Hodson, Gerda Isenberg, Yves Jarreau, Robert Keeffe, Sandra Landers, Barry Lopez, Judith Lowry, Roger Raiche, Wayne Roderick, Jennifer Scarano, Cliff Schmidt, Jake Sigg, and Philip Van Soelen, for the insight of their observations;

Steve Boyd, Bruce Delgado, Barbara Ertter, Holly Forbes, Jim Henrickson, Michael Honer, Tom Howell, Jon Keeley, Steve Junak, Elizabeth Painter, John Sawyer, Cliff Schmidt, Jim Shevock, John Strother, Tom van Devender, Gary Wallace, Margriet Wetherwax, and Vern Yadon, who each, in his or her own way, provided help, guidance, and constructive criticism on a wide array of ecological and taxonomic issues;

Jonathan Beacon, Howard Brown, Barbara Coe, Steven Edwards, Lorrae Fuentes, Barry Lehrman, Bart O'Brien, Warren Roberts, M. Nevin Smith, Ken Taylor, Matt Teel, and Ellen Zagory, for clarification and assistance with the cultivar stories;

Laurie Hannah, Isabelle Sterling, Bea Beck, and Barbara Hellenthal, for their kind guidance with library and herbarium research;

Neil Lucas, who provided an informed and essential British perspective;

Sherwin Carlquist, for securing photomicrographs and sharing his knowledge and thoughts on parts of the text;

Janine Beckert, for new illustrations of *Ceanothus bolensis, C. cuneatus* var. *fascicularis, C. ophiochilus,* and *C. roderickii;*

the staff of Native Sons nursery for covering in their colleague's absence and growing more selections of *Ceanothus* than practical;

the staff and trustees of the Santa Barbara Botanic Garden for their understanding and encouragement;

the many other gardeners, botanists, horticulturists, maintenance professionals, students, and landscape contractors who have shared their experiences and knowledge. Our debt here is large and speaks to the willing and charitable nature of those involved with horticulture, ecology, and taxonomy;

and our wives, Rainie and Beth, for sensitive editing and the depth of their support.

PART 1

Ceanothus in the Garden and Landscape

Plants in the genus *Ceanothus* are known by a number of common names, including wild lilac, mountain lilac, California lilac, blueblossom, and buckbrush. The genus name itself is also used as a common name: "ceanothuses" is the traditional plural form though it is not uncommon to see "ceanothus" treated that way, too.

Blue, the rarest color in nature, is primary. The color of desire, melancholy, and Levi's jeans, it is ripe with emotion and contradiction—sorrow, loneliness, and the brooding blue-black sky of Vincent van Gogh's *Crows Flying over a Cornfield*—but also hope, introspection, and serenity. Sought by gardeners to cool and settle the landscape, blue affords a soothing pause and depth to the garden. *Ceanothus* offers an abundance of blue, "the color of all colors" as Pablo Picasso said. Each spring, tints and shades of azure, cobalt, indigo, and cerulean surface in the chaparral of California as if to offer a new name for the Golden State. Madder blue, milk-blue, and lavender, and then there are the blues of the sea—aqua, ultramarine, and a hue found only in the Sea of Cortés. The genus includes plants with flowers of each of these colors, and more: cyanine, sky-blue, and the flinty hues of slate.

Beyond this wealth and range of flower color, *Ceanothus* offers the gardener a remarkable selection of enduring, functional shrubs and ground covers suitable for a comprehensive variety of garden and landscape situations. In California, they are frequently used as screens, specimens, and patio trees but are best known as indispensable ground covers on dry banks and slopes. British gardeners have long espaliered *Ceanothus* on south-facing walls to shelter plants through cold winters, and included the plants in mixed borders with perennials, grasses, and other flowering shrubs. Large specimens are found woven through woodland gardens in French landscapes, and some selections are carefully trained up courtyard trellises in a fashion North American gardeners rarely attempt. Along the northern border of the Mediterranean Sea in Italy, France, and Spain, *Ceanothus* can be found defining a garden axis, or planted for transition to the garrigue, the European equivalent of chaparral.

Although *Ceanothus* offers the gardener a range of durable habits and forms suit-

Ceanothus maritimus 'Frosty Dawn', Fross garden, Arroyo Grande, California

Ceanothus 'Gentian Plume', Santa Barbara Botanic Garden, California

able in landscapes from Brittany to California, it is the extraordinary variety of blue flowers that continues to draw attention to the genus. Cultivar selection since the mid-20th century has intensified color and clarity in plants, enhancing their appeal. New colors include a blue as sheer as silver and as dark as a crepuscular sky, and a dusky pink turning blue again and pale unlike anything known from the sky. And as if these new colors were not quite enough, horticulturists continue to look for new tints in the wild and evaluate intriguing hybrids that germinate in gardens and nurseries.

Natural Distribution

Ceanothus is a North American genus found across much of the temperate areas of the continent. Species occupy an astonishing range of environments, from subtropical rain forests in southern Mexico to the open woodlands of the eastern United States, and from snow-covered ridges in the mountains of the West to windswept coastal bluffs. This diversity of habitats has resulted in a wide array of morphological and ecological adaptations from which a startling assortment of horticultural variety has been selected.

Although the genus ranges widely across North America, it is concentrated in the

Ceanothus thyrsiflorus var. *griseus*, Big Sur, California

western portions of the continent and centered in the Mediterranean climatic core of California. The concentration of *Ceanothus* species in California is part of the unique distribution pattern that characterizes the entire flora of the state. Diverse habitats result from the varied climatic, topographic, and edaphic features found in the state, and species endemism is common in a number of genera found in the California Floristic Province. *Ceanothus* has evolved in this complex floristic area, responding to the changing environmental gradients with a rich array of species and varieties, many of which have restricted natural distributions.

California's diverse physical and climatic features provide a multitude of habitats suitable for the genus *Ceanothus*. Species occupy many different ecological niches, and a range of morphological forms has resulted from this diversity. Mat-forming species of *Ceanothus* can be found growing on the foggy, exposed headlands just above the Pacific Ocean, or in shallow soils on exposed ridges in the Coast Ranges. Arborescent forms are found in the closed-cone pine forests of the Channel Islands or woven into the complex, mixed chaparral communities of the Santa Lucia Range. Rigid, thorny varieties occur in desert woodlands at the edge of the Mojave Desert or laced together in pure stands of *Ceanothus* chaparral a few miles from the civic center of Los Angeles.

There are 50 species of *Ceanothus* in North America, 41 of which are found in California. Restricted natural distributions are common. For example, *C. hearstiorum* and

C. maritimus occur together exclusively on the coastal terraces of the Hearst property in northern San Luis Obispo County. *Ceanothus ferrisiae* grows on a few acres in Santa Clara County at the base of the Mount Hamilton Range, and *C. arboreus* is limited to Guadalupe Island, Mexico, and three of the Channel Islands off the coast of southern California. Wide-ranging species, such as *C. cuneatus, C. leucodermis,* and *C. spinosus,* occupy a broad spectrum of habitats. They inhabit large areas from San Diego County to Siskiyou County yet remain within the boundaries of the Mediterranean climatic core of California. Collectively, these distribution patterns demonstrate the ecological complexity of the genus and reflect California's position as the center of distribution of the genus.

History of Cultivation

The native people of North America were the first humans to use *Ceanothus* as a resource. Uses varied regionally and by species. In California the flowers of many species served as a detergent, the inflorescence being lathered in water to remove dirt and oil. Young, flexible stems of some forms provided the circular withes for baskets, and both leaves and roots offered medicinal remedies for a variety of ailments. Eastern groups used the roots and leaves, preparing a tea-like beverage that was consumed by the colonists during the Revolutionary War as a substitute for English tea.

Ceanothus thyrsiflorus var. *griseus* 'Santa Ana', Rancho Santa Ana Botanic Garden, California

The long cultural association of native people with the genus likely led to other uses. This may have been as simple as the seasonal signal of the flowering, leading to a deeper spiritual connection to place and regional identity. Perhaps flowers were cut for ornament or used in spring ceremonies. Young children may have developed hunting skills by catching the wide range of pollinating insects that frequent the spring flowers. Surely the blue flowers and strong scents evoked a response not unlike that of gardeners who covet the plants today. Native people taught the Franciscan monks of the California missions the cleansing properties of *Ceanothus* flowers, and though there are records indicating the padres' appreciation for the beauty of the plants, there is little record of their use as ornamentals in mission gardens. It is difficult to imagine, however, the missionaries not attempting to cultivate the many different species found in the hills surrounding their settlements.

The extraordinary diversity in both flower color and form led naturally to horticultural interest by Europeans as they explored North America. Horticultural evaluation began as early as 1713 with the introduction of *Ceanothus americanus* to Europe. This common species could be found growing in many of the original American colonies. It did not, however, gain favor in Europe as a garden subject and might have been of little horticultural importance beyond novelty were it not for the discovery of *C. caeruleus* from Mexico.

Ceanothus caeruleus is a large-leaved shrub with brilliant blue flowers that was discovered in south-central Mexico a century after the introduction of *C. americanus* into Europe. This new species offered Europeans bold blue colors that were lacking in the two white-flowered species, *C. americanus* and *C. herbaceus* (then called *C. ovatus*) common to eastern North America, but *C. caeruleus* lacked the hardiness necessary to endure winters in European gardens. After its introduction into Europe in 1818, a series of hybrids were developed combining the desirable traits of all three species. *Ceanothus americanus* and *C. herbaceus* provided hardiness and a larger leaf size while *C. caeruleus* offered a palette of blue colors from which breeders selected a range of hues from violet to pink. Most of these early breeding efforts took place in French and Belgian nurseries before 1830, and the resulting crosses were named *C. ×delilianus*— 'Gloire de Versailles' is perhaps the best known. The French continued to develop beautifully named hybrids from this cross through the remainder of the 19th

Ceanothus ×delilianus 'Gloire de Versailles' on a wall, Richmond Hill, England

century. Unfortunately, most have been lost through the years, and we are left, in many cases, with only the compelling cultivar names and our imagination.

Ceanothus thyrsiflorus, blueblossom, was the first of the California species to receive both botanical and horticultural recognition. It was during the Russian expedition on the *Rurik,* under the command of Otto von Kotzebue, that ship botanist Adelbert von Chamisso and his companion, ship doctor Johann Friedrich Gustav von Eschscholtz, collected plants. Among the collections, from a brief visit to San Francisco in October 1816, was the first of a California *Ceanothus* species. *Ceanothus thyrsiflorus* would not have been flowering heavily in October, yet it is still possible to imagine Chamisso and Eschscholtz attracted to sporadic clusters of blue flowers in the autumn light.

The Royal Horticultural Society of England received seeds of *Ceanothus thyrsiflorus* from Richard Brinsley Hinds, surgeon-naturalist on the expedition of H.M.S. *Sulphur,* in 1837, making it the first California species introduced into European gardens. It remains common in British gardens to this day, with a number of cultivars. One of these, 'El Dorado', was introduced in 2002 into North American cultivation from the Pershore College of Horticulture. 'El Dorado' is a variegated sport selected from a stem found on 'Zanzibar'. 'Zanzibar' is a variegated sport discovered growing on a specimen of *C. thyrsiflorus* in a local garden near the college. Thus from the original seed sent to England in 1837, *C. thyrsiflorus* has returned to California in the variegated 'El Dorado'.

Ceanothus thyrsiflorus var. *thyrsiflorus* 'El Dorado', Fross garden, Arroyo Grande, California

The intriguing material reaching England from California early in the 19th century persuaded the Royal Horticultural Society to send a young Scotsman, David Douglas, to the West Coast of North America in search of "any interesting plants or seeds he found." Douglas became famous for his collecting efforts, adding a wealth of new plants to horticulture during his short life. His West Coast collections included a number of species, including *Ceanothus dentatus, C. incanus, C. integerrimus,* and *C. papillosus.* The only seed from his collections that is documented to have reached England is from *C. velutinus* collected in Oregon and Washington. The records from his time in California were lost in an unfortunate accident, and the full extent of his travels while there remains unknown.

As collecting continued in California, additional samples were sent to England. In 1836, Thomas Nuttall found *Ceanothus megacarpus, C. oliganthus, C. rigidus, C. spinosus,* and *C. verrucosus.* His collections were of pressed samples but did not include seed. Learning of this, a German plant collector working for the Horticultural Society of London, Karl Theodor Hartweg, traveled in California in the 1840s, collecting seeds of *C. cuneatus, C. dentatus,* and *C. rigidus* among other plants. The seeds added to the English collections and fueled horticultural interest in the genus. Evaluation of these new species in British nurseries led to many fine selections such as *C. arboreus* 'Trewithen Blue' and the hybrids 'Cynthia Postan' and 'Edinburgh'.

These early collections created enough horticultural attention to justify Veitch nurseries' employment of a collector. Their choice, William Lobb, was sent in 1849 to gather *Ceanothus* specimens and seeds in California. He collected extensively from 1849 to 1863 and managed to acquire a number of new species as well as to secure seeds of previously discovered species. Among the many plants he sent to England were *C. floribundus* (now considered a synonym of *C. dentatus*), *C. ×lobbianus, C. papillosus,* and *C. ×veitchianus. Ceanothus ×veitchianus* became a popular and widely cultivated evergreen shrub in British gardens, remaining a favorite to this day. Interestingly, this intersubgeneric hybrid—*C. thyrsiflorus* var. *griseus* (subgenus *Ceanothus*) × *C. cuneatus* var. *rigidus* (subgenus *Cerastes*)—from the Monterey area has only been found

Ceanothus foliosus var. *medius,* Leaning Pine Arboretum, California Polytechnic University, San Luis Obispo

in the wild since on rare occasions and remains a testament to William Lobb's expertise as a collector.

Discoveries in California continued sporadically to the end of the 19th century with Edward Lee Greene collecting *Ceanothus arboreus* from Santa Cruz Island, Sara A. Plummer gathering *C. impressus* from Burton Mesa in northern Santa Barbara County, and Charles C. Parry finding both *C. foliosus* and *C. parryi*. Interestingly, Parry first found *C. parryi* in a garden near Calistoga. *Ceanothus arboreus* was not cultivated until 1908, and *C. impressus* found its way into gardens in 1934, almost 50 years after its discovery when it was first offered by Calles Nursery of Lompoc.

Ceanothus 'Concha', churchyard, New Milton, England

In California, recognition of the horticultural value of the genus was left to 20th century plantsmen and plantswomen. Pioneer nurseryman Theodore Payne was the first to grow and sell *Ceanothus*, in his Los Angeles nursery. His enthusiastic advocacy and interest in the garden application of California's flora helped focus attention on the genus. This awareness was part of a general awakening to the horticultural wealth of the California flora, and the first expression of the use of California native plants in the gardens of the state.

Howard E. McMinn began the first living collection of *Ceanothus* on the campus of Mills College in Oakland, intent on adding "to the botanical and horticultural knowledge of the genus" (Van Rensselaer 1942). Hundreds of seedlings were transplanted to the gardens of Mills College for observation between 1923 and 1928. From these trials came invaluable information regarding garden performance, growth rate, longevity, and maintenance requirements. This initial testing helped to popularize the genus and influenced the spectrum of cultivars available today.

During this same period, Lester Rowntree, an extraordinary horticulturist and field botanist, traveled widely throughout California, gleaning seeds and eagerly distributing them to nursery people and gardeners. Her collecting efforts, informed writings, and contagious enthusiasm helped expand the number of species of *Ceanothus* used in California gardens. Her Carmel Highlands home also served as a test site for the specimens she gathered from the wild, providing a living laboratory for her thoughtful opinions about the use of the genus in the landscape.

Collecting and discovery continued through the 1920s and 1930s, resulting in additional introductions of promising and unusual specimens. In 1923 McMinn discovered *Ceanothus masonii* (included here with *C. gloriosus*) in Marin County, and a few years later Milo Baker found *C. sonomensis* in Sonoma County. In Santa Barbara County, E. Denys Rowe located and introduced *C. papillosus* var. *roweanus* (now considered only a compact form of the species), and *C. gloriosus* var. *porrectus* was discovered in Marin County by James B. Roof and Louis L. Edmunds. Each discovery helped stimulate interest in the genus.

McMinn's collecting and taxonomic work led to the classic book on the subject, *Ceanothus,* by Maunsell Van Rensselaer and McMinn, published in 1942 by the Santa

Ceanothus 'Dark Star', private garden, Santa Barbara, California

Barbara Botanic Garden. Van Rensselaer's part, "Ceanothus for Gardens, Parks and Roadsides," was the first attempt to evaluate the entire genus from a horticultural perspective and helped focus attention on the landscape and garden potential of the genus.

Hybrids found in nurseries and gardens began to appear in the nursery trade after the Second World War. 'Concha' from Bee Line Nursery and 'Ray Hartman' from Leonard Coates Nurseries are two classics from this period and remain standards in the industry today. Other nurseries added to the hybrids entering the nursery trade. Louis Edmunds, an eminent California nurseryman, introduced 'Blue Cloud' in the 1940s, which was followed by an equally respected nurseryman, Ken Taylor, and his popular garden hybrid 'Dark Star'.

California's distinguished botanical gardens actively selected, evaluated, and introduced both garden hybrids and selected clones of *Ceanothus* from the wild during this dynamic period of cultivar development. Rancho Santa Ana Botanic Garden in Claremont introduced a number of hybrids, including 'Blue Jeans' in 1963 and 'Blue Cascade' and 'Sierra Snow' in 1979. Santa Barbara Botanic Garden introduced the hybrids 'Far Horizons' and 'Wheeler Canyon' in the 1970s, and the Regional Parks Botanic Garden in Berkeley selected and introduced *C. cuneatus* var. *ramulosus* 'Rodeo Marin' in 1986 and the hybrid 'Tilden Park' in 1991. This legacy of cultivar development continues today with introductions such as *C. tomentosus* var. *olivaceus* 'Cielo' from Rancho Santa Ana Botanic Garden and *C. arboreus* 'Powder Blue' from Santa Barbara Botanic Garden.

Ceanothus thyrsiflorus var. *griseus* 'Yankee Point', Mission Oaks, Santa Ynez, California

Saratoga Horticultural Research Foundation, originally located in Saratoga and later in San Martin, California, was also instrumental in the development of some of the most popular ceanothuses in the trade. Its evaluations and introductions include the hybrid 'Julia Phelps' in 1952, *Ceanothus thyrsiflorus* var. *griseus* (at the time called *C. griseus* var. *horizontalis*) 'Yankee Point' in 1958, and the hybrid 'Joyce Coulter' in 1962. All remain popular in the California landscape trade and are common in gardens.

Additional horticultural efforts by individuals, nurseries, botanical gardens, and other institutions toward the close of the 20th century resulted in an array of interesting *Ceanothus* cultivars. Roger Raiche, formerly with the University of California Botanical Garden in Berkeley, selected and introduced the hybrid 'Centennial' and *C. thyrsiflorus* var. *griseus* 'Kurt Zadnik'. Native Sons nursery in Arroyo Grande collected a number of clones of *C. maritimus* from Arroyo de la Cruz in San Luis Obispo County, resulting in the introduction of 'Frosty Dawn' and 'Point Sierra'. Horticulturist and respected nurseryman M. Nevin Smith introduced the unique *C. foliosus* 'Berryhill' and *C. impressus* var. *impressus* 'Vandenberg' in the 1980s. Phil Van Soelen of California Flora Nursery in Fulton discovered a rare intersubgeneric hybrid—*C. thyrsiflorus* var. *griseus* (subgenus *Ceanothus*) × *C. gloriosus* (subgenus *Cerastes*)—near Salt Point in Sonoma County that he named 'Coronado' and introduced in 1991. He later added the low-growing *C. gloriosus* var. *gloriosus* 'Heart's Desire' into the trade.

Growing Ceanothus

Ceanothus is best suited to gardens where conditions match or approach those of where the plants are found in the wild. In many of the native California habitats of *Ceanothus* there are a number of ecological similarities, whether plants grow on the coastal bluffs of Mendocino County, sandstone ridges of the Santa Lucia Range, or brushy slopes above the San Gabriel Valley. In all these sites, the soils drain well and the summers are dry. *Ceanothus* grows in a range of soil types but often is found on steep slopes in soils with low or marginal fertility. Nitrogen-fixing bacteria are found in nodules on their wide-spreading roots, helping the plants adapt to dry, nutrient-poor conditions. Considering their natural habitats, it is not surprising that most California species will endure long periods of drought, are intolerant of summer-wet environments, and require little or no fertilization when planted in gardens.

Many of the selections originating from California species can be grown successfully outside their native habitats and have demonstrated broad cultural tolerances particularly in regions that are cooler and moister than the Mediterranean climate portions of California. British gardeners have long used a diverse range of evergreen and deciduous cultivars as specimens, screens, and ground covers. *Ceanothus* is frequently espaliered along south-facing walls and included in the perennial borders of England, Ireland, and northern France. Species and cultivars are typically longer-lived and grow larger in these environments than is typical in California gardens.

Other areas with moderate winter temperatures, like the Pacific Northwest of North America, and New Zealand, have been successful growing selected evergreen cultivars such as the hybrids 'Concha', 'Edinburgh', and 'Skylark'. In the eastern United States, *Ceanothus americanus* has been valuable in woodland gardens and tolerates drier conditions than many other woodland shrubs. The deciduous hybrids, such as *C.* ×*delilianus* 'Gloire de Versailles' and *C.* ×*pallidus* 'Marie Simon' are also effective in the warmer portions of the eastern United States or with frost protection in colder regions.

Most cultivated species and hybrids originated in the Mediterranean climate portion of California with its extended summer drought. The length and severity of this seasonal drought is moderated in the northern portion of the state by a shorter rainless period, and in coastal areas by persistent summer fog that reduces the evapotranspiration rates of plants found in those habitats. Species that occur at higher elevations receive some dry-season moisture from occasional summer thunderstorms, but as a group, most California species receive little or no precipitation when evapotranspiration rates are highest, in summer.

The primary requirement for garden success with these plants is a well-drained soil. Numerous fungal organisms (water molds, rots, and wilts such as *Fusarium*, *Phoma*, *Phytophthora*, *Rhizoctonia*, and *Vertcillium dahliae*) damage or kill plants in poorly drained soils. Frequent summer irrigation and warm soil temperatures favor these pathogens. Occasional summer watering is accept-

Ceanothus impressus var. *nipomensis* trained on a wall, private garden, England

able for established plantings and may improve the appearance of most selections, but soils should be allowed to dry between waterings.

Most *Ceanothus* species and cultivars follow a similar pattern of growth and flowering. During their first few years, plants grow rapidly and flowering is modest. This is typically followed by a period of slower growth with exceedingly heavy flower production. From 7 to 12 years in age, they continue to flower but with less profusion, and the size of the flower clusters decreases in a number of cultivars. Plant structure often begins to open during this period, and specimens develop a more pronounced woody character. This is a generalized time line, and it may vary, depending on the site, species, or cultivar. Gardening practices also influence plant development. In favorable sites, many cultivars and species will continue living many years.

The reputation of *Ceanothus* as short-lived is often based on poor site selection rather than an inherent problem with the genus. Poorly drained soils combined with frequent summer irrigation will kill plants in a few years. Some species and cultivars, such as *C. hearstiorum* and the hybrid 'Dark Star', are naturally shorter-lived than other selections. *Ceanothus arboreus* and *C. thyrsiflorus* var. *griseus,* however, can live 25 years or more in a garden setting. Most of the California species (and resulting cultivars) have evolved in fire-active plant communities such as chaparral and coastal scrub. These communities are subject to periodic fires that remove senescent stands, activate the dormant seed bank, and cover the charred earth with fresh young seedlings. In

Ceanothus ×*pallidus* 'Marie Simon', Knoll Gardens, Dorset, England

their native habitats, many species lose vigor and decline as they age, based on an evolved adaptation to fire or as part of community succession. This natural successional process renews the older stands in rhythmic fire cycles that might have 20-, 35-, or 50-year cadences.

In addition to its stunning spring flowers, *Ceanothus* fulfills many practical landscape and garden requirements. The broad diversity found in the genus offers a multitude of sizes and forms from which to choose. Larger selections are useful as quick screens, growing to 10 feet tall or more in a few years, or as solitary specimens. They can serve equally well as small trees or even formal hedges when properly and routinely pruned. With detailed attention they can also be espaliered on walls or fences. Medium-sized shrubs are useful as informal hedges, and with knowledgeable cultivar selection flowering can extend from winter to midsummer. Many new ground-cover selections have been added since the 1980s to an existing palette of well-known favorites. They range from low, creeping types like the hybrid 'Centennial', suitable for use in the dappled shade of a woodland garden, to large, sprawling forms like *C. thyrsiflorus* var. *griseus* (at the time called *C. griseus* var. *horizontalis*) 'Yankee Point', com-

Ceanothus foliosus var. *medius* following fire, Cuesta Ridge, San Luis Obispo County, California

monly used to cover sunny, south-facing slopes. Some of these lower-growing types are useful in rock gardens or spilling over walls. Although uncommon and labor intensive, a number of ceanothuses can be pruned into small hedges or trained to climb a trellis.

An annual trimming of the new growth will maintain a more compact form and improve the appearance of most species. The removal of spent flowers and fruit improves the vigor of many cultivars and will produce a tidier form. Taller species can be trained into small trees with early pruning, and the removal of interior dead wood as plants age produces a cleaner appearance. Once this arborescent character is achieved it is easily maintained and requires minimal effort. Shearing for hedges and formal effect is tolerated by most species and cultivars if cutting into woody tissue is avoided. Prune immediately after flowering, and only back to the new year's flush of growth.

Fast-growing selections sited in fertile soils and receiving typical garden irrigation can be subject to "wind rock," especially in winter. Specimens become sail-like and blow over in the wind. This contributes to the reputation of the genus as short-lived. Pruning the young stems to reduce size, encourage a denser form, and reduce the amount of available water may help avert this problem. Heavy pruning into woody tis-

Ceanothus 'Concha' topiary, Monterey, California

Ceanothus thyrsiflorus var. *thyrsiflorus* 'Snow Flurry', Long Beach, California

sue can lead to branch dieback, which is caused by the fungal disease apricot dieback (*Eutypa armeniacae*). Air-borne spores spread this pathogen primarily during the rainy season, and entry to the plant is gained through open wounds that expose xylem tissue. Heavy pruning with multiple cuts provides the ideal condition for the disease and should be avoided especially during the rainy season. If the disease is present, remove the infected wood well below any cankers and close the wound with a sealing compound. Always disinfect pruning tools after working with diseased specimens.

Ceanothus attracts myriad insects. Many are beneficial and significantly improve garden habitats. Bees, both native and domestic, and other pollinating insects cloud the plants when in bloom, and the larval forms of a number of butterflies and moths use *Ceanothus* species for food. Ceanothus silk moth, California tortoiseshell, California hairstreak, and artful dusky wing skipper are just a few of the California native insects that depend on the genus. Some farm operations have begun using *Ceanothus* species in windrows to attract beneficial predatory insects as part of integrated pest management programs. As a result, birds are attracted to these insect populations and use *Ceanothus* for cover. Quail, rabbits, chipmunks, and ground squirrels consume the small hard seeds, and many other animals use the shelter they provide.

Disease and Pests

Insect pests can pose a number of problems for *Ceanothus* in garden settings if left uncontrolled. Aphids, mealybug, scale, and whitefly are the most common and can disfigure and distort populations. Stem gall moth (*Periploca ceanothiella*) can pose a potentially serious problem in some regions of California. Swollen stems and branches indicate the presence of larvae that will often girdle the distal portion of the infected tissue. Portions of the state are relatively free of the pest, while in other areas it would be prudent to avoid the use of the preferred larger-leaved species in subgenus *Ceanothus* such as *C. thyrsiflorus* var. *griseus* and *C. arboreus*. Environmentally friendly

Ceanothus subg. *Ceanothus,* clockwise from upper left: *C. thyrsiflorus* var. *griseus* 'Yankee Point', 'Dark Star', *C. hearstiorum, C. arboreus* 'Cliff Schmidt', *C. thyrsiflorus* var. *thyrsiflorus* 'Snow Flurry', and 'Concha'

Ceanothus subg. *Cerastes,* left to right: 'Blue Jeans', *C. cuneatus* var. *ramulosus* 'Rodeo Lagoon', *C. gloriosus, C. maritimus* 'Frosty Dawn', and *C. cuneatus* var. *rigidus* 'Snowball'

controls are not available, but close monitoring of irrigation and fertilization to prevent off-season (summer–fall) flushes of growth will help avoid serious damage.

Boring insects are a potentially serious problem. Sycamore borer (*Synanthedon resplendens*) and Pacific flatheaded borer (*Chrysobothris mali*) are particularly widespread. Shallow, irregular mines or burrows just under the bark of the main trunk or larger branches indicate these pests (Dreistadt et al. 1994). The area above the burrow is dark-colored and often has sap exuding from the wound. If left untreated, borers will usually kill the plants; a systemic insecticide is the only effective control. Early detection and treatment will moderate the problem. Like stem gall moth, the occurrence of borers has a regional pattern and is problematic in some areas yet uncommon in others.

Deer present a challenge when gardening with *Ceanothus* as they often browse heavily on plants, often deforming or even killing young plants. Large-leaved species and cultivars of subgenus *Ceanothus* are particularly subject to deer predation. Some of the smaller-leaved types, and those of subgenus *Cerastes,* are less likely to attract deer, but any will be eaten when fresh from nursery containers or during periods when other browse material is scarce. Protection of young plants is strongly recommended in deer-prone areas. After establishment, deer are less likely to kill the plants but will browse lightly even on older, well-established plants. Mice, rabbits, and rats can also be a problem, especially with young plantings, which may require protection.

The numerous fungal organisms that attack *Ceanothus* in the garden are usually a result of moist conditions common in many summer gardens. Summer moisture provides a favorable environment for these pathogens. One strategy that can limit or prevent these problems in the landscape is the selection of resistant species and cultivars, careful irrigation, and the recognition that in some situations another plant might be more appropriate. Inappropriate spacing of ground-cover selections can create two problems commonly encountered in large-scale plantings. First and most obvious is planting *Ceanothus* on 3-foot centers for "quick cover." After a few years such a stand is 5 feet tall, covering walkways and climbing up the fence or adjacent vegetation. This mass then provides ideal conditions for a second problem—fungi that can cause twig and stem dieback as well as plant disfiguration. Proper spacing, appropriate cultivar selection, and a small measure of patience will prevent both problems.

Cultivar Development

Opportunities remain for additional cultivar testing and selection. Garden-tolerant plants that perform well in summer heat, such as that of interior valleys, would be desirable, as would additional selections of the delightfully fragrant and slower-growing members of subgenus *Cerastes.* Smaller shrubs and lower ground covers would be

Ceanothus 'Ray Hartman', Mission Oaks, Santa Ynez, California

suitable for the smaller gardens typical of new housing developments, as many popular selections of *Ceanothus* are simply too large for many residential gardens. Most hybrids common in the nursery trade are a result of crosses that would not have occurred outside of garden or nursery conditions and that would not be possible in the wild. Intentional hybridization holds enormous potential for new cultivar development, although little has been achieved to that end as yet.

Propagation

Most ceanothuses are readily propagated from seed, and many can be grown successfully from cuttings. Cultivar development since the 1950s has focused most commercial efforts on cutting propagation. Restoration practitioners, botanical gardens, collectors, and some native nurseries concerned with site specificity and the genetic diversity of wild populations favor seed propagation.

Seed maturation depends on the weather, but fruits are typically ripe 4–8 eight weeks after flowering. Warm or hot weather hastens the ripening process and should be monitored carefully near the time of expected maturation. Check fruits for ripeness as the color begins to change from ruby or burgundy to dull brown or black. Collect

Ceanothus tomentosus var. olivaceus 'Cielo', Fross garden, Arroyo Grande, California

fruit into a closed container when 2–5 percent have shattered on a specimen or in a selected population. As the fruits dry and dehisce, the seeds are projected a considerable distance. Place the drying fruit in containers or trays covered with shade cloth or fine screen to contain the seed. Seed treatment depends on the species. Fresh seed typically produces the best results. Stored seed requires scarification and in some cases stratification, especially species from higher elevations. For production purposes a hot water treatment—placing seeds in water at 180–200°F (82–93°C) and left to cool for 24 hours—is often more practical than scarification. For specific recommendations see *Seed Propagation of Native California Plants* (Emery 1988).

All *Ceanothus* species and cultivars can be propagated from cuttings, but some are very difficult. Cutting success depends on timing; semihardwood cuttings from new seasonal growth following flowering typically yield the highest rooting percentages. However, many species and cultivars can be propagated successfully most of the year though they may take significantly longer to root, and rooting percentages are typically much lower.

Softwood and hardwood cuttings may also yield satisfactory results. Softwood cuttings are quicker to root, more susceptible to fungal pathogens, and typically require a mist system to complete the rooting process. Hardwood cuttings are harvested in the least desirable season, are commonly slower to root, and yield lower rooting percentages. All cuttings should be collected from vigorous, healthy plants free of insect pests, disease, or nutrient deficiencies.

Tip cuttings typically produce roots faster and yield the highest rooting percentages. They produce greater uniformity and can be grown on to a larger container sooner. Any cutting with an axillary bud (the intersection of a leaf and stem, that is, a node) can be used as well, producing equally successful results. Cuttings are best collected in the morning when humidity is higher and temperature is lower, and processed while fresh. If storage is necessary, place the cuttings in a moist plastic bag and refrigerate. Fresh cuttings produce the greatest yield.

Ceanothus Species and Cultivars
for the Garden and Landscape

Additional information on species, including keys to varieties and subspecies when these are recognized, may be found in Part 2.

Ceanothus americanus

New Jersey tea, redroot, wild snowball

Ceanothus americanus is a wide-ranging species found across the central and eastern portions of North America from southern Canada to northern Florida. It is typically a member of shrubland, woodland, and prairie communities and is commonly seen after a disturbance such as fire. Although New Jersey tea was the first ceanothus to be cultivated—introduced into British gardens early in the 18th century—showier horticultural varieties are more commonly grown today. First described by Carl Linnaeus and named for its American origin, it was the first species of the genus to be given a scientific name. The common name New Jersey tea derives from its use as a tea substitute during the Revolutionary War.

New Jersey tea is a rounded, deciduous shrub 3–4 feet high and 5 feet wide with medium-green, ovate leaves $1^{1}/_{2}$ inches long. Dense, cylindrical, 1- to 2-inch-long clusters of fragrant, clear white flowers form on new growth from May to August, followed by purple to black fruits in July and August. Young twigs are yellow and add winter interest to the leafless plants. As with many widely ranging species, *Ceanothus americanus* is variable, and regional differences have been observed and recognized in local floras.

Cultural requirements include full sun or partial shade and soils with good drainage. One of the hardiest species in the genus, it can be grown successfully in U.S. Department of Agriculture hardiness zone 4. Although tolerant of dry conditions, plants have a fresher appearance when provided some water during summer. The plant is effective in native gardens, habitat gardens, or combined with other shrubs as an informal hedge, and it is used in restoration projects across the eastern United States.

Three distinct varieties of *Ceanothus americanus* have been recognized: *pitcheri,* a densely downy form found in the Mississippi basin; *intermedius,* with smaller leaves and found on the coastal plain of the eastern seaboard; and *americanus,* with nearly glabrous leaves.

Ceanothus arboreus

island ceanothus, felt-leaf ceanothus, Catalina ceanothus

Ceanothus arboreus is one of the tallest members of the genus. Mature specimens are capable of reaching 25–30 feet with broad, rounded crowns much like small oak trees. The leaves are equal to the largest found in the genus, to 3 inches long and $1\frac{1}{2}$ inches wide, with felted white undersides, dark slate-green surfaces, and black, gland-tipped teeth along the margins. Flowers form in lavender-pink buds and open into 4- to 6-inch-long, compound panicles of scented blossoms ranging in color from pale blue-gray to luminous hues of blue. Flowers are generally produced from late winter to early spring, but fall flowering is also common. In mild years along the coast of California, *C. arboreus* frequently blooms from October to March, the autumn flowers continuing into spring.

Island ceanothus has a long history of cultivation in both California and Europe. Introduced early in the 20th century, landscape uses included informal hedges, screening, and roadside plantings in coastal southern California. The popularity of the species faded in the 1930s as the introduction of additional species with darker blue flowers, such as *Ceanothus cyaneus*, gained favor over the pale blue colors typical of *C. arboreus*.

In Britain and Ireland, however, island ceanothus remains a popular subject due to the introduction of the darker blue-flowered 'Trewithen Blue'. Although tender in many parts of the British Isles, 'Trewithen Blue' can still be found espaliered on south-facing walls or mixed with other flowering shrubs in woodland gardens.

California gardeners have enjoyed a hybrid involving *Ceanothus arboreus* parentage since the early 1950s in much the same manner. The introduction of 'Ray Hartman', with the large arborescent habit of *C. arboreus* and radiant blue flowers of its other parent, *C. thyrsiflorus* var. *griseus*, shifted attention away from *C. arboreus*, which dropped out of the horticultural trade in California until the 1970s. A few growers and botanical gardens have renewed interest in the species in more recent years, and a number of selections are now available. In cultivation, island ceanothus prefers well-drained soils, full or partial sun, and a maritime climate but is often successfully grown away from the coast, especially in the British Isles. In California it requires protection from the hot temperatures of interior locations, whereas in Britain or Ireland a warm, south-facing wall would be practical protection against winter cold. Healthy specimens will tolerate minimum winter temperatures as low as $14\,°F$ ($-10\,°C$) for short periods. The plant is useful as a screen or specimen and is easily trained into a handsome small tree.

Island ceanothus occurs naturally on Santa Rosa, Santa Cruz, and Santa Catalina Islands in California and on Guadalupe Island off the western coast of Baja California, Mexico. On the California islands, it is a common constituent in chaparral, woodlands, and pine forests on rocky slopes and exposed ridges, where plants vary in height, 8–30 feet.

Ceanothus arboreus 'Blue Mist'
'Blue Mist' originated in the Chelsea Physic Garden and is occasionally grown in the

British Isles. It has an upright, rounded form to 15 feet tall and 12 feet wide. The leaves and light blue flowers are typical of the species.

Ceanothus arboreus 'Cliff Schmidt'

'Cliff Schmidt' is an upright selection from Santa Cruz Island made in the spring of 1983 by David Fross. In the wild it was 10 feet tall with a wide, spreading habit and had darker blue flowers than other individuals in the vicinity. It was found growing on a rocky ridge in an open forest of *Pinus muricata* var. *remorata* (Santa Cruz Island pine) with an understory of *Arctostaphylos insularis* (island manzanita).

Ceanothus arboreus 'Cliff Schmidt', Fross garden, Arroyo Grande, California

In the garden, mature plants can reach 15–20 feet high with an equal width. The broad, 2-inch-long leaves have a felted white underside and a dark glossy green surface. Fine, gland-tipped teeth subtly highlight the margin of each leaf. Young stems blush rose before turning gray with age, adding contrast to the rich green foliage. Budding flowers are milk-blue flecked with small rust-colored bracts that expand into open 5-inch-long sprays of powder-blue blossoms in early spring. Autumn flowering is common in this selection, and in some years specimens bloom from September to March or April.

Handsome and stately, 'Cliff Schmidt' is suited to coastal gardens in California that can accommodate its size. Outside California, frost sensitivity will limit its use as it is damaged at about 15°F (−9°C). When planted in warmer inland climates, it performs best with some afternoon shade or on north- and east-facing slopes. Slower growing relative to other larger-leaved species, it is longer-lived than most; 20–30 years is not uncommon.

Ceanothus arboreus 'Powder Blue'

The distinctive 'Powder Blue' features 4- to 5-inch-long clusters of pendulous, powder-blue flowers that cascade like tears down the dark green foliage. Early flowering, specimens begin to bloom by late February and frequently flower again in fall. It is smaller than typical island ceanothus, growing 6–9 feet high with a 10- to 15-foot spread. Broad, 2- to 3-inch-long leaves offer a bold texture that combines well with many fine-textured shrubs and perennials. 'Powder Blue' was selected by Carol Bornstein from a

Ceanothus arboreus 'Powder Blue', Santa Barbara Botanic Garden, California

low-growing specimen (3 feet tall in the wild) on the western end of Santa Cruz Island and was introduced by the Santa Barbara Botanic Garden in 2002.

Ceanothus arboreus 'Thundercloud'

A selection provided by the Chelsea Physic Garden to one of the National *Ceanothus* Collections held for many years at Cannington College in Somerset, England, 'Thundercloud' features light blue-gray flowers held in open panicles to 6 inches long. Upright and tree-like to 15 feet at maturity, it is suitable as a specimen, trained on walls, or as a screen.

Ceanothus arboreus 'Trewithen Blue'

'Trewithen Blue' was selected from Trewithen Gardens in Cornwall, England, and was granted the Award of Merit in 1967 and the Award of Garden Merit in 1984 by the Royal Horticultural Society. It exhibits an upright, arching habit to 15 feet tall with vivid blue flowers held in compound clusters 4–6 inches long. More recently reintroduced into the California nursery trade, 'Trewithen Blue' also remains a popular garden subject in the British Isles, where it is frequently encountered as a specimen or espaliered on walls.

Ceanothus 'A. T. Johnson'

'A. T. Johnson' is a garden hybrid selected in England early in the 20th century and named for garden writer Arthur Tysilio Johnson. An evergreen shrub with an arching, open habit to 6 feet high and 8 feet wide, it was recognized with the Award of Merit from the Royal Horticultural Society in 1934. The alternate leaves are $^1/_2$–$^3/_4$ inches long with three conspicuous veins, serrated margins, and noticeably pointed tips. Both foliage and form strongly suggest *Ceanothus thyrsiflorus* parentage. Flowers form in narrow, 2-inch-long slate-blue clusters before maturing to a flat, medium-blue.

'A. T. Johnson' is known for its dependable garden performance and second flowering period in late summer and early fall. Spring flowering is not as profuse as other selections, but gardeners are compensated with periodic blossoms through summer, particularly in cool coastal climates. The open nature of this cultivar can be improved upon with an annual pruning, to shape and clean specimens. 'A. T. Johnson' is popular in the British Isles and has more recently been reintroduced into the United States. In California, some flowers are present most of the year, with heavier blooming in spring and early fall. It is reliably hardy to 15°F (−9°C).

Ceanothus 'Autumnal Blue'

'Autumnal Blue' is a fall-blooming garden hybrid introduced early in the 20th century by Burkwood and Skipwith Nursery of London. It received the Award of Merit in 1929 and Award of Garden Merit in 1984 from the Royal Horticultural Society and is considered one of the hardiest evergreen selections available. *Ceanothus* ×*delilianus* parentage is thought to be the source of the summer to fall flowering, and the handsome dark green foliage results from *C. thyrsiflorus.*

'Autumnal Blue' features an open, upright habit to 8 feet tall with an equal spread. Slate-blue flower buds open in summer and early fall into 2$^1/_2$-inch-long clusters of lavender-blue blossoms. In California, intermittent flowering commonly occurs all year long, and occasionally, spring flowering is equal to the fall display. The ovate, three-veined leaves are 1$^1/_2$ inches long and 1 inch wide, and held on ruby-colored stems. They have a distinct, oily appearance that adds an appealing sheen to the foliage. Attractive burgundy fruits form through the season, offering a brief period of additional interest before turning dark brown, then black.

Like many other evergreen selections, 'Autumnal Blue' is best grown in full sun and well-drained soils, although it has proven remarkably tolerant of heavy soils. Light pruning after flowering will help tighten its open habit as well as remove the old fruits. More recently reintroduced into North America, the summer to fall flowers offer design opportunities with an evergreen cultivar unavailable in most other ceanothuses.

Ceanothus 'Bamico'

Horace Colby selected 'Bamico' from an open-pollinated *Ceanothus thyrsiflorus* var. *griseus* seedling found at Bamico Nursery in Pasadena, California. It was later named by Coolridge Rare Plant Gardens in the 1960s. Similar to, but smaller than *C. thyrsi-*

Ceanothus 'Bamico', Leaning Pine Arboretum, California Polytechnic University, San Luis Obispo

florus var. *griseus* 'Yankee Point', it grows to 4 feet high and 6–8 feet wide. The leaves are $3/4$–1 inch long with glossy, dark green surfaces and slightly curled margins. Cylindrical 3-inch-long panicles hold rich violet-blue flowers that open from buds with pale pink scales.

A versatile and garden-tolerant selection, 'Bamico' has demonstrated remarkable longevity in heavy soils with summer watering. The size and form—more mounding than spreading—make it suitable for smaller gardens that might be overwhelmed by *Ceanothus thyrsiflorus* var. *griseus* 'Hurricane Point' or 'Yankee Point'. It is excellent as a bank cover or when used in combination with perennials in a dry border. Adaptable to pruning and shearing, it can be grown as a low hedge or formal mound. When planted in the hotter summer temperatures of interior California, partial shade is recommended, and it is hardy to at least 15 °F (−9 °C).

Ceanothus 'Blue Buttons'
A garden hybrid of unknown parentage, 'Blue Buttons' ceanothus was selected by John Dourley and introduced by Rancho Santa Ana Botanic Garden in 1975. It appears to have characteristics of *Ceanothus oliganthus* crossed with *C. spinosus* or *C. impressus*. Dense and rigidly branched, 'Blue Buttons' grows 10–12 feet tall with an equal spread. It typically forms a single trunk with a spreading crown similar to a small coast live oak (*Quercus agrifolia*) in silhouette. The dark green, $1/4$- to $1/2$-inch-long leaves are

rounded, with a slightly wrinkled surface, and held on maroon-purple stems. Creamy green buds form along the stem in early spring and open into small, button-like heads of dusty blue flowers.

Handsome and floriferous, 'Blue Buttons' can be grown as a specimen, informal screen, or small tree. It has demonstrated excellent garden tolerance in both interior and coastal plantings in California and is useful in partial shade as well as full sun. Although it has yet to achieve significant attention from gardeners in North America or Europe, it is garden worthy for its striking form alone, and an excellent choice planted as a focal point.

Ceanothus 'Blue Cascade'

'Blue Cascade' is another of the fine hybrids originating from Rancho Santa Ana Botanic Garden. A chance garden seedling collected and named by John Dourley and introduced in 1979, it is similar in form and size to the reliable and popular hybrid 'Concha'. Parentage is unknown, but *Ceanothus papillosus* (the compact form once called variety *roweanus*) and *C. thyrsiflorus* are thought to have played a role in its origin.

Growing to 10 feet high and 16 feet wide with arching branches and a distinct mounding form, 'Blue Cascade' requires ample space to accommodate its wide, spreading habit. The flower buds have burgundy scales and open into 2-inch-long cascading spikes of radiant sky-blue blossoms that offer a luminous complement against the bright green $^3/_4$-inch-long leaves. The narrow, wrinkled foliage has an attractive polished sheen.

The impressive size of 'Blue Cascade' hinders its potential in small gardens, but it is suitable for large landscapes, parks, and roadways. Garden tolerant, it has performed well in a wide range of climates and is useful both along the coast and in the interior of California. Its rapid growth can be used to create quick screens and windbreaks, and 'Blue Cascade' combines well with other large-scale shrubs such as *Fremontodendron* 'Ken Taylor' and *Salvia leucophylla* 'Amethyst Bluff'. Hardiness has not been reliably tested, but 15°F (−9°C) can be expected.

Ceanothus 'Blue Cloud'

Prominent California native plant nurseryman Louis Edmunds selected 'Blue Cloud' in 1940 and considered it a likely cross between *Ceanothus impressus* and *C. spinosus*. A vigorous, fast-growing shrub, it grows 8–12 feet high with a slightly wider spread. The leaves are oblong to elliptic, $^1/_2$–$^3/_4$ inches long, and have a glossy surface. Mature plants are floriferous, covering the foliage with 4- to 7-inch-long compound clusters of sky-blue flowers that fade with age to a pale blue-gray. Some horticulturists consider this hybrid one of the most profusely flowering selections introduced into the nursery trade.

'Blue Cloud' is a garden-tolerant cultivar that has performed well in heavy soils and the interior heat of southern California and the Central Valley. Its rapid growth can leave the basal portions of the plants open, but this is easily alleviated with foreground plantings. Although only occasionally available, 'Blue Cloud' is worth the effort to locate, as it accurately lives up to its name, filling the garden with a billowing blue cloud in early spring.

Ceanothus 'Blue Cushion'

'Blue Cushion' was selected by Louis Edmunds at his Danville, California, nursery and introduced into the landscape trade in 1958. A garden hybrid, parentage is thought to be *Ceanothus dentatus* crossed with a low-growing form of *C. thyrsiflorus* var. *thyrsiflorus* (previously called variety *repens*). It features a compact, arching habit to 3 feet tall with a 5- to 8-foot spread. Abundant pale blue flowers form in button-like clusters from late winter to the middle of spring. The dark, evergreen leaves are $^1/_2$–$^3/_4$ inches long and have finely serrated margins.

'Blue Cushion' is a commonly used plant in British gardens but is seldom grown in California. Its smaller size and compact habit are useful in landscapes with limited space. The rounded form is effective mixed in dry borders with other California natives such as *Salvia* 'Bee's Bliss', *Eriogonum fasciculatum* 'Theodore Payne', and *Leymus condensatus* 'Canyon Prince', or fronting gray-foliaged plants such as *Constancea nevinii*

Ceanothus 'Blue Cushion', Royal Horticultural Society Garden Wisley, England

(formerly *Eriophyllum nevinii*) 'Canyon Silver'. Hardy to at least 15°F (−9°C), it does best in full sun and well-drained soils.

Ceanothus 'Blue Jeans'

'Blue Jeans' originated as a seedling found at Rancho Santa Ana Botanic Garden in 1951, the progeny of seed presented to the garden by Louis Edmunds as *Ceanothus purpureus*. Clearly a hybrid, it was later named by John Dourley and introduced in 1979. Vigorous and fast growing, it can reach 7 feet tall with an equal spread in just a few years. Stiff, arching branches diverge from the base, creating a vase-shaped or fountain-like form. The dark, olive-green leaves are leathery, $^{1}/_{2}$ inch long, with serrated margins and a distinctive, flattened tip. In early spring, sprays of violet, diamond-shaped buds line the stems, opening into lavender-blue blossoms.

The medium size and graceful form of 'Blue Jeans' is valuable in residential gardens as an informal or natural hedge. Combined with Mediterranean shrubs such as *Artemisia* (sagebrush), *Cistus* (rockrose), and *Lavandula* (lavender), or other California natives such as *Salvia leucophylla* (purple sage) and *Leymus condensatus* 'Canyon Prince', it provides early-season flowers in a water-conserving garden. It is a good option in landscapes frequented by deer, although it is not deer-proof. Garden and drought tolerant, it is hardy to 10°F (−12°C) and does best in full sun.

Ceanothus 'Blue Mound'

'Blue Mound' is an open-pollinated seedling of *Ceanothus thyrsiflorus* var. *griseus* selected and introduced by the famed Hillier Nursery of Hampshire, England

Ceanothus 'Blue Jeans', Leaning Pine Arboretum, California Polytechnic University, San Luis Obispo

Ceanothus 'Blue Mound' with *Chamaecyparis lawsoniana* 'Lutea', London, England

(Hillier and Coombert 2002). The second parent is believed to be *C. impressus*. Released in 1960, it quickly became a popular shrub in the British Isles and was given an Award of Garden Merit by the Royal Horticultural Society. It remains a commonly grown plant in the United Kingdom and is also available from a few nurseries on the Pacific coast.

'Blue Mound' is well named with its dense, mounding habit, 3 feet high and 6 feet wide. The dark green, elliptic leaves are $^1/_2$–$^3/_4$ inch long with a glossy sheen and undulating margins. Later flowering than many other ceanothuses, bright blue flowers form in tight, crowded clusters in late spring and often again in fall. The tidy, rounded form and smaller size of 'Blue Mound' are useful in gardens with limited space, and if desired it can be maintained in a formal or semiformal appearance with modest pruning. Garden tolerant, it is used with confidence by many British horticulturists and is considered "an excellent mounding shrub" (Lucas 1996). Performing best in full sun along the coast, it is hardy to 15°F (−9°C).

Ceanothus 'Blue Sapphire'
Karen and Warick Wilson selected 'Blue Sapphire' from a single plant of 'Blue Cushion' growing in a Rotorua, New Zealand, garden center. Cuttings were taken in 1994 from a dark-colored shoot growing from the side of the plant and propagated at their nursery in Drury. The unique, black-green color proved to be a stable trait, and plants were

distributed by Lyndale Nurseries of Auckland, New Zealand, to Europe and the United States.

'Blue Sapphire' has a spreading habit, growing to 3 feet high and 5 feet wide, and features an unusual combination of compelling traits. The oblong to elliptic, $^{1}/_{4}$- to $^{3}/_{8}$-inch-long leaves are crinkled and have distinctive, burgundy-green surfaces and finely serrated edges. Open, 2- to 3-inch-long sprays of violet-blue flowers add a bold complement to the foliage in early spring.

Stunning in bloom, 'Blue Sapphire' has not proven particularly garden tolerant. Open and rangy, plants tend to be leafless in their interior, revealing the gray stems and branches. Plants respond to tip pruning, and some cleaning of the interior wood is necessary to improve the general appearance of specimens. Full sun is recommended. 'Blue Sapphire' is reported to be resistant to downy and powdery mildew and has tolerated temperatures as low as 18°F (−8°C).

Ceanothus bolensis
Cerro Bola ceanothus

Described and named in 2003 by Steve Boyd and Jon Keeley, *Ceanothus bolensis* is a narrow endemic, restricted to Cerro Bola in northwestern Baja California, Mexico. An erect shrub to 8 feet high with rigid stems, it is found primarily in chaparral at 1,800–4,200 feet (550–1,275 m) in elevation. The leathery, wedge-shaped leaves are folded along the midvein and are $^{1}/_{4}$ inch long. Pale blue to white flowers are held in small, rounded clusters from late winter to early spring. Cerro Bola ceanothus has not been cultivated outside of a few botanical gardens, and little is known of its garden potential. The threat of development within the area of its limited distribution makes it a species of special concern to conservationists.

Ceanothus 'Burkwoodii'

'Burkwoodii' is a garden hybrid selected and introduced in 1929 by Burkwood and Skipwith Nursery of London. One parent is believed to be *Ceanothus* ×*delilianus* 'Indigo' with the second parent uncertain, perhaps *C. dentatus* or *C.* ×*veitchianus*. 'Burkwoodii' was the first hybrid to combine the characteristics of the evergreen species—flowering in spring on stems from the preceding year—with characteristics of the deciduous species that flower in late summer and fall on growth of the current year. Like the hybrid 'Autumnal Blue', it received the Award of Merit, in 1930, and the Award of Garden Merit in 1984 from the Royal Horticultural Society.

'Burkwoodii' is a compact, rounded shrub to 5–6 feet tall with an equal spread. The oval leaves are $^{1}/_{2}$–1$^{1}/_{4}$ inches long and have serrated margins and glossy, dark green surfaces. Dark blue flowers are abundant through summer and fall in 1- to 2-inch-long sprays. Although 'Burkwoodii' was introduced into the United States in 1936

Ceanothus 'Burtonensis', private garden, London, England

and reported to perform well in California, nurseries in the state seldom offer it for sale. In the United Kingdom, however, it remains a favorite and is considered by many British gardeners one of the best and most reliable of the evergreen cultivars. Tolerant of heavier soils, it requires full sun and is hardy to about 10°F (−12°C).

Ceanothus 'Burtonensis'
Burton ceanothus

'Burtonensis' originated from a naturally occurring hybrid, *Ceanothus impressus* var. *impressus* × *C. thyrsiflorus* var. *thyrsiflorus,* on Burton Mesa in northern Santa Barbara County, California. Propagated at the Santa Barbara Botanic Garden in 1941, plants were sent to England and later introduced into cultivation by Francis P. Knight, director of the Royal Horticultural Society, in 1963.

'Burtonensis' is similar to Santa Barbara ceanothus (*Ceanothus impressus*) with an arching, upright habit to 6–8 feet tall with an equal spread. The evergreen leaves have depressed veins and a glossy surface like Santa Barbara ceanothus but are more rounded in outline. A floriferous, early-blooming selection, the bright blue flowers are held in dense, rounded, 3/4- to 1 1/2-inch-long clusters that completely cover the foliage.

Although 'Burtonensis' is seldom cultivated, plants can still be found in British nurseries and gardens, where it is seen on walls and along fences. Its billowing habit and bright blue flowers have a frothy, almost fountain-like character, recommending it as a specimen or informal hedge. Tolerant of temperatures as low as 15°F (−9°C), it does best in full sun and well-drained soils.

Ceanothus buxifolius
boxleaf ceanothus, binorilla, chaparro prieto, guasapul, junco

Ceanothus buxifolius is a broad-ranging species from north-central Mexico, growing in montane shrubland, pine and oak woodlands, and conifer forests at 4,500–10,400 feet (1,360–3,150 m) in elevation. Habit varies from spreading to erect, 2–12 feet tall, with stiff, open, spine-like stems. The evergreen to deciduous leaves are variable, 1/2–3/4 inch long, and have a flat, dull green surface. White to pink-tinged flowers are held in rounded heads to $\frac{1}{2}$ inch long. *Ceanothus buxifolius* is seldom cultivated, and little is known of its garden potential.

Ceanothus caeruleus

azure ceanothus, chaquira, cuaicuastle, tlaxiste, sayolistle

Ceanothus caeruleus is broadly distributed throughout the mountains of Sonora, Mexico, south to Chiriquí province, Panama, at elevations of 3,300–9,950 feet (1,000–3,025 m). It occurs in clearings and open sites among oak woodlands, pine forests, cloud forests, and mixed oak-pine forests. An evergreen shrub 3–15 feet tall, it exhibits an upright to spreading habit with flexible stems. The dark green, alternate leaves are 1–3 inches long and have a leathery, downy texture. Three-veined and ovate, the lower leaf surface has dense, matted hairs that become rust-colored with age. Medium to dark blue flowers are held in 3- to 6-inch-long, frothy sprays from March to September, depending on latitude and elevation.

French breeders used *Ceanothus caeruleus* early in the 19th century to develop the extraordinary *C. ×delilianus* hybrid series. It is one of the parents—the others being *C. americanus* and *C. herbaceus*—of such notable selections as 'Gloire de Versailles', 'Henri Desfosse', and 'Topaze'. Rarely cultivated in the United States or Europe, it is still grown in Mexico. Frost tender, it would not survive except in the warmest portions of United States and is occasionally listed as *C. ×azureus.*

Ceanothus 'Cal Poly'

Howard Brown selected 'Cal Poly' from a seedling he found near an open-pollinated *Ceanothus cyaneus* growing on the campus of California Polytechnic University, San Luis Obispo. It was later introduced into the nursery trade at the horticulture refresher course in 1958. Similar in many respects to *C. cyaneus*, it features glossy green leaves 1–2 inches long held on an open, upright form to 8 feet high with an equal spread. Long-stalked panicles of violet-blue flowers, 6–8 inches long, form from dark, amber-blue buds in the middle of spring and again sparingly in fall.

Fast growing to a fault, 'Cal Poly' usually requires some pruning to achieve a desirable form. It is useful on dry slopes mixed with *Fremontodendron* 'California Glory' or *Romneya coulteri* (matilija poppy), as a quick screen, or it can even be pruned into a formal hedge. Planting in well-drained soils along the coast is recommended as it is not as garden tolerant or frost hardy as many other ceanothuses.

Ceanothus 'Cascade'

'Cascade' is commonly seen in nurseries and landscapes throughout much of Great Britain. It was selected, named, and introduced by Rowland Jackman, of Rowland Jackman Nursery, Woking, England, in 1938. Believed by many to be a *Ceanothus thyrsi-*

florus hybrid, it exhibits similar characteristics with glossy green, elliptic leaves to 2 inches long and powder-blue flowers held in loose heads to 3 inches long. A rounded shrub with arching branches, it will grow to 6–8 feet high with an equal spread and has been reported to reach a height of 25 feet against walls. 'Cascade' serves many garden functions in Great Britain, from specimens and hedges, to borders and screens. Garden tolerant, it does best in full sun, although partial shade is tolerated. 'Cascade' received an Award of Merit in 1946 and an Award of Garden Merit in 1984 from the Royal Horticultural Society.

Ceanothus 'Celestial Blue'
Bert and Celeste Wilson selected the seedling 'Celestial Blue' from the growing grounds of their Las Pilitas Nursery in Santa Margarita, California, in the mid-1990s. Parentage is unknown, although the rounded, $1/2$- to $3/4$-inch leaves strongly suggest *Ceanothus impressus* var. *nipomensis* in this evergreen hybrid. Matte-green and flat, the margins have finely toothed edges. Luminous, rich blue flowers are held in tight, conical clusters from late winter to spring. In California, sporadic flowering often continues through summer and well into fall.

'Celestial Blue' has a mounding habit 6–8 feet tall with a similar spread. It is useful as an informal hedge or medium-sized screen and is effective as a specimen or accent shrub. Full sun and well-drained soils are recommended, and it is hardy to at least 10°F (−12°C).

Ceanothus 'Centennial', private garden, Santa Barbara, California

Ceanothus 'Centennial'

'Centennial' is a naturally occurring hybrid, *Ceanothus foliosus* × *C. thyrsiflorus* var. *griseus,* grown from seed that was collected at Salt Point on the Sonoma County coast by Roger Raiche in 1985. It was named and introduced into the nursery trade in 1992. Low and spreading, 'Centennial' features creeping stems 8–12 inches high and rounded, $\frac{1}{4}$- to $\frac{1}{2}$-inch-long leaves with undulating, polished green surfaces. In early spring, cobalt-blue flowers are concentrated in tight, 1- to 2-inch-long, rounded or cylindrical heads. The glistening, wrinkled foliage presents an appealing water-like quality in mature specimens.

'Centennial' is surprisingly tolerant of considerable shade and is particularly useful in the filtered light common in woodland gardens. Heavy leaf drop in the understory can easily bury specimens, however, and plants should be thoughtfully placed. It can be used in full sun in cooler climates but requires some protection from the sun in warmer regions of Mediterranean climate. Well-drained soils are required for longevity, and it is hardy to about 15°F (−9°C).

Ceanothus 'Concha'

'Concha' is a striking hybrid discovered by Charles Samms in his San Dimas, California, nursery in 1946. Named in 1949, it is thought to be a cross between *Ceanothus impressus* and *C. papillosus* var. *roweanus* (now considered only a compact form of *C. papillosus*), and many California gardeners and nursery professionals believe it is one

Ceanothus 'Concha', private garden, Newport Beach, California; also see pages 18 and 25

of the finest cultivars the genus has to offer. Variable in size, it typically reaches 6–9 feet tall with an equal spread, although specimens in sheltered British gardens can achieve much larger sizes, with one individual measuring 21 feet tall and 24 feet wide. The branches arch gracefully, forming a dense, symmetrical mound of lustrous green foliage. Narrow, 1-inch-long leaves are dark green and have depressed veins and finely serrated edges. Vibrant, dark blue flowers in 1-inch-long clusters form in early spring from magenta buds, giving plants a distinctive bicolored appearance while in bloom.

A dependable and heavy bloomer, 'Concha' is well known for its excellent garden tolerance and adaptable form. Specimens can be pruned or even sheared to conform to smaller gardens. It is more reliable than many other common cultivars of equal size, such as the hybrids 'Julia Phelps' and 'Dark Star', and will endure heavier soils and summer watering. Although best suited for and longer-lived in coastal environments, it can be planted in warmer inland conditions with confidence. 'Concha' is reliably hardy to 15°F (−9°C) and has survived temperatures as low as 10°F (−12°C).

Ceanothus cordulatus

mountain whitethorn, snowbush

Mountain whitethorn is a mounding or spreading evergreen shrub to 6 feet high with a 12- to 15-foot spread. It is found in most of the higher mountains of California at 1,450–10,400 feet (450–3,150 m), where it occurs on ridges, slopes, and dry flats. Forming dense stands in montane chaparral or billowing thickets in the understory of mixed and coniferous forests, Ceanothus cordulatus is one of the most commonly encountered species in California.

Mature plants have an open appearance, often with a flattened top that is in part genetic and in part resulting from the weight of snow. The branches and stems are rigid, gray to nearly white, and form a pleasing, intricate pattern. Widely spaced, 1/2- to 3/4-inch-long leaves are blue-green, oval, and three-veined. The cream-white flowers are borne in late spring or early summer in dense 1-inch-long heads and have a strong, pungent fragrance.

Mountain whitethorn is seldom grown at lower elevations, and little is known of its tolerances as a landscape subject. A tough and durable species, it is useful in mountain communities along roadsides, cut slopes, and golf courses or as a drought-tolerant shrub for landscaping at higher elevations. Enduring winter snowdrifts, it is one of the hardiest species grown.

Ceanothus 'Coronado'

'Coronado' is an uncommon intersubgeneric hybrid—Ceanothus thyrsiflorus var. griseus (subgenus Ceanothus) × C. gloriosus (subgenus Cerastes)—that was collected near Anchor Bay on the Sonoma County coast by Phil Van Soelen. California Flora Nursery introduced it into the nursery trade in 1991. The deeply veined leaves are held tightly along the stems and have the characteristic shape and teeth of *C. gloriosus*. Glossy, dark green surfaces derive from the *C. thyrsiflorus* var. *griseus* parentage. Frosty blue buds open in late winter and early spring into oval clusters of luminous, azure-blue flowers.

Ceanothus 'Coronado', University of California Botanical Garden in Berkeley

Relatively new to the nursery trade, its size and slower growth rate make 'Coronado' a good candidate for smaller gardens. Plants sited in warmer interior climates tend to open with age and display considerable wood. Coastal plantings are more compact, and some garden professionals along the central coast of California have been effusive with their compliments. 'Coronado' combines beautifully with gray-foliaged plants such as *Stachys* 'Helen von Stein' and *Artemisia* 'Powis Castle'. Hardiness remains unknown, but 10–15°F (−12 to −9°C) can be anticipated.

Ceanothus crassifolius
hoaryleaf ceanothus

Ceanothus crassifolius is a common associate of low-elevation chaparral, 200–3,700 feet (60–1,100 m) in southern California, where it occasionally forms nearly pure stands on coastal slopes. Two varieties of *C. crassifolius* have been recognized: *planus,* with flat leaf blades and entire margins, and *crassifolius,* with revolute margins and dense hairs on the underside of the leaves. Variety *planus* is found in the western Transverse Ranges from Santa Barbara County to Los Angeles County. Variety *crassifolius* occupies the southern portion of the range from the San Gabriel Mountains through the Peninsular Ranges and into northwestern Baja California, Mexico.

Stiffly branched and open, hoaryleaf ceanothus has a rounded form to 5–10 feet tall with an equal spread. The evergreen leaves are leathery, to 1 inch long, and with dull, olive-green surfaces. A coating of fine white hairs covers the younger stems and undersides of the leaves, giving plants an appealing grayish cast. The flat, woolly gray buds give rise to round, 1-inch clusters of dusty white flowers in late winter and early spring.

Hoaryleaf ceanothus has never been widely cultivated and is rarely recommended as an ornamental. The bright blue flower colors and dense habits of many of the more recent introductions are considered more desirable, but the grand dame of California horticulture, Lester Rowntree, considered it one of the most beautiful plants in her *Ceanothus* collection. Its olive-gray foliage can be contrasted against the dark green foliage of other *Ceanothus* selections. This slow-growing species is useful in hot interior gardens for erosion control, or as transition into chaparral or coastal scrub. It is best grown in full sun and well-drained soils.

Ceanothus 'Cuesta'

'Cuesta' is a naturally occurring hybrid, *Ceanothus cuneatus* × *C. prostratus*, collected from a native population in the foothills of the Sierra Nevada near Grass Valley in Nevada County, California. After evaluating 60 different offspring, George Edmondson of the U.S. Department of Agriculture Soil Conservation Service, made this selection in 1974 for its superior performance and revegetation potential. It has proven easy to establish and maintain, and has an enduring, handsome presence.

'Cuesta' is an open, evergreen shrub to 4 feet tall with a spreading habit to 8 feet wide. Leaves are opposite and favor its *Ceanothus cuneatus* parentage. Arching gray stems support rose-colored branchlets and complement the loosely arranged olive-green leaves. Flowers are pale, milk-blue in open clusters, and form in mid to late spring from dusty white buds.

'Cuesta' was developed for use as a ground cover to provide a low-maintenance option for roadsides and slopes around rural and mountain homes in the Sierra Nevada. It is well adapted to environments up to 6,000 feet (1,815 m) in elevation with well-drained soils and is an excellent choice for erosion control, deer resistance, and drought tolerance. Although not as showy as some cultivars in flower, 'Cuesta' offers solid landscape function in difficult circumstances and has a subtle, geometric beauty.

Ceanothus cuneatus
buckbrush

Ceanothus cuneatus is one of California's most widespread species. It is so common in portions of the state that the terms chaparral and buckbrush are often used synonymously. As might be expected with a broad-ranging species, buckbrush is variable in habit, leaf morphology, and flower color, and taxonomic distinctions have shifted through the years. Five naturally occurring varieties are recognized, based primarily on leaf morphology and life form. Typically, *C. cuneatus* has intricately branched stiff gray stems with thick leathery leaves that vary in color from olive to dark green. The specific epithet refers to the shape of the leaf, which is usually wedge-shaped with a blunt or pointed tip. Flowers are most commonly white and held in small, tight clusters. Some coastal populations of *C. cuneatus* var. *fascicularis* have pale blue to lavender flowers.

Size and form are also variable and related to habitat. *Ceanothus cuneatus* growing in the coastal dunes of Montana de Oro State Park on the central coast of California is

Ceanothus cuneatus var. *fascicularis,* San Luis Obispo County, California

a sprawling shrub to 5 feet high. On the hot, dry slopes of Figueroa Mountain in Santa Barbara County, buckbrush has an arching, vase-shaped form to 12 feet tall or more. The Figueroa Mountain populations all have white flowers while the Montana de Oro populations display a range of flower colors from pale blue to lavender, and varying shades of white.

Although *Ceanothus cuneatus* is seldom used as a garden subject, it is frequently a required element in restoration and revegetation projects in its native range. Most of these projects require seeds and/or cuttings collected from specific sites. In the garden, buckbrush has a compliant, durable nature and is an excellent choice for difficult sites. A number of California horticulturists believe this species has far greater garden potential, and further selection may yield promising new cultivars.

Ceanothus cuneatus 'Mount Madonna'
'Mount Madonna' was selected and introduced by M. Nevin Smith from material collected on Mount Madonna in the Santa Cruz Mountains. It has a mounding, open form with arching branches to 8 feet tall and 10 feet wide. The leaves are held tightly along the stems and give 'Mount Madonna' a *Pyracantha*-like appearance. Fragrant, smoky white flowers are held in small, round clusters in late winter or early spring.

Ceanothus cuneatus var. *ramulosus* 'Rodeo Lagoon'
'Rodeo Lagoon' is a sprawling ground cover 1–2 feet high, spreading to 10 feet or more. Collected by Steven Edwards of the Regional Parks Botanic Garden, Berkeley, from a windswept ridgeline north of Rodeo Lagoon in Marin County, it was introduced into

the California nursery trade by Native Sons nursery. The dark, olive-green leaves are held in whorls of three along felted gray stems, and new growth has a rusty hue that adds an ornamental quality to the spring foliage. Clear white flowers open from amber-colored buds in the middle of spring.

'Rodeo Lagoon' has demonstrated remarkable garden tolerance when grown in heavier soils that receive frequent watering and is highly recommended for sunny coastal gardens. The graceful branching pattern is attractively displayed on slopes and banks with other drought-tolerant ground covers, and the plant combines well with grasses and perennials in a coastal meadow. Light tip pruning will help tighten the typically open growth pattern.

Ceanothus cuneatus var. *ramulosus* 'Rodeo Marin'
'Rodeo Marin' was selected from the same ridgetop colony as *Ceanothus cuneatus* var. *ramulosus* 'Rodeo Lagoon' by Steven Edwards in 1986 and introduced by the Regional Parks Botanic Garden, Berkeley, in 1999. Equally vigorous, it has medium-blue flowers and a dense, prostrate form 1–2 feet high with a 6- to 10-foot spread.

Ceanothus cuneatus var. *rigidus* 'Snowball'
One of the earliest cultivars to bloom, 'Snowball' is commonly in flower by the end of January or early February, lending a wintry appeal to the California landscape. The

Ceanothus cuneatus var. *rigidus* 'Snowball', private garden, Morro Bay, California

budding flower clusters have tawny-colored bracts that add an attractive stripe against the emerging white blossoms. Opening into tight, $^3/_4$-inch spheres, the flowers cover the foliage in a shower of snow-white blossoms. Gray, stiffly arching branches offer contrast to the thick and leathery texture of the wedge shaped, olive-green, $^1/_4$-inch leaves.

Forming mounds 4–6 feet tall and 6–10 feet wide, 'Snowball' is useful mixed in a sunny, dry garden with other drought-tolerant shrubs and perennials, or it can be combined for a splash of winter color with other winter-blooming California natives such as *Garrya elliptica* (silk-tassel bush), *Ribes sanguineum* var. *glutinosum* (flowering currant), and *Arctostaphylos* 'Austin Griffiths'. It tolerates a wide range of soils and summer watering but becomes open and woody in extremely dry sites. Hardy to 15°F (−9°C), it has not survived in the colder portions of the British Isles without winter protection.

Ceanothus cyaneus

San Diego ceanothus, Lakeside ceanothus

Kate Sessions introduced *Ceanothus cyaneus* into the California nursery trade in the 1920s, and it quickly gained popularity in southern California where its frost-tender nature is seldom a garden consideration. Through the 1930s and 1940s it was one of the most common native shrubs encountered but eventually lost favor with the development of smaller, more refined cultivars in the last half of the century. It is still grown in limited quantities and for restoration and revegetation efforts. San Diego ceanothus has, however, been a parental source of a number of large-flowered hybrids, including 'Cal Poly', 'Gentian Plume', and 'Sierra Blue'.

San Diego ceanothus is an erect shrub to 12 feet tall with an open, spreading habit. The young stems are lime-green and mature into arching gray-green branches that rise from a thick gray-brown trunk. The 1-inch-long, evergreen leaves are thin, glossy, and ovate. Flower clusters form from buds of indigo, pink, and silver on terminal branchlets. These buds open into brilliant, 10-inch-long panicles of radiant blue flowers, which vary from pale to deep blue. Flowering typically occurs in late spring, although sporadic flowers often appear through summer and into fall.

Fast growing to a fault, San Diego ceanothus requires pruning to control its exuberant growth. It is useful as a screen or trained against walls and fences. It does not respond favorably to summer watering and should be sited in well-drained soils. Frost sensitive, plants are damaged when temperatures drop below 25°F (−4°C).

Ceanothus cyaneus 'YBN Blue'

'YBN Blue' originated in the Yerba Buena Nursery Demonstration Garden in Redwood City, California, and was named by Eleanor Williams in 1989. It is occasionally seen listed as *Ceanothus thyrsiflorus* or as a hybrid, but *C. cyaneus* is clearly indicated by the 6- to 10-inch-long compound sprays of medium-blue flowers and the evergreen, elliptic to ovate, $1^{1}/_{2}$- to 2-inch-long leaves with a bright green upper surface and finely serrated margins.

Fast growing, 'YBN Blue' can reach a height of 10 feet with a 12- to 14-foot spread in a few years. Suitable as a screen or specimen, it is also effective as a pruned hedge or trained as a small tree. Full sun and coastal environments are recommended as it not as hardy (only down to 18–20°F, −8 to −7°C) as many other upright selections.

Ceanothus 'Cynthia Postan', private garden, Arroyo Grande, California

Ceanothus 'Cynthia Postan'

'Cynthia Postan' was developed at the University Botanic Garden, Cambridge, England, from seed collected in 1965 by Lady Cynthia Postan in the Regional Parks Botanic Garden, Berkeley, California. The seed was collected from a specimen of *Ceanothus papillosus* var. *roweanus* (now considered only a compact form of the species) originating from the Tranquillon Mountain area of northern Santa Barbara County, California. Based on the observations of Peter Yeo of Cambridge, the other parent is believed to be *C. thyrsiflorus* var. *griseus*.

Yeo based his conclusion on the leaf morphology of 'Cynthia Postan' and a sibling seedling from the original seed collected by Lady Postan. He believed that the overall general resemblance is great enough to conclude that the two hybrids have the same parentage and that *Ceanothus griseus* var. *horizontalis* (treated here as *C. thyrsiflorus* var. *griseus*) is the pollen parent. Lady Postan grew plants from the same group of seed that was given to the Cambridge Botanic Garden, both in her garden at Cambridge and in another garden at Blaenau, Ffestiniog, northern Wales. Specimens are preserved in the herbarium of the Cambridge Botanic Garden.

'Cynthia Postan' is a rounded shrub to 8 feet tall with dense, stout stems and branches that arch and spread as wide as 10 feet. Leaf blades are narrowly oblong and $^3/_4$–$1^1/_2$ inches long. The upper leaf surfaces are wrinkled, dark green, and glossy, with strongly depressed primary and midrib veins, while the lower surfaces are gray-green, with fine, tangled hairs. Leaf margins are wavy, with glandular hairs at the tips of shallow teeth. Bronze-blue bud clusters open into slightly elongated panicles of fine, violet-blue flowers. At the peak of the flowering season, from May to early June, the blossoms obscure the foliage.

Although 'Cynthia Postan' has circulated among gardeners and nursery people since the 1970s and a specimen was featured in an exhibit at the 1988 Chelsea Flower Show, it has yet to achieve significant popularity. The tight, arching, almost brooding habit and extended floral display alone is a strong endorsement, and it has proven quite hardy in the British Isles. Plants have been regularly exposed to 14°F (−10°C) with little damage. 'Cynthia Postan' has now been introduced into the California nursery trade and demonstrates remarkable tolerance of heavy soils along the coast.

Ceanothus 'Dark Star'

One of the most commonly encountered selections in California gardens, 'Dark Star' remains exceedingly popular with gardeners across the state. Selected from seedlings

Ceanothus 'Dark Star' as a hedge, San Luis Obispo, California; also see page 19

planted in 1968 by Ken Taylor in his Aromas, California, garden, it is believed to be a cross between *Ceanothus impressus* and *C. papillosus* var. *roweanus* (now considered only a compact form of *C. papillosus*). 'Dark Star' was introduced through Ken Taylor Nursery in 1971.

'Dark Star' has a dense, arching habit 6–8 feet tall with an 8- to 12-foot spread. The evergreen leaves are deeply veined, as long as $^1/_2$ inch, and have a dark, muted character, appearing almost black from a distance. In early spring, masses of burgundy buds give a rose-colored glow to specimens before opening into cylindrical heads of brilliant, cobalt-blue flowers.

'Dark Star' is useful as an informal screen, at the back of a dry border, or featured as a specimen. In the British Isles it is occasionally seen as an espalier or trained loosely along a fence. Sensitive to water molds in poorly drained soils, it is best grown in coastal gardens with well-drained soil. Flowering is stronger in full sun, but 'Dark Star' will tolerate moderate shade. Short-lived in interior gardens, the abundant flowers make its ephemeral nature acceptable to some gardeners. Hardy to 15°F (−9°C), it is less attractive to deer than some selections, although it is far from deer-proof.

Ceanothus 'Delight'

'Delight' is an intersubgeneric garden hybrid of English origin: *Ceanothus papillosus* (subgenus *Ceanothus*) × *C. cuneatus* var. *rigidus* (at the time considered a separate species, *C. rigidus*; subgenus *Cerastes*). It was introduced by Burkwood and Skipwith Nursery of London early in the 20th century and received an Award of Merit in 1933 and Award of Garden Merit in 1984 from the Royal Horticultural Society. 'Delight' has an upright form to 12 feet tall with spreading branches to 15 feet wide. The elliptic leaves are dark green, $1^1/_2$–2 inches long, and have a glossy surface. Dark blue flowers are held in cylindrical panicles 3–5 inches long from late winter to early spring. Many British gardeners consider 'Delight' one of the best large cultivars available and frequently train specimens along walls and fences. Garden tolerant, handsome specimens are often encountered in gardens. Hardy to 10°F (−12°C), it is considered one of the most frost tolerant of the evergreen selections. Unfortunately, it has not been grown in the United States.

Ceanothus ×delilianus

Delilianus hybrid ceanothus

Ceanothus ×*delilianus* represents a group of hybrids that were originally created in France by crossing the deciduous, white-flowered *C. americanus* of the eastern United States with the evergreen, blue-flowered *C. caeruleus* of Mexico and Guatemala. The introduction into Europe in 1818 of the frost-tender *C. caeruleus* renewed interest in the genus and offered breeders a chance to add more desirable colors to the previously introduced

Ceanothus ×delilianus 'Gloire de Versailles', private garden, Arroyo Grande, California

C. americanus. Primarily through the work of French breeders and the Lemoine Nursery, the *C. ×delilianus* hybrid line resulted in many attractive blue and pink cultivars throughout the 19th century.

As many as 40 different cultivars of Delilianus hybrids were available in the 19th and early 20th centuries, several with compelling, imaginative names like 'Coquetterie', 'Madame Furtado', or 'Sceptre d'Azur'. Regrettably, much of this horticultural legacy has been lost, although the remaining selections offer a sampling of this significant early breeding work. Deciduous *Ceanothus* species and cultivars

Ceanothus ×delilianus 'Gloire de Versailles', showing pruning, Knoll Gardens, Dorset, England; also see page 15

bloom on the current season's growth and consequently flower later than the evergreen varieties. Most hybrids flower in flushes from midsummer to fall. Deadheading spent flowers during the season encourages additional flowers. Allowing the late-season flowers to persist provides an attractive display of seedpods.

The deciduous selections do best in full sun, although many will tolerate partial shade. As a group they are much more tolerant of summer watering and not as demanding of well-drained soils as their evergreen counterparts. Hardiness varies by cultivar, but most will tolerate temperatures of 10°F (−12°C) or less. Specimens should be cut back each season to encourage greater flowering the following year. Size and form can be controlled with this annual trimming as well. Pruning is best performed in early spring or can be accomplished in late fall or early winter in California as these hybrids are often not fully deciduous in warmer climates:

'Basil Fox' has an open habit 3–5 feet tall. Flowers open from slate-blue buds into compound heads of light blue flowers.

'Ceres' features a rounded habit to 3 feet tall and as wide as 6 feet. Flowers buds are suffused lavender-pink and open a pale lilac-pink. The 3 $^1/_2$-inch-long leaves are the largest in the hybrid series.

'Comtesse de Paris' is a vigorous selection with a tidy form to 3 feet high and dark blue flowers held in open, 5-inch-long clusters.

'Gloire de Versailles' is the best known and most commonly grown of the group and is perhaps the largest, growing to 12 feet tall. It features powder-blue flowers on 6-inch-long panicles and a vigorous though somewhat awkward habit. The leaves open dark green and become paler with age. 'Gloire de Versailles' was granted the Award of Garden Merit by the Royal Horticultural Society in 1984.

Ceanothus ×delilianus 'Indigo', Knoll Gardens, Dorset, England

'Fincham' is a white-flowered selection with delicate pale pink buds and thin, *Ceanothus americanus*-like leaves as long as 2½ inches. Although not as vigorous as some selections, it has a subtle, unassuming appeal.

'Henri Desfosse' is a compact selection with a rounded habit to 3 feet high. Burgundy-red stems offer a strong contrast to the pallid green leaves. Dark blue flowers are held in tight, 3- to 5-inch-long panicles.

'Indigo' has the darkest blue flowers of the group and a narrow, tapered form to 4 feet tall. It is not as hardy as many of the others and is often found groomed along walls in the British Isles, in part as winter protection.

'Topaze' has a compact, almost pyramidal form to 5 feet tall and medium-blue flowers with a distinctive topaz-hued sheen.

Ceanothus dentatus
cropleaf ceanothus

While collecting seed for the Horticultural Society of London in California at the beginning of the Gold Rush, Karl Theodor Hartweg included *Ceanothus dentatus* among his many contributions to gardens. Although not commonly cultivated in California, it has a long and somewhat confused history in the British nursery trade, where it remains popular in garden centers to this day.

Cropleaf ceanothus is an upright, spreading shrub 2–5 feet tall and 3–6 feet wide that forms a dense mound. Leathery and dark forest-green, the evergreen leaves are narrowly elliptic to ¾ inch long with depressed veins and wavy, finely toothed margins. From mid to late spring the dark blue flowers form in ½- to 1-inch-long clusters in the axils of 1- or 2-year-old branchlets. Cropleaf ceanothus is best grown in full sun but will tolerate the light shade of trees. It will accept a wide range of garden conditions, although plants sited in well-drained soils along the coast usually live longer and have a more attractive form. British gardeners use *Ceanothus dentatus* along walls and in open plantings in the southern portion of the country.

Ceanothus divergens
Calistoga ceanothus

A variable, narrow endemic found in scattered localities in the North Coast Range of California, *Ceanothus divergens* is a chaparral and woodland associate typically growing in dry, rocky habitats. It has a convoluted taxonomic history (see Part 2), and what were once called *C. confusus* and *C. prostratus* var. *occidentalis* are included here as synonyms of *C. divergens*. Three subspecies are recognized based primarily on habit and the number of teeth along the margins: subspecies *divergens* has an ascending to erect habit to 3 feet tall and leaf blades with five to nine teeth along the margins; subspecies *confusus* (Rincon Ridge ceanothus) is trailing to mat-like and has decumbent branches as tall as 18 inches and leaf blades with three to seven teeth; and subspecies *occidentalis* is a flat, creeping form with spreading stems that root at the nodes and leaves with three to seven marginal teeth. All three subspecies share opposite, evergreen leaves that are evenly spaced along the stems. Thick and leathery, the upper surfaces are green to gray-green, and the blades are $1/2$–1 inch long with toothed, occasionally revolute margins. Small, flat-topped clusters of blue to lavender flowers form in early spring.

The two low-growing subspecies, *confusus* and *occidentalis,* offer the greatest garden potential. Low and creeping, they both could be used in rock gardens, along banks as a ground cover, or spilling gently over a low wall. Well-drained soils, full sun or partial shade, and light watering are the cultural requirements. Calistoga ceanothus is seldom available, and restoration nurseries might offer the best chance to locate specimens. Hardy to at least 10°F (−12°C), it can be expected to endure both cold and hot interior sites.

Ceanothus diversifolius
pine mat

Ceanothus diversifolius is a California endemic that grows along the western slopes of the Cascade, Sierra Nevada, and North Coast Ranges at elevations of 2,500–7,600 feet (760–2,300 m). Typically on open ridges, flats, and talus slopes in mixed evergreen and coniferous forests, it hugs the earth with a creeping, vine-like character and is usually less than 1 foot high. The trailing stems root as they travel and can reach lengths of as much as 6 feet. Blue to pale green leaves are thin and broadly elliptic, with soft hairs across the $1/2$- to $1^1/4$-inch-long surface. They lack the luster common in many alternate-leaved ceanothuses but have a soft, attractive texture. Pale to gray-blue flowers are held in small, rounded clusters from mid to late spring.

Although pine mat is not commonly grown, it is a fine rock garden subject or small-scale ground cover. Native to open forests, it tolerates partial shade and is valuable in woodland gardens as a cover for slopes. A slower-growing, shy bloomer, pine mat is used more for its subtle, elegant habit than a vivid display of flowers. Hardy to 5°F (−16°C), it performs best with some summer watering and partial shade away from the coast.

Ceanothus 'Ebbets Field'

Nurseryman Robert Keeffe selected this garden seedling in Ebbets Field, one of the growing grounds at Native Sons nursery in Arroyo Grande, California. Observed and evaluated for 6 years, it was introduced into the nursery trade in 2002. Parentage is unknown, but it has many characteristics consistent with *Ceanothus impressus* var. *impressus.*

'Ebbets Field' has a dense, compact habit to 4 feet tall with a 4- to 6-foot spread. The rounded, dark green leaves are deeply veined and as long as ¼ inch. At a distance, and much like the hybrid 'Dark Star', the foliage appears as if cast in perennial shadow. Spring flowers open from ruby-colored buds into rounded, ½-inch-long heads of bright blue flowers. In early spring the bud and flower sequence provides an intriguing bicolored appearance against the foliage.

A useful cultivar in smaller gardens, 'Ebbets Field' is suitable for dry borders, trained along a fence, or pruned into a tidy hedge. Well-drained soils and full sun are recommended, as it has not been tested in heavier soils to date. Hardy to at least 15°F (−9°C), it will require partial shade in warmer interior sites due to its *Ceanothus impressus* lineage.

Ceanothus 'Edinburgh'

'Edinburgh' originated around 1934 from seedlings of *Ceanothus foliosus* var. *medius* (at that time called *C. austromontanus*) found growing in the Royal Botanic Garden of Edinburgh, Scotland. Clearly a hybrid, some have suggested *C. thyrsiflorus* var. *griseus* as the other parent. In the past it has been known also as "Edinensis."

'Edinburgh' has an open, upright habit to 10 feet tall and 8 feet wide. The ovate, ¾- to 1¼-inch-long leaves are dark green, have entire, slightly revolute margins, and are held loosely along the stems. Rich blue flowers form in cylindrical clusters 1–2 inches long from early to the middle of spring.

Often trained along walls in the British Isles, 'Edinburgh' is a versatile garden subject suitable for use against fences or pruned into an informal hedge. It does best in full sun but will tolerate modest shade and heavier soils. Granted an Award of Garden Merit by the Royal Horticultural Society in 1984, it is hardy to 10°F (−12°C).

Ceanothus 'Edinburgh' on a wall, Royal Horticultural Society Garden Wisley, England

Ceanothus 'Edward Stevens', East Dudley, England

Ceanothus 'Edward Stevens'

'Edward Stevens' is a hybrid that originated in England. The rounded, deeply veined leaves are strongly suggestive of *Ceanothus impressus*. Smoky white-blue buds give rise to sky-blue flowers that bloom in 1- to 2-inch-long panicles from mid to late spring.

A spreading, evergreen shrub 4–8 feet tall and wide, 'Edward Stevens' is useful as a screen or for large-scale mass plantings. In more recent years it has not been listed in the Royal Horticultural Society's *Plant Finder*, although it is seen in gardens and two of the national *Ceanothus* collections in the United Kingdom; it is not grown in the United States. 'Edward Stevens' does best in full sun and is hardy to 10–15°F (−12 to −9°C).

Ceanothus 'Eleanor Taylor'

'Eleanor Taylor' originated from a seedling in Ken Taylor's Aromas, California, garden. Discovered with the better known and more commonly grown hybrid 'Dark Star', it is believed to be a cross between *Ceanothus impressus* and *C. papillosus* var. *roweanus* (now considered only a compact form of *C. papillosus*). Although a sibling of 'Dark Star' it is considerably different, with much larger leaves and a massive, rambling habit.

Evergreen and fast-growing, 'Eleanor Taylor' has arching stems to 12 feet high with an expansive 20-foot spread. The leaves are broadly ovate, $^{1}/_{2}$–$1^{1}/_{4}$ inches long, and have glossy green surfaces, serrated margins, and deeply depressed veins. Young stems are slightly pubescent and burgundy-rose in color, providing a pleasant contrast to the dark foliage. Attractive raspberry-colored buds form in early spring, followed by chalky blue flowers with a faint hint of pink in tight, 2-inch-long clusters.

'Eleanor Taylor' is a robust selection that is difficult to place in the garden due to its wide-spreading nature. It can be sheared to control its size but is best suited for use on hillsides or banks that can accommodate its robust form. Garden tolerant, it can be grown in full sun to light shade and heavy soils. 'Eleanor Taylor' is available from a few nurseries in California and Europe and is hardy to approximately 15°F (−9°C).

Ceanothus 'Ernie Bryant'

'Ernie Bryant' originated as a garden seedling at Rancho Santa Ana Botanic Garden in Claremont, California. It was introduced in the fall of 2003 and named in honor of a trustee of the garden for his long service. A mounding, evergreen shrub to 5 feet tall with a 10-foot spread, the arching branches have long internodes, giving the plants an open, airy character. The oval, three-veined leaves are $1-1^{1}/_{2}$ inches long, with finely serrated edges and a glossy surface. The dark blue flowers are displayed in early spring in branched sprays as long as 12 inches.

'Ernie Bryant' is not widely distributed and remains untested in the California landscape outside of a few gardens. Its handsome habit and large flower clusters would be useful as a specimen, bank cover, or trained to spill over a wall. Full sun and well-drained soils are recommended.

Ceanothus 'Everett's Choice'

Percy Everett selected 'Everett's Choice' in 1966 from seed collected from a specimen of *Ceanothus gloriosus* growing at Rancho Santa Ana Botanic Garden in Claremont, California. The second parent is believed to be *C. papillosus* (Everett 1957). The hybrid was later named by John Dourley and introduced into the nursery trade by the garden.

'Everett's Choice' is a decumbent shrub 2–3 feet tall with spreading branches to 6 feet wide. Evergreen, oblong leaves are $1-1^{1}/_{2}$ inches long, arranged openly along the stem, revealing the light gray branches. China-blue flowers open in late winter and early spring from rose-green buds into rounded heads as much as 1 inch in diameter. Mature specimens are commonly open, revealing a considerable amount of wood, and have been characterized as "awkward" by some gardeners. Although unusual, 'Everett's Choice' is superb in rock gardens or spilling gracefully over retaining walls and fences. Tip-pruning young plants can moderate the open habit, although it removes a good portion of its appeal. Well suited to both coastal and interior sites, it does best in full sun but tolerates light shade.

Ceanothus 'Far Horizons'

'Far Horizons' originated from a group of open-pollinated seedlings of *Ceanothus ×burtonensis,* a hybrid from Burton Mesa in northern Santa Barbara County, *C. impressus × C. thyrsiflorus,* which were growing in the Santa Barbara Botanic Garden. Selected by

Ceanothus 'Far Horizons', Fross garden, Arroyo Grande, California

Dara Emery in 1965 and introduced by the garden in 1981, it features a graceful, arching habit, reaching 4–6 feet high with an 8-foot spread, and warty, dark green leaves similar to Santa Barbara ceanothus (*C. impressus*). An early-flowering selection, the swelling buds open in late February and early March into distinctive, pebble-like heads of bright, clear blue flowers.

'Far Horizons' is best grown in coastal climates but can also be used in interior climates with partial shade and prudent watering. Although a practical midsized shrub with an appealing form, it has not become as popular in the nursery trade as cultivars such as 'Dark Star' or 'Julia Phelps'. Garden tolerant, this handsome, reliable shrub deserves greater use. It is hardy to approximately 15°F (−9°C).

Ceanothus fendleri

Fendler ceanothus

Ceanothus fendleri is common in the Rocky Mountains from northern Mexico to southern Wyoming on steep slopes, ridges, and mesas in chaparral, oak woodlands, and coniferous forests. Evergreen at lower elevations and semievergreen higher up, it grows at 4,500–8,700 feet (1,360–2,650 m). The alternate, matte-green leaves are oblong to elliptic, $^1/_3$–$^3/_4$ inch long, and spaced widely along the stems. Muted white flowers, some with a hint of pink, are held in umbel-like clusters $^1/_3$–1 inch long. Flowering depends on the site at which it is grown, beginning as early as January or as late as July.

The form of Fendler ceanothus varies from an erect shrub that stands 6 feet tall to a low mound 6 feet or more across. Often open and flat-topped, specimens are usually intricately branched, with stiff stems that can be spine-like. Used primarily in restoration, it is grown for habitat value, in transition to wild lands, or massed on dry slopes. One of the hardiest species of the genus, it is also tolerant of summer watering.

Ceanothus ferrisiae

coyote ceanothus, Ferris's ceanothus

A narrow California endemic, *Ceanothus ferrisiae* is found on serpentinitic soils in the western foothills of the Mount Hamilton Range of Santa Clara County. Growing in coastal scrub, chaparral, and oak and pine woodlands, it has also been collected in the adjacent Santa Cruz Mountains. An upright shrub 3–8 feet tall, it has ascending branches that arch to form a rounded crown. The evergreen, $^1/_2$- to $^3/_4$-inch-long leaves have a thick leathery texture and are dark green above and pale green below, with entire to finely toothed margins. Pale lavender to white flowers open from cream-colored buds into rounded heads $^1/_2$ inch long from January to May. Coyote ceanothus is not commonly cultivated but is occasionally available at specialty plant sales and in revegetation and restoration nurseries. Like many other narrow endemics, it is a species of special concern and has been listed as endangered by the U.S. Fish and Wildlife Service.

Ceanothus foliosus
wavyleaf ceanothus

Ceanothus foliosus is an evergreen species that varies markedly in form, from low and mat-like to upright, arching, and 10 feet high. The common name is derived from the leathery, dark green, $^1/_2$-inch-long leaves that typically have an undulating surface and a pleasing, sweet scent. From mid to late spring, blossoms are held in dense, occasionally open, round clusters of pale to purple-blue flowers. A California endemic, wavyleaf ceanothus is found in the Coast Ranges and Cuyamaca Mountains to 5,000 feet (1,510 m) in elevation, on ridges and open, rocky slopes. It grows in a variety of soils, including those derived from serpentinite, and is found primarily in chaparral communities, although it also occurs in redwood, mixed evergreen, and conifer forests.

Three varieties, based primarily on habit and leaf shape, of *Ceanothus foliosus* have been recognized: variety *foliosus* is typically the most erect of the three, forming a compact mound 6–10 feet high; variety *medius* (La Cuesta ceanothus; see pages 17 and 24) is commonly less than 6 feet high; and variety *vineatus* (Vine Hill ceanothus) is mounding or mat-like, usually less than 3 feet tall. All three are useful garden subjects and have been in the nursery trade for years. They are best grown in full sun but will tolerate considerable shade when sited in hotter, interior climates. Cold tolerance depends on the variety, but most plants will endure short periods of 10°F (−12°C).

Ceanothus foliosus 'Berryhill'

A curious cultivar selected by nurseryman M. Nevin Smith in 1976 on the slope of Hood Mountain in Sonoma County, California, 'Berryhill' was introduced by Leonard Coates Nurseries of Watsonville in 1978. It is unlike any other ceanothus available in the nursery trade. Wiry stems are lined with tiny, pebbled leaves that have a glossy, polished appearance. Plants mound to 2 feet high with a 4- to 6-foot spread and are covered each spring with small, round clusters of vivid blue flowers. Although it is not a particularly garden tolerant selection and often short-lived, its distinctive character is compelling. 'Berryhill' is useful in rock gardens, perennial borders, and on dry slopes, the bright, shiny leaves adding year-round interest in all applications.

Ceanothus fresnensis
Fresno mat

Ceanothus fresnensis is found on ridges and slopes at elevations of 3,200–7,000 feet (970–2,300 m) in the western Sierra Nevada. As Maunsell Van Rensselaer said in a letter to Howard McMinn, it is seen "creeping along the ground and hugging the stones" in clearings and open sites in conifer forests. Dense, carpet-like, and reaching a width of as much as 10 feet, it has rigid gray stems clothed in evergreen, $^1/_4$- to $^1/_2$-inch-long leaves. Pallid green above and paler below, the narrow blades are thick and leathery, with entire margins. Short-stalked, clusters of blue to white flowers as long as $^1/_2$ inch are abundant from mid to late spring. Glossy red seedpods follow in early summer and offer a sharp contrast to the flat gray foliage.

Fresno mat is seldom cultivated and is a difficult garden subject, especially at lower elevations. A hardy species and tolerant of snow cover, it has significant potential as a ground cover in the mountains of western North America. Rock gardens and road cuts offer opportunities for this appealing species, although some evaluation is needed to overcome its temperamental garden performance to date.

Ceanothus 'Frosty Blue'

Percy Everett selected 'Frosty Blue' at Rancho Santa Ana Botanic Garden in Claremont, California, from a plant of uncertain origin in 1965. It was named in 1970 by John Dourley and introduced into the nursery trade in 1974. *Ceanothus impressus* and *C. thyrsiflorus* var. *griseus* appear to play a part in the parentage of this robust, evergreen cultivar.

'Frosty Blue' exhibits an upright habit with a rigid, fountain-like appearance 8–12 feet high. Dense and vigorous, specimens can spread 15 feet or more. Textured, $^3/_4$-inch-long leaves are deeply veined and have glossy green surfaces. The frosted appearance of the 2- to 4-inch-long panicles of luminous blue flowers is a result of the white bracts on the buds. It blooms later than many other cultivars and has an extended flowering period, through spring.

Garden tolerant, 'Frosty Blue' is considered one of the more reliable cultivars for heavy soils. Useful as a screen or specimen, its vase-shaped form can be trained into an attractive small tree or espaliered against a wall. Robust and fast growing, timely pruning will help control and shape its exuberant nature. Hardy to 10°F (−12°C), its garden appeal is strongest when plants are grown in full sun.

Ceanothus 'Gentian Plume'

'Gentian Plume' is a garden seedling selected by Walter Lammerts in 1970 and introduced by Ken Taylor Nursery 4 years later. Parentage is unknown, although it clearly has many characteristics consistent with *Ceanothus cyaneus*. It is grown primarily for the branched, 8- to 14-inch-long sprays of dark, gentian-blue flowers produced through spring. The evergreen ovate leaves are $2^1/2$ inches long and have glossy surfaces.

Fast-growing young plants can reach 6–8 feet in a single year—it is sparsely branched and may reach 20 feet in height with an equal spread. The untrained form is rangy and awkward, and the leggy stems of young plants require pinching to achieve a desirable structure. Useful as a fast-growing screen or thoughtfully sited specimen, the large, frothy blossoms make a stunning fountain-like display of intense blue. Durable and garden tolerant, it is suitable for sunny coastal gardens or in hotter valleys with partial shade. Foliage is damaged when exposed to prolonged temperatures below 20°F (−7°C).

Ceanothus 'Gerda Isenberg'

'Gerda Isenberg' is an evergreen hybrid found at Yerba Buena Nursery in Redwood City, California, and is believed to have originated from *Ceanothus* ×*regius*, a naturally occurring hybrid, *C. papillosus* × *C. thyrsiflorus* var. *thyrsiflorus*. Roxana Ferris recognized its garden merit in the 1970s, and Cathy Bordi named it in honor of an eminent nurserywoman who influenced and guided the careers of a number of prominent California horticulturists.

'Gerda Isenberg' is a mounding shrub similar to the hybrid 'Concha', growing to 8 feet tall and 8–12 feet wide. At maturity, it often has an open habit with an oak-like form. The glossy green leaves are $1/2$–1 inch long, with depressed veins and finely serrated margins. Floriferous, it is

Ceanothus 'Gentian Plume' border, Santa Barbara Botanic Garden, California; also see page 12

covered in bright blue flowers from late winter to the middle of spring, held in cylindrical, 3- to 4-inch-long heads.

Although 'Gerda Isenberg' is not commonly available, it is a useful midsized selection with a handsome form. Heavy flowering, it makes an excellent specimen or can be combined with other early- and late-flowering selections to create a spectrum of blue in early spring. Full sun is recommended as plants sited in even partial shade perform poorly. It does best planted in well-drained soils along the coast and is hardy to at least 15°F (−9°C).

Ceanothus gloriosus

Point Reyes ceanothus

Point Reyes ceanothus has long been a favorite in coastal California gardens. As the name of the species suggests, it is a stunning sight in bloom, with fragrant lavender-blue to blue-purple flowers held in rounded, short-stalked clusters in early spring. The dark green, elliptic leaves are thick and stiff, with fine teeth along the margins and reminiscent of holly. Form and habit are variable, but most plants are low growing or creeping, usually less than 5 feet tall.

A narrow endemic from the coastal bluffs and dunes of Marin, Mendocino, and Sonoma Counties, *Ceanothus gloriosus* is an excellent choice for coastal gardens. Plants grown in interior sites require afternoon shade and some additional watering. Its

Ceanothus gloriosus var. *gloriosus* used as a ground cover, Santa Ynez, California

widely spreading habit may necessitate pruning when it is grown in smaller gardens. Sprawling selections are effective cascading over walls and banks.

Three varieties of *Ceanothus gloriosus* are recognized based primarily on leaf size and form. Varieties *gloriosus* and *porrectus* form low-growing mats or mounds; variety *porrectus* (Mount Vision ceanothus) has narrower leaves than variety *gloriosus* (glory mat) and fewer teeth. Variety *exaltatus* (Navarro ceanothus, glory bush) and plants referable to *C. masonii* (Mason's ceanothus) have upright habits, the former with broader leaves and more spines along the margins.

Ceanothus gloriosus var. *exaltatus* 'Emily Brown'

'Emily Brown' is a mounding shrub to 4 feet high (occasionally higher) with an 8- to 10-foot spread selected from *Ceanothus gloriosus* var. *exaltatus,* Navarro ceanothus. The rigid, wide-spreading stems are covered in thick, rounded, dark green leaves and hold bright displays of blue-violet flowers from early to middle spring.

A strong, garden-tolerant cultivar, 'Emily Brown' can be used in both coastal and interior gardens and has survived short episodes of temperatures as low as 10°F (−12°C). The broadly spreading habit of 'Emily Brown' is useful on banks and slopes, or plants can be combined with other mounding shrubs such as *Fremontodendron* 'Dara's Gold' and *Salvia leucophylla* 'Point Sal' to make a colorful dry border.

Ceanothus gloriosus var. *exaltatus* 'Emily Brown', private garden, Palo Alto, California

Ceanothus gloriosus var. *gloriosus* 'Anchor Bay', lightly pruned, Santa Ynez, California

Ceanothus gloriosus var. *gloriosus* 'Anchor Bay'

'Anchor Bay' was selected from seed collected near Anchor Bay in southern Mendocino County, California, by Roman Gankin and Andrew Leiser of the University of California at Davis. Three hundred seedlings were grown and evaluated from these collections by UC Davis Arboretum in the early 1970s. 'Anchor Bay' was chosen and named in this process for its larger leaves and dense habit. It was introduced into the nursery trade in 1976 by the Saratoga Horticultural Research Foundation and has become a popular selection in California gardens.

'Anchor Bay' is a garden-tolerant cultivar, to 3 feet high with a 6-foot spread and *Campanula*-blue flowers. It has performed admirably in both coastal and interior portions of California and is considered one of the best ground-cover selections available. The 1-inch-long leaves are larger than typically found in the species but have the same leather-like texture, dark glossy green surfaces, and short teeth. Arching branches carry these holly-like leaves closely along the tangled stems, forming a rigid mass of foliage that appears as if it were laced together.

Flower production of 'Anchor Bay' is modest, as it was selected more for the fresh, lustrous appearance of the foliage than for its flowering. Held in small panicles, the flowers are carried on short peduncles and open a fresh, dark blue before quickly fading to a flat sky-blue. They offer a pleasing contrast to the prickly leaves in March or early April in California, May in the British Isles and other northern latitudes.

'Anchor Bay' is a superb choice for coastal California gardens. It tolerates salt spray and can be used with confidence in heavier soils when provided with adequate drainage. Cultivation in climates away from the coast with increased heat and aridity require additional irrigation and some shade. East- and north-facing slopes offer desirable protection in interior regions of California. It is not as common in the British Isles and continental Europe as other California cultivars, but it is capable of enduring short periods of 10°F (−12°C).

Ceanothus gloriosus var. gloriosus 'Fallen Skies'

A Rancho Santa Ana Botanic Garden introduction, 'Fallen Skies' was selected based on growth habit and flower color by Percy Everett in 1956. Introduced in 1974, it features a prostrate form to 14 inches high and can spread to as wide as 15 feet. The leaves are typical of the species, dark green and leathery, with numerous teeth along the margins. In late winter and early spring, lavender-blue flowers are held in rounded umbels $1/2$ inch across. 'Fallen Skies' is a floriferous selection, and the flowers, though pale, are prominent against the dark foliage.

'Fallen Skies' has not achieved the popularity of the other Ceanothus gloriosus cultivars. The low habit and stout stems are useful as a ground cover or trained to spill over a low wall. It is best in coastal gardens with well-drained soils but can be grown in interior sites when protected from the afternoon sun.

Ceanothus gloriosus var. gloriosus 'Heart's Desire'

'Heart's Desire' is an exceptional ground-cover selection made by Phil Van Soelen of California Flora Nursery in Fulton and was found on a rocky outcropping above Heart's Desire Beach in the Point Reyes National Seashore in Marin County. It forms a dense ground cover 6–12 inches high and can spread as much as 5 feet across. The dark green leaves are typical of the species, with strongly spined margins and russet-tinted edges. Flower color is a bit darker than other Ceanothus gloriosus cultivars: a muddy, velvet blue. Although not a heavily flowering cultivar, it is an excellent choice for coastal gardens and has demonstrated notable promise in interior sites when provided partial shade.

Ceanothus gloriosus var. porrectus

Mount Vision ceanothus

The narrow endemic Ceanothus gloriosus var. porrectus in found at Point Reyes National Seashore, growing along the edges of closed-cone pine forests. The leaves are typically smaller than those of varieties gloriosus and exaltatus, giving plants a correspondingly finer texture. Mount Vision ceanothus has a rounded or sprawling habit to 2 feet high with rigid, angular stems that can spread as wide as 7 feet. The rounded flower clusters are bright blue but are seldom displayed in profusion.

Mount Vision ceanothus is a durable garden subject and has proven tolerant of a wide range of soil types. Full sun is recommended in coastal gardens, and partial shade in warmer interior sites. Suitable as a ground cover for banks and slopes, it can also be used in medians and parking areas if moderate pruning is anticipated.

Mount Vision ceanothus is reliably hardy to 15°F (−9°C), although it has survived brief periods of temperatures as low as 10°F (−12°C). Most of the plants grown in the California nursery trade originated from an unnamed selection introduced by the Saratoga Horticultural Research Foundation.

Ceanothus hearstiorum
Hearst ceanothus

Ceanothus hearstiorum is a rare, narrow endemic from the coastal hills surrounding Arroyo de la Cruz in northern San Luis Obispo County, California, where it grows in association with another rare species, *C. maritimus.* Low growing to mat forming, plants are typically only 12 inches high and spread widely to as much as 8 feet. Young plants develop a star-like pattern as the branches radiate rapidly away from the center. As plants age, this pattern typically matures into a loosely mounding habit. The shiny green leaves are narrow, $^{1}/_{2}$–1 inch long, and have a warty texture much like that of *C. papillosus.* Flowers form in the middle of spring in rounded, $^{1}/_{2}$- to $1^{1}/_{2}$-inch-long clusters and open a pastel or medium shade of blue.

Hearst ceanothus is temperamental in garden settings and has demanding require-

Ceanothus hearstiorum ground-cover planting, Lester Rowntree Garden, Carmel, California

ments, especially if longevity is desired. In cool coastal climates and extremely well-drained soils, plants can be expected to live 10–15 years. Plants grown in warmer inland climates are best suited to situations with light to moderate shade. In soils that lack adequate drainage, plants rarely live more than a few years.

Although not the best choice for large-scale ground-cover applications, Hearst ceanothus can certainly be used in a variety of situations. The interesting branching pattern alone is intriguing, and the pale blue flowers across the surface of the leaves is captivating. It is one of the lowest-growing species available, and its shade tolerance recommends it in the dappled light under mature trees. It is hardy to about 15°F (−9°C).

Ceanothus herbaceus
inland Jersey tea

Known widely in botanical and horticultural literature as *Ceanothus ovatus,* inland Jersey tea (*C. herbaceus*) is a deciduous shrub to 3 feet tall and similar to *C. americanus* and *C. sanguineus* with its serrated, 1¹/2- to 3-inch-long, narrowly oval leaves. Dull to clear white flowers form in rounded heads ¹/2–1¹/4 inches long on the current year's stems.

Ceanothus herbaceus is not commonly grown in the United States or Europe. It was crossed by early French breeders with *C. ×delilianus* to produce some of the rose-colored forms of the hybrid series such as 'Ceres', 'Marie Simon', and 'Perle Rose'. Ranging across temperate North America from Montana to southeastern Canada and south to Louisiana and northern Mexico, inland Jersey tea can be grown with confidence in some of the colder portions of the United States.

Ceanothus impressus
Santa Barbara ceanothus

A California endemic found on Burton Mesa of northern Santa Barbara County and Nipomo Mesa of southern San Luis Obispo County, the dark blue flowers of *Ceanothus impressus* have long drawn horticultural attention. First offered

Ceanothus impressus var. *impressus* container planting, Richmond Hill, England

Ceanothus impressus var. *nipomensis,* threatened by development, Nipomo, California; also see page 22

for sale in 1934, its popularity with gardeners and wide use eventually led to two of California's most popular hybrids, 'Dark Star' and 'Julia Phelps', both derived in part from *C. impressus* parentage.

Santa Barbara ceanothus is an upright, spreading, evergreen shrub 4–6 feet tall with a similar width. The dense, arching stems hold wrinkled, dark green leaves $1/4$–$1/2$ inch long. Abundant cobalt-blue flowers form in 1-inch-long clusters, contrasting vividly with the dark green-black foliage in early spring. Russet-red seedpods follow the flowers in late spring and offer a brief ornamental quality before shattering.

Ceanothus impressus var. *impressus* 'Vandenberg'

'Vandenberg' is a compact selection from Burton Mesa in northern Santa Barbara County, California. Made by M. Nevin Smith in 1982, it forms a dense mound 3–5 feet tall with a 5- to 8-foot spread. The small black-green leaves are round and crinkled, with sparkling surfaces. Panicles of bright blue flowers in the middle of spring complement the dark glossy foliage.

The intensely green leaves appear almost black from a distance and are effective combined with silver- or gray-leaved plants such as agave, lavender, and sage. Like other *Ceanothus impressus* selections and hybrids, 'Vandenberg' does best in well-drained soils and full sun.

Ceanothus impressus var. nipomensis 'Mesa Lilac'

'Mesa Lilac' was selected in 1986 from "Ceanothus Corner" on Nipomo Mesa in southern San Luis Obispo County by botanist Austin Griffiths and introduced the following year by Native Sons nursery. A graceful, arching cultivar, it can quickly reach 10 feet high and 10–15 feet wide. The olive-green leaves are larger and flatter than typical *Ceanothus impressus* and are closely spaced along the stems. Lavender, 2-inch flower clusters are abundant in early spring and often again in fall.

Ceanothus incanus
coast whitethorn

In the British Isles the handsome, appropriately named *Ceanothus incanus* ("hoary gray") is found occasionally trained on red brick walls, the whitish stems providing an appealing contrast. Although coast whitethorn is seldom grown in California, it is recommended for its garden tolerance and frothy sprays of white flowers. As Lester Rowntree, the first lady of California horticulture, said, "It has the most beautiful twigs and young boughs of any *Ceanothus*" (Rowntree 1939).

Coast whitethorn is a large upright shrub 5–10 feet tall with an equal, occasionally wider spread. The broad, open crown is rounded in outline, typically presenting a billowing form. Grayish green, ovate leaves are up to $2^1/_2$ inches long and $1^1/_2$ inches wide and have entire margins. Flowers form in the middle of spring on 1- to 3-year-old branches in 1- to 2-inch clusters, ranging in color from a cream-yellow to a bright, clear white. Blossoms have a robust, pungent fragrance that some gardeners find disagreeable.

Ceanothus incanus is found in the Santa Cruz Mountains and North Coast Range of California in chaparral and coniferous and mixed evergreen forests. These forest environments suggest its use in lightly shaded woodland gardens, although it performs equally well on sunny slopes. Tolerant of summer watering in well-drained sites, it can be grown with confidence in most soils. The young ornamental stems mature into stout thorns, making coast whitethorn an effective barrier specimen, so thoughtful placement is recommended in gardens visited by children and pets.

Ceanothus incanus, Mayacmas Mountains, Sonoma County, California

Ceanothus integerrimus
deer brush

Ceanothus integerrimus, pink flowers, Mayacmas Mountains, Sonoma County, California

Ceanothus integerrimus is a variable, widespread species found along the Pacific slope from southwestern Washington to the northern Peninsular Ranges in California and east to Arizona and southwestern New Mexico. It occupies a bewildering range of habitats, primarily in upland communities of chaparral, oak woodland, and conifer and mixed evergreen forest. Two varieties are recognized: variety *integerrimus* has elliptic leaf blades with a single vein from the base and is restricted to the southern Santa Cruz Mountains, and the more commonly encountered variety *macrothyrsus* has leaf blades with three prominent veins from the base.

Deer brush is an open, upright shrub 5–12 feet tall that can take a number of forms. Some are tree-like; others form flattened mounds. Deciduous to semideciduous, the soft green leaves are thin and egg-shaped in outline, 1–3 inches long, and have entire margins. Flowers are typically white or blue, but in some populations pink specimens can be found. Held in profuse, feathery panicles as long as 6 inches, the flowers open from late spring to early summer, depending on location.

Discovered by David Douglas in the early 1830s, *Ceanothus integerrimus* was sent to England and introduced into the nursery trade in 1850. It was grown for many years as an "elegant wall plant" (Bean 1936) but has lost favor and is no longer listed in the Royal Horticultural Society's *Plant Finder*. It is seldom used in gardens In California, but in its native range it is often included in restoration efforts. Deer brush performs best in montane environments. Plants are usually poorly developed and short-lived at lower elevations. Tolerant of summer watering in well-drained soils, it is a good choice for mountain landscapes that can accommodate its size.

Ceanothus 'Italian Skies'

'Italian Skies' is a seedling selected by Edward Bertram Anderson of Gloucestershire, England, from seed of open-pollinated *Ceanothus foliosus* supplied by the University of Washington Arboretum, Seattle, in 1956. It features a dense, mounding habit 6–8 feet high and can spread to 12 feet. The narrow, dark green leaves are $^1\!/_2$–1 inch long and have depressed veins and slightly rolled margins. Gray-blue buds form in the middle of spring before opening into conical, 1- to 2-inch-long racemes of luminous blue flowers.

A popular cultivar in Europe, 'Italian Skies' is seen frequently in gardens and public landscapes from England to Italy. Its spreading form is useful on dry slopes and banks, and the rich blue flowers complement gray- or silver-foliaged plants such as *Artemisia* 'Powis Castle', *Salvia dolomitica,* and *Plectranthus argentatus* 'Longwood Silver'. Garden tolerant, it does best in full sun and will abide heavier soils and moderate garden watering. 'Italian Skies' was granted an Award of Garden Merit by the Royal Horticultural Society in 1984. It is seldom grown in the United States, although it has more recently been made available in California.

Ceanothus jepsonii

musk brush, Jepson's ceanothus

Ceanothus jepsonii is another of California's narrow endemics found on serpentinitic soils. Occurring in the southern portion of the North Coast Range from Mendocino and Tehama Counties south

Ceanothus 'Italian Skies', Chateau de Montmarin, Dinard, France

to Marin and Napa Counties, it typically grows on slopes and ridges in coastal scrub, chaparral, or in open sites among oak and pine woodlands at 200–2,900 feet (60–880 m) in elevation. The habit is variable, from upright and mounding to 3 feet tall, to prostrate and spreading and less than 1 foot tall. Similar in many respects to *C. purpureus,* the opposite, holly-like leaves are leathery and wavy with sharply dentate margins. The leaves of *C. jepsonii* differ in color, from pale green to yellow-green, compared to the darker green of *C. purpureus.* Blue-violet to white flowers are held in rounded, $1/2$-inch-long heads that have a musk-like aroma. The individual flowers are the largest in the genus, and the six sepals and six petals are also unique in the genus. White-flowered forms tend to occur in the eastern portion of its range, while those with blue flowers grow in the west.

Notoriously difficult to cultivate, Jepson's ceanothus is seldom grown and usually only available at specialty nurseries and botanical garden plant sales. Garden subjects typically have an open habit and lack vigor, appearing to reject garden conditions with a willful disregard for the care given. First discovered by the legendary botanist Willis Linn Jepson in 1893, it was named in his honor, a tribute to his dedication to the study and preservation of the California flora.

Ceanothus 'Joan Mirov'

A naturally occurring hybrid, 'Joan Mirov' is a cross between *Ceanothus thyrsiflorus* var. *griseus* and *C. foliosus*. It was collected on the Sonoma County coast near Salt Point by Roger Raiche and introduced in 1991 by the University of California Botanical Garden in Berkeley. Mature specimens have a billowing, cloud-like appearance, spreading to as much as 20 feet across and reaching a height of 4–6 feet. The intricate branches and stems hold small, crinkled, green leaves with deeply depressed veins. A floriferous cultivar, the rose-burgundy buds open into luminous cobalt-blue flower clusters in early spring.

'Joan Mirov' has proven an excellent selection for use in coastal gardens of northern California and would be suitable for gardens of the Pacific Northwest and the British Isles. In southern California and interior sites it has not been a reliable choice as the plants tend to be woody and short-lived. The low , spreading habit combined with the dense form make it a useful ground or bank cover. The vivid blue flowers are enhanced when combined with gray- or silver-foliaged plants. Hardiness has not been reliably tested, but at least 15°F (−9°C) can be expected.

Ceanothus 'Joyce Coulter'

'Joyce Coulter' was selected by John E. Coulter at his San Carlos, California, nursery in 1956. Evaluated in his garden and by Saratoga Horticultural Research Foundation, it was named in honor of Coulter's wife, Joyce, and introduced into the nursery trade in 1962. An evergreen hybrid, it appears to have the characteristics of *Ceanothus papillosus* and *C. thyrsiflorus* var. *griseus*. It quickly gained popularity with California gardeners and remains a popular ground cover to this day.

Low and spreading, well-spaced plantings are typically 2–3 feet high with trailing branches that occasionally reach 25 feet or more across. The elliptic, 3/4- to 1 1/2-inch-long leaves appear almost rectangular and have polished, textured, green surfaces that sparkle in bright sunlight. Gentian-blue flowers are produced for many weeks through late winter and spring in 3- to 5-inch heads, and some flowering is not uncommon in the fall.

Ceanothus 'Joyce Coulter', Saratoga, California

'Joyce Coulter' is a reliably garden tolerant ground-cover selection and can be easily grown as a low, pruned hedge. Occasional vertical shoots should be removed to maintain a prostrate form. The trailing branches are effective spilling over walls or covering broad banks with *Fremontodendron* 'Ken Taylor' and *Salvia leucophylla* 'Point Sal'. It is best grown in coastal gardens but in interior sites requires supplemental irrigation. Not as hardy as some cultivars, it will not tolerate temperatures below 15°F (−9°C).

Ceanothus 'Julia Phelps'

'Julia Phelps' (see photograph on page 2) is another cultivar with a long horticultural pedigree descending from seed collected by the intrepid Lester Rowntree. Leonard Coates Nurseries, then in Morgan Hill, California, purchased seed of *Ceanothus papillosus* var. *roweanus* (now considered only a compact form of the species) from Ms. Rowntree in 1945. Dudley Phelps—then propagator of Saratoga Experimental Garden, also in Morgan Hill—planted a distinctly different seedling from the group in 1947. Saratoga Horticultural Research Foundation evaluated the planting in 1951 and released it late that year, stating, "this plant has such splendid possibilities as a garden ornamental" (Van Rensselaer 1952). It remains one of the most popular and commonly grown ceanothus cultivars found in California gardens.

'Julia Phelps' is similar to the hybrid 'Dark Star' with deep cobalt-blue flowers in abundant, 1-inch clusters. Also comparable in size, it grows to 8 feet tall but with a wider, expansive habit to 12 feet or more. The leaves are a little darker but of equal size, and in containers it is extremely difficult to distinguish the difference between the two. Like 'Dark Star' it is a short-lived selection and temperamental when used away from the coast and in heavier soils. Full sun and well-drained soil are recommended, and it is hardy to 15°F (−9°C).

Ceanothus 'Knowles Ryerson'

'Knowles Ryerson' originated from open-pollinated seed collected by botanist Don Sexton from a *Ceanothus papillosus* var. *roweanus* (now considered only a compact form of the species) growing at UC Davis Arboretum in the 1950s. He named the cultivar in honor of a benefactor and former dean of the agriculture school. Plants were introduced into the nursery trade in the late 1970s.

A mounding hybrid similar to 'Concha', it grows to 6 feet tall and spreads as wide as 6 feet but with a more irregular form. Dark green, textured leaves are narrow and as long as 2 inches. In spring it bears a profusion of bright, true-blue flowers in crowded heads. Drought and heat tolerant, it does best in full sun. Pruning helps tighten its open habit. 'Knowles Ryerson' is not commonly available in California, although this may change as it has more recently been listed in a number of West Coast nursery catalogs. It is hardy to at least 15°F (−9°C).

Ceanothus lemmonii

Lemmon's ceanothus

Growing in some of the warmer environments of northern California, *Ceanothus lemmonii* is found along the inner North Coast Range and western slopes of the southern Cascade Range and Sierra Nevada. It occurs in chaparral and open sites found in oak and pine woodlands at 590–4,300 feet (180–1,300 m). It is a low, spreading shrub 1–3 feet tall with pale gray to almost white stems that provide an attractive contrast to the evergreen, $1/2$- to 1-inch-long leaves. Elliptic and flat, the blades have finely serrated margins and pale green undersides. Bright blue flowers in $1/2$- to $2 1/2$-inch-long clusters complement the light-colored stems.

Lemmon's ceanothus is a defiant garden subject and has not performed well in cultivation. It is available from revegetation and restoration growers but is seldom produced for the landscape trade. Lester Rowntree thought it required full sun and plenty of heat, but James Roof believed it needed a rocky soil. Maunsell Van Rensselaer suggested that hot, dry climates might present a problem. An attractive species with significant potential as a ground cover in hot interior areas, *Ceanothus lemmonii* would benefit from greater evaluation by the horticultural community of California.

Ceanothus leucodermis
chaparral whitethorn

Chaparral whitethorn is appropriately named for its light gray to white bark and stiff, spiny stems ending in sharp spurs. It grows on dry, rocky slopes in the South Coast Range, along the western slopes of the Sierra Nevada, and in the coastal mountains of southern California into Baja California, Mexico. Often a member of chaparral communities, it is also found in openings within oak woodlands and conifer forests below 6,000 feet (1,810 m).

Ceanothus leucodermis, Cuyamaca Mountains, San Diego County, California

A rigid, evergreen shrub, chaparral whitethorn ranges in height, 5–10 feet, and can have an erect or spreading form. Some forms are dense while others are open, and many populations have a flattened crown. The alternate, $^1/_2$- to $1^1/_4$-inch-long leaves are gray-green with a smooth, leathery texture and offer an appealing contrast to the coloring of the stems and branches. Fragrant flowers form from steely blue buds that vary in color when open from pale blue to white. Blooming occurs from April to June.

Ceanothus leucodermis is seldom grown as a landscape ornamental but is used in restoration plantings. Requiring full sun and well-drained soils, it is well suited to dry gardens and thrives in the heat of interior sites. The gray-green leaves, white trunk, and rigid symmetry combine to make chaparral whitethorn a handsome specimen. It can be grown as a natural or pruned hedge, and the white bark can be featured at the back of a dry border. Chaparral whitethorn is not a good choice for coastal gardens.

Ceanothus ×lobbianus
Lobb's ceanothus

Collected by William Lobb in the early 1850s near Monterey, California, *Ceanothus ×lobbianus* is a naturally occurring hybrid, believed to be a cross between *C. thyrsiflorus* var. *griseus* and *C. dentatus.* Erect, with an arching habit, 5–8 feet tall and spreading to 10 feet wide, it is often confused in the British nursery trade, at times labeled *dentatus* or *veitchianus.* The oblong, 1-inch-long leaves are distinctly three-veined and have revolute and toothed margins. Bright blue flowers are held in rounded heads $^3/_4$–1 inch long from March to May.

Ceanothus ×*lobbianus* is commonly grown in the British Isles, often against walls or as a specimen. *Ceanothus dentatus* and *C. thyrsiflorus* var. *griseus* occasionally grow together on the Monterey Peninsula, but Lobb's ceanothus is rarely cultivated in the United States. It does best in full sun and is hardy to 15°F (−9°C).

Ceanothus maritimus
maritime ceanothus

Ceanothus maritimus is a narrow endemic that grows on the coastal bluffs and low hills surrounding Arroyo de la Cruz in northern San Luis Obispo County, California. This evergreen shrub typically stands less than 2 feet high and has rigid stems and a thick, intricately branched habit. Both creeping and mounding forms are found in its windswept native habitat. The thick leathery leaves are as long as $^{1}/_{2}$ inch and have flat or folded olive-green surfaces and dense, hairy undersides. Earlier flowering and slower growing than many other species, blooms usually begin appearing in late January or early February in California. Flowers are held in small umbel-shaped heads and range from white through a spectrum of blues and lavenders.

Maritime ceanothus is an excellent choice for a small-scale ground cover, accenting dry borders or featured in rock gardens. Adaptable and long-lived, it can be used in both coastal and interior sites but benefits from partial shade in warmer interior gardens. It tolerates heavy soils with adequate drainage and requires minimal maintenance once established. A number of selections have been made from seeds and cuttings collected from Arroyo de la Cruz.

Ceanothus maritimus 'Frosty Dawn', Santa Barbara, California; also see page 10

Ceanothus maritimus 'Claremont'

Introduced in 1972 by Rancho Santa Ana Botanic Garden from a plant growing in the garden since 1956, 'Claremont' is dense and spreading, reaching 8–12 inches high and 3–4 feet wide. Olive-green leaves are typical of the species, and flowers form in late winter, opening into oval, pale gray-blue heads as much as 1 inch in diameter.

Ceanothus maritimus 'Frosty Dawn'

'Frosty Dawn' is one of two cultivars (the other is 'Point Sierra') selected in 1985 from a group of 35 cuttings collected in the hills just south of Arroyo de la Cruz by

Austin Griffiths and David Fross. Low growing and compact, the gray-green leaves are held tightly on spreading branches. Lavender-blue flowers appear in rounded heads crowded along the younger stems in late winter. Mature plants can reach 2 feet high with a spread of as much as 5 feet. 'Frosty Dawn' is useful in rock gardens or as a small or medium-sized ground cover on open banks, in parkways, and along median strips. This tough and durable cultivar has been grown successfully in the interior of California with some shade but is best planted in coastal climates.

Ceanothus maritimus 'Point Sierra'

'Point Sierra' was selected from Arroyo de la Cruz in 1985 along with 'Frosty Dawn'. It exhibits a similar habit but is slightly taller at 2–3 feet. The leaves are ash-green above with hairy white undersides. The arching branches combined with the small-ranked leaves give 'Point Sierra' the appearance of a *Cotoneaster*. Blue-violet flowers held in small, rounded clusters break from dusty white buds in late winter.

Ceanothus maritimus 'Popcorn'

A mounding selection with light olive-green leaves, 'Popcorn' grows to 3 feet high with a 5-foot spread. Late winter flowers are held in tight, rounded heads and open from cloudy white buds into clear, brilliant white blossoms reminiscent of popcorn, hence the name. A floriferous selection, it is useful in rock gardens or massed with the blue-flowered forms of *Ceanothus maritimus.*

Ceanothus maritimus 'Spring Skies'

Roger Raiche and Warren Roberts selected 'Spring Skies' in 1982 on bluffs above Arroyo de la Cruz in northern San Luis Obispo County, California. Like other *Ceanothus maritimus* selections, the flowers open in mid to late winter from rounded buds that open into umbels as wide as $1^{1}/_{4}$ inches. The flowers are the darkest blue of the of the *C. maritimus* selections.

'Spring Skies' has a compact, prostrate form 12–18 inches high and 3–5 feet wide. It is effective in perennial borders and median strips as well as on banks and slopes. Slower growing and with a smaller profile than many other *Ceanothus maritimus* selections, it is a good choice in landscapes and gardens with limited space. Garden tolerant, it performs best in full sun along the coast and with some shade in interior sites.

Ceanothus martinii

Utah mountain lilac, Martin's ceanothus

The distribution of *Ceanothus martinii* is centered on the Colorado Plateau of Utah, northwestern Arizona, and portions of Colorado, Nevada, and Wyoming, at 6,000–10,500 feet (1,810–3,200 m) in elevation. Growing on ridges, slopes, and mesas, it is found in shrublands, pine-oak woodlands, and pine-juniper woodlands. Utah mountain lilac has a mounding to erect habit 3–4 feet tall and 5–6 feet wide. Deciduous to semideciduous leaves are as much as 1 inch long, alternate, three-veined, and have a rounded outline. White flowers are held in open, $^3/_4$- to $1^1/_4$-inch-long clusters from May to July, depending on elevation.

Ceanothus martinii is listed by a number of growers in the Intermountain West. The neat, rounded form of plants in some populations has a formal appeal, or plants can be grown on dry, exposed sites in transition to the natural landscape. Tolerating full sun or partial shade and hardy to at least 10°F (−12°C), it does best in well-drained soils with some supplemental summer watering.

Ceanothus megacarpus var. megacarpus, chaparral above Santa Barbara, California

Ceanothus megacarpus
big-pod ceanothus

The robust, arching *Ceanothus megacarpus* is common on the lower slopes and foothills of cismontane southern California, forming broad thickets in the chaparral. Known for its early flowering, some years the white flowers form as early as mid-December, offering a distinctly Californian perspective to the song line, "I'm dreaming of a white Christmas."

Mature specimens have an open crown and erect habit up to 15 feet tall and wide. The dull green leaves are evergreen and can be both alternate and opposite on the same plant. Evenly spaced along the stems, they are thick and broadly elliptic, typically with entire margins. Clear white flowers form in dense, umbel-shaped clusters on the terminal and upper stems of 1- or 2-year-old branchlets. Fruits, as the common name implies, are large, $^1/_4$ to nearly $^1/_2$ inch wide, and offer a brief period of decorative interest in mid to late spring. Two varieties of *Ceanothus megacarpus* have been recognized: variety *megacarpus* has mostly alternate leaves (a characteristic it shares with *C. verrucosus,* also a member of subgenus *Cerastes*), and fruit with prominent ridges or horns; variety *insularis* has mostly opposite leaves, and fruit with a smooth surface or weakly developed horns.

Big-pod ceanothus can be trained into a small tree that features the handsome gray-brown bark. Variety *pendulus,* a form recognized by McMinn (1942), with long, pendulous flowering branches, can be pruned into a weeping specimen. The arching stems are suitable as an espalier for gardeners willing to make the effort. Hardy to 15°F (−9°C), it will tolerate modest shade and extremely dry garden conditions.

Ceanothus microphyllus
sandflat ceanothus, thymeleaf ceanothus

Ceanothus microphyllus is a deciduous shrub 6–18 inches tall with spreading stems that bear the smallest leaves found in the genus. Flat and three-veined, the leaves are 1/8 inch long and have finely toothed margins. White flowers open into rounded clusters 1/4–3/4 inch long from March to June. Sandflat ceanothus is found in sand barrens and flats from southern Alabama and Georgia to Florida, in clearings and open sites in shrublands, oak woodlands, and pine forests.

Sandflat ceanothus is listed occasionally in nurseries in the southeastern

Ceanothus megacarpus var. *megacarpus* bark, private garden, Santa Barbara, California

Ceanothus megacarpus var. *insularis,* Santa Cruz Island, California

United States and is used primarily for revegetation and restoration. Native plant enthusiasts have increased demand regionally in more recent years, but it is rarely grown elsewhere in the country.

Ceanothus 'Mountain Haze'

Walter E. Lammerts selected 'Mountain Haze' in 1941 from a group of seedlings grown from open-pollinated 'La Primavera'. The male parent is believed by many to be *Ceanothus impressus*. At the time of its introduction, in 1948, it was believed to be a dwarf or low growing, but plants commonly reach heights of 6–8 feet with an equal spread. The branches are angled, have fine hairs, and hold dark, evergreen leaves up to $^3/_4$ inch long. Deeply veined and oval, the upper leaf surfaces are glossy green and the undersides a villous light green. Clear, medium-blue flowers are borne in the middle of spring in $1^1/_2$- to 3-inch-long panicles.

'Mountain Haze' is not exceptionally heavy flowering, although it was a fashionable cultivar with California gardeners during and after the drought of 1976–1977. Remnant plantings can still be seen along Highway 101 in central California, where a few of the specimens are as old as 25 years. The size and fast growth make it useful for the back of a border, as an informal hedge, or with light pruning, to soften a fence or building. 'Mountain Haze' is rarely grown today as stronger flowering and deeper blue selections have superseded its popularity. Hardy to at least 15°F (−9°C), it is garden tolerant and best grown in full sun to maintain a dense form.

Ceanothus ochraceus
ochre-leaf ceanothus

Ceanothus ochraceus a spreading evergreen shrub 1–2$^1/_2$ feet tall, similar to *C. caeruleus* but with white flowers and smaller inflorescences and leaves. It occurs through the western mountains of Mexico from Sonora to Oaxaca among oak and pine woodlands and forests at 5,900–8,800 feet (1,790–2,670 m). Ochre-leaf ceanothus is not cultivated to our knowledge.

Ceanothus oliganthus
hairy ceanothus

A widespread species in California, *Ceanothus oliganthus* is found from the North Coast Range through the western Transverse and Peninsular Ranges into northwestern Baja California, Mexico, at 520–6,300 feet (160–1,900 m) in elevation. It grows on rocky slopes, ridges, and flats in chaparral, oak woodland, mixed evergreen forest, and open sites in pine forest. Three varieties are recognized: *orcuttii, oliganthus,* and *sorediatus* (see Part 2). Variety *sorediatus*, commonly called Jim brush, is the most frequently encountered of the three in garden applications.

An upright, intricately branched shrub to 12 feet tall with a spreading crown, hairy ceanothus will occasionally form a thick, tree-like trunk. The evergreen, alternate leaves are broadly oblong, $1/2$–$1 1/4$ inches long, distinctly three-veined, and with a leathery texture. Flowers vary from pale to purple-blue and are produced in abundant, 1- to 2-inch-long, rounded to cylindrical clusters from February to April.

Although used sparingly today, hairy ceanothus was cultivated frequently in California in the past and has performed well in a broad range of garden conditions. Tolerant of heat, clay soils, and some summer watering, it can be used as a screen, specimen, or trained into a small tree. Fast growing and vigorous, light pruning will help moderate its robust nature. Hardy to 10°F (−12°C), it can be grown in partial shade as well as full sun.

Ceanothus ophiochilus
Vail Lake ceanothus

Ceanothus ophiochilus is a narrow endemic restricted to three populations in the hills immediately west of Vail Lake and on the northern slopes of Agua Tibia Mountain in the Agua Tibia Wilderness in Riverside County, California. Growing on unusual, nutrient-poor soils in chaparral, Vail Lake ceanothus is difficult to distinguish from *Adenostoma fasciculatum* (chamise) when not in bloom. Discovered in 1989, *C. ophiochilus* was listed as endangered by the state in 1994 and as threatened by the U.S. Fish and Wildlife Service in 1998.

An upright shrub to 12 feet tall, Vail Lake ceanothus has an open crown and broadly mounding habit. The thick, evergreen leaves are pale to yellow-green, $1/8$–$1/4$ inch long, and clustered along the stems. Pale blue or occasionally pink-lavender flowers in rounded heads $1/2$–$3/4$ inch long are held in the upper axils or at the end of the branches.

The horticultural potential of Vail Lake ceanothus is unknown, although the spider-like stems, appealing texture, and pink-lavender flower color in some individuals warrant further evaluation. It is not grown outside of botanical gardens as yet, but threatened development in the Vail Lake area will likely result in production for restoration and revegetation.

Ceanothus otayensis
Otay Mountain ceanothus

An erect evergreen shrub 3–5 feet tall, *Ceanothus otayensis* is found on Otay and San Miguel Mountains in southern San Diego County, California. It occurs in chaparral at 1,670–3,700 feet 510–1,100 m) and is considered a species of special concern due to its limited distribution and the threat of habitat loss.

The thick, evergreen leaves are oval, $1/4$–$1/2$ inch long, with revolute, often toothed margins. Dull green to gray above and white to rusty-brown below, they are evenly spaced along the stems in an opposite arrangement. Held in terminal or upper axils, white to pale blue flowers bloom from January to April in umbel-shaped heads $^1/_4$–$^1/_2$ inch long.

Otay Mountain ceanothus is occasionally grown in southern California and is available from specialty growers and at botanical garden plant sales. Relatively untested as a garden subject, the handsome gray foliage is useful combined in gardens with silver-, blue-, and other gray-leaved plants. It could be used in dry borders with rosemary, lavender, and rockrose. Full sun is recommended along the coast, and partial shade in interior sites. Otay Mountain ceanothus is hardy to at least 15 °F (−9 °C).

Ceanothus 'Owlswood Blue'

A large, spreading hybrid, 'Owlswood Blue' was selected in the 1950s from seed collected in an Oakland, California, garden by Malcolm G. Smith. The parentage is believed to be *Ceanothus arboreus* × *C. thyrsiflorus* var. *griseus*, as the leaves and large spreading habit suggest. 'Owlswood Blue' was selected, named, and subsequently presented to the Saratoga Horticultural Research Foundation for further evaluation in 1972. Plants were introduced by the foundation into the commercial nursery and landscape trade in 1975.

Mature plants can reach 10 feet high with a spread of 20 feet or more. The rounded, 2- to 3-inch-long leaves are dark green and have waxy, polished surfaces. Budding flower clusters lack the pink or burgundy bud scales and bracts common in other cultivars, but the blue coloring is intensified as a result. In full flower the compound trusses can reach 9 inches in length with a 3-inch spread. Flower color is similar to the reputed parents, a pleasing deep-sea blue.

Vigorous and fast growing, 'Owlswood Blue' is reliably heavy blooming, often flowering again in fall. Periodic pinching of new growth will help shape and control its spreading habit. It is useful as a screen, bank cover, or informal hedge for sunny, well-drained gardens and has regained favor among a number of California growers.

Ceanothus ×pallidus

Pallidus hybrid ceanothus

Ceanothus ×pallidus is a hybrid series named by John Lindley (1840) that resulted from a cross between *C. herbaceus* (at the time called *C. ovatus*) and *C. ×delilianus*. Similar to the *C. ×delilianus* hybrids, they are all deciduous, bear flowers on new wood in late spring and summer, and benefit from a hard annual pruning. Rose- and pink-flowered selections are common in the *C. ×pallidus* series, due in part to the dilution of the *C. caeruleus* influence in *C. ×delilianus*:

'Golden Elan' is the only hybrid in the series with variegated foliage. The ovate, 2-inch-long leaves have dark green centers with margins of yellow-green variegation. Ruby stems and pink flowers add a delicate rosy glow to the foliage. Only occasionally available, it is worth the effort to locate.

'Marie Simon' has the strongest pink flowers of the series, opening from deep rose-colored buds into panicles as long as 5 inches. Colorful red stems complement both the bright green 3-inch-long leaves and the pink flowers. It is a strong, robust shrub to 5 feet high with an equal spread.

'Perle Rose' is striking, featuring large plumes of rose-carmine flowers on an upright form to 8 feet tall. Flower color is reportedly weak in some soil types.

Ceanothus papillosus

wartleaf ceanothus, Tranquillon Mountain ceanothus, Rowe ceanothus

Ceanothus papillosus is another species discovered by the tenacious plant collector David Douglas while traveling through California in 1832. It was introduced into English gardens in 1850 by William Lobb and was regarded as "one of the most desirable species" (Van Rensselaer 1942) for many years. Although still listed in the Royal Horticultural Society's *Plant Finder,* it has lost favor compared to some of the newer

Ceanothus ×pallidus 'Perle Rose' with *C. ×delilianus* 'Henri Desfosse', Knoll Gardens, Dorset, England

hybrid cultivars and is no longer commonly grown in the British Isles. The popularity and availability of wartleaf ceanothus have followed a similar course in California, resulting in its use being primarily in restoration.

Wartleaf ceanothus is an erect shrub 3–12 feet tall, often with arching branches to 10 feet wide. The dark green, distinctly narrow leaves can reach $2^{1}/_{2}$ inches in length and have a blistered or warty surface. Sticky to the touch and leathery, the leaves have blunt or notched tips with revolute margins and pale green undersides. From March to May, dense heads of red-purple buds open into rounded, dark blue to purple flower clusters 1–2 inches across.

Two varieties of *Ceanothus papillosus* are sometimes recognized, based primarily on size, form, and geographical range. Variety *papillosus* is found in the South Coast Range from San Francisco south to the western Transverse Ranges, Santa Ana Mountains, and into northwestern Baja California, Mexico. Variety *roweanus* has a compact form less than 5 feet tall and is apparently restricted to the western slopes of the Santa Ynez Mountains in Santa Barbara County. E. Denys Rowe, a leading California horticulturist in the mid-20th century, discovered it on Tranquillon Mountain in 1935, and variety *roweanus* rapidly became the more favored garden form.

The interesting leaves of wartleaf ceanothus would be reason enough to grow the species. Some selections have radiant, dark blue flowers, and the smaller, more compact forms of variety *roweanus* make excellent specimens in mixed borders or on dry, open hillsides. It will tolerate some shade and can be mixed effectively into woodland gardens or used to border mature oaks. Best sited in coastal gardens, wartleaf ceanothus requires light pruning to control wayward stems and encourage compact growth.

Ceanothus parryi
Parry's ceanothus

Praise for the graceful *Ceanothus parryi* is woven through the literature of the genus. Maunsell Van Rensselaer (1942) called it "one of the most beautiful of all." Howard McMinn believed it would replace the then popular *C. thyrsiflorus*, particularly in interior gardens. Lester Rowntree (1939) remarked, "*C. parryi* is well nicknamed Ladybloom; there is something very graceful about the shrub and its growth habit." Nurseryman M. Nevin Smith (1979) expressed a frustration of many California horticulturists when he stated, "In my view, lady bloom has been unfairly overlooked for landscape use." Viewing specimens growing in the chaparral in the North Coast Range of California and in west-central Oregon only confirms these collective voices.

Similar to *Ceanothus thyrsiflorus*, Parry's ceanothus has an upright habit with delicate, arching branches typically 8–12 feet tall. The dark green, oblong leaves are three-veined, $^{1}/_{2}$–$1^{1}/_{2}$ inches long, with dense hairs on the pale green undersides. The foliage, though fragrant, lacks the bright, lustrous quality of *C. thyrsiflorus*. Flowers form in conical, 1¼- to 2¾-inch-long trusses in colors from pale to deep blue.

The potential of *Ceanothus parryi* remains unexplored, as few West Coast nurseries grow it. It would certainly make a fine screen, specimen, or informal hedge, and it tolerates interior heat much better than *C. thyrsiflorus*. Selection for form and dark blue flower color would add to the appeal. Full to partial sun and well-drained soils are recommended, as ideal garden conditions and hardiness are not certain.

Ceanothus parvifolius

littleleaf ceanothus

Ceanothus parvifolius is a deciduous, flat-topped shrub to 4 feet tall with spreading olive-green to reddish branches. The alternate, medium-green leaves are oblong to elliptic, ¼–1 inch long, and three-veined with entire margins. Pale to dark blue flowers open from smoky blue buds into 1- to 3-inch-long simple or compound clusters. It grows on wooded mountain slopes and flats at 4,500–7,300 feet (1,360–2,210 m) along the western slope of the Sierra Nevada from Plumas County to Tulare County, California.

Flexible branches radiate away from the central axis of the main stem, creating an intriguing form in mature specimens. The small glossy leaves, bright blue flowers, green to reddish branches, and manageable size combined with the interesting lines suggest significant horticultural potential. Unfortunately, littleleaf ceanothus is seldom cultivated, in part because it is deciduous, and also due to poor performance at lower elevations. Maunsell Van Rensselaer suggested it might be suitable in the Pacific Northwest or the eastern United States, but there is little evidence of any significant testing.

Ceanothus pauciflorus

woolly ceanothus, Gregg's ceanothus

Ceanothus pauciflorus is a widely scattered species found in desert and montane shrublands, woodlands, and forests from southwestern Texas to Tamaulipas and San Luis Potosí, Mexico. An erect shrub with a mounding or occasionally tree-like form, it produces spreading or ascending stems 3–10 feet tall and 5–8 feet wide. The opposite, leathery, thick, ¼- to ½-inch-long leaves have pallid green to gray-green upper surfaces. Leaf shape is variable, and some populations have leaf blades that are folded lengthwise. White to pale blue or pink-tinged flowers are held in loose rounded heads as wide as 1 inch.

Some plants previously grown as *Ceanothus greggii* vars. *perplexans* and *vestitus* are treated here as *C. vestitus*. *Ceanothus pauciflorus* is rarely grown in the United States, although it is heat and drought tolerant, and taller-growing specimens could be trained into attractive small trees.

Ceanothus 'Percy Picton'

A cultivar originating in the United Kingdom and named for the owner of Old Court Nursery, Worcestershire, England, 'Percy Picton' is believed to be a cross between *Ceanothus impressus* and *C. papillosus;* it exhibits the rich blue flowers and dark green, wrinkled leaves common to both parents.

'Percy Picton' is a dense, rounded shrub 6–10 feet tall with a 10- to 14-foot spread. Like the hybrids 'Dark Star' and 'Julia Phelps', it has arching stems and is covered in early spring with small clusters of dark, cobalt-blue flowers. Fast growing yet dense, it is excellent as a screen or informal hedge or can be sited as a specimen. 'Percy Picton' is occasionally grown in the British Isles and to our knowledge has not been introduced into North America. It is hardy to at least 15°F (−9°C).

Ceanothus 'Picnic Day'

'Picnic Day' originated in the 1960s as a seedling selected by botanist Don Sexton at UC Davis Arboretum. It is believed to be a hybrid, *Ceanothus thyrsiflorus* var. *griseus* × *C. arboreus,* and was introduced into the nursery trade in 1974. The three-veined, dark green, elliptic leaves and rich blue flowers held in 6- to 7-inch-long pyramidal trusses are consistent with other hybrids of this parentage, such as 'Ray Hartman'.

Named 'Picnic Day' for it habit of blooming in late April, it is an upright shrub to 12 feet high with a spread of 10–14 feet. Like many fast-growing cultivars, it benefits from pruning particularly when young and is useful as a screen, informal hedge, or specimen. 'Picnic Day' has not been widely grown and is available primarily through botanical garden plant sales. It has been grown successfully at UC Davis Arboretum for many years, demonstrating good heat and drought tolerance. Hardiness has not been widely tested, but it will likely tolerate short periods to as low as 15°F (−9°C).

Ceanothus pinetorum

Kern Plateau ceanothus, Coville's ceanothus

Ceanothus pinetorum is a California endemic found on the Kern Plateau in the southern Sierra Nevada and in the southern Trinity Mountains of Trinity and Shasta Counties of northern California. It grows on wooded slopes and flats in openings in conifer forests—often in the pine forests for which it was named—at 5,400–8,500 feet (1,630–2,570 m) in elevation, frequently in the company of *C. prostratus* in the Trinity Mountains. Low and spreading, 6 inches to 3 feet tall and to 12 feet wide, the rigid gray stems hold evenly spaced, evergreen, rounded leaves $1/2$–1 inch long with prickly toothed margins. Pale blue to lavender-blue flower clusters are held in short-stalked umbels $1/4$–$1/2$ inch long.

Kern Plateau ceanothus is rarely cultivated, although it is infrequently grown for restoration and revegetation purposes in its native range. Tolerant of heavy snowfall and cold temperatures, the lower-growing forms hold potential for use in mountain environments as ground covers or massed on road cuts for erosion control.

Ceanothus prostratus
mahala mat

Ceanothus prostratus is typically found under the canopy of mixed coniferous forest in mountains of Washington, Oregon, and northern California at 2,600–9,000 feet (790–2,720 m). Growing in rocky or gravelly soils, mahala mat forms broad, dense carpets 2–6 inches tall and 2–8 feet across. In these appealing, open forests it resembles a green blanket pulled tightly over the forest floor, and in many populations a light dusting of pine needles adds to the allure.

The young red branches bear leathery, wedge-shaped leaves as long as 1 inch. The blunt leaf tips are distinctly toothed in some populations, nearly smooth in others. Flowers are held in rounded umbels of lavender to blue from mid to late spring. Horned, bright red fruit follows flowering and adds an attractive seasonal interest.

As a garden subject, mahala mat is quite another matter—it has been characterized as maddeningly difficult. Perhaps Lester Rowntree (1939) stated it best: "I have tried it in sandy soil and in red clay-like soil, in humus and grit, and in loam. And I have decided that the secret of its culture rests in the laps of the gods and that they are keeping it a secret." Nursery people and gardeners continue to experiment with mahala mat, and perhaps one day we will have a selection more tolerant of garden conditions. Still, for those seeking a challenge, *Ceanothus prostratus* is waiting.

Ceanothus 'Puget Blue'

A selection made from the Washington Park Arboretum in Seattle, 'Puget Blue' is at times listed as a cultivar of *Ceanothus impressus*. Although similar in appearance to that species, it is believed to have originated from open-pollinated seed of *C. papillosus* var. *roweanus* (now considered only a compact form of the species) sent to the arboretum by Lester Rowntree. The longer, narrower leaves, revolute margins, and depressed veins appear to confirm the parentage.

'Puget Blue' has been a favorite in the Pacific Northwest for many years and has demonstrated remarkable garden tolerance. Some plants have been reported to live in excess of 20 years, reaching heights of 8–12 feet and spreading as wide as 15 feet. Arching branches add grace to its dense, rounded form. Sprays of luminous lavender-blue flowers obscure the warty, $^1/_2$- to $^3/_4$-inch-long leaves in early spring. Considered one of the hardiest of the evergreen cultivars, it has tolerated 10°F (−12°C) with little damage. 'Puget Blue' received an Award of Merit in 1971 and an Award of Garden Merit in 1984 from the Royal Horticultural Society.

Ceanothus pumilus

Siskiyou mat, Siskiyou ceanothus

Ceanothus pumilus is a prostrate species that grows on serpentinitic soils from south-western Oregon south through the Klamath Mountains and North Coast Range to Mendocino County, California. Found on slopes, summits, and ridges at elevations of 460–7,400 feet (140–2,240 m), it is common in chaparral and open sites in conifer forests. Similar in appearance to *C. cuneatus*, the thick, flat green leaves are oblong, $^{1}/_{4}$–$^{1}/_{2}$ inch long, and usually have a few distal teeth along the margins. Rounded, $^{1}/_{2}$-inch-long clusters of pale blue to lavender-blue flowers form in late spring and continue into early summer.

Siskiyou mat is occasionally grown in the Pacific Northwest, primarily as a rock garden subject. The creeping stems root occasionally, making Siskiyou mat effective as a small-scale ground cover or spilling down a steep bank. Temperamental and slow growing, it does best in full sun or partial shade with well-drained soils and some summer moisture. The range and elevation of Siskiyou mat suggest hardiness to at least 0°F (−18°C).

Ceanothus purpureus

hollyleaf ceanothus, Napa ceanothus

A narrow endemic from the Vaca Mountains of Napa and Solano Counties, California, *Ceanothus purpureus* is typically found in chaparral and open woodlands on dry, rocky ridges and slopes. Erect or spreading, specimens typically have an open, rounded form 3–6 feet tall and spread 3–9 feet wide, with stiff, gray-barked stems. The dark green, rounded leaves are as long as 2 inches and have sharp teeth lining the wavy margins, probably accounting for its lack of appeal to deer. Strikingly beautiful in bloom, the swollen flower buds are silver-lavender, opening into flattened 1-inch-wide umbels of purple-lavender blossoms.

Hollyleaf ceanothus has a temperamental reputation and is rarely grown by California gardeners. It does best in well-drained soils with sun or filtered shade and requires supplemental water in hotter, drier locations. Young stems should be tipped to prevent the legginess common in older specimens.

Ceanothus 'Ray Hartman'

'Ray Hartman' is one of the best known and most commonly grown selections in California. A cross between *Ceanothus arboreus* and *C. thyrsiflorus* var. *griseus*, the original seedling was collected in Saratoga and grown at Leonard Coates Nurseries in Morgan Hill. Howard McMinn was the first to evaluate and distribute plants, and for a brief period in the late 1940s it carried the cultivar name 'Blue Sky'. Saratoga Horticultural Research Foundation eventually renamed and introduced it in 1954 with the approval of the Coates Nurseries and Everett Far-well of Oak Knoll Nursery, who had sold it as 'Blue Sky'. It was named in honor of Ray Hartman for his lifelong interest and advocacy of California native plants.

One of the largest-growing cultivars available, 'Ray Hartman' can reach a height of 12–20 feet and be equally wide. Young plants have a spherical, upright form, eventually becoming a tall, willow-like mound. The evergreen, $1^1/_2$- to 3-inch-long and $^1/_2$- to $^3/_4$-inch-wide leaves are alternate, modestly revolute, and three-veined from the base. Dark green, they have a bright sheen on their upper surfaces and are gray below with silky pubescence. Compound clusters 3–5 inches long of medium-blue flowers form from decorative lavender-rose buds that are covered with silky hairs. The blue flowers combined with the rosy buds and dark green foliage give mature spec-imens a bright lavender cast. Three-lobed fruits are at first burgundy and quickly turn a dark chocolate-brown.

'Ray Hartman' is considered by many to be one of the most reliable and gar-den-tolerant ceanothuses in cultivation and deserves its nickname "old depend-able." Due to its rapid growth, careful and frequent pruning may be required to keep specimens restrained. It tolerates heavy soils, summer watering, and the

Ceanothus 'Ray Hartman' freeway planting, Atascadero, California; also see page 29

hotter, drier conditions found in interior gardens. Best grown in full sun, it can be used in partial shade though flowering is not as profuse. Useful as a screen, specimen, or small tree, "Even in this favored land, where all types of plants grow readily, a blue-flowering tree is something to behold," noted Marjorie Schmidt (1980). 'Ray Hart-man' will also tolerate heavy pruning and can be trained into a hedge, but with inhib-ited flower production. Hardy to 15°F (−9°C), it gets frost burn with consistent nights

Ceanothus 'Ray Hartman', pruned, Carmel, California

of temperatures below 20°F(−7°C). The California Horticultural Society granted its Award of Merit to 'Ray Hartman' in 1957.

Ceanothus 'Remote Blue'

An evergreen hybrid from the grounds of Las Pilitas Nursery in Santa Margarita, California, 'Remote Blue' is believed to be a cross between *Ceanothus oliganthus* var. *sorediatus* and *C. thyrsiflorus* var. *griseus.* Introduced in 1991 by the nursery's owners, Bert and Celeste Wilson, it has been successfully grown in a wide range of sites and has demonstrated remarkable garden tolerance.

A mounding shrub to 8 feet tall with an equal spread, it features oval, 1- to 1$^1/_4$-inch-long leaves with lustrous green surfaces held on attractive lime-green and gray stems. Flowers form from charcoal-blue buds before opening into clear blue, 2- to 3-inch-long clusters that complement the glistening leaves.

'Remote Blue' is useful as an informal hedge, or with light pruning it would be suitable in a formal garden as a screen or specimen. The bright, gleaming foliage adds sparkle to the garden and is effective when sited against the flat foliage color of conifers. Full sun and well-drained soils are recommended, although it has performed well in a wide range of soil types, including heavy clay. It is known to be hardy to 15°F (−9°C) without suffering damage.

Ceanothus roderickii
Pine Hill ceanothus, Roderick's ceanothus

Ceanothus roderickii is a narrow endemic found on gabbro-derived soils in the Sierra Nevada foothills of western El Dorado County, California. Growing in chaparral and woodlands at elevations of 850–2,070 feet (260–630 m), it occurs with a number of rare plants that are restricted to the unusual soils of Pine Hill State Ecological Reserve. *Ceanothus roderickii* is listed under the federal Endangered Species Act as endangered, and with the state of California as rare. The species was named for Wayne Roderick, raconteur, gardener, plant collector, mentor to a generation of native plant advocates, and the first to cultivate Pine Hill ceanothus in 1963.

Pine Hill ceanothus is a prostrate or mounding shrub to 18 inches tall and 9 feet wide, with rooting stems. The evergreen, elliptic leaves are thick, $^1/_6$–$^1/_3$ inch long, and have entire margins occasionally toothed at the apex. Soft green above and pale green below, the leaf blades ascend along radiating stems, presenting the lower surface almost as clearly as the upper surface. White to pale blue flowers are held in short-stalked, rounded clusters $^1/_4$–$^1/_2$ inch long, making the stems appear as if adorned with cotton balls from April to June.

Pine Hill ceanothus is not commonly grown but has a novel appeal. It has been characterized by some as odd, and Roderick (personal communication, 1997) considered it "the homeliest species in the genus." Available at specialty nurseries and botanical garden plant sales, Pine Hill ceanothus is suitable in rock gardens or sited on dry banks, and for some it is a simple reminder of the extraordinary man for whom it was named.

Ceanothus 'Russellianus'
Russell ceanothus

A hybrid of similar parentage as *Ceanothus ×lobbianus*, 'Russellianus' is sometimes listed as a cultivar of *C. dentatus* in the United Kingdom. Vigorous and mounding, it grows to 6 feet tall and 6–8 feet wide. The dark green, $^1/_2$- to $^3/_4$-inch-long leaves are elliptic to oblanceolate and have a bright, glossy surface and gland-tipped teeth along the margins. Silver-blue buds open into tight, 2- to 4-inch-long clusters of slate-blue flowers. A floriferous cultivar, the foliage is covered with blossoms from late winter to the middle of spring.

'Russellianus' is confusing in the nursery trade—*Ceanothus ×lobbianus*, *C. dentatus*, and the hybrid 'Southmead' are at times sold under the name. A handsome midsized shrub, it can be combined at the back of dry border with Mediterranean shrubs and grasses or sited on a south-facing slope with other ceanothuses. Full sun or partial shade and well-drained soils are recommended. It is rarely grown in the United States and has become harder to find in the United Kingdom. It is hardy to at least 15°F (−9°C).

Ceanothus sanguineus

redstem ceanothus, Oregon tea-tree, northern buckbrush

Ceanothus sanguineus is a deciduous shrub found in the Pacific Northwest from northern California to southern British Columbia, Canada, east to Montana and with a disjunct population in Michigan. Growing in forest openings, along forest edges, and on prairie margins from near sea level to 4,500 feet (1,360 m), it frequently colonizes abandoned lots, clearings, and roadsides. Mounding and 5–10 feet in height, redstem ceanothus has an open habit and flexible, green to reddish stems. The flat, three-veined leaves are ovate, 1–2³/₄ inch long, and have pallid to shiny green surfaces. Flowers bloom from the middle of spring to early summer in loose, 1- to 2-inch-long clusters of dull white to occasionally pink-tinged blossoms on side shoots of the previous season's growth.

Redstem ceanothus is used primarily for revegetation and habitat restoration in its native range. A few nurseries in the Pacific Northwest offer it for sale, where it can be cultivated with ease for erosion control or in transition to native habitats. It was discovered and collected by Meriwether Lewis in 1806 and later introduced into England by the resolute William Lobb, who collected it for Veitch nurseries in 1853.

Ceanothus 'Sierra Blue'

Selected by Walter Lammerts in 1948, 'Sierra Blue' is an open-pollinated seedling of 'La Primavera', an evergreen garden hybrid from the Santa Barbara Botanic Garden chosen from open-pollinated seedlings of *Ceanothus cyaneus* in 1935 by Maunsell Van Rensselaer. Its primary characteristics are clearly those of *C. cyaneus.*

Open and free-formed, 'Sierra Blue' can reach 15–20 feet tall and spread to 25 feet wide. Young stems and branches are light green and hold polished, three-veined leaves to 2¹/₂ inches long. Silver-blue buds form on terminal stems before opening into compound, 6- to 8-inch-long sprays of vivid blue-violet flowers. Hanging like blue lanterns from April to mid-May, the abundant flowers cast a soothing calm.

Fast growing, 'Sierra Blue' benefits from selective pruning to improve its form. It is best grown in full sun as plants in shade tend to be sparsely foliaged. Useful as a

Ceanothus 'Sierra Blue', Rancho Santa Ana Botanic Garden, California

specimen, open screen, informal hedge, or small tree, it is garden tolerant and has a reputation for longevity. 'Sierra Blue' is an excellent selection for southern California in both coastal and interior gardens and is hardy to about 18°F (−8°C).

Ceanothus 'Sierra Snow'

An evergreen hybrid collected in Rancho Santa Ana Botanic Garden by Lee Lenz and named for its attractive white flowers, 'Sierra Snow' was introduced in 1979. Parentage is unknown, but it is presumed to be a cross between *Ceanothus cuneatus* and perhaps *C. fresnensis*. The olive-green $1/2$-inch-long leaves are thick, leathery, and wedge-shaped, appearing to fit with the *C. cuneatus* complex.

'Sierra Snow' is a stiffly upright shrub 8–10 feet tall with an equal spread. Open and woody, mature plants have handsome, muted gray stems. In late winter and early spring the branchlets and stems are covered with dusty white floral buds that open into dome-shaped, $1/2$- to 1-inch-wide clusters of milky white flowers. A floriferous cultivar, plants in full bloom have a captivating lathered or frothy appearance.

The erect form of 'Sierra Snow' makes it useful as a specimen or mixed with other hybrids such as 'Frosty Blue' or 'Ray Hartman' to form an attractive informal hedge or screen. Slower growing than many of the other upright cultivars, it can be trained to con-

Ceanothus 'Sierra Snow', Leaning Pine Arboretum, California Polytechnic University, San Luis Obispo

form to a narrow corner with light pruning, or it might be espaliered on a dark wall. It has demonstrated exceptional garden tolerance and can be used in both coastal and interior gardens. Full sun is recommended, and plants are hardy to at least 10°F (−12°C).

Ceanothus 'Skylark'

The origin of 'Skylark' remains ambiguous. Introduced by Mitch Nursery of Aurora, Oregon, the cultivar filtered through West Coast nursery channels until it was finally named by M. Nevin Smith with "a desire to distinguish it from others in the trade" (Smith 1979). Parentage is thought to be *Ceanothus thyrsiflorus* var. *thyrsiflorus* × *C. velutinus,* which is consistent with the broad physical characteristics of the plant. It is believed by many to be the same plant grown in the nursery trade as *C. thyrsiflorus* 'Victoria'.

Dense and compact, 'Skylark' has a dome-shaped form to 4 feet tall and 6 feet wide, making it a good choice for smaller gardens. The dark green, 2-inch-long leaves are curled and have a thick, resinous texture. Cerulean blue flowers are produced later than in most other cultivars, from late spring to early summer. Light pruning of spent flowers will improve the appearance, as it tends to hold old inflorescence stalks longer than other cultivars. 'Skylark' has demonstrated a wide tolerance of climate and soil types and performs well in both coastal and interior sites. In 1972, plants survived repeated nights of 10°F (−12°C) with daytime temperatures not rising above 30°F (−1°C).

Ceanothus sonomensis

Sonoma ceanothus

Ceanothus sonomensis is another of California's narrow endemics and is found in the Hood mountains separating the Napa and Sonoma Valleys on summits, ridges and slopes primarily in chaparral. It is an erect evergreen shrub 2–4 feet tall with spreading or upright gray to gray-brown stems. Thick, holly-like leaves with spined margins are $^1/_4$–$^1/_2$ inch long and have a dark green upper surface and pale green underside. The short-stalked, blue to lavender flower clusters are rounded, $^1/_4$–$^1/_2$ inch long, and open in early spring.

Ceanothus sonomensis was discovered by Milo Baker in 1933 and planted in his garden and on the campus of Santa Rosa Junior College. Maunsell Van Rensselaer thought Sonoma ceanothus might achieve some measure of popularity with gardeners, but it is seldom cultivated and is used primarily in revegetation and restoration applications.

Ceanothus 'Southmead'

'Southmead' is similar to *Ceanothus* ×*lobbianus* and the hybrid 'Russellianus' and is believed to be a cross between *C. dentatus* and *C. thyrsiflorus* var. *griseus.* Selected and named by Captain C. K. Mooney, it was given and Award of Merit at Chelsea in 1964 and an Award of Garden Merit in 1984 by the Royal Horticultural Society.

Dense and rounded, 'Southmead' grows to 6 feet tall with a similar width. The evergreen elliptic leaves are $^3/_4$–$1^1/_4$ inches long and have glandular-toothed margins. Distinctly three-veined with a lustrous sheen, they are a handsome balance of the parentage. Rich blue flowers form in the middle of spring in oblong, 2- to 4-inch-long clusters.

Garden tolerant and durable, 'Southmead' was a popular selection in the British Isles for many years. Used commonly in the landscape and nursery trade, it is still seen, frequently against walls. It is rarely grown in the United States but has been reintroduced into California. It is hardy to a least 15°F (−9°C).

Ceanothus spinosus
green-bark ceanothus

Ceanothus spinosus is a large, sprawling shrub that can reach 20 feet tall with a broad, open crown. The stiff, yellow-green stems are blunt-tipped but can be spine-like, as the name of the species implies. Bright, glossy green leaves are flat, oblong, and $^1/_2$–1 inch long. Typically evergreen, it can also be semideciduous in exceptionally dry years. Sprays of frothy, gray-blue to white flowers are held in loose, 2- to 6-inch-long trusses from late winter to early spring. Darker blue forms are occasionally found, but the

Ceanothus spinosus var. *spinosus* in chaparral above Santa Barbara, California

flower colors in mass are usually a hazy blue or, as Lester Rowntree (1939) suggested, "like a sea of fog or a great drift of smoke, caught against the hillsides."

Green-bark ceanothus is fast growing and may require some pruning to control its expansive character. It can be shaped into an open tree form and is suitable as a coarse screen or in transition to chaparral or woodland. Older specimens have a shabby, disheveled appearance, but they can be faced with silver-leaved shrubs such as *Salvia leucophylla* or *Constancea nevinii* (formerly *Eriophyllum nevinii*) 'Canyon Silver' to cover the lower branches and complement the billowing flowers. Coppicing is also an option with older plants as *Ceanothus spinosus* is one of the few species that will reliably crown sprout, producing new branches when the plant is cut back to the ground. Full sun to partial shade and well-drained soil are recommended.

Ceanothus 'Tassajara Blue'

Introduced in 1996, 'Tassajara Blue' is a garden hybrid selected by Bert and Celeste Wilson of Las Pilitas Nursery in Santa Margarita, California. Similar to 'Ray Hartman', the parentage is believed to be *Ceanothus arboreus* × *C. thyrsiflorus* var. *griseus*, which is validated by the broad, dark green, 2- to 3-inch-long leaves, and the frothy, cone-shaped flower clusters. Robust and upright, 'Tassajara Blue' can grow 6–8 feet high and 12 feet wide. The spring buds are dark rose-blue before opening into bright, 3- to 5-inch-long sprays of bright blue.

Although relatively new to the nursery trade, 'Tassajara Blue' has demonstrated good garden tolerance in limited trials. It is useful as a screen or hedge, massed on dry

Ceanothus 'Tassajara Blue', private garden, Arroyo Grande, California

slopes, or even in woodland gardens with half-day sun. The bud and flower combination is striking and is often repeated, though not as heavily, in fall. It performs best in full or partial sun and is hardy to a least 15°F (−9°C).

Ceanothus thyrsiflorus

blueblossom

Ceanothus thyrsiflorus is a common shrub along the coast of California from near Point Conception in Santa Barbara County to southern Oregon, and it is found in a broad range of forms and habitats. Specimens in protected canyons can be massive, reaching 20 feet high and spreading as wide as 40 feet in tangled thickets of maritime chaparral, while others are wind-sculpted into dense, low hedges on rocky headlands. The ever-green leaves range in size, $1/2$–$1^1/2$ inches long and $1/4$–1 inch wide. All are three-veined from the base but can vary in color from dark forest-green to shiny yellow-green. Leaf margins are weakly rolled or plane, with a faint row of teeth along the edge. The dark to pale blue or rarely white flowers are held in $1/2$- to $2^1/2$-inch-long clusters that vary in form from open to dense. Flowering depends on the site and ranges from early March to June.

Ceanothus thyrsiflorus var. *thyrsiflorus,* private garden, Carmel Valley, California

Howard McMinn distinguished *Ceanothus thyrsiflorus* from what he called *C. griseus* on leaf margin and absence or presence of fine hairs on the leaf surface. These differences appear to intergrade, and plants show considerable variation. Consequently, *griseus* is treated here as a variety of *C. thyrsiflorus.* Variety *griseus* is distinguished by revolute margins throughout the length of the blade and the presence of short hairs on the underside of the leaves. Variety *thyrsiflorus* has plane margins, and the lower leaf surfaces are sparsely hairy or lack hair altogether.

Ceanothus thyrsiflorus var. *griseus* hedge, London, England

Ceanothus thyrsiflorus var. *griseus*
Carmel ceanothus

Ceanothus thyrsiflorus var. *griseus* is the most commonly planted ceanothus species in California. It is found along the coast of California from Santa Barbara to Mendocino Counties in a variety of habitats including exposed bluffs and headlands, steep canyon slopes, and dunes. Plants are typically wide spreading and vary in height, 1–15 feet. The leaves are ovate to elliptic, 1–2 inches long and feature glossy, dark green surfaces with revolute margins. Flower colors vary from luminous indigo to pale, denim blue. Most of the selections made from Carmel ceanothus are durable, garden tolerant subjects when used in coastal sites. They require supplemental summer watering and are often short-lived when planted in warmer, interior environments.

A number of outstanding ground-cover cultivars have been made from the low-growing forms of Carmel ceanothus that occur along the ocean bluffs between Hurricane Point and Carmel in northern Monterey County—'Diamond Heights', 'Hurricane Point', and 'Yankee Point'—from what at the time was called *Ceanothus griseus* var. *horizontalis*. Variety *horizontalis* is not recognized here as the gradient of low-growing to arborescent forms found in the wild provides insufficient evidence to justify these prostrate forms as distinct. Plants grown under the name variety *horizontalis* in the nursery trade are variable, but most are large-leaved, have pale blue flowers, and reach 3–5 feet high with a 12-foot spread. They can be easily pruned to maintain a lower form by removing upright and arching branches. They make exceptional choices for seaside gardens

Ceanothus thyrsiflorus var. *griseus,* private garden, Santa Barbara, California; also see page 13

Ceanothus thyrsiflorus var. *griseus* on a wall, Richmond Hill, England

as most of the lower-growing selections originate from habitats with strong prevailing winds and salt spray. Hardiness is variable, but most will survive frosts of short duration to 15°F (−9°C).

Ceanothus thyrsiflorus var. *griseus* 'Blue and Gold'

David McCrory discovered the variegated 'Blue and Gold' in 1999 growing on a stem of *Ceanothus thyrsiflorus* var. *griseus* at a gas station in San Raphael, California. It was sold for a brief period in the California nursery trade without a cultivar name, and Maggie Wych of Western Hills Nursery gave it the cultivar name.

A sprawling shrub 2–4 feet high with a 6- to 8-foot spread, 'Blue and Gold' features highly variable yellow-gold variegation—some leaves with no variegation, some entirely yellow-gold, others intermediate. The evergreen leaves are typical of *Ceanothus thyrsiflorus* var. *griseus*: three-veined, elliptic, and 1–1^1/$_2$ inches long. From February to May, medium-blue flowers are held in cylindrical sprays 1–2 inches long. Occasional flowers form in later summer and fall as well.

'Blue and Gold' is a vigorous cultivar suitable mixed in large-scale plantings of Carmel ceanothus (*Ceanothus thyrsiflorus* var. *griseus*) for contrast and interest. The unpredictable variegation adds appeal and character to otherwise broad masses of green and can be woven into a low hedge of Carmel ceanothus with the same effect. Culturally similar to Carmel ceanothus, 'Blue and Gold' is best in full sun along the coast and partial shade in interior sites.

Ceanothus thyrsiflorus var. *griseus* 'Diamond Heights', Fross garden, Arroyo Grande, California

Ceanothus thyrsiflorus var. *griseus* 'Diamond Heights'

A variegated, prostrate cultivar 6–12 inches tall with a 3- to 5-foot spread, Barry Lehrman selected 'Diamond Heights' in 1985 from a cultivated population of *Ceanothus thyrsiflorus* var. *griseus* (at the time called *C. griseus* var. *horizontalis*) in the Mount Davidson area of San Francisco. Named for the housing development where it was found, it was introduced into the California nursery trade a few years later. The leaves have a marbled yellow variegation at the margins and are of typical size for *C. thyrsiflorus* var. *griseus*. Plants are generally grown for their foliage as the rounded, 2-

inch-long flower clusters are a peculiar blue against the variegation. 'Diamond Heights' is suited to mild coastal climates and requires some shading to prevent burning, especially in warmer, interior gardens. The variegation is stable, although reverting stems are not uncommon, as are other interesting sports. It is particularly effective with dark-green-foliaged plants such as *Rhamnus californica* 'Leatherleaf' and *Carex tumulicola*, or paired with *Chamaecyparis lawsoniana* 'Lutea'.

Ceanothus thyrsiflorus var. *griseus* 'All Gold', Fross garden, Arroyo Grande, California

An occasionally cultivated selection from 'Diamond Heights' has been named 'All Gold'. As the name implies, the leaves are gold with an absence of the green found in 'Diamond Heights'. 'All Gold' is considerably slower growing than 'Diamond Heights', forming a prostrate ground cover 6–12 inches high with a 2- to 4-foot spread. Plants seldom flower but when they do are a dusty pale blue, held in 1-inch-long clusters. 'All Gold' has proven surprisingly garden tolerant but requires partial to full shade to prevent leaf burn. It is useful in woodland gardens and will grow through the leaf fall common in these gardens. It is hardy to at least 17°F (−8°C).

Ceanothus thyrsiflorus var. griseus 'Hurricane Point'

'Hurricane Point' originated from seeds collected near Hurricane Point along California Highway 1 south of the Little Sur River by Louis Edmunds prior to 1960. He later introduced this large-leaved, wide-spreading form through his influential Native Plant Nursery in Danville. Many of the plants in the California nursery trade labeled 'Carmel Creeper' are Louis Edmunds' original selection, 'Hurricane Point'.

'Hurricane Point' is a vigorous, sprawling selection 2–3 feet tall with a 15- to 30-foot spread. The oval leaves are 2 inches long and have polished, dark green surfaces held on lime-green stems. It is not particularly floriferous; pale blue flowers form in cylindrical 1-inch-long clusters in late winter and early spring.

Lower growing than most other previously recognized *Ceanothus thyrsiflorus* var. *griseus* (at the time called *C. griseus* var. *horizontalis*) cultivars, 'Hurricane Point' will quickly cover a large bank and can be combined with other spreading native shrubs such as *Salvia leucophylla* 'Point Sal' and *Fremontodendron* 'Dara's Gold' to form a drought-tolerant mosaic. Pruning will control its rampant growth, or it can be sheared into a dense low hedge. Like other *C. thyrsiflorus* var. *griseus* clones, it is highly suscepti-

Ceanothus thyrsiflorus var. *griseus* 'Kurt Zadnik', private garden, Berkeley, California

ble to deer damage and should not be sited in areas with large deer populations. It is a reliable, garden-tolerant selection for coastal gardens and hardy to about 15°F (−9°C).

Ceanothus thyrsiflorus var. *griseus* 'Kurt Zadnik'

Selected in 1986 by Roger Raiche from the northern Sonoma County coast near Horseshoe Cove, this cultivar was named for his coworker at the University of California Botanical Garden in Berkeley and introduced in 1991. Fast growing and vigorous, a specimen can reach 3 feet high and 18 feet wide in 5 years or less. Leaf size and color are typical for *Ceanothus thyrsiflorus* var. *griseus*. Blue-black buds form with silvery bracts in the middle of spring and open into deep, brooding blue blossoms. The depth of the color in the flowers provides little contrast against the dark leaves, and flowering plants appear as if cast in perennial shadow. Found growing on a crumbling bluff only 30 feet above the Pacific Ocean, 'Kurt Zadnik' is well suited to coastal gardens and tolerates wind, salt spray, and fog.

Ceanothus thyrsiflorus var. *griseus* 'Louis Edmunds'

'Louis Edmunds' is a wide-spreading selection made in 1942 by distinguished nurseryman Louis Edmunds from a group of plants located at the entrance of the Regional Parks Botanic Garden in Berkeley, California. Attracted by the profuse, deep blue flowers and glossy foliage, he produced plants and distributed stock beginning in 1945 from his Danville, California, nursery. The clone was presented to Saratoga Horticultural Research Foundation in 1952, where it was soon produced in quantity as *Ceanothus griseus* 'Louis Edmunds'. It was granted an Award of Merit in 1956 by the California Horticultural Society.

'Louis Edmunds' is a dense, evergreen shrub growing to 6 feet high and spreading 25 feet or more. Fast growing, specimens can achieve enormous proportions, and light pruning to shape and control growth is recommended. Dark green, oblong to oval, 1-to 2-inch-long leaves are light gray-green underneath and held on green stems. Three-veined from the base, they have a wavy surface and slightly revolute, serrated margins. Flower buds have prominent triangular bud scales colored gray-green with a

Ceanothus thyrsiflorus var. *griseus* 'Santa Ana', Royal Horticultural Society Garden Wisley, England; also see page 14

hint of purple. Compound, 2- to 4-inch heads of flowers open sea-blue in March and April.

'Louis Edmunds' is useful in large coastal gardens where its rambling habit can be fully expressed. It tolerates heavy pruning and can be used as a formal or informal hedge. Garden tolerant, it will abide heavier soils and summer watering but requires full sun. Some shade is required in interior sites, and it is hardy to approximately 15°F (−9°C).

Ceanothus thyrsiflorus var. *griseus* 'Santa Ana'

'Santa Ana' is another selection originating from the attentive observations of Louis Edmunds. It was chosen from seeds of *Ceanothus thyrsiflorus* var. *griseus* collected by him near Point Arena in 1949. It has an open, mounding form 4–8 feet tall with a 6- to 12-foot spread. The rich blue flowers are held in dense clusters and are considered by some to be among the darkest found in the genus. Rounded leaves are an intense, dark green, to 1¹/₂ inches long, and combined with the deep blue flowers present a bold complement to gray- or silver-foliaged plants. Garden tolerant, 'Santa Ana' is useful on banks and slopes, in dry borders, or as a formal hedge when regularly pruned.

Ceanothus thyrsiflorus var. *griseus* 'Silver Surprise'

Discovered in 1995 by Simon Smith of Hatfield, England, 'Silver Surprise' originated as a variegated stem growing on *Ceanothus thyrsiflorus* var. *griseus* (at the time called *C.*

griseus var. *horizontalis*) 'Yankee Point'. Repeated cycles of vegetative propagation and selection led to the stable clone that was patented as *C. griseus* 'Brass'. Introduced into the English nursery trade in 2000 with the cultivar name 'Silver Surprise', it became available in the United States in 2002.

A mounding shrub 3–4 feet high and as much as 5 feet wide, 'Silver Surprise' is much slower growing than typical *Ceanothus thyrsiflorus* var. *griseus*. The dark green, $1/2$- to 1-inch-long leaves are irregularly variegated, with revolute, cream-white margins. From March to May dense panicles of pale blue flowers $3/4$–1 inch long add an attractive complement to the mottled foliage.

'Silver Surprise' is effective in containers, mixed in perennial borders, or planted in combination with dark-foliaged hybrids such as 'Centennial' and 'Ebbets Field'. Like many other variegated plants, occasional stems will revert to green and should be removed at the base of the plant. 'Silver Surprise' has performed well in full sun along the coast of California and requires partial shade in warmer, inland gardens.

Ceanothus thyrsiflorus var. *griseus* 'Yankee Point'

'Yankee Point' was developed from cuttings of four individual plants (called *Ceanothus griseus* var. *horizontalis* at the time) in northern Monterey County, California, by Maunsell Van Rensselaer in 1954. Yankee Point is a rocky bluff fully exposed to the power of the Pacific Ocean with a population of low-growing *C. thyrsiflorus* var. *griseus* that reflects the maritime extremes of the site. After a 2-year evaluation process, Van Rensselaer selected and named 'Yankee Point' from the original four plants. The newly named cultivar was the lowest growing of the four and offered the most floriferous form and darkest blue flowers of the group. Its relatively low habit and rapid growth proved useful as a ground cover, and 'Yankee Point' quickly developed into the most commonly grown selection in California gardens. It remains an exceedingly popular cultivar, although in more recent years a number of the plants sold under the name are not true to the original, causing considerable confusion in the California nursery trade.

The dense, arching branches of 'Yankee Point' will spread quickly 10–12 feet wide and 3 feet high. Plants typically achieve a greater height when climbing on other plants, and it is not unusual to see some populations reach 5 feet in height under these circumstances. Selective early pruning is recommended to control rapid growth, remove upright stems, and maintain a dense habit. If desired, a clean, low hedge can be maintained with frequent pruning to extend the functional application of this versatile shrub.

The leaves of 'Yankee Point' are smaller than typical *Ceanothus thyrsiflorus* var. *griseus*, to 2 inches long and $1^1/4$ inches wide, with polished upper surfaces and slightly glaucous below. Dusty white buds develop into 2-inch-long panicles with China-blue flowers. In early spring the abundant flowers provide a rich contrast to the dark green

Ceanothus thyrsiflorus var. *griseus* 'Yankee Point', London, England; also see page 20

foliage. For a selection from an extreme maritime habit, 'Yankee Point' is surprisingly tolerant of a wide range of garden environments, including the heat of interior valleys. Full sun is recommended along the coast, partial shade inland, and it is hardy to about 15°F (−9°C).

Ceanothus thyrsiflorus var. *thyrsiflorus* 'Arroyo de la Cruz'

'Arroyo de la Cruz' was collected by nurseryman M. Nevin Smith in 1981 from Arroyo de la Cruz in northern San Luis Obispo County, California, and introduced by Winter-green Nursery in Aromas, California, a few years later. It displays a low, mounding form to 4 feet tall and 6–10 feet wide. The three-veined leaves are typical for *Ceanothus thyrsiflorus* var. *thyrsiflorus* but with a bright, glossy sheen. Spring flowers open from pale blue buds into ¹/₂- to 2-inch-long clusters of sky-blue blossoms.

'Arroyo de la Cruz' is an excellent specimen in smaller gardens and is useful as a low, informal hedge or massed on slopes and banks. The lustrous leaves add a rich sparkle to the garden and combine well with larger-leaved forms such as *Ceanothus arboreus*

'Cliff Schmidt' or the hybrid 'Ray Hartman'. Garden tolerant, plants perform well in coastal gardens with full sun, and at interior sites when sited in partial shade. Hardiness is not well tested, although plants have tolerated 17°F (−8°C) without damage.

Ceanothus thyrsiflorus var. *thyrsiflorus* 'Borne Again'

'Borne Again' is a variegated form similar to *Ceanothus thyrsiflorus* var. *thyrsiflorus* 'Zanzibar', selected by Jonathan Beacon from a plant found growing near Pershore, Worcestershire, England. Introduced in the 1990s by Beacon's Nurseries, 'Borne Again' has the greatest degree of variegation compared to the other gold-foliaged *C. thyrsiflorus* var. *thyrsiflorus* selections from the British Isles, 'Zanzibar' and 'El Dorado'.

Upright and rounded, 'Borne Again' has a dense, tidy habit to 8 feet tall and 6 feet wide. The yellow-gold leaves have a small, irregular band of green along the midvein and are otherwise typical for *Ceanothus thyrsiflorus* var. *thyrsiflorus*. Sky-blue flowers are held in cylindrical heads 1–2 inches long.

'Borne Again' has demonstrated remarkable tolerance of heavy soils and summer watering in limited garden trials. Not as commonly grown as 'Zanzibar' and 'El Dorado', it has an engaging appeal, particularly when combined with dark-foliaged cultivars such as the hybrids 'Dark Star' and 'Ebbets Field', and *Ceanothus arboreus*

Ceanothus thyrsiflorus var. *thyrsiflorus* 'Borne Again', Leaning Pine Arboretum, California Polytechnic University, San Luis Obispo

'Powder Blue'. Full sun along the coast and partial to full shade inland is recommended to protect the foliage from burning. Frost tender, the leaves are damaged at temperatures below 20°F (−7°C).

Ceanothus thyrsiflorus var. *thyrsiflorus* 'El Dorado'

'El Dorado' (see page 16) is a patented selection (Plant Patent Number 13433, as *Ceanothus thyrsiflorus* 'Perado') discovered in 1996 at Yoder Toddington (Farplants Sales) of Littlehampton, England. It originated as a branch sport growing on an individual plant of *C. thyrsiflorus* var. *thyrsiflorus* 'Zanzibar'. The leaves are typical of *C. thyrsiflorus* var. *thyrsiflorus* but have irregular, dark green centers with yellow-gold margins. Medium-blue flowers are held in cylindrical, 1- to 3-inch-long clusters on slightly extended stems and provide contrast to the variegated foliage in late winter to the middle of spring.

Mature plants have an upright habit to 6–10 feet tall with an equal spread. The vivid yellow-gold foliage is effective as a specimen or combined with other dark-foliaged shrubs. 'El Dorado' is a good choice for coastal California and the Pacific Northwest in full sun and well-drained soils. In hotter interior sites, some shade is required to prevent foliage burn. Occasional reversions require removal to keep the variegated foliage uniform. Vigorous and fast growing, it is hardy to about 10°F (−12°C).

Ceanothus thyrsiflorus var. *thyrsiflorus* 'Millerton Point'

'Millerton Point' was selected from Millerton Point on Tomales Bay in Marin County, California, from a drift of white-flowered *Ceanothus thyrsiflorus* var. *thyrsiflorus* by Malcolm G. Smith and later introduced by the Saratoga Horticultural Research Foundation. It is a large, mounding shrub with a tree-like form 10–12 feet tall and 12–14 wide, featuring glossy leaves $1^{1}/_{2}$–$2^{1}/_{2}$ inches long. Ashen-white buds form in late winter and open into 3- to 5-inch-long masses of bright white flowers.

Like many cultivars selected from *Ceanothus thyrsiflorus* var. *thyrsiflorus*, 'Millerton Point' has demonstrated exceptional garden tolerance, but it is not commonly grown in the California nursery trade. It is useful as a fast-growing screen, specimen, or informal hedge and can add refreshing contrast to a group of blue-flowered selections. A number of California horticulturists consider it the most graceful of the white-flowered *C. thyrsiflorus* forms. Interior sites require light shade and supplemental summer irrigation to maintain an attractive appearance. Hardiness is not tested, but at least 20°F (−7°C) can be anticipated.

Ceanothus thyrsiflorus var. *thyrsiflorus* 'Snow Flurry'

'Snow Flurry' is large, sprawling selection collected along the Big Sur coast by Joseph Solomone in 1975. It was introduced in 1977 and has become one of the most com-

Ceanothus thyrsiflorus var. *thyrsiflorus* 'Snow Flurry', Pismo Beach, California; also see page 26

monly grown white-flowered cultivars available in California. Fast growing with a rounded habit, it can reach a height of 20 feet with a 35-foot spread in favorable sites. The bright green leaves are 2 inches long and have a glossy, polished appearance. Radiant white flowers are produced on $2^1/_2$-inch-long panicles, adding to the attraction of the reflective foliage. A heavy bloomer in youth, 'Snow Flurry' lives up to its name with swirling sprays of white flowers in early spring.

Adaptable and best grown as a tree, 'Snow Flurry' is a dependable, garden-tolerant cultivar in both coastal and inland situations in California. It has also been used successfully in the British Isles on south-facing walls, where its arching branches can be groomed into an espalier. Light pruning in youth will help control its form and ultimate size. Arching branches will root on occasion, and some older specimens begin to form sprawling thickets. In warmer, drier sites, partial shade and modest summer watering will improve garden appearance. It is hardy to 15°F (−9°C) and has survived temperatures as low as 10°F (−12°C) though with significant leaf and stem damage.

Ceanothus thyrsiflorus var. *thyrsiflorus* 'Spring Valley'

Collected by Al Ottoboni from the San Francisco watershed property at Crystal Springs in 1974, 'Spring Valley' was named for the water company that operated in the area for many years. Selected for bright white flowers and a vigorous habit, it was evaluated at Strybing Arboretum and introduced into the nursery trade late in the 1970s.

'Spring Valley' has an upright, spreading form to 12 feet tall and 15 feet wide. The dark green leaves are typical for *Ceanothus thyrsiflorus* var. *thyrsiflorus* and have a lustrous sheen. In early spring, fresh white flowers bloom in dense, 1$^1/_2$- to 2$^1/_2$-inch-long clusters. 'Spring Valley' is not as floriferous as *C. thyrsiflorus* var. *thyrsiflorus* 'Snow Flurry', which may account for its limited availability. Fast growing, 'Spring Valley' is suitable for planting in full sun or partial shade and performs best in well-drained soils along the coast. It is hardy to 15°F (−9°C).

Ceanothus thyrsiflorus var. *thyrsiflorus* 'Taylor's Blue'

'Taylor's Blue' has circulated in the nursery trade for many years under three names: *Ceanothus thyrsiflorus* var. *repens,* and *C. thyrsiflorus* var. *repens* 'Ken Taylor' and 'Louis Edmunds'. It is still grown by most nurseries as variety *repens,* but the existence of intermediate forms in the wild precludes recognizing it as a distinct natural taxon. Some nurseries list this

Ceanothus thyrsiflorus var. *thyrsiflorus* 'Taylor's Blue', campus planting, California Polytechnic University, San Luis Obispo

clone as *C. thyrsiflorus* var. *repens* 'Louis Edmunds' in an effort to identify the source of the selection (not to be confused with *C. thyrsiflorus* var. *griseus* 'Louis Edmunds'). Louis Edmunds made the original selection, and plants were later grown in Ken Taylor's Aromas, California, garden. Barbara Coe and Philip McMillan Browse of the Saratoga Horticultural Research Foundation viewed the plant in Taylor's garden and introduced this clone in 1981 as *C. thyrsiflorus* var. *repens.*

Nomenclature notwithstanding, this distinctive selection forms an open 3-foot mound 10–15 feet wide with gracefully arching branches. The medium-green, $^3/_4$-

inch-long leaves are held loosely along pale green stems. 'Taylor's Blue' flowers over a long period—late winter to the middle of spring—with powder-blue blossoms in cylindrical, 2- to 3-inch-long clusters. In coastal gardens, sporadic flowering occurs most of the year.

The Royal Horticultural Society granted this selection an Award of Garden Merit in 1984, and it remains a popular selection in the United Kingdom to this day, although at least three clones are offered under the name. Vigorous and garden tolerant, 'Taylor's Blue' is useful fronting other shrubs or on slopes and banks as a ground cover. It does best in full sun but tolerates a surprising amount of shade along the coast. Partial shade is recommended in interior valleys. It is hardy to 10°F (−12°C).

Ceanothus thyrsiflorus var. thyrsiflorus 'Variegata'
variegated blueblossom

Three separate selections, all made by Roger Raiche in the 1980s, have been grown under the name 'Variegata' in California. The most commonly encountered is from San Bruno Mountain in San Mateo County. Another was discovered on Montara Mountain in the same county, and a third, believed to be extinct, was collected at Point Reyes in Marin County. The mottled variegation on each is similar and variable, some stems heavily variegated and others with only a few variegated leaves. Occasional branches are free of all variegation but seldom dominate the entire plant. All are vigorous, upright shrubs, 6–8 feet tall with an 8- to 12-foot spread. The three-veined leaves have varied variegation and are $^1/_2$–$1^1/_4$ inches long, with finely serrated margins. Medium-blue flowers are held in 2- to 4-inch-long clusters from February to April.

Variegated blueblossom is effective as a specimen or facing dark green conifers such as *Sequoia sempervirens* (coast redwood) or mixed with shrubs like *Rhamnus californica* (coffeeberry) and *Garrya elliptica* (silk-tassel bush). The inconsistency of the variegation adds an intriguing element against fences and walls, and the arching stems can be trained to lace and weave through lattice. Garden tolerant, the three selections have preformed well in a wide range of soil types, but they do best when grown in coastal climates. Full sun is recommended along the coast, and partial to full shade in interior sites. Variegated blueblossom is hardy to 15°F (−9°C).

Ceanothus thyrsiflorus var. thyrsiflorus 'Zanzibar'

Bob Hares of Pershore College of Horticulture selected 'Zanzibar' in 1992 from a garden in Pershore in Worcestershire, England. Evaluated in the college garden, it was introduced into the British nursery trade in 1997. Similar in many respects to *Ceanothus thyrsiflorus* var. *thyrsiflorus* 'Borne Again', it has a little more green at the center of the yellow-gold leaves, along with lax, arching branches. 'Zanzibar' produced the branch sport that became 'El Dorado'.

'Zanzibar' is an upright shrub, growing 6–10 feet tall with a similar spread. The variegated, elliptic leaves are 1½–2 inches long and have irregular bands of dark green, typically along the veins. Color varies from cream to lime-yellow, depending on the amount of green at the center of each leaf. Cylindrical heads of 1- to 2-inch-long, light blue flowers bloom sporadically from late winter to the middle of spring.

Used primarily for its foliage, 'Zanzibar' provides contrast when woven among dark-green-foliaged plants, and it will lighten a shady wall. Slower growing and considerably less vigorous than *Ceanothus thyrsiflorus* var. *thyrsiflorus,* it can easily be maintained at a reduced size in small gardens. Remove any green stems that develop to maintain the variegated form. It does best in partial shade away from the coast, and it is hardy to 15–20°F (−9 to −7°C).

Ceanothus 'Tilden Park'

Wayne Roderick selected 'Tilden Park' from a seedling found growing through *Ceanothus thyrsiflorus* var. *griseus* (at the time called *C. griseus* var. *horizontalis*) in Mendocino County, California, and planted at the Regional Parks Botanic Garden, Tilden Regional Park, in Berkeley. Roderick (1991) considered one parent *C. griseus* var. *horizontalis*

Ceanothus 'Tilden Park', Royal Horticultural Society Garden Wisley, England

and said, "the other must be a small-leaved, medium-blue, compact plant belonging to the same section (*Euceanothus*)," that is, belonging to subgenus *Ceanothus*.

Vigorous and fast growing, 'Tilden Park' is a mounding shrub 3–5 feet tall with a spreading habit 6–8 feet wide. The dark green, three-veined leaves are as long as 1 inch and have finely serrated margins. A floriferous cultivar, rose-pink buds form in early spring and open into 2- to 4-inch-long sprays of violet-blue flowers.

'Tilden Park' is grown occasionally on the West Coast of North America and in the British Isles. Its dense, arching form is useful as a specimen, on slopes and banks, or as an informal hedge. Mature plants in Britain are typically taller (8–10 feet) than those grown in California. Specimens have demonstrated good garden tolerance and maintain a handsome, dense habit as they mature. Hardiness is similar to other *Ceanothus thyrsiflorus* var. *griseus* hybrids, 15°F (−9°C).

Ceanothus tomentosus
woollyleaf ceanothus

Ceanothus tomentosus is found in a variety of habitats along the western slope of the Sierra Nevada from Nevada County to Mariposa County and in the Transverse and Peninsular Ranges from San Bernardino County to northwestern Baja California, Mexico. Growing at 150–6,800 feet (45–2,060 m) in elevation, woollyleaf ceanothus is found in chaparral, woodlands, and pine forests with a diverse mix of associate species. An erect to arborescent shrub with an open crown, plants vary greatly in height, 3–12 feet, with a similar width. Form is variable, from rounded to pear-like, with ascending to spreading stems that are first white, then brown. The evergreen leaves are thin, elliptic, as long as 1¼ inches, and have fine, gland-tipped margins. White to luminous blue flower are held in open clusters, ¾–1½ inches long. Two varieties of *C. tomentosus* are recognized: variety *tomentosus* has hairy leaves and grows in the Sierra Nevada, and variety *olivaceus* has hairless leaf blades and is found in southern California.

Until the introduction of *Ceanothus tomentosus* var. *olivaceus* 'Cielo', woollyleaf ceanothus was grown by only a few California nurseries. It tolerates the warmer interior climates of southern California and is effective as a specimen, screen, or bank cover. Fast growing, plants may require modest pruning to maintain a desirable form. Full sun in well-drained soils is recommended, although plants tolerate light shade. Woollyleaf ceanothus is hardy to 10–15°F (−12 to −9°C).

Ceanothus tomentosus var. *olivaceus* 'Cielo'

'Cielo' was selected from a planting of *Ceanothus tomentosus* var. *olivaceus* growing near the cultivar collection at Rancho Santa Ana Botanic Garden in Claremont, California. Each spring a large specimen drew comments from visitors for its luminous, bright blue flowers. Introduced by the garden in 1998, it has yet to receive much attention

Ceanothus tomentosus var. *olivaceus* 'Cielo', Rancho Santa Ana Botanic Garden, California; also see page 30

from the nursery trade in California, although it features one of the most radiant flower colors available in the genus.

Vase-shaped and airy, 'Cielo' has an upright habit to 12 feet tall with a 10-foot spread. Flowers develop from dusty maroon buds into cylindrical, 3- to 5-inch-long flower clusters of glowing, bright blue flowers—a blue so vivid that flowering plants seem to tremble with color. The 1-inch leaves are bright green and have pointed tips, prominent veins, and finely serrated edges. Young stems are burgundy before maturing silver-gray, contrasting pleasantly with the rich green foliage.

Although 'Cielo' is relatively new to the nursery trade, experience from Rancho Santa Ana Botanic Garden and the wild environment of *Ceanothus tomentosus* var. *olivaceus*—a chaparral component in the Peninsular Ranges of southern California—suggests a strong tolerance of heat and drought. Fast growing, with a woody appearance even in youth, 'Cielo' can be used as a screen or a specimen at the back of mixed border. Its relatively narrow, upright habit offers opportunities for broad walkways and in smaller gardens where some of the wider-spreading forms can outgrow their welcome. The alluring flowers are enticement enough to try this selection. Hardiness is still unknown, but 15–18°F (−9 to −8°C) can be expected.

Ceanothus 'Treasure Island'

A handsome cultivar of unknown origin, 'Treasure Island' was dedicated by Maunsell Van Rensselaer (1942) to "the many Californians whose ingenuity resulted in the magnificent Golden Gate International Exposition of 1939 and 1940 on Treasure Island in San Francisco Bay." An evergreen hybrid, *Ceanothus arboreus* × *C. thyrsiflorus* var. *thyrsiflorus*, 'Treasure Island' has been close to extinction on a number of occasions. More recent interest by botanical gardens and a few nurseries may help ensure future availability.

Ceanothus 'Treasure Island', Santa Barbara Botanic Garden, California

Upright with a rounded form, 'Treasure Island' grows to 8–12 feet tall with a slightly wider spread. The three-veined, glossy green leaves are 1–3 inches long and favor the *Ceanothus arboreus* parentage. Silvery pink-blue buds open into 4- to 7-inch-long compound sprays of bright blue flowers. It does best along the coast in full sun but can also be grown in woodland gardens with partial shade. Hardiness is not well tested, but 15°F (−9°C) can be expected.

Ceanothus ×veitchianus

Veitch ceanothus

Veitch ceanothus is a storied naturally occurring hybrid collected near Monterey, California, by William Lobb on his travels through California. He made a number of trips to the state during the Gold Rush and located this uncommon intersubgeneric hybrid in 1853. A number of renowned horticulturists have offered opinions as to the parentage, leaving *Ceanothus thyrsiflorus* var. *griseus* (subgenus *Ceanothus*) × *C. cuneatus* var. *rigidus* (subgenus *Cerastes*) as the consensus. It was named for nurseryman John Gould Veitch, a member of the renowned English nursery family, and has rarely been found in the wild since its discovery.

Long a favored garden subject in the British Isles, Veitch ceanothus is an upright evergreen shrub to 10 feet tall with a similar spread. The dark green, 1/2- to 3/4-inch-long leaves are wedge-shaped and have glandular toothed margins and a varnish-like surface. Free-flowering, it displays cylindrical, 1-inch-long clusters of bright blue blossoms in the middle of spring.

Size and form are easily controlled with light pruning following flowering. Reliable and garden tolerant, Veitch ceanothus can be grown as an informal hedge, specimen, or combined in a perennial border. In the British Isles it is frequently seen trained up walls and along fences. *Ceanothus* ×*veitchianus* is often confused by the nursery trade, and *C. dentatus* and *C.* ×*lobbianus* are frequently grown under this name.

Ceanothus velutinus

snow brush, mountain balm, sticky laurel, tobacco brush, varnish-leaf ceanothus

Ceanothus velutinus var. *velutinus,* Cascade Range, Oregon

Widespread in the mountains of western North America, *Ceanothus velutinus* is found from central California north to British Columbia and east to the Black Hills of South Dakota. Although it occurs near sea level in the Pacific Northwest, it is most commonly encountered in the mountains as high as 11,200 feet (3,400 m) in montane chaparral and in the understory of coniferous forests. Often forming dense thickets, snow brush is easily recognized by its glossy green leaves, which exhibit a viscid sheen. The epithet *velutinus* refers to the velvety appearance of the lower surface of the leaves.

The habit of snow brush varies from open, arborescent forms up to 18 feet tall to dense, flat-topped mounds 3 feet tall and 6 feet wide. The glistening oval leaves are 1–3 inches long, 1–2 inches wide, and have finely serrated margins. When crushed, they emit a cinnamon-like fragrance. Flowers open from crowded cauliflower-like buds into stout, dull white clusters 2–4 inches long from the middle of spring into summer. Two varieties of *Ceanothus velutinus* are recognized: variety *velutinus* has microscopic hairs on the veins of the lower leaf surface and a mounding habit, and variety *hookeri* lacks hairs on the lower leaf veins and exhibits an upright or arborescent habit.

Snow brush tolerates partial shade and root competition, recommending it for woodland gardens. It makes a considerably better garden subject in mountain habitats and will take more watering than most other members of the genus. Although it is not commonly grown in California, snow brush can be used in cooler, wetter environments such as those of the British Isles and Pacific Northwest.

Ceanothus verrucosus

wart-stemmed ceanothus, barranca brush

Ceanothus verrucosus is similar to *C. megacarpus* var. *megacarpus* in appearance and with which it shares the unique characteristic of alternate leaves as a member of subgenus *Cerastes*. A narrow endemic, *C. verrucosus* is found along the coast of San Diego County south into northwestern Baja California, Mexico, in chaparral and coastal pine woodland. Much of its original range in California has been lost to development, and its limited distribution makes it a species of concern among conservationists.

Wart-stemmed ceanothus offers gardeners an intricately branched shrub 5–8 feet high with an equal spread that is suitable for slopes or dry borders. The dense, rounded form looks as though it is sheared in some populations, and plants can easily be trained for use in a semiformal application. One of the earliest ceanothuses to bloom, its white flowers can be seen in the hills around San Diego as early as January. The emerging flower buds are lime-white before opening into rounded umbels of white flowers with prominent yellow anthers. Heart-shaped leaves $^1/_4$–$^1/_2$ inch long are shiny green above, gray-green below, and have entire or toothed margins. Wart-stemmed ceanothus is suitable for use in coastal gardens in full sun and can be grown in interior landscapes with some shade.

Ceanothus vestitus

cupleaf ceanothus, Mojave ceanothus

Ceanothus vestitus is a variable species of the western United States, growing at elevations of 2,960–7,000 feet (900–2,330 m) in transmontane California and in the interior mountains surrounding the San Joaquin Valley through the mountains of the Mojave Desert, central Nevada, southern Utah, northern Arizona, southwestern New Mexico, and western Texas. There are also wide scattered populations in the mountains of northern Mexico, including Baja California. Typically found in desert and montane shrublands and open woodlands and forests, cupleaf ceanothus is an upright, evergreen shrub 3–12 feet tall. Intricately branched, the rigid, ascending to spreading stems are gray to gray-brown, with some appearing almost white. The thick, oppositely arranged leaves are rounded and $^1/_4$–$^1/_2$ inch long with an equal width. The upper surfaces can vary in color from green to gray-green or even yellow-green while the lower surfaces are typically paler. Leaf blades are often folded along a single midvein, creating a cup-like appearance as the common name suggests, and they have entire margins with occasional teeth. White flowers, at times pale blue or pink-tinged, open from ball-like heads $^1/_4$–$^1/_2$ inch long in February through April.

Ceanothus vestitus is most commonly identified in the nursery trade as *C. greggii* var. *vestitus* or var. *perplexans*. Tolerant of hot, dry, interior sites, it is useful along the desert margins of the West in transition to the natural landscape or mixed in dry borders with *Fremontodendron* 'California Glory', *Rhus trilobata* (sumac), and *Fallugia paradoxa* (Apache plume). Arborescent forms can be trained into handsome small trees with broad, rounded crowns suggestive of oaks and planted with a skirt of *Aristida purpurea* (purple three-awn grass) or *Bouteloua gracilis* (blue grama) to accentuate this attractive character. Cupleaf ceanothus does best in full sun and well-drained soils, although specimens have performed well in heavier soils. A hardy species, it will endure temperatures as low as 0°F (−18°C).

Ceanothus 'Wheeler Canyon'

A dense, mounding shrub to 6 feet tall with a slightly wider spread, 'Wheeler Canyon' was selected by Dara Emery in 1981 from a plant found along the road in Wheeler Gorge, Ventura County, California. It is thought to be a hybrid involving *Ceanothus papillosus* var. *roweanus* (now considered only a compact form of the species) as one parent and was introduced by the Santa Barbara Botanic Garden. The narrow, 1- to 1 1/2-inch-long leaves have textured surfaces with a lustrous dark green sheen. Attractive, violet-pink buds open into profuse 2-inch-long heads of medium-blue flowers. The floral buds offer an arresting contrast to the lighter blue flowers, and a brief bicolored phase results in early spring.

'Wheeler Canyon' has been grown successfully in heavier soils as well as in gardens with routine summer watering. The dense form and compact habit make it useful in smaller gardens, and with an annual pruning specimens can be maintained at a height

Ceanothus 'Wheeler Canyon', private garden, Santa Cruz, California

of 4–5 feet. Suitable on dry banks and slopes, as a natural hedge, or defining the back of a perennial border, 'Wheeler Canyon' is a handsome, versatile selection deserving of a wider gardening audience. Plantings along the coast or in cooler climates have exhibited much greater longevity than those planted in hot interior gardens, with some specimens living 15 years or more. It is hardy to at least 15°F (−9°C).

Other Ceanothus Cultivars

The following are believed to be extinct or are no longer commercially cultivated. Those known to still exist in gardens are indicated parenthetically.

Ceanothus 'Appleblossom', pink in bud, white in flower

Ceanothus 'Berkeley Skies', light blue flowers (Rancho Santa Ana Botanic Garden, Claremont, California, and University of California Botanical Garden in Berkeley)

Ceanothus 'Blue Lolita', blue flowers (Las Pilitas Nursery, Santa Margarita, California)

Ceanothus 'Blue Whisp', evergreen with ice-blue flowers

Ceanothus 'Brilliant', evergreen with blue flowers (East Dudley, England)

Ceanothus 'Cielito Lindo', blue flowers

Ceanothus 'Consuella', rich blue flowers

Ceanothus cordulatus 'Maleza', white flowers

Ceanothus ×*cyam*, light blue flowers

Ceanothus ×*delilianus*
  'Aramis', mauve flowers
  'Astéroïde', azure-blue flowers
  'Bertini', azure-blue flowers
  'Biela', slate-blue flowers
  'Bijou', blue flowers tinged with pink
  'Bleu Céleste', soft blue flowers
  'Boule Bleue', pale blue flowers
  'Charles Detriche', deep blue flowers

  'Ciel de Provence', sky-blue flowers
  'Crépuscule', gray-blue flowers
  'Croix du Sud', dark blue flowers
  'Distinction', flowers white with blue highlights
  'Esther', large blue flowers
  'Fantaisie', violet-blue flowers
  'Gloire de Plantieres', deep azure-blue flowers
  'La Condamine', mauve flowers
  'Léon Simon', gray-blue flowers
  'Lucie Simon', blue flowers'
  'Maguerite Aubusson', blue flowers
  'Melusine', deep brilliant blue flowers
  'Rosamonde', azure-blue flowers
  'Saphir', blue flowers
  'Sceptre d'Azur', blue flowers
  'Sirius', metallic blue flowers
  'Victor Jouin', blue flowers

Ceanothus 'Dignity', deep blue flowers (East Dudley, England)

Ceanothus gloriosus 'Alba', white flowers (various California gardens)

Ceanothus gloriosus 'Tuttle', blue flowers

Ceanothus incanus 'Owen Pearce', white flowers

Ceanothus 'James Roof', spreading evergreen with rich blue flowers

Ceanothus 'La Primavera', blue flowers

Ceanothus 'La Purisima', bright blue flowers

Ceanothus 'Lester Rowntree', bright blue flowers

Ceanothus maritimus 'Arroyo Azul', dark blue flowers

Ceanothus maritimus 'R. F. Hoover', pale blue flowers

Ceanothus 'Mary Lake', medium-blue flowers

Ceanothus 'Mary Simpson', blue flowers

Ceanothus 'Mills Glory', a selection by Howard McMinn with light blue flowers

Ceanothus 'Olympic Lake', dark blue flowers

Ceanothus ×*pallidus*

  'Albert Pittet', light pink flowers

  'Albidus', white flowers

  'Albus Plenus', white to cream-colored flowers

  'Attraction', rose-pink flowers

  'Caprice', pink flowers

  'Carmen', carmine flowers

  'Cigale', lilac-blue flowers

  'Coquetterie', rose-carmine flowers

  'Esperanto', pink flowers

  'Fleur d'Été', grayish carmine flowers

  'Gaulois', violet-rose flowers

  'Georges Simon', rose-carmine flowers

  'Gladiateur', grayish rose flowers

  'Gracieux', violet-carmine flowers

  'Ibis Rosé', pink flowers

  'Jocelyn', light pink flowers

  'Le Géant', rose-pink flowers

  'Lucie Moser', blue flowers

  'Lustre', carmine flowers

  'Madame Furtado', pink flowers

  'Mérimée', rose-pink flowers

  'Mina', rose-white flowers

  'Névé', white flowers

  'Palmyre', violet-rose flowers

  'Pénombre', carmine flowers

  'Pinguet-Guindan', carmine flowers

  'Pole Nord', white flowers

  'Président Réveil', rose flowers

  'Richesse', rose flowers

  'Rose Carmin', carmine-pink flowers

  'Spicatus', rose flowers

  'Uranus', rose-carmine flowers

  'Virginal', white flowers

Ceanothus 'Pansy Canham', blue flowers

Ceanothus pumilus 'French Hill', blue flowers

Ceanothus purpureus 'Mount George', chalk-blue flowers

Ceanothus 'Royal Blue', dark blue flowers

Ceanothus ×*roseus*, name occasionally applied to *C.* ×*pallidus* hybrids

Ceanothus 'Theodore Payne', upright evergreen with deep blue flowers

Ceanothus thyrsiflorus 'Castleford Variety', blue flowers

Ceanothus thyrsiflorus 'Fort Ross', brilliant blue flowers

Ceanothus thyrsiflorus 'San Andreas', bright blue flowers (various California gardens)

Ceanothus thyrsiflorus var. *griseus* 'Compacta', blue flowers

Ceanothus thyrsiflorus var. *thyrsiflorus* 'Compactus', dense evergreen with medium-blue flowers

Ceanothus ×*vanrensselaeri*, a naturally occurring hybrid, *C. incanus* × *C. thyrsiflorus*, with white flowers (Rancho Santa Ana Botanic Garden, Claremont, California)

Additional *Ceanothus* ×*delilianus* and *C.* ×*pallidus* hybrids listed in European nursery catalogs at the end of the 19th century without designation of the parent species:

'Aérostat'
'Albert Moser'
'Diamant'
'Elegans'
'Eleusis'
'Félibre'
'Gloire de Vaise', blue flowers
'Gloire d'Orléans'
'Leviathan'

'Madame Émile Bertin'
'Manzoni'
'Météore'
'Monsieur Verlot'
'Monument'
'Multiflore'
'Othello'
'Panthéon'
'Vesta'

Ceanothus Selection Guide

Here, recommendations are given for species and cultivars of *Ceanothus* that are particularly good choices according to these criteria: garden tolerant, fast growing, bank covers, ground covers, informal hedges, screens, specimens and small trees, small gardens, seashore gardens, shade tolerant, variegated foliage, summer flowering, large trusses, white flowers.

Garden Tolerant

Demonstrating broad cultural tolerance and consistently performing well in a wide range of soils and climates.

Ceanothus 'A. T. Johnson'
Ceanothus 'Autumnal Blue'
Ceanothus 'Blue Buttons'
Ceanothus 'Blue Cloud'
Ceanothus 'Burkwoodii'
Ceanothus 'Concha'
Ceanothus 'Cynthia Postan'
C. ×*delilianus* 'Gloire de Versailles'
Ceanothus 'Frosty Blue'
C. incanus
C. ×*pallidus* 'Marie Simon'
Ceanothus 'Puget Blue'
Ceanothus 'Ray Hartman'
Ceanothus 'Skylark'
C. thyrsiflorus var. *griseus* 'Yankee Point'

Fast Growing

Typically reaching mature size rapidly.

C. arboreus and cultivars
Ceanothus 'A. T. Johnson'
Ceanothus 'Blue Cascade'
Ceanothus 'Blue Cloud'
Ceanothus 'Cal Poly'

C. cyaneus and 'YBN Blue'
Ceanothus 'Eleanor Taylor'
Ceanothus 'Ernie Bryant'
Ceanothus 'Frosty Blue'
Ceanothus 'Gentian Plume'
C. impressus and cultivars
Ceanothus 'Joyce Coulter'
Ceanothus 'Owlswood Blue'
Ceanothus 'Puget Blue'
Ceanothus 'Ray Hartman'
Ceanothus 'Sierra Blue'
C. spinosus
Ceanothus 'Tassajara Blue'
C. thyrsiflorus var. *griseus,* and 'Louis Edmunds', 'Hurricane Point', and 'Yankee Point'
C. thyrsiflorus var. *thyrsiflorus* 'Millerton Point', 'Snow Flurry', and 'Spring Valley'
Ceanothus 'Treasure Island'

Bank Covers

Vigorous, broadly spreading, suitable for use on slopes and banks.

Ceanothus 'Bamico'
Ceanothus 'Blue Mound'
Ceanothus 'Cuesta'
Ceanothus 'Ernie Bryant'

Bank Covers (continued)

Ceanothus 'Far Horizons'
C. foliosus vars. *medius* and *vineatus*
C. gloriosus var. *exaltatus* 'Emily Brown'
Ceanothus 'Joan Mirov'
Ceanothus 'Joyce Coulter'
C. thyrsiflorus var. *griseus* 'Kurt Zadnik',
  'Louis Edmunds', 'Yankee Point', and
  'Hurricane Point'
C. thyrsiflorus var. *thyrsiflorus* 'Arroyo de
  la Cruz' and 'Taylor's Blue'
Ceanothus 'Tilden Park'

Ground Covers

Can be grown as ground cover less than
2 feet tall.

Ceanothus 'Centennial'
C. cuneatus var. *ramulosus* 'Rodeo
  Lagoon' and 'Rodeo Marin'
C. divergens subspp. *confusus* and *occi-
  dentalis*
C. diversifolius
C. foliosus 'Berryhill'
C. fresnensis
C. gloriosus var. *gloriosus* 'Fallen Skies',
  'Heart's Desire', and var. *porrectus*
C. hearstiorum
C. maritimus 'Claremont', 'Frosty
  Dawn', 'Point Sierra', and 'Spring
  Skies'
C. pinetorum, some forms
C. prostratus
C. pumilus
C. roderickii
C. thyrsiflorus var. *griseus* 'Diamond
  Heights'

Informal Hedges

With a rounded form suitable for use as
an informal hedge.

Ceanothus 'Blue Mound'
Ceanothus 'Burkwoodii'
Ceanothus 'Celestial Blue'
Ceanothus 'Concha'
C. cuneatus var. *rigidus* 'Snowball'
Ceanothus 'Cynthia Postan'
Ceanothus 'Dark Star'
C. dentatus
Ceanothus 'Ebbets Field'
Ceanothus 'Far Horizons'
C. foliosus var. *medius*
C. impressus var. *impressus* 'Vandenberg'
Ceanothus 'Italian Skies'
C. maritimus 'Popcorn'
Ceanothus 'Mountain Haze'
Ceanothus 'Puget Blue'
Ceanothus 'Ray Hartman'
Ceanothus 'Remote Blue'
Ceanothus 'Sierra Snow'
Ceanothus 'Skylark'
Ceanothus 'Southmead'
Ceanothus 'Wheeler Canyon'

Screens

Large evergreens that rapidly provide
visual privacy.

C. arboreus and 'Blue Mist', 'Cliff
  Schmidt', 'Thundercloud', and
  'Trewithen Blue'
Ceanothus 'Blue Buttons'
C. cyaneus and 'YBN Blue'
Ceanothus 'Delight'
Ceanothus 'Frosty Blue'

Ceanothus 'Gentian Plume'

C. impressus 'Mesa Lilac'

C. oliganthus var. *sorediatus*

Ceanothus 'Owlswood Blue'

C. parryi

Ceanothus 'Puget Blue'

Ceanothus 'Ray Hartman'

Ceanothus 'Sierra Blue'

C. spinosus

C. thyrsiflorus var. *thyrsiflorus* 'Millerton Point', 'Snow Flurry', and 'Spring Valley'

C. tomentosus var. *olivaceus* 'Cielo'

Ceanothus 'Treasure Island'

Specimens and Small Trees

Large and upright, can become tree-like either naturally or with modest pruning.

C. arboreus and 'Blue Mist', 'Cliff Schmidt', 'Thundercloud', and 'Trewithen Blue'

Ceanothus 'Blue Buttons'

Ceanothus 'Delight'

Ceanothus 'Frosty Blue'

Ceanothus 'Gentian Plume'

C. incanus

C. megacarpus

Ceanothus 'Owlswood Blue'

C. parryi

Ceanothus 'Ray Hartman'

Ceanothus 'Sierra Blue'

C. thyrsiflorus var. *thyrsiflorus* 'Millerton Point', 'Snow Flurry', and 'Spring Valley'

C. tomentosus var. *olivaceus* 'Cielo'

Ceanothus 'Treasure Island'

Small Gardens

Useful in gardens with limited space. Many of those listed will require some pruning to conform to particularly small situations.

Ceanothus 'Bamico'

Ceanothus 'Blue Cushion'

Ceanothus 'Blue Mound'

Ceanothus 'Blue Sapphire'

Ceanothus 'Centennial'

Ceanothus 'Coronado'

C. ×delilianus 'Ceres', 'Henri Desfosse', and 'Indigo'

Ceanothus 'Ebbets Field'

Ceanothus 'Everett's Choice'

Ceanothus 'Far Horizons'

C. foliosus 'Berryhill'

C. gloriosus var. *gloriosus* 'Heart's Desire' and var. *porrectus*

C. hearstiorum

C. impressus var. *impressus* 'Vandenberg'

C. maritimus and cultivars

C. otayensis

C. ×pallidus 'Golden Elan' and 'Marie Simon'

C. prostratus

C. pumilus

C. roderickii

Ceanothus 'Skylark'

C. thyrsiflorus var. *griseus* 'All Gold', 'Blue and Gold', 'Diamond Heights', and 'Silver Surprise'

Ceanothus 'Wheeler Canyon'

Seashore Gardens

Tolerant of areas exposed to ocean winds and salt spray.

Ceanothus 'Bamico'
Ceanothus 'Centennial'
Ceanothus 'Coronado'
C. cuneatus var. *ramulosus* 'Rodeo Lagoon' and 'Rodeo Marin'
C. gloriosus cultivars and var. *porrectus*
C. hearstiorum
C. maritimus and cultivars
C. thyrsiflorus var. *griseus* 'Kurt Zadnik', 'Hurricane Point', 'Santa Ana', and 'Yankee Point'
C. thyrsiflorus var. *thyrsiflorus* 'Arroyo de la Cruz' and 'Millerton Point'

Shade Tolerant

Can be successfully grown in partial shade. Shade tolerance varies according to climate and the character of the shade. Ceanothus is typically better suited to the light, partial shade of deciduous woodlands than the dense shade of a conifer forest. All ceanothuses demonstrate greater shade tolerance in warmer, drier climates such as California and less shade tolerance in cooler, moister regions such as England and the Pacific Northwest. Plants with an asterisk (*) tolerate full shade in California.

C. arboreus and cultivars
Ceanothus 'Bamico'
*Ceanothus 'Centennial'
C. cordulatus
Ceanothus 'Coronado'
Ceanothus 'Delight'

C. ×*delilianus* and cultivars
Ceanothus 'Far Horizons'
C. foliosus 'Berryhill'
C. gloriosus and cultivars
C. hearstiorum
C. impressus var. *impressus* 'Mesa Lilac'
C. incanus
C. integerrimus
Ceanothus 'Joyce Coulter'
C. oliganthus
C. ×*pallidus* and cultivars
C. pinetorum
C. prostratus
Ceanothus 'Ray Hartman'
Ceanothus 'Skylark'
*C. thyrsiflorus var. *griseus* 'Blue and Gold' and 'Diamond Heights'
*C. thyrsiflorus var. *thyrsiflorus* 'Borne Again', 'El Dorado', 'Variegata', and 'Zanzibar'
C. velutinus

Variegated Foliage

C. thyrsiflorus var. *griseus* 'All Gold', 'Blue and Gold', 'Diamond Heights', and 'Silver Surprise'
C. thyrsiflorus var. *thyrsiflorus* 'Borne Again', 'El Dorado', 'Variegata', and 'Zanzibar'

Summer Flowering

Blooming primarily in the summer. Plants marked with an asterisk (*) bloom from late spring into summer.

C. americanus
Ceanothus 'Autumnal Blue'
Ceanothus 'Burkwoodii'
*C. caeruleus

C. cordulatus
C. ×*delilianus* cultivars
C. *herbaceus*
*C. *integerrimus*
*C. *martinii*
C. ×*pallidus* cultivars
*C. *sanguineus*
Ceanothus 'Skylark'
*C. *velutinus*

Large Trusses

Plants with large inflorescences.

C. *arboreus* and cultivars
Ceanothus 'Blue Cloud'
Ceanothus 'Cal Poly'
C. *cyaneus* and 'YBN Blue'
C. ×*delilianus* cultivars
Ceanothus 'Ernie Bryant'
Ceanothus 'Gentian Plume'
C. *integerrimus*
Ceanothus 'Owlswood Blue'
C. ×*pallidus* cultivars
Ceanothus 'Sierra Blue'
Ceanothus 'Treasure Island'

White Flowers

Plants with white or cream flowers. Plants marked with an asterisk (*) are primarily white-flowered, but lavender, pale blue, and pink-tinged flowers are possible in some populations.

C. *americanus*
C. *cordulatus*
C. *crassifolius*
C. *cuneatus* 'Mount Madonna'
C. *cuneatus* var. *ramulosus* 'Rodeo Lagoon'
C. *cuneatus* var. *rigidus* 'Snowball'
C. *fendleri*
C. *ferrisiae*
C. *herbaceus*
C. *incanus*
*C. *integerrimus*
*C. *jepsonii*
*C. *leucodermis*
C. *maritimus* 'Popcorn'
C. *martinii*
C. *megacarpus*
C. *ochraceus*
*C. *otayensis*
*C. *pauciflorus*
*C. *roderickii*
C. *sanguineus*
Ceanothus 'Sierra Snow'
C. *thyrsiflorus* var. *thyrsiflorus* 'Millerton Point', 'Snow Flurry', and 'Spring Valley'
C. *velutinus*
C. *verrucosus*
*C. *vestitus*

PART 2

Ceanothus in the Wild

Ceanothus belongs to the buckthorn family (Rhamnaceae), which includes about 50 genera and more than 900 species worldwide (Medan and Schirarend 2004). As treated here, the genus comprises 50 species, some that are well defined, some that are ecologically and geographically restricted but differ by relatively few morphological traits, and others that are widespread and show considerable variation. Molecular analyses and reevaluations of morphology suggest that *Ceanothus* may be a very old genus, perhaps first evolving more than 65 million years ago, and thus with an origin near the base of evolutionary lineages leading to the ancestors of other modern genera in the family (Richardson et al. 2000a, b). *Ceanothus* is restricted entirely to North and Central America, but interestingly, its closest relatives may be genera such as *Colletia* and *Discaria*, which are found in the southern hemisphere. Another relative, *Adolphia*, occurs in arid regions of southwestern North America.

The genus is of considerable botanical interest for several reasons. Many *Ceanothus* species are considered to be adapted to fire, based on their ability to sprout from burls or from long-lived seed banks (Hanes 1971, Keeley 1987). They often appear in early stages of succession in abandoned agricultural or deforested areas. *Ceanothus americanus, C. herbaceus,* and *C. sanguineus* are considered important members of woodlands and prairies, often colonizing and occupying cleared areas or open sites but declining in frequency with succession. Some species, such as *C. cuneatus, C. integerrimus,* and *C. leucodermis,* often form extensive colonies or thickets and may dominate local stands of chaparral for many decades after disturbance. The persistent occurrence of large stands or thickets of *C. velutinus* on mountain slopes in the Cascade Range and Rocky Mountains has been attributed to its ability to rapidly regenerate from both burls and seeds following recurrent fires. Other species, including *C. megacarpus, C. oliganthus, C. papillosus,* and *C. spinosus,* are often important members of fire-adapted chaparral communities in coastal or interior habitats, where they regenerate entirely from seeds after fire. Under natural conditions, some species, such as *C. integerrimus, C. leucodermis,* and *C. thyrsiflorus,* may live many decades, dying only in

Ceanothus spinosus var. *palmeri,* Upper Sespe River, Ventura County, California

Ceanothus integerrimus var. *macrothyrsus,* Yuba Gap, Sierra Nevada, California

response to competition from other chaparral species (Mooney and Conrad 1977, Conrad and Oechel 1982, Conard et al. 1985).

Most members of the genus have the rare capacity to nitrify the soils in which they grow through symbiotic relationships with nitrogen-fixing fungi of the genus *Frankia,* which occurs primarily in root swellings or nodules (Delwiche et al. 1965, Schwintzer and Tjepkema 1990, Baker and Mullen 1994). Such root nodules can develop in the first few years and may appear as intricately branched swellings or appendages of the mature root system. The nitrogen-fixing capacity of *Ceanothus* is not as great as that found in legumes but contributes significantly to total available soil nitrogen. The ability to fix nitrogen is important to the success of plant growth and establishment during early stages of succession in addition to contributing to the nutrient budget of associated herbaceous and woody species.

The genus has been a model for evolutionary biologists interested in the evolutionary radiation and divergence of taxa at the diploid chromosomal level and in the absence of intrinsic barriers to hybridization. Charles C. Parry was the first student of *Ceanothus* to bring attention to the existence of hybrids, which were increasingly recognized in later decades. Based on field observations in the late 19th century, Parry suggested that both *C.* ×*lobbianus* and *C.* ×*veitchianus* are hybrids involving *C. thyrsiflorus* as one parent. By the mid-1940s, Howard McMinn (1944) had tallied at least 30 natural interspecific combinations. At least 14 combinations have been documented subsequently in the literature and from herbarium specimens. Many involve wide-ranging species such as *C. cuneatus, C. integerrimus,* and *C. thyrsiflorus* as one parent because they come into contact with other species throughout parts their range. In contrast, hybrids between members of the two subgenera are rare.

Experimental studies, conducted primarily by Malcolm Nobs and Howard McMinn, showed that hybrids between pairs of species in each of the subgenera are highly fertile, nearly always producing fertile seeds when self-pollinated or crossed with other plants. All species are believed to have 24 chromosomes, which form 12 pairs during meiosis. Pairing of chromosomes in interspecific hybrids is often normal, and pollen fertility in such hybrids is almost as high as in the parents. Hybrids between representatives of the two subgenera, however, are rare, limited in distribution, and nearly always sterile. Some such naturally occurring hybrids, by virtue of their morphological distinctiveness, have been named. *Ceanothus ×rugosus,* a naturally occurring hybrid between *C. prostratus* (subg. *Cerastes*) and *C. velutinus* (subg. *Ceanothus*), has been reported from only two localities, in the Cascade Range and in the Sierra Nevada of California. *Ceanothus ×serrulatus,* once known only from a single small population near Lake Tahoe in Eldorado County, California, is considered a hybrid, *C. prostratus* (subg. *Cerastes*) × *C. cordulatus* (subg. *Ceanothus*), both of which occurred with the hybrids. *Ceanothus ×veitchianus* is a naturally occurring hybrid—*C. cuneatus* var. *rigidus* (subg. *Cerastes*) × *C. thyrsiflorus* var. *griseus* (subg. *Ceanothus*)—and presumably known only from near Monterey, California, where the two parents occur together. Other intersubgeneric hybrids include *C. purpureus* (subg. *Cerastes*) × *C. thyrsiflorus* (subg. *Ceanothus*), named 'James Roof'; *C. masonii* (subg. *Cerastes* and considered part of *C. gloriosus* in this book) × *C. foliosus* (subg. *Ceanothus*); *C. crassifolius* (subg. *Cerastes*) × *C. spinosus* (subg. *Ceanothus*); and *C. cuneatus* (subg. *Cerastes*) × *C. tomentosus* (subg. *Ceanothus*). Each of these naturally occurring hybrids is represented by one or a few, apparently sterile plants found in the presence of both parents (Nobs 1963, Hannan 1974).

The widespread occurrence of hybridization in *Ceanothus* can be attributed partly to the lack of barriers to gene flow. Most *Ceanothus* species attract a wide range of pollinators at the time of flowering, and it is common to observe small flies, bees, and even butterflies simultaneously visiting plants in flower. The occurrence of *Ceanothus* species in close proximity to each other, often enhanced by natural and artificial disturbance along boundaries between plant communities, and pollination by widely foraging insects both increase the probability of hybridization. Molecular studies provide evidence that seemingly unrelated species share unique gene sequences in common, suggesting that hybridization played a significant role in the early evolutionary history of some modern species. Alternatively, the same evidence also suggests the potential for survival of evolutionary lineages derived independently from a more variable ancestral milieu of genotypes (Hardig et al. 2000, 2002).

The earliest clearly identifiable fossil records of *Ceanothus* are leaf impressions found in early to middle Miocene rocks of western North America that are 14.5 million to 13 million years old. Among them are plants that resemble modern *C. cuneatus* (subg. *Cerastes*) and *C. spinosus* (subg. *Ceanothus*), and a third extinct species, *C. leitchii*, which had three principal veins similar to other members of subgenus *Ceanothus*. The existence of both subgenera in the Miocene suggests that diversification into two distinct phylogenetic lineages probably took place much earlier. Fossils of plants similar to *C. cuneatus* and *C. spinosus* were associated with ancestors of modern *Cercocarpus* (mountain mahogany), *Heteromeles* (toyon), and *Arctostaphylos* (manzanita), which are common associates in modern chaparral communities. *Ceanothus leitchii*, found only in western Nevada rocks, was associated with *Sequoiadendron* (giant sequoia) and other species that occur today on the western slopes of the Sierra Nevada. Fossil leaf impressions of species similar to *C. cuneatus* and *C. spinosus* occur widely in Pliocene fossil assemblages between 10 million and 2.5 million years ago. Species similar to modern *C. cuneatus*, *C. integerrimus*, *C. leucodermis*, and *C. tomentosus* have been found together in the same rocks of the early Pleistocene, some 2 million years ago, and at sites where some of these species are absent today.

Based on interpretation of fossils, geological history, and the paleoclimates of western North America, maximum diversification within *Ceanothus* may have coincided with the middle to late Pliocene (Raven and Axelrod 1978). Diversification during this time probably resulted from several factors. During this time, the Mediterranean climate became firmly established in what is now the California Floristic Province and contributed significantly to the evolution of species adapted to dry summers and moist to wet winters. The geological record shows that many species of plants and animals that were adapted to more equitable climates with higher rates of precipitation gradually disappeared from western North America, partly in response to increasing summer aridity and the restriction of precipitation to winter months. Many of their closest North American relatives survive today either in eastern North America or in subtropical Mexico. Thus greater fluctuation in seasonal precipitation, coupled with summer aridity, probably represented a strong selective agent, contributing to the success of new genetic combinations and subsequent adaptation.

The Pliocene and Pleistocene of western North America were periods of intensive tectonic activity, resulting in the development of extensive mountain ranges composed of diverse rock types, ranging from volcanic magmas or ash deposits to the massive granitic batholiths of the Sierra Nevada. These same mountain ranges became separated by basins of considerable size, formed either through erosion or, as in the case of the Great Basin, by vertical fault blocks. Deep-lying sedimentary or metamorphic rocks and formations containing serpentinized rocks derived from deep-sea oceanic plates were thrust upward. These processes resulted in considerable regional and local geological variation, exposing rocks with different chemical and physical properties and juxtaposing them through regional and local folding or faulting. The same geological activity resulted in regional and local landscapes with considerable topographic relief, including slopes with varying aspects and erosion features that included elevated marine terraces and alluvial or colluvial deposits. Much of western North America, especially that of the California Floristic Province, can be considered a complex three-dimensional mosaic of climatic, topographic, and geological diversity. Dramatic fluctuations in temperature and precipitation occurred during the Pleistocene, which probably resulted in local or regional extinctions and migration of different evolutionary lineages.

Ceanothus has been somewhat perplexing to both professional and amateur botanists who attempt to identify individual specimens or plants in the wild. Most recognized taxa are distinguished by combinations of traits, of which some show a broad range of almost continuous variation and thus are often difficult to quantify or describe using discrete terminology. Other taxa display local variation over a broad range of habitats and geography, which may result from hybridization, the regional and local effects of diverse environmental factors, or the consequences of a long evolutionary history under isolation. As a result, *Ceanothus* presents continuing challenges and questions regarding its evolutionary history and taxonomic disposition as new hypotheses of origins and speciation are examined. Most species of *Ceanothus* have been recognized by suites of several characters, which include life form, inflorescence architecture, leaf shape, margin, and venation, flower color, and fruit morphology. The various species in subgenus *Ceanothus* are separated by contrasting character states such as three-veined versus one-veined leaves, deciduous versus evergreen leaves, short versus long peduncles, white versus blue flowers, and smooth versus appendaged fruits, among others. In subgenus *Cerastes,* species are separated by white versus blue or purple flowers, smooth versus appendaged fruits, dense versus open canopies, and entire versus toothed leaves, in addition to quantitative differences in other traits. However, not all these traits can be observed on a single specimen or during a single visit to a natural population.

Early treatments by Charles C. Parry, William Trelease, and Katherine Brandegee essentially circumscribed most of the currently recognized species and their natural varieties. Later treatments, especially those by John Thomas Howell and Howard McMinn, recognized additional species but circumscribed and discussed them from the additional perspectives of ecological and geographical distribution and evolutionary processes, including hybridization. McMinn was strongly influenced by the elegant ecogenetic studies conducted by Jens Clausen, David Keck, and William Hiesey during the 1930s and 1940s at the Carnegie Institution at Stanford University. Their studies resulted in a theory of speciation that included concepts of different environmental distributions, modes of morphological variation, and levels of gene exchange. Distinct species were treated as occupying different habitats, were generally recognized by unique combinations of several morphological traits, and their hybrids with other such groups were partially sterile and had lower fitness. Morphologically different plants that occupy different habitats but that yield fertile hybrids with relatively high fitness were treated at a lower level of the taxonomic hierarchy (e.g., subspecies or varieties). Although this theory has been used to explain some patterns of variation in plants, it has not been universally applicable. In some cases, clearly defined ecological and morphological differences have not been accompanied by reproductive barriers. In other situations, reproductive barriers evolved without clearly defined morphological or ecological differences. Regardless, McMinn (1942, 1944) applied this theory to his classification of *Ceanothus* and paid special attention to hybridization and intergradation among plants he recognized as species. He also expressed doubt regarding some species, noting that "the number of existing distinct species (ecospecies) is much fewer than represented by the number of binomials given in manuals, and that more subspecies (ecotypes) and local variations (biotypes) will be recognized when sufficient knowledge of the behavior of hybrids is known."

The circumscriptions of taxa recognized as species here do not differ very much from those recognized by McMinn. Plants that share a common and unique pattern of several morphological traits are recognized as species. Such taxa occur in distinctive habitats generally restricted to a particular geographical region or physiographic province and are separated from their putatively nearest relatives by well-defined gaps in quantitative morphological traits. There are numerous exceptions, especially with respect to geographical distribution. *Ceanothus pinetorum,* for example, occurs in the Trinity Mountains and in the southern Sierra Nevada of California. *Ceanothus parryi* occurs near the coast of northwestern California and in a small area of west-central Oregon. *Ceanothus spinosus* var. *palmeri* occurs primarily in the mountains of southern California but also is represented by a few small populations in the western foothills of the Sierra Nevada.

In some cases, species may show several modes of variation for a few traits that may be either ecologically or geographically restricted and in which there exists evidence for intergradation other than occasional or local hybridization. Such modes are recognized here at the level of variety or subspecies, depending on currently available names. The varieties of *Ceanothus americanus,* for example, differ almost entirely by the shape, size, and hairiness of their leaves, but many plants with intermediate conditions occur, especially in areas where two varieties occur together. Plants assignable to *C. cuneatus* vars. *fascicularis, rigidus,* or *ramulosus* can occur in close proximity and often in association with intermediate forms. Although *C. megacarpus* vars. *megacarpus* and *insularis* usually differ with respect to leaf arrangement and fruit size, there exist plants and populations with intermediate patterns that cannot be currently attributed to hybridization. In a few cases, previously recognized species (e.g., *C. arcuatus, C. divergens,* and *C. masonii*), which differ only by a few traits from their putatively closest relative, are treated as part of the species with the earlier available name (i.e., *C. fresnensis, C. confusus, C. gloriosus,* respectively). Some broadly defined species show considerable variation. Among them are *C. cuneatus, C. pauciflorus,* and *C. vestitus,* each of which show patterns of variation related partly to geographical and ecological distribution but in which recognizable morphological gaps are not apparent. In each of these species, particular modes of variation have been treated as varieties, or attention is given to names that might apply to such modes.

Cladistic (phylogenetic) analyses of gene sequences are somewhat disappointing from the perspective of resolving phylogenetic relationships, primarily because of a lack of consensus among different phylogenetic trees (Jeong et al. 1997, Hardig et al. 2000, 2002). These studies, however, clearly support the divergence of subgenus *Ceanothus* from subgenus *Cerastes* and in some cases either confirm previously suspected relationships or provide new hypotheses deserving attention. Strong relationships were found between *C. verrucosus* and both varieties of *C. megacarpus,* which is consistent with their close morphological relationships. *Ceanothus divergens* (including *C. confusus*) and *C. purpureus* share unique sequences in common, a pattern that is consistent with previous studies of naturally occurring hybridization and their overlapping geographical distribution. However, although *C. jepsonii* var. *jepsonii* was found to be most closely related to both *C. gloriosus* vars. *gloriosus* and *exaltatus,* molecular evidence excluded *C. jepsonii* var. *albiflorus. Ceanothus cyaneus, C. leucodermis,* and *C. parvifolius* were also found to be closely related to each other, even though these species are each morphologically more similar to other species. In some cases, especially in subgenus *Cerastes,* molecular evidence also suggests close relationships between some species based on geographical distribution rather than traditional morphological variation. This evidence has been interpreted as supporting the influence of hybridization over a longer period of evolutionary history than previously hypothesized. Alternatively, the evidence is also consistent with the idea that some gene sequences have survived in seemingly independent evolutionary lineages (Hardig 2002).

Morphological and anatomical traits have been traditionally used to estimate phylogenetic relationships and develop taxonomic hierarchies. However, the differences that lead taxonomists to recognize taxa as species, subspecies, or varieties remain subjective because the relative amount of genetic divergence between such traits as opposite versus alternate leaves, globose versus conic glands, and prostrate versus erect life forms, among others, remains unknown. The number of times a particular trait has evolved independently (i.e., convergent evolution) remains unknown. As additional, phylogenetically informative gene sequences are uncovered, and as evolutionary biologists unravel the genetic causes of morphological variation, we may someday understand more precisely the evolutionary relationships among the various taxa and appreciate the relative influences of phenomena such as hybridization, geographical isolation, and ecological adaptation.

Ecological and Geographic Distribution

Ceanothus is restricted almost entirely to North America, with the greatest concentration of species occurring in the California Floristic Province, an area extending from southwestern Oregon to central Baja California. Most of the remaining species occur in regions that experience colder winters and relatively moist, warm to hot summers. A few species, such as *C. caeruleus* and *C. ochraceus,* also occur in the seasonally more equitable climates of southern Mexico and Central America. Most members of subgenus *Ceanothus* occur in forest and woodland communities that experience relatively high amounts of precipitation. In contrast, most species of subgenus *Cerastes* occur in dry habitats, often as members of shrublands or woodlands and forests at higher elevations.

Ceanothus americanus, C. herbaceus, and *C. microphyllus,* all members of subgenus *Ceanothus,* are the only species that occur entirely east of the Rocky Mountains and in a region with moist summers and relatively cool to cold winters. *Ceanothus herbaceus* has perhaps the widest geographical distribution in the genus, ranging from the Great Plains of Manitoba, Canada, to the Atlantic coast, southward to the Gulf of Mexico, and as far west as the Rocky Mountain front ranges of Montana to northern Coahuila, Mexico. *Ceanothus americanus* shares a similar distribution but is generally absent west of the central Great Plains in Canada and the United States. *Ceanothus microphyllus,* in contrast, is restricted to sandy soils of southern Alabama and Georgia, and northern Florida. *Ceanothus sanguineus,* a close relative of *C. americanus,* occurs primarily in the Pacific Northwest, from British Columbia east to Montana, and south to northwestern California, but has disjunct populations in northern Michigan. Most of this region experiences relatively cool summers and cool to cold, moist winters.

Three other species occur in part of the Pacific Northwest: *Ceanothus velutinus* and *C. integerrimus* in subgenus *Ceanothus,* and *C. prostratus* in subgenus *Cerastes. Ceanothus velutinus* occurs as far east as the northern Rocky Mountains and as far south as the Sierra Nevada in California. *Ceanothus prostratus* extends from southern Washington and western Idaho through the Cascade Range of Oregon southward to the northern Sierra Nevada. *Ceanothus integerrimus* has a wider distribution, ranging from the Coast Ranges and Cascade Range of Washington south through Oregon and much of California, with a disjunct distribution in the mountains of northern Arizona and southwestern New Mexico. In California and Oregon, *C. integerrimus* occurs primarily on the western slopes of the major, interior mountain ranges, but *C. velutinus* reaches its southernmost distribution on the drier, eastern side of the Sierra Nevada.

Five species occur almost exclusively in the Great Basin, Rocky Mountains, and Sierra Madre of Mexico, but one, *Ceanothus caeruleus,* extends as far south as Panama. *Ceanothus ochraceus* and *C. caeruleus* occur in a broad range of woodlands and forests throughout Mexico, ones with relatively cool, dry to moist winters and warm, moist summers. Notably, *C. caeruleus* ranges as far south as Costa Rica and northern Panama, where it occurs in cloud forests. *Ceanothus buxifolius* and *C. pauciflorus* (including plants previously referred to *C. greggii*) each display considerable variation and have a broad distribution in the region, and are often associated with a broad diversity of arid shrublands and woodlands (Fernández Nava 1986, 1996, González Elizondo et al. 1991, Villareal Quintanilla 2001). The seasons are generally more equitable with respect to precipitation than in the California Floristic Province, especially in Mexico, although the total precipitation is generally less than elsewhere within the geographical range of the genus; temperatures vary from cold to cool during the winter, and warm to hot during the summer. *Ceanothus martinii* is restricted to the eastern Great Basin and part of the Colorado Plateau, in shrublands and woodlands with cold winters and relatively dry summers.

Among the 50 species in the genus, 42 are primarily restricted to the California Floristic Province, including 22 of the 29 species in subgenus *Ceanothus,* and 20 of the 21 species in subgenus *Cerastes.* The California Floristic Province is characterized by a Mediterranean climate, with cool, moist to wet winters and warm to hot, dry summers (Di Castri and Mooney 1973, Barbour and Major 1977). Members of the two subgenera can often be found in the same general area, with representatives of subgenus *Ceanothus* closer to the coast or in somewhat moist habitats of canyons and north-facing slopes, and most members of subgenus *Cerastes* at slightly higher elevations toward the interior or on south-facing slopes. The greatest concentration of diversity is found in the Coast Range immediately north of San Francisco Bay, where as many as 13 species are distributed within an area less than 50 km (30 miles) wide, including *C. foliosus, C. incanus, C. integerrimus, C. oliganthus, C. parryi, C. thyrsiflorus,* and *C. velutinus* in subgenus *Ceanothus,* and *C. cuneatus, C. divergens, C. gloriosus, C. jepsonii, C. purpureus,* and *C. sonomensis* in subgenus *Cerastes.*

Some species are almost entirely restricted to coastal bluffs and foothills, with distributions lying almost entirely within the summer fog belt. Among them are members of both subgenus *Ceanothus* (e.g., *C. dentatus, C. hearstiorum, C. impressus,* and *C. thyrsiflorus*) and subgenus *Cerastes* (e.g., *C. gloriosus, C. maritimus,* and *C. megacarpus*). Some species such as *C. spinosus* and *C. foliosus* include morphologically distinguishable ecological races that are either coastal (e.g., varieties *spinosus* and *foliosus,* respectively) or occur at higher elevations immediately toward the interior (e.g., varieties *palmeri* and *medius,* respectively). Other species are restricted to the Sierra Nevada, or the southern California Transverse and Peninsular Ranges, where summers are drier and warmer. Relatively widespread taxa include *C. diversifolius, C. leucodermis, C. parvifolius,* and *C. tomentosus* in subgenus *Ceanothus,* and *C. cuneatus* var. *cuneatus* and *C. fresnensis* in subgenus *Cerastes.* At higher elevations in the Sierra Nevada and Transverse Ranges, *C. cordulatus* is a common member of montane chaparral. In contrast, the wide-ranging *C. cuneatus,* which includes a number of regional varieties, occurs over a broad range of habitats, from low-elevation coastal chaparral from near sea level to over 1,815 m (6,000 feet) in drier, colder sites of montane chaparral or open conifer forests.

Several Californian species have highly restricted geographical ranges, often associated with specific geological substrates. *Ceanothus roderickii* occurs only on a few outcrops of decomposed gabbro in the Sierra Nevada foothills of El Dorado County. *Ceanothus purpureus* and *C. bolensis* are restricted to volcanic substrates in the Vaca Mountains of Napa and Solano Counties, and Cerro Bola, northern Baja California, respectively. *Ceanothus ferrisiae, C. jepsonii,* and *C. pumilus* occur almost exclusively on thin soils derived from ultramafic rocks, of which the most common type in California is serpentinite. Ultramafic rocks are composed of minerals rich in iron, magnesium, silicates, and heavy metals but poor in calcium and other essential plant nutrients (Kruckeberg 1984). *Ceanothus pinetorum* occurs on loose granitic substrates in the Sierra Nevada but is found on both granitic and ultramafic rocks in the Trinity Mountains of northwestern California. At least two narrowly restricted taxa, *C. dentatus* and *C. impressus,* occur on Pleistocene terraces or bluffs composed primarily of sandy soils along the coasts of Monterey and Santa Barbara Counties, respectively.

Form and Function in Ceanothus

Two well-recognized groups of species have been treated as sections or, as here, subgenera: *Ceanothus* (often referred to by the informal, taxonomically incorrect name *Euceanothus* or "true *Ceanothus*") and *Cerastes.* Although members of subgenus *Cerastes* were once considered to have been derived from within subgenus *Ceanothus,* molecular and morphological evidence suggests that the two groups evolved and radiated independently from a single common ancestor. Members of subgenus *Ceanothus* have relatively thin, alternate leaves and deciduous stipules, and many have relatively smooth fruits. In contrast, most members of subgenus *Cerastes* have relatively thick, opposite leaves and stipules that develop swollen bases, which remain persistent until eventually sloughed off or enveloped by the expanding stem. Most species have horn-like projections on the fruits, the source of the name (*ceras,* Greek for horn). The two subgenera are also distinguished by other traits, including mode of reproduction, leaf structure, distribution of the stomates, architecture of the inflorescence, and fruit and seed size.

Most species of subgenus *Ceanothus* are capable of sprouting vegetatively after fire has consumed the crown and trunks or following severe frost damage. Some species, including *C. americanus, C. cordulatus, C. incanus, C. integerrimus, C. leucodermis, C. microphyllus, C. spinosus,* and *C. velutinus,* have well-developed underground burls, sometimes called lignotubers, which serve to store food reserves and which bear dormant buds that sprout after fire or damage to the crown and basal stems (James 1984). Some species are polymorphic for sprouting ability, including *C. oliganthus* and *C. tomentosus.* Sprouting from root crowns has been reported in populations of *C. oliganthus* var. *sorediatus* and *C. tomentosus* var. *olivaceus* (but apparently is absent in the typical varieties), which are found primarily north of the Transverse Ranges in California. In contrast, all species of subgenus *Cerastes* lack burls and reproduce strictly from seeds (Keeley 1975, Schlesinger et al. 1982).

Most species are erect shrubs with a canopy or crown that is hemispheric to obovoid in outline. Such plants are characterized by several basal trunks that give rise to additional branches, the number and intricacy of branching depending on the species and the age and size of the plant. In some species, single-trunked plants may develop under competitive conditions in mature vegetation, but following fires, the same plants may sprout with shoots that give rise to multiple trunks. In low-growing, erect species such as *Ceanothus americanus, C. herbaceus,* and *C. microphyllus,* the dominant, conspicuous stems are strictly erect to ascending. In other species, such as *C. cordulatus, C. parvifolius,* and *C. pinetorum,* plants have several to many weakly ascending stems that radiate conspicuously from the central subterranean axis. Several species in both subgenera are composed of mat-like shrubs with strictly prostrate branches (e.g., *C. diversifolius, C. fresnensis, C. prostratus,* and some forms of *C. gloriosus*). Other low-growing taxa, such as *C. arcuatus* (see under *C. fresnensis*), *C. hearstiorum, C. pinetorum,* and *C. pumilus,* are mound-like and often flat-topped, growing extensively by means of spreading to weakly ascending branches. A few species, including *C. maritimus* and *C. roderickii,* often have both low-growing, spreading stems and ascending to erect central branches. *Ceanothus arboreus* and *C. caeruleus* are often arborescent, with single trunks and elevated crowns. Some species, including *C. cuneatus, C. gloriosus,* and *C. thyrsiflorus,* range from nearly prostrate to erect. The latter species can have both shrub-like and arborescent forms, often in close proximity. The various cultivated forms of variable species such as *C. foliosus, C. gloriosus,* and *C. thyrsiflorus* often retain their natural life form under uniform horticultural conditions, suggesting underlying genetic differences.

Branches arising from the central trunks in many species angle upward (ascending), and their lateral branches often spread or arch outward. Prostrate species such as

Ceanothus cordulatus, with spinose branches, Yuba Gap, Sierra Nevada, California

Ceanothus diversifolius, C. fresnensis, and *C. prostratus* generally have strictly spreading branches, rooting at nodes covered by soil and leaf litter. Each of these species produce short, erect, leafy shoots that may give rise to inflorescences but that do not continue to grow upward. Other species with mat- or mound-like habits (e.g., *C. pumilus* and *C. roderickii*) may produce roots at relatively remote nodes either near the tips of branches or near their bases. In some species the branching pattern may be more intricate and widely spreading (divaricate), with many relatively short internodes (e.g., *C. buxifolius, C. cordulatus, C. dentatus,* and some forms of *C. cuneatus*). In species such as *C. buxifolius, C. cordulatus,* and *C. incanus* the terminal branchlets become rigid with age and lose most or all their leaves, becoming sharp-pointed and spine-like in appearance. Several species, including *C. buxifolius, C. incanus,* and *C. spinosus,* are polymorphic, with some plants bearing predominantly spine-like branchlets and others with blunt-tipped branchlets.

The bark of twigs or young branchlets, especially those formed during the first few years of growth, varies from green to brown or gray, depending on the species. Most species have smooth branchlets that are round in cross section, but others, such as *Ceanothus gloriosus* and *C. thyrsiflorus,* may have slightly elevated ridges that give them an angled appearance. The branchlets of a few species (e.g., *C. cyaneus*) have a rough or papillose (wart-like) surface. The youngest branchlets are either glabrous or bear short hairs that are straight, curly, or densely entangled (i.e., tomentulose). The hairs are often similar to those found on leaves, and are sloughed off with the developing bark. The older bark of trunks and secondary branches in subgenus *Ceanothus* is either smooth or moderately rough in texture and varies in most species from gray to dark brown, although some species, such as *C. spinosus* and *C. integerrimus,* retain a greenish bark for many years. In some members of subgenus *Cerastes,* the older bark gradually dies back, leaving vertical, elevated, often narrow ribbons of living bark.

Leaves are either alternate or opposite, with each leaf blade subtended by two stipules. Stipules are either thin, leaf-like, and deciduous, or their bases are persistent and swollen, often looking like minute knobs with a cork-like texture. Thin, deciduous stipules are associated with the alternate-leaved species that belong to subgenus *Ceanothus.* All species of subgenus *Cerastes* bear thick, persistent stipules, and most have opposite leaves. In subgenus *Cerastes* the distal deciduous portion of each stipule may spread or reflex when young, with an orientation that often characterizes individual species. In *C. gloriosus,* for example, the young stipule apices are reflexed, but in *C. cuneatus* they are short and erect. Stipule size, shape, and orientation have not been fully studied, mainly because the complete structure is poorly represented on most herbarium specimens. *Ceanothus megacarpus* var. *megacarpus* and *C. verrucosus* are the only members of subgenus *Cerastes* with alternate leaves. Interestingly, in some species of subgenus *Ceanothus* the first few leaves are opposite, but the shoot soon develops internodes with alternate leaves. In some species of subgenus *Cerastes* the lateral shoots on older branches are suppressed and remain short, so that their leaves appear to be clustered. Such species include *C. gloriosus, C. prostratus, C. roderickii,* and *C. verrucosus.* Most species of subgenus *Ceanothus* and all species of subgenus *Cerastes* have evergreen leaves. Although different species show varying patterns of leaf longevity, a few, such as *C. americanus, C. integerrimus,* and *C. sanguineus,* are completely deciduous during the winter. In other species, especially in subgenus *Cerastes,* some leaves are apparently retained for many years.

All leaves of *Ceanothus* have pinnate venation, with a prominent central vein and from five to nine prominent lateral veins on each side. Leaf blades of subgenus *Ceanothus* are typically thin, with well-developed raised veins on the lower surface. Several species (e.g., *C. integerrimus, C. thyrsiflorus,* and *C. velutinus*) have leaves that are often described as being three-veined from the base. The lower pair of lateral veins may extend to near the midpoint of the blade or approach the length of the midvein, often curving parallel with the leaf margin and often much longer than those above. In large-leaved species such as *C. integerrimus, C. thyrsiflorus,* and *C. velutinus,* prominent secondary veins diverge from them and extend to the margin. *Ceanothus foliosus, C. integerrimus,* and *C. lemmonii* have both one- and three-veined leaves, sometimes on the same plant. In *C. dentatus* and *C. impressus* the veins are deeply furrowed when viewed from above. In most species of subgenus *Ceanothus,* most of the venation system, including the tertiary veins or veinlets, is visible under relatively low magnification.

Ceanothus microphyllus is a notable exception in often having only three minute veins visible on the lower surface. Tertiary veins and terminal veins or veinlets in subgenus *Cerastes* are not often clearly visible, because the thickness of the blade obscures them.

In subgenus *Ceanothus* the stomates are generally distributed evenly over the lower surface of the blades between the veins, but in subgenus *Cerastes* the stomates are restricted to sunken, crypt-like invaginations of the lower leaf surface that are bordered or covered by microscopic tomentulose hairs. Stomatal crypts provide opportunities for enhanced photosynthesis and gas exchange under the water-limiting conditions imposed by dry, hot summers in the areas where most members of subgenus *Cerastes* occur. Nobs (1963) classified stomatal crypts into three types, based on anatomical structure and the distribution of associated hairs. However, their taxonomic distribution is not completely consistent with relationships inferred from molecular evidence or other morphological traits. The stomatal crypts and associated hairs are often arranged in regular patches (areoles) surrounded by the terminal veinlets. The pattern of distribution of the stomatal crypts varies among species, but their architecture has not been systematically studied throughout all members of subgenus *Cerastes*.

The largest leaves in the genus are found on both shrubs (e.g., *Ceanothus americanus*, *C. sanguineus*, and *C. velutinus*) and arborescent taxa such as *C. arboreus* and *C. caeruleus*, all members of subgenus *Ceanothus*. The leaves of *C. americanus*, *C. herbaceus*, and *C. sanguineus* are also relatively thin, whereas relatively thick leathery (i.e., coriaceous) leaves are characteristic of *C. arboreus* and most forms of *C. caeruleus*. The leaves of subgenus *Cerastes* are usually small and thick, although the smallest leaves in the genus are found in *C. microphyllus*, a member of subgenus *Ceanothus*. Broad or large, thin-leaved species occur in relatively moist climates or habitats. The small, thick

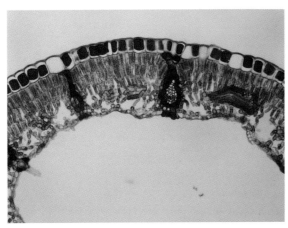

Cross section of leaf with surface stomata (*Ceanothus papillosus*, subgenus *Ceanothus*)

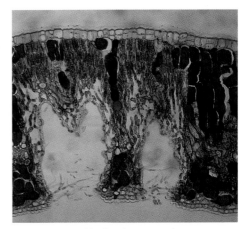

Cross section of leaf with stomatal crypts (*Ceanothus gloriosus*, subgenus *Cerastes*)

leaves (i.e., sclerophylls) of subgenus *Cerastes* are generally believed to be an adaptation to the summer dry climate of Mediterranean and desert ecosystems, because they reduce water loss while permitting photosynthesis.

Leaf blade shape generally ranges from elliptic or ovate to lanceolate. The blades of some species are notably oblong or linear in outline, as in *Ceanothus ophiochilus* and some forms of *C. hearstiorum* and *C. papillosus.* In some taxa, such as *C. cuneatus,* there exist numerous leaf shapes, ranging from elliptic or oblanceolate to almost round (i.e., orbicular), which are often correlated with geographical and ecological distribution. In *C. cuneatus* var. *fascicularis* the leaves of the main shoots can be broadly obovate or almost round, but the clustered leaves of short, axillary shoots are narrowly oblanceolate. Relatively broad, almost orbicular leaves can be found in some forms of *C. buxifolius* and *C. vestitus.* Leaf blades in most members of subgenus *Ceanothus* are generally flat. Notable exceptions include *C. dentatus, C. hearstiorum,* and *C. papillosus,* which appear convex when viewed from above and whose margins are also conspicuously revolute. Subgenus *Cerastes* includes species with leaf blades that are flat, convex, concave, or folded lengthwise when viewed from above. Leaf blades with concave upper surfaces have often been described as cupped.

Leaves may be either glabrous or hairy, often with different densities of hairs on the upper and lower surfaces. One of the most common forms consists of sparsely to moderately distributed short, straight, hairs composed of a single row of cells that are borne parallel to the leaf surface (i.e., appressed-puberulent or strigulose). In a few species, the hairs of the lower leaf surfaces are relatively long and densely entangled (i.e., tomentulose, as in *Ceanothus tomentosus, C. caeruleus,* and *C. pauciflorus*). Short, somewhat curly hairs are a diagnostic trait for *C. vestitus.* Although most hairs on *Ceanothus* leaves are generally white or grayish in aggregate, rust-colored or brownish hairs are typical of *C. caeruleus, C. ochraceus,* and the young leaves of *C. otayensis.* Hair density varies from species to species, usually with fewer hairs on the upper surface than on the lower. In general, the youngest leaves often have the highest densities of hairs, depending on the species. Although many members of subgenus *Cerastes* develop nearly glabrous leaves with age, the distinctive microscopic hairs of the stomatal crypts are retained throughout the life of the leaf.

Leaf margins may be entire or toothed, with the teeth pointed toward the apex (i.e., serrulate) or pointed somewhat outward, perpendicular to the leaf axis (i.e., denticulate). Most members of subgenus *Ceanothus* have serrulate to denticulate leaves and usually bear deciduous to persistent, multicellular, glandular appendages that often become dark with age. These glands vary from narrowly conic in *C. americanus* and *C. caeruleus* to broadly conic or subglobose in such species as *C. cordulatus, C. foliosus,* and *C. thyrsiflorus.* Short-stalked or sessile globose glands occur on the margins and upper leaf surfaces in *C. hearstiorum* and *C. papillosus* but are apparently restricted

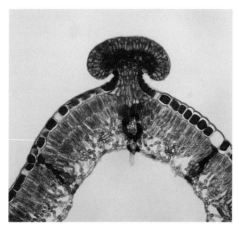

Cross section of leaf with globose gland
(*Ceanothus papillosus*, subgenus *Ceanothus*)

only to the upper surfaces of leaves in *C. dentatus*. The slender, stalked glands of *C. diversifolius* appear unique in the genus. Some species, including *C. parvifolius* and *C. spinosus*, have uniformly entire leaves on most branches, but even these species have microscopic deciduous glands near the tips of the developing leaves. Toothed leaves also occur on young shoots of juvenile plants or on shoots developed from burls after fires. When present, the teeth in leaves of subgenus *Cerastes* are thick, persistent, and spinulose. In some species, such as *C. jepsonii* and *C. purpureus,* the spinulose tips are relatively narrow and sharp, giving the leaves a somewhat holly-like appearance. Some members of subgenus *Cerastes* have teeth restricted to the upper half of the blade while others have teeth that are evenly distributed. Strongly thickened or revolute leaves occur in both subgenera and are diagnostic traits in unrelated species such as *C. papillosus, C. parryi, C. impressus,* and most plants of *C. pauciflorus.*

As inflorescences expand following dormancy, they reveal a dense aggregation of bracts that senesce and fall with the expanding flowers. In both subgenera the arrangement is complex, with bracts subtending small units usually consisting of three flowers, even in the few-flowered umbels of subgenus *Cerastes.* Aggregates of these units are often accompanied by additional bracts. The large number of bracts in each inflorescence suggests congestion of a more complex, open shoot system. Bracts in most species of *Ceanothus* are ovate to almost orbicular and usually are moderately to densely pubescent. Patterns of variation in the size, shape, pubescence, and relationship to branching have not been studied but may be prove useful in analyzing systematic relationships.

Following expansion of the inflorescence and loss of subtending bracts, the flowers appear arranged in umbels, racemes, or panicles in which all or most pedicels are equal in length and attached to single nodes of the inflorescence axis. In many members of subgenus *Cerastes*, the umbels are either solitary or aggregated into dense clusters at the top of a short peduncle whose buds develop during the late spring of the year prior to flowering. Clusters are usually borne on short peduncles, sometimes with two minute bracts near the base of the pedicels. In subgenus *Ceanothus* the umbels or subumbellate racemes are aggregated into compound raceme- or panicle-like inflorescences. Such inflorescences usually develop from the tips of growing shoots and are borne on peduncles with relatively well developed bracts or leaves. In some species, such as *C. buxifolius*, *C. cordulatus*, *C. martinii*, and *C. sanguineus*, inflorescences are produced on short shoots borne in the upper axils of older woody branches.

The flower of *Ceanothus* has five sepals, five petals, and five stamens. The ovary is considered to be half-inferior, with the receptacle forming a ring around the ovary. Each ovary usually has three separate locules, each enclosing a single ovule. The flower bears a prominent annular disk around the upper portion of the ovary and between the style and the insertion of the stamens and perianth. The disk serves as a nectar gland and often glistens in sunlight when the flower is mature. The outer sepals are generally lanceolate to elliptic, flat, and have acute or obtuse tips. The petals of *Ceanothus* are obovate in outline, with narrow claws and distinctly cupped, hood-like blades that have strongly concave upper surfaces. The petals alternate with the sepals, and the stamens are located opposite the petals. Each stamen appears enclosed by the blade of the adjacent petal as the flower opens, but they separate at maturity. As the petals reflex, the stamens remaining erect or ascending. The style is short and usually bears three linear lobes. Flowers with floral parts in series of four have been found in some species but not uniformly throughout the plant. *Ceanothus jepsonii* appears to be unique in the genus in uniformly having perianth parts and stamens in sets of six or eight. Flower size varies throughout the genus but has not been systematically surveyed. The smallest flowers apparently occur in *C. microphyllus* and *C. pauciflorus*; *C. jepsonii* has the largest flowers.

The distinctive fruit of *Ceanothus*, which opens explosively at maturity, has been variously interpreted as either a capsule or a drupe composed of three pyrenes, but its structure does not match the traditional definitions of either type. Following fertilization and initiation of seed development, the outer fruit walls become leathery, sometimes developing a thick, resinous secretion. In some species of subgenus *Ceanothus* the outer wall breaks apart and sloughs off prior to dehiscence; in other species, especially in subgenus *Cerastes*, the outer wall remains attached until dehiscence. The outer wall and resinous secretions of *C. incanus* are notably thick relative to the inner portion of the fruit and often break apart uniformly into many small granular pieces. At the time of dehiscence each fruit opens along three sutures that develop along the contiguous walls of the locules enclosing the seeds. The inner walls that surround each of the three seeds become hard at maturity and develop with sufficient tension such that they uncurl almost instantaneously during dehiscence. The lower, woody half of the fruit remains intact and may provide a structurally resistant platform for each of the dehiscent units. This action contributes to a rapid, explosive expulsion of the seed and its dispersal several meters from the source. Fruit dehiscence usually takes place during warm or hot days and often when relative humidity is lowest. On such days it is possible to hear the fruits exploding, followed by a light rain of seeds beneath the canopy.

Ceanothus fruits are generally globose, often with weakly to well-developed lobes

Ceanothus megacarpus var. insularis fruits, Santa Cruz Island, California

when viewed in cross section. Fruits with prominent lobes appear somewhat triangular in cross section. The fruits of subgenus *Ceanothus* are usually smooth or have weakly developed dorsal ridges and are 2–6 mm wide. Some species have knob-like protuberances or swellings on the dorsal surface of each lobe. In contrast, fruits of most species of subgenus *Cerastes* are 4–9 mm wide and often bear prominent, horn-like appendages. The appendages sometimes appear as extensions of dorsal ridges, when present. In other species, such as *C. fresnensis* and *C. purpureus,* they can arise directly from the rounded surface of each lobe. The function of the ridges and horns is poorly understood. Although they often appear to be the sources of resinous secretions in some species, they also may be structurally related to fruit dehiscence.

Seeds range from ellipsoid to obovoid and are usually somewhat compressed. In some species the outer seed surface (i.e., the surface facing the fruit wall) can have a weakly developed ridge. Although appendages (i.e., arils) have been reported in some species of *Ceanothus,* they appear too small to be especially attractive to ants. Regardless, harvesting and storage by ants has been reported in at least one species, *C. vestitus* (called *C. greggii* by Mills and Kummerow 1989). Most seeds are shiny and can vary from brown to black. The thick walls of the seeds are impermeable to water unless gradually eroded (i.e., scarified) by soil particles and microbial activity, or cracked open by the heat of natural fires (Quick and Quick 1961, Evans et al. 1987, Keeley 1991). This physical dormancy is combined with physiological dormancy, which is overcome under natural conditions by exposure to short periods of cool or cold temperatures preceded by the imbibition of water during winter precipitation. Seed size seems correlated with fruit size. Seeds of subgenus *Ceanothus* average 2.5–3 mm in length, but those of subgenus *Cerastes* are often 4–5 mm long. The somewhat larger seed size in subgenus *Cerastes* may be a function of larger food reserves required for long-term dormancy or for rapid germination and establishment germination, especially after fires.

Species of *Ceanothus* have been and continue to be difficult to identify by means of traditional dichotomous keys, because many of them cannot be organized into a hierarchical order using unique or distinct combinations of morphological characters. Overlapping variation in several characters, the influence of hybridization, the lack of information concerning whole-plant architecture on many specimens, and the frequent inaccessibility to both flowers and mature fruits from the same plant also contribute to difficulty in identification. The following keys attempt to use, as much as possible, those diagnostic characters that are readily accessible most of the time between flowering and fruiting, including young shoots and leaves. Certain species may appear more than once in the key because of variation in one or more characters (e.g., number of leaf veins, pubescence, leaf shape, and plant architecture) or because some species have two or more varieties or subspecies. Consequently, it is very important to compare specimens and the locality from which the plant was obtained, including ecological and geographical distribution, with the full description in the text. Although the key to species sometimes results in groups of taxa with similar combinations of characters, it does not necessarily indicate close evolutionary relationships. Taxa treated as varieties or subspecies are keyed out separately in the treatment of the species in which they are included.

Subgenera of *Ceanothus* Linnaeus

1 Stipules thin, deciduous at an early stage of shoot elongation; inflorescences usually racemose or paniculate; leaves alternate, the margins in most species with teeth tipped with dark, conic to globose glands, at least when young . . . .*Ceanothus* subg. *Ceanothus*
1 Stipules thick and persistent, becoming knob-like and corky, their upper leaf-like portion disintegrating; inflorescences usually umbellate, solitary or in dense clusters; leaves usually opposite (alternate only in *C. megacarpus* and *C. verrucosus*), the margins either entire or with pale, opaque, spinulose teeth . . . .*Ceanothus* subg. *Cerastes*, p. 156

Ceanothus subg. *Ceanothus*

Stipules thin, scale-like, completely deciduous. Leaves alternate. Leaf blades relatively thin; lower surfaces usually with raised veins and usually with somewhat evenly distributed stomates; margins entire or with teeth usually terminated by minute conic to globose glands, especially when young. Inflorescences usually racemose to paniculate. Fruit globose to lobed, smooth to evidently ridged near or above the middle, rarely with horns. Reproducing from seeds and, in some species, from basal shoots following fire.

1 Flowering or terminal branches with rigid, often spine-like branchlets 2
1 Flowering or terminal branches with flexible to somewhat rigid, blunt-tipped (not spine-like) branchlets 7
2 Branchlets pale gray to almost white; older bark usually light gray to light grayish brown, sometimes grayish green or almost white 3
2 Branchlets green to grayish green; older bark grayish green to dark gray or brown 5

3 Inflorescences sessile to subsessile or peduncles to 6 mm long; plants usually less than 1.5 m tall . . . . *C. cordulatus*

3 Inflorescences on peduncles 9–30 mm long; plants usually 1.5–4 m tall 4

4 Rachises and peduncles moderately puberulent; most leaf blades 10–30 mm wide; lower surfaces usually appressed-puberulent; outer surface of fruits strongly wrinkled when dry; North Coast Range and Santa Cruz Mountains of California . . . . *C. incanus*

4 Rachises and peduncles sparsely puberulent to glabrous; most leaf blades 5–15 mm wide; lower surfaces usually glabrous, sometimes sparsely puberulent; outer surface of fruits smooth to weakly wrinkled when dry; Sierra Nevada, South Coast Range, Transverse, and Peninsular Ranges of California, and northern Baja California . . . . *C. leucodermis*

5 Most leaves with a single principal vein from the base, lateral veins more or less equal in length; spine-like branchlets leafy; inflorescences racemose to paniculate, 30–150 mm long; coastal mountains of southern California and northern Baja California . . . .*C. spinosus*

5 Most leaves with 3 veins from the base, the lowest lateral pair clearly longer than those above; spine-like branchlets often becoming leafless; inflorescences umbellate to subumbellate, sometimes racemose, 10–27 mm long; Rocky Mountains of the United States south to the Sierra Madre of central Mexico 6

6 Leaf blades usually oval, orbicular, or broadly elliptic, the margins often with persistent dark glands, the lower surfaces glabrous to sparsely appressed-puberulent between the veins . . . . *C. buxifolius*

6 Leaf blades usually oblong, elliptic-oblong, or elliptic, the margins rarely with persistent glands, the lower surfaces sparsely appressed-puberulent to densely short-wavy-hairy between the veins . . . . *C. fendleri*

7 Leaves with a single central vein, the lowest pair of lateral veins not much longer than those immediately above (sometimes 3-veined from the base in *C. diversifolius, C. foliosus,* and *C. lemmonii*) 8

7 Leaves with 3 principal veins from the base, the basal pair of lateral veins longer than the pair above, often extending a third or more of the blade length, sometimes equaling the central vein 22

8 Shrubs mat- to mound-like, often flat-topped, usually less than 0.5 m tall; branches widely spreading 9

8 Shrubs erect to semierect, hemispheric to broadly obovoid, 0.5–2.5+ m tall 12

9 Leaf blades somewhat convex above lengthwise; upper leaf surface papillose or with persistent, sessile to subsessile, globose glands; coastal slopes of the Santa Lucia Range, northern San Luis Obispo County, California . . . . *C. hearstiorum*

9 Leaf blades flat or folded lengthwise or slightly wavy; upper leaf surfaces sparsely appressed-puberulent or short-villous, sometimes becoming glabrous 10

10 Leaf blades usually wavy and slightly folded lengthwise, the upper surface dark green; most petioles 1–3 mm long; leaf margins with broadly conic or subglobose glands . . . .*C. foliosus*

10 Leaf blades flat to slightly wavy but not folded lengthwise, the upper surface green to pale to bluish green; most petioles 3–11 mm long; leaf margins, especially of young leaves, with narrowly conic or short-stalked glands 11

11 Plants mat-like, usually less than 30 cm tall; twigs usually green to reddish green; most leaf blades obovate or ovate, sometimes almost orbicular, their length usually less than twice their width . . . . *C. diversifolius*

11 Plants mound-like, usually more than 30 cm tall; branchlets pale grayish green, often glaucous and light gray; most leaf blades elliptic to oblong-elliptic, their length at least twice their width . . . . *C. lemmonii*

12 Leaf blades somewhat convex above (concave below), the margins revolute to thickened 13

12 Leaf blades mostly flat, sometimes wavy or slightly folded lengthwise, the margins entire to denticulate or serrulate, sometimes thickened or revolute in *C. parryi* 15

13 Leaf blades elliptic to almost orbicular, the upper surfaces with the secondary veins in well-developed furrows . . . . *C. impressus*

13 Leaf blades linear to oblong, sometimes narrowly elliptic, the upper surfaces irregularly roughened, appearing somewhat corrugated but not conspicuously furrowed 14

14 Globose to subglobose glands restricted to or near the leaf blade margins; plants usually 0.5–1.5 m tall; crown dense; branchlet internodes 6–10 mm long, brown to grayish brown . . . . *C. dentatus*

14 Globose to subglobose glands present on the upper surfaces and margins of the leaf blades; plants usually 1–3.5 m tall; crown open; branchlet internodes 15–28 mm long, green . . . . *C. papillosus*

15 Mature leaf margins denticulate to serrulate, the teeth tipped with deciduous to semi-persistent glands 16

15 Mature leaf margins entire or weakly serrulate, glands rarely present and then only on young, developing leaves 18

16 Lower surfaces of leaf blades densely white-tomentulose but becoming rust-colored with age; marginal glands narrowly conic; flowers usually white; mountains of Mexico . . . . *C. ochraceus*

16 Lower surfaces of leaf blades moderately to densely short-villous, marginal glands subglobose to globose; flowers usually blue; California 17

17 Branchlets pale grayish green to light gray; older bark gray; leaf blades usually flat with plane margins; inner North Coast Range, southern Cascade Range, and Sierra Nevada of California . . . . *C. lemmonii*

17 Branchlets greenish to reddish green; older bark brown; leaf blades flat to more often wavy, sometimes folded lengthwise; outer Coast Ranges and Cuyamaca Mountains of California . . . . *C. foliosus*

18 Leaf blade margins slightly revolute, at least below the middle; lower surfaces of leaf blades white-villous to loosely tomentulose, the hairs cobwebby . . . . *C. parryi*

18 Leaf blade margins entire, sometimes slightly thickened; lower surfaces of leaves glabrous to sparsely puberulent, often appressed-puberulent or more strigulose along the veins 19

19 Older stems weakly ascending to spreading and radiating from the central trunk; spreading shrubs usually less than 1.5 m tall; inflorescence usually racemose, the rachis 19–38 mm long . . . . *C. parvifolius*

19 Central trunk and older stems erect to ascending; erect shrubs, sometimes arborescent, 1–6 m tall; inflorescence racemose to paniculate, the rachis 30–180 mm long 20

20 Upper surfaces of leaves green, shiny, remaining somewhat shiny but becoming purplish when dry; flowers usually blue; coastal slopes at elevations less than 910 m (3,000 feet), from San Luis Obispo County, California, south to northwestern Baja California . . . . *C. spinosus*

20 Upper surfaces of leaves usually dull green, sometimes somewhat shiny, usually dull to pale green when dry, sometimes appearing glaucous; flowers white 21

21 Leaves elliptic to elliptic-oblong, completely deciduous, thin and pliable; fruits 4–6.5 mm wide, their lobes usually smooth, sometimes with a minute glandular bulge or ridge; southern Santa Cruz Mountains and northern Santa Lucia Range of California . . . .*C. integerrimus*

21 Leaves elliptic to oblong-ovate, semideciduous, some leaves persisting longer than others, thick and somewhat stiff; fruits·6–9 mm wide, their lobes usually with a glandular bulge or ridge; western slope of the Sierra Nevada and inner Coast Ranges from San Benito County, California, south to northwestern Baja California . . . . *C. spinosus*

22 Mature leaf margins usually entire, very rarely denticulate or serrulate and then the teeth minute or present only as dark deciduous glands on young leaves 23

22 Mature leaf margins denticulate to serrulate or serrate, the teeth often tipped with somewhat persistent dark glands 28

23 Leaf blades 2–6(–11) mm long, 1.5–4(–6) mm wide; lateral veins minute or obscure; internodes 3–9(–12) mm long; southeastern United States . . . . *C. microphyllus*

23 Leaf blades usually 12–75 mm long, 5–40 mm wide; lateral veins evident; internodes 5–23 mm long; western North America 24

24 Plants usually 1–4.5 m tall; inflorescences usually paniculate, rachis 21–180 mm long . . . 25

24 Plants usually less than 1.5 m tall; inflorescences usually subumbellate to racemose, rarely paniculate, rachis 11–38 mm long 26

25 Branchlets stiff, widely spreading; young internodes pale gray; lower surfaces of leaves light grayish green, evenly appressed-puberulent; fruits appearing strongly wrinkled when dry . . . . *C. incanus*

25 Branchlets flexible, ascending to spreading; young internodes green to yellowish green; lower surfaces of leaves dull green, glabrous to sparsely puberulent, often more puberulent on the veins; fruits smooth or with 3 dorsal ridges but not strongly wrinkled when dry . . . . *C. integerrimus*

26 Flowers blue; crown mound-shaped, sometimes flat-topped, the main branches radiating from the center; leaf blades elliptic to narrowly elliptic; Sierra Nevada of California . . . . *C. parvifolius*

26 Flowers white; crown hemispheric to broadly obovoid, the main branches erect to ascending upward; leaf blades elliptic or elliptic-oblong to almost orbicular in outline; Great Basin ranges and Rocky Mountains 27

27 Leaf blades elliptic to elliptic-oblong, 4–9 mm wide; upper surfaces sparsely puberulent to tomentulose; lower surfaces sparsely puberulent to tomentulose . . . . *C. fendleri*

27 Leaf blades broadly elliptic to almost orbicular in outline, 9–21 mm wide; upper surfaces glabrous to sparsely appressed-puberulent; lower surfaces glabrous to sometimes appressed-puberulent on the veins . . . . *C. martinii*

28 Lower surfaces of leaves uniformly and densely tomentulose to densely puberulent, the veins sometimes obscured by the hairs 29

28 Lower surfaces of leaves subglabrous to sparsely or moderately puberulent or short-villous but neither tomentulose nor densely hairy; in most species the veins often more hairy than the surfaces between the veins 34

29 Leaf blades usually 8–30 mm long, 3–25 mm wide 30

29 Leaf blades usually 35–125 mm long, 10–65 mm wide 32

30 Lower surfaces of leaves usually uniformly tomentulose, white when young but becoming rust-colored with age; marginal teeth 9–29 per leaf; pedicels usually puberulent when young; mountains of central Mexico . . . . *C. ochraceus*

30 Lower surfaces of leaves tomentulose to densely short-villous, pale green, if tomentulose then usually remaining white, often more densely hairy on the veins; marginal teeth 19–71 per leaf; pedicels glabrous; California and Baja California, Mexico 31

31 Upper surfaces of leaves glabrous to sparsely short-villous or puberulent; lower surfaces short-villous, the marginal glands usually broadly conic to subglobose . . . . . *C. oliganthus*

31 Upper surfaces of leaves usually moderately short-villous or puberulent, sometimes becoming glabrous; lower surfaces tomentulose, the marginal glands usually conic . . . . *C. tomentosus*

32 Leaf blades narrowly elliptic to lanceolate; flowers white; inflorescences hemispheric and terminal on the current year's shoot; peduncle usually longer than the inflorescence . . . . *C. herbaceus*

32 Leaf blades elliptic to broadly ovate, sometimes lanceolate; flowers pale blue to blue; inflorescences racemose to paniculate, usually borne in the uppermost axils of 1- or 2-year-old branchlets, peduncle usually shorter than the inflorescence 33

33 Lower leaf surfaces pale green to grayish green with age; pedicels glabrous; fruits 5–8 mm wide; California Channel Islands . . . . *C. arboreus*

33 Lower leaf surfaces rust-colored with age; pedicels often puberulent when young; fruits 4–5 mm wide; mountains of central Mexico south to Panama . . . . *C. caeruleus*

34 Most leaf blades 40–100 mm long, 25–60 mm wide, usually broadly elliptic to broadly ovate (elliptic to lanceolate in *C. herbaceus*), the margins usually with more than 50 teeth per leaf 35

34 Most leaf blades 5–40 mm long, 5–25 mm wide, elliptic, oblong-elliptic, oblanceolate, rarely ovate, the margins usually with fewer than 50 teeth per leaf 39

35 Upper surfaces of leaves somewhat sticky, appearing resinous and shiny, usually with a distinctive pungent or spicy odor when crushed . . . . *C. velutinus*

35 Upper surfaces of leaves not sticky, neither resinous nor shiny, and without a distinctive odor when crushed 36

36 Leaves narrowly elliptic to lanceolate; inflorescences usually hemispheric and terminal on the current year's shoot . . . . *C. herbaceus*

36 Leaves elliptic to ovate; inflorescences usually longer than wide, racemose to paniculate, borne in the upper axils of the current year's or older shoots 37

37 Inflorescences borne on the current year's shoots; peduncles usually longer than the inflorescences; plants usually less than 1.5 m tall; eastern North America . . . *C. americanus*

37 Inflorescences borne in the upper axils of older, somewhat woody stems or branchlets; peduncles usually shorter than the inflorescences; plants 1–7 m tall; western North America (*C. sanguineus* disjunct in northern Michigan) 38

38 Flowers pale blue to blue; branchlet internodes 11–25 mm long, brown, tomentulose, becoming glabrous with age; fruits 5–8 mm wide; California Channel Islands . . . .
. . . .*C. arboreus*

38 Flowers white; branchlet internodes 25–45 mm long, green or reddish brown, puberulent but becoming glabrous with age; fruits 3–4.5 mm wide; southern British Columbia east to South Dakota, south to northwestern California, disjunct in Michigan . . . *C. sanguineus*

39 Plants usually less than 1 m tall, either hemispheric with older stems erect to ascending, or mat- to mound-like with weakly ascending to widely spreading stems 40

39 Plants usually 1–4 m tall, usually obovoid, sometimes hemispheric or arborescent, with erect to ascending stems 45

40 Plants mat- to mound-like, often flat-topped, the main stems prostrate to and widely spreading or weakly ascending 41

40 Plants hemispheric, the stems erect to stiffly ascending 43

41 Youngest or current year's branchlets usually angled, often with prominent longitudinal

ridges at least along the distal internodes; main veins on the lower surfaces of leaf blades raised and relatively prominent . . . . *C. thyrsiflorus*

41 Youngest or current year's branchlets cylindrical and smooth; main veins on lower surfaces of leaf blades not prominently raised 42

42 Branchlets usually green to reddish green; leaf blades elliptic to obovate or ovate, sometimes almost orbicular, their length usually twice their width or less; plants usually carpet- or mat-like, usually less than 50 cm tall . . . . *C. diversifolius*

42 Branchlets pale grayish green, often glaucous and light gray; leaf blades elliptic to oblong-elliptic, their length twice their width or more; plants usually mound-like but often flat-topped, usually more than 50 cm tall . . . . *C. lemmonii*

43 Inflorescences usually hemispheric and terminal on the current year's shoots; leaves usually lanceolate to narrowly elliptic . . . . *C. herbaceus*

43 Inflorescences racemose to paniculate, usually longer than wide, borne in the upper axils of the current year's or older branchlets; leaves usually ovate or broadly lanceolate . . . 44

44 Inflorescences borne on the current year's shoots; peduncles usually longer than the inflorescences; eastern North America . . . . *C. americanus*

44 Inflorescences borne in the upper axils of older, somewhat woody stems or branchlets; peduncles usually shorter than the inflorescences; western North America, disjunct in northern Michigan . . . . *C. sanguineus*

45 Youngest or current year's branchlets usually angled, often with prominent longitudinal ridges along the distal internodes 46

45 Youngest or current year's branchlets smooth and cylindrical, not prominently angled or ridged longitudinally 48

46 Lower surfaces of leaf blades white-villous to white-villous-tomentulose, especially when young but often becoming subglabrous with age . . . . *C. parryi*

46 Lower surfaces of leaf blades surfaces pale green, glabrous to puberulent or short-villous, sometimes strigulose on the veins, the veins often more puberulent than the surfaces . . 47

47 Inflorescences paniculate; rachises 35–190 mm long; peduncles 20–150 mm long; veins on lower surfaces of leaf blades not prominently raised; mature fruits brown to reddish brown . . . . *C. cyaneus*

47 Inflorescences racemose, sometimes paniculate; rachises 15–53(–75) mm long; peduncles 12–33 mm long; veins on lower surfaces of leaf blades prominently raised; mature fruits dark brown to black . . . . *C. thyrsiflorus*

48 Leaf blades usually wavy, sometimes slightly folded lengthwise and weakly concave above; petioles 1–3 mm long . . . . *C. foliosus*

48 Leaf blades usually flat or slightly convex above; petioles 3–7 mm long 49

49 Lower surfaces of leaf blades sparsely to densely short-villous or strigulose, especially on the veins . . . . *C. oliganthus*

49 Lower surfaces of leaf blades uniformly tomentulose . . . . *C. tomentosus*

Ceanothus subg. *Cerastes* (Watson) Weberbauer

Stipules thick, the apical portion deciduous, the basal portion persistent and often conspicuously thick, appearing swollen. Leaves usually opposite, rarely alternate. Leaf blades relatively thick; lower surfaces usually with main veins evident but not raised, stomates sunken in crypts that are usually distributed in patches among the terminal veinlets and covered by minute tomentulose hairs; margins entire or with spinulose teeth. Inflorescences usually umbellate, solitary or in dense clusters. Fruit globose to lobed, smooth to evidently ridged or horned near or above the middle. Reproducing entirely from seeds.

1 Leaves alternate (1 per node) at most nodes, with a single pair of stipules present at each node 2
1 Leaves opposite (2 per node) at most nodes, with 2 pairs of stipules present at each node 3
2 Leaf blades obovate to broadly elliptic, flat to slightly convex above, the tips rounded to truncate or slightly notched, the margins thick to slightly revolute, usually entire, sometimes remotely denticulate with 3–5 teeth per leaf; mature fruits 7–12 mm wide . . . .
. . . .*C. megacarpus*
2 Leaf blades broadly obovate to somewhat deltate or almost orbicular, flat or concave above, the tips truncate to notched, rarely obtuse, the margins thick, entire to obscurely denticulate with 9–16 teeth per leaf; mature fruits 4–6 mm wide . . . . *C. verrucosus*
3 Plants mat- to mound-like, usually less than 1 m tall, the main stems spreading or weakly ascending, sometimes rooting at buried nodes 4
3 Plants erect, 0.5–3(–4) m tall, the main stems erect to ascending, the older lateral branches sometimes widely spreading from the central axis but not rooting at the nodes 13
4 Leaf blade margins usually entire, sometimes with 1–3 minute or weakly developed teeth 5
4 Leaf blade margins usually evidently denticulate, usually with 3–30 teeth per blade 8
5 Leaf blades usually obovate, 8–21 mm long, 4–15 mm wide, the margins thickened to somewhat revolute, the lower surfaces densely tomentulose; coastal bluffs of Santa Lucia Range, California, at elevations below 60 m (200 feet) . . . . *C. maritimus*
5 Leaf blades usually elliptic to oblanceolate or narrowly obovate, 4–12 mm long, 2–8 mm wide, the margins plane to only slightly thickened, the lower surfaces sparsely to moderately puberulent or tomentulose and often becoming glabrous; interior mountains at elevations above 260 m (850 feet) 6
6 Upper surfaces of leaf blades dull green, puberulent when young, the lower surfaces pale green to glaucous, appressed-puberulent or tomentulose; fruits with slender, somewhat spreading horns 1.5–2 mm long . . . . *C. fresnensis*
6 Upper surfaces dark green and somewhat shiny, glabrous, the lower surfaces paler than

the upper surfaces but not evidently glaucous; fruits hornless or with erect horns less than 1 mm long 7

7 Leaves usually evenly spaced, sometimes clustered on short lateral shoots, the leaves mostly spreading; flowers white; widespread in mountains of Oregon, California, and Baja California, Mexico . . . . *C. cuneatus*

7 Leaves mostly clustered on short lateral shoots, the clustered leaves ascending to erect; flowers blue to pale blue, or white with age; restricted to the Sierra Nevada foothills of El Dorado County, California . . . . *C. roderickii*

8 Leaf blades usually broadly elliptic, broadly obovate, or orbicular, their length usually less than twice their width; marginal teeth 9–30 per leaf 9

8 Leaf blades usually elliptic to obovate or oblanceolate, their length usually twice their width or more; marginal teeth 3–11 per leaf 10

9 Young internodes often angled near the tips, aging brown to purplish brown; stipules 2.5–4.5 mm wide; upper surfaces of leaf blades bright green, the lower surfaces only slightly paler in color than the upper; fruits 4–6 mm wide; North Coast Range, Mendocino to Marin Counties, California . . . . *C. gloriosus*

9 Young internodes smooth throughout, aging gray or glaucous; stipules 1–2 mm wide; upper surfaces of leaf blades dull green, the lower surfaces pale green; fruits 6–9 mm wide; southern Sierra Nevada and southern Trinity Mountains, California . . . *C. pinetorum*

10 Leaves obovate or orbicular to broadly elliptic, 5–16 mm wide; most leaf blades with 5–11 teeth distributed along the distal two-thirds of the blade 11

10 Leaves oblanceolate to narrowly elliptic, 2–5 mm wide; most leaf blades with 3–5 teeth (sometimes 7 on large blades) restricted to the distal one-third of the blade 12

11 Leaf blades usually dentate above the middle, the margins often somewhat wavy and conspicuously thickened; fruits 4–6 mm wide, the horns slender, 1.5–2.5 mm long . . . .*C. divergens*

11 Leaf blades usually dentate from below the middle, the margins plane, not conspicuously thickened; fruits 6–9 mm wide, the horns thick, wrinkled, 1–2 mm long . . . . .*C. prostratus*

12 Leaf blades usually evenly spaced, spreading, the upper surfaces pale or dull green, the tips truncate to acute, with 2–3 apical teeth; Klamath Mountains of Oregon and California . . . . *C. pumilus*

12 Leaf blades mostly clustered on short lateral shoots, often ascending, the upper surfaces darker than the lower, the tips obtuse to slightly notched, the teeth if present somewhat remote; Sierra Nevada foothills of Eldorado County, California . . . . *C. roderickii*

13 Leaf blade margins with sharply spinulose teeth (leaf blades holly-like, at least above the middle); restricted to the southern North Coast Range of California 14

13 Leaf blade margins entire or denticulate but with the teeth not sharply tipped (i.e., not holly-like); widespread but not in the southern North Coast Range of California except *C. cuneatus* and *C. sonomensis* 17

14 Petals and sepals 6–8; most leaves somewhat deflexed; fruit horns broadly conical, conspicuously wrinkled . . . . *C. jepsonii*

14 Petals and sepals 5; most leaves spreading to ascending (sometimes deflexed in *C. sonomensis*); fruit horns relatively slender, smooth to somewhat wrinkled 15

15 Petioles less than 1 mm long, the leaf blades sessile to subsessile, broadly obovate, usually 5–11 mm long, 2–5 mm wide; flowers blue to lavender . . . . *C. sonomensis*

15 Petioles 1–2 mm long, the leaf blades elliptic, obovate, or orbicular, usually 10–21 mm long, 5–14 mm wide; flowers deep blue to purple 16

16 Leaf blades flat to more often with the upper surface somewhat convex, the tips sharply acute and spine-like or notched between adjacent teeth; stipules 1–2 mm wide; leaf blade margins thick, somewhat revolute, with 3–11 teeth per leaf . . . . *C. divergens*

16 Leaf blades wavy to slightly folded (concave above), the tips rounded but often sharply acute; stipules 2–3 mm wide; leaf blade margins neither conspicuously thick nor revolute, with 7–15 teeth per leaf . . . . *C. purpureus*

17 Lower surfaces of leaf blades usually densely tomentulose, the tomentum obscuring the surface, the margins evidently thickened or revolute 18

17 Lower surfaces of leaf blades usually glabrous to sparsely strigulose or puberulent, the surface evident and appearing under magnification as a mosaic of minute, light-colored patches between the secondary veins, the blade margins flat to slightly thickened or revolute 19

18 Leaf blades usually broadly elliptic to obovate, with 8–19 teeth per blade; nectar disk black or at least much darker than the white petals; coastal slopes of southern California and northern Baja California, Mexico . . . . *C. crassifolius*

18 Leaf blades usually elliptic to narrowly elliptic, entire or with 2–7 teeth per blade; nectar disk white to cream, not obviously darker than petals; mountains of northern Mexico
. . . . *C. pauciflorus*

19 Leaf blades usually with entire margins, if toothed then with fewer than 5 teeth that are often unevenly or remotely distributed 20

19 Leaf blades usually denticulate to serrulate, the teeth evenly distributed along the margin, above the middle, or near the apex, the teeth sometimes obscure in *C. bolensis, C. crassifolius,* and *C. vestitus* 23

20 Most leaf blades 3–7 mm long, 1.5–3 mm wide, narrowly oblanceolate to narrowly obovate, the lateral veins obscure or not visible on the surface . . . . *C. ophiochilus*

20 Most leaf blades 8–25 mm long, 5–12 mm wide, obovate to broadly obovate or broadly elliptic, the lateral veins evident 21

21 Sepals and petals white, the nectar disk often almost black; fruits 7–12 mm wide . . . .
. . . . *C. megacarpus*

21 Sepals, petals, and nectar disk white to blue or lavender, the disk usually not much darker than the perianth except when dry; fruits 3.5–9 mm wide 22

22 Upper surfaces of leaf blades yellow-green, moderately short-curly-villous to sparsely tomentulose when young but becoming glabrous with age; lower surfaces often glabrous at maturity; branchlet internodes often becoming glaucous and pale gray . . . .*C. vestitus*

22 Upper surfaces of leaf blades green, glabrous to sometimes sparsely appressed-puberulent but becoming glabrous with age; lower surfaces often appressed-puberulent to strigulose, especially on the veins; branchlet internodes gray to grayish brown . . . .*C. cuneatus*

23 Uppermost internodes of terminal branchlets conspicuously angled in cross section, appearing to have longitudinal ridges or striations, green to reddish or purplish brown . . . . *C. gloriosus*

23 Uppermost internodes of terminal branchlets cylindrical, appearing smooth, grayish brown to brown to gray or pale gray and glaucous 24

24 Most leaf blades usually 12–25+ mm long, more than 8 mm wide 25

24 Most leaf blades usually less than 12 mm long, less than 8 mm wide (sometimes slightly larger in *C. otayensis*) 29

25 Leaf blades usually elliptic to narrowly obovate, sometimes oblong-obovate, the teeth sharply acute, the blade tip usually sharply toothed; flowers dark blue to purple . . . .*C. divergens*

25 Leaf blades usually broadly elliptic to broadly obovate or suborbicular, the teeth not sharply acute, the blade tip rounded to minutely toothed; flowers white or blue to bluish lavender in *C. pinetorum* 26

26 Plants mound-like, sometimes erect, usually less than 1.5 m tall, the main stems spreading to weakly ascending; stipules often confluent; southern Sierra Nevada and Trinity Mountains, California . . . . *C. pinetorum*

26 Plants erect, hemispheric to broadly obovoid, 1–4 m tall, the main stems erect to strongly ascending; stipules usually not confluent 27

27 Leaves petiolate, the petioles 2–5 mm long, the margins evidently thickened or revolute; lower leaf surfaces very pale green to almost white, much paler than the upper surface . . . .*C. crassifolius*

27 Leaves sessile to subsessile, the petioles less than 2 mm long, the margins plane or somewhat thickened; lower leaf surfaces yellow-green to pale green but not much paler than the upper surface 28

28 Upper surfaces of leaf blades dark green; lower surfaces grayish or dull green; fruits 6–9 mm wide, horned above widest part of the fruits, the horns erect . . . . *C. ferrisiae*

28 Both leaf surfaces somewhat yellow-green, especially near the margins; fruits 3.5–6 mm wide; horns absent or weakly developed as a bulge or short horn near the widest part of the fruit, the horns spreading . . . .*C. vestitus*

29 Leaf blade margins usually conspicuously thickened or revolute, at least near the base
. . . . 30

29 Leaf blade margins usually plane to somewhat thickened but not evidently revolute . . . 31

30 Stipules 2–3 mm wide; lower surfaces of leaf blades white- to brown-tomentulose when
   young but becoming glabrous; fruits smooth or very weakly horned; southern San Diego
   County, California . . . . *C. otayensis*

30 Stipules 1–1.5 mm wide; lower surfaces of leaf blades glabrous except for microscopic
   tomentulose patches between the secondary veins; fruits with slender horns 2–3 mm
   long; Napa and Sonoma Counties, California . . . . *C. sonomensis*

31 Plants with compact crowns, sometimes flat-topped, with spreading branches; leaf blade
   margins with evident teeth, these 0.5–1 mm long; horns on mature fruits near the tip
   and erect . . . . *C. cuneatus*

31 Plants with open crowns, with both ascending and spreading branches; leaf blade margins with obscure teeth less than 0.5 mm long; horns on mature fruits absent or weakly
   developed as a bulge near the middle 32

32 Leaf blades usually obovate to oblanceolate; upper surfaces dull green, sparsely puberulent when young but becoming glabrous with age; branchlets reddish brown to gray but
   not strongly glaucous; peduncles 1–2 mm long; Cerro Bola, northern Baja California,
   Mexico . . . . *C. bolensis*

32 Leaf blades usually elliptic, sometimes oblanceolate; upper surfaces grayish green,
   moderately short-curly-villous to sparsely tomentulose when young but becoming
   glabrous with age; branchlets gray to pale gray and glaucous; peduncles 2–5 mm long;
   desert slopes and interior mountains of California and Baja California, Mexico, east to
   the southern Rocky Mountains . . . . *C. vestitus*

Ceanothus Species

Each description of a species is followed by a brief summary of its general habitat, elevation range, general geographical distribution, a discussion of patterns of variation,
and nomenclatural references, including synonyms. Keys to varieties or subspecies are
provided when such taxa are recognized here. All species descriptions have been writ-
ten in a parallel format for ease of comparison. Some species of *Ceanothus* have been
given more than one common name, based on regional usage; in such cases the first
one is that most often used.

Ceanothus americanus Linnaeus
   New Jersey tea, redroot, wild snowball
Subgenus *Ceanothus*. Erect shrubs, 0.5–1 m tall; crown open, hemispheric to obovoid,

the main branches mostly ascending; distal branchlets flexible, their internodes 21–43(–50) mm long, smooth, sometimes slightly angled, green to yellow-green, sometimes becoming red-tinged, sparsely puberulent to short-villous, often becoming glabrous; mature bark brown to grayish brown. Stipules thin, deciduous. Leaves alternate, deciduous, evenly spaced; petioles 4–11 mm long. Leaf blades 18–100 mm long, 8–60 mm wide, usually ovate, sometimes broadly elliptic, flat, thin, three-veined from the base; upper surfaces green, glabrous, veins often sparsely puberulent; lower surfaces pale green, subglabrous to puberulent or sparsely short-villous, especially on the veins; tips acute to obtuse, sometimes acuminate; bases rounded, sometimes obtuse; margins plane, serrate to serrulate; teeth 54–130+ per leaf, with minute, somewhat persistent, conic glands. Inflorescences in upper axils of the current year's branchlets, sometimes terminal, racemose to paniculate; rachises 14–52 mm long; peduncles 31–91 mm long; peduncles and rachises glabrous to puberulent. Pedicels 5–9 mm long, glabrous; sepals and petals five; perianth and disk white to cream. Fruit 3.5–5 mm wide, globose to lobed, brown to dark brown; lobes smooth, ridged near or above the middle; horns absent. Seeds 2.5–3 mm long, subglobose to ovoid, dark reddish brown. Flowering May–August; fruiting July–October; reproducing from seeds, and basal shoots following fire.

Well-drained soils derived from various substrates; open sites, abandoned clearings, and margins of mixed conifer-deciduous forest; 15–770 m (50–2,550 feet). In Canada from Ontario to southwestern Quebec; in the United States from Minnesota east to Maine, south through eastern Nebraska and Oklahoma to Texas and northern Florida.

Three intergrading varieties, based on leaf shape and pubescence, have been recognized in several regional manuals (Fernald 1950, Steyermark 1963, Correll and Johnston 1970, Gleason and Cronquist 1991), but Coile (1988) provided evidence for substantial intergradation among them. Plants with lanceolate to narrowly ovate leaf blades, usually less than 50 mm long, are referable to variety *intermedius*. Such plants occur mostly from Massachusetts south to northern Florida but extend as far west as the lower Mississippi River Valley. Plants with ovate to somewhat elliptic leaves longer than 50 mm and glabrous to sparsely puberulent lower leaf surfaces are referable to variety *americanus*. Such plants occur primarily in the northern portion of the species' range. The name variety *pitcheri* has been applied to plants with leaf blades

Ceanothus americanus var. *americanus*

that have uniformly puberulent to short-villous lower leaf surfaces. Such plants are more common in the western part of the species' range. The name *Ceanothus serpyllifolius*, considered here a synonym of *C. microphyllus*, has been applied to small-leaved forms of variety *intermedius*. Hybridization and subsequent introgression between *C. americanus* and *C. herbaceus* or *C. microphyllus* should not be discounted in explaining some of the variation in *C. americanus*. Most plants assignable to the three varieties can be separated by the accompanying key.

Varieties of *Ceanothus americanus*

1 Leaf blades usually lanceolate to narrowly ovate, less than 5 cm long . . . .
. . . .*C. americanus* var. *intermedius*
1 Leaf blades usually ovate to somewhat elliptic, more than 5 cm long 2
2 Lower surfaces of leaf blades glabrous to sparsely puberulent . . . .
. . . .*C. americanus* var. *americanus*
2 Lower surfaces of leaf blades uniformly puberulent to short-villous . . . .
. . . .*C. americanus* var. *pitcheri*

Close relatives include *Ceanothus herbaceus* and *C. sanguineus*, based on habit, inflorescence architecture, overall fruit morphology, and the relatively large, deciduous, serrate to serrulate leaves (McMinn 1942, Coile 1988). *Ceanothus herbaceus* usually differs by its hemispheric inflorescences and elliptic to lanceolate leaves; *C. sanguineus* differs primarily by its taller stature and inflorescences borne on branchlets older than the current year's.

References. *Ceanothus americanus* Linnaeus, *Species Plantarum* 1: 195 (1753); *C. perennis* Pursh, *Flora Americae Septentrionalis*, 167 (1814).

Ceanothus americanus var. *intermedius* (Pursh) Torrey & A. Gray, *Flora of North America* 1: 264 (1838), based on *C. intermedius* Pursh, *Flora Amer. Sept.*, 167 (1814); *C. macrophyllus* Desfontaines, *Tableau de École de Botanique*, ed. 2, 232 (1815); *C. ellipticifolius* Wenderoth, *Schriften Gesellschaft Beförderung Gesammten Naturwissenschaften zu Marburg* 2: 247 (1830); *C. americanus* var. *glaber* Alph. Wood, *Class-Book of Botany*, 291 (1861); *C. americanus* var. *intermedius* (Pursh) Trelease in A. Gray, *Synoptical Flora of North America* 1: 410 (1897; Trelease's name is a later homonym and illegitimate).

Ceanothus americanus var. *pitcheri* Pickering ex Torrey & A. Gray, *Fl. N. Amer.* 1: 264 (1838).

The following names were validly published but without reference to specimens. They have been considered synonyms to *Ceanothus americanus*, but some of them may refer to *C. herbaceus*. Their application to the three varieties remains unresolved: *C. trinervus* Moench, *Methodus Plantas Horti*, 651 (1794); *C. tardiflorus* Hornemann, *Hortus Regius Botanicus Hafniensis*, 230 (1813); *C. officinalis* Rafinesque, *Medical Flora* 2: 205 (1830); *C. glomeratus* Rafinesque, *New Flora and Botany of North America* 3: 55 (1836); *C. glomeratus* var. *fuscatus* Rafinesque, *idem* 3: 55 (1836); *C. latifolius* Rafinesque, *idem* 3: 55 (1836); *C. virgatus* Rafinesque, *idem* 3: 56 (1836); *C. ellipticus* Rafinesque, *idem* 3: 56 (1836); *C. glandulosus* Rafinesque, *idem* 3: 57 (1836; based on Rafinesque's descriptions, the names *C. ellipticus* and *C. glandulosus* may also refer to *C. herbaceus*); *C. decumbens* Steudel, *Nomenclator Botanicus,* ed. 2, 1: 313 (1840). Rafinesque also described four varieties of *C. officinalis* without citation of specimens: var. *ovatus, idem* 3: 54 (1836); var. *acutus, idem* 3: 54 (1836); var. *paniculatus, idem* 3: 55 (1836); and var. *foliosus, idem* 3: 55 (1836).

Ceanothus arboreus E. L. Greene
island ceanothus, felt-leaf ceanothus, Catalina ceanothus

Subgenus *Ceanothus.* Shrubs or trees, 2–7 m tall; crown open, hemispheric to obovoid, the main branches ascending to spreading; distal branchlets flexible, their internodes 11–25 mm long, smooth to slightly angled, brown, tomentulose, becoming glabrous; mature bark gray to grayish brown. Stipules thin, deciduous. Leaves alternate, evergreen, evenly spaced; petioles 10–25 mm long. Leaf blades 25–80 mm long, 19–38 mm wide, elliptic to broadly ovate, flat, leathery, three-veined from the base; upper surfaces dark green, dull to somewhat shiny, glabrous to sparsely puberulent; lower surfaces pale green, densely white-tomentulose, especially when young, sometimes subglabrous with appressed-puberulent veins; tips acute to obtuse; bases rounded to subcordate; margins plane, serrulate; teeth 35–65 per leaf, tipped with minute conic glands when young. Inflorescences racemose to paniculate usually in the upper axils of 1- or 2-year-old branchlets, sometimes terminal, 54–83 mm long; peduncles 12–31 mm long; peduncles and rachises puberulent. Pedicels 5–7.5 mm long, glabrous; sepals and petals five; perianth pale to deep blue; disks similar or somewhat darker. Fruits 5–8 mm wide, globose to weakly lobed, viscid when young, black; lobes smooth to weakly ridged; horns absent. Seeds 2.5–3 mm long, subglobose to broadly ovoid, dark brown. Flowering February–May; fruiting June–August; usually reproducing from seeds, sometimes from basal shoots.

Rocky soils derived from various geological substrates; ridges and steep, mostly north-facing slopes and canyons; chaparral, oak woodland, and closed-cone pine woodland; 60–580 m (200–1,900 feet). Santa Catalina, Santa Cruz, and Santa Rosa Islands, California, and Guadalupe Island, Mexico.

Ceanothus arboreus is a common species in chaparral, woodland, and forest communities on the northern California Channel Islands. Both arborescent and low-growing plants retain their habit under common cultivation, suggesting genetic differentiation for growth form. Plants from Santa Rosa Island with sparsely appressed-puberulent veins on the lower surfaces of leaves were named variety *glaber,* but plants with similar leaves are also found on Santa Cruz Island. A few plants on Santa Cruz Island may represent hybrids with *C. spinosus,* which has not been reported from the island. Some plants grown at the Santa Barbara Botanic Garden from wild-collected seed produced by such plants are strikingly similar to *C. spinosus* of the mainland. Although Raven and Axelrod (1978) suggested a relationship with *C. caeruleus,* some features of leaf and fruit morphology suggest that *C. arboreus* may also be related to species such as *C. thyrsiflorus* and *C. oliganthus*.

References. *Ceanothus arboreus* E. L. Greene, *Bulletin of the California Academy of Sciences* 2: 144 (1886); *C. velutinus* Douglas ex Hooker var. *arboreus* (E. L. Greene) Sargent, *Garden and Forest* 2: 364 (1889); *C. arboreus* var. *glaber* Jepson, *Manual of the Flowering Plants of California*, 619 (1925). Note that some publications have incorrectly used the spelling *glabra*.

Ceanothus bolensis S. Boyd & J. Keeley

Cerro Bola ceanothus

Subgenus *Cerastes*. Erect shrubs, 1–1.5 m tall; crown open to somewhat dense, hemispheric to broadly obovoid; main branches erect to spreading; distal branchlets stiff, their internodes 7–12 mm long, smooth, gray to reddish gray when young, becoming gray and somewhat glaucous, sparsely puberulent; mature bark gray. Stipules thick, persistent, 1–2 mm wide, sometimes confluent. Leaves opposite, evergreen, evenly spaced or clustered at nodes, subsessile; petioles less than 1 mm long. Leaf blades 3–6 (–10) mm long, 3–4(–9) mm wide, broadly obovate to broadly oblanceolate, folded, concave above and convex below, thick, stiff, one-veined; upper surfaces dull green, sparsely puberulent to glabrous; lower surfaces pale green, sparsely puberulent or appearing glabrous except for microscopic tomentulose patches between the secondary veins; tips rounded to somewhat truncate; bases obtuse; margins somewhat thickened, entire to denticulate above the middle; teeth four to six per leaf, spinulose. Inflorescences terminal and in upper axils of 1- or 2-year-old branchlets, umbellate to subumbellate, 9–14 mm long, subsessile; peduncles 1–2 mm long; peduncles and rachises puberulent. Pedicels 3–5 mm long, glabrous; sepals and petals five; perianth and disks pale blue or white. Fruits 3–4 mm wide, globose to weakly lobed, dark reddish brown; lobe smooth, sometimes weakly ridged or weakly horned near the middle. Seeds 2.5–3 mm long, broadly ellipsoid to ovoid, slightly compressed, dark brown. Flowering February–April; fruiting April–June; reproducing entirely from seeds.

Slopes and outcrops of volcanic substrates in chaparral; 550–1,275 m (1,800–4,200 feet); restricted to Cerro Bola, northern Baja California, Mexico. A species of special conservation concern because of its limited distribution and potential habitat loss.

Ceanothus bolensis appears most closely related to *C. ophiochilus*, although Boyd and Keeley, in describing *C. bolensis*, also suggested relationships to what has been called *C. perplexans*, treated here as part of *C. vestitus*.

Ceanothus bolensis, leaf detail ×2

The short internodes and relatively large stipules are also similar to those of *C. otayensis* and some forms of *C. pauciflorus*.

Reference. *Ceanothus bolensis* S. Boyd & J. Keeley, *Madroño* 49: 291 (2003).

Ceanothus buxifolius J. A. Schultes

boxleaf ceanothus, binorilla, chaparro prieto, guasapul, junco

Subgenus *Ceanothus*. Erect to spreading shrubs, 0.5–2 m tall; crown somewhat open to compact, hemispheric to broadly obovoid, sometimes mound-like, often intricately branched; main branches broadly ascending to widely spreading; distal branchlets stiff, often becoming strongly spine-like, their internodes (5–)8–19 mm long, smooth to slightly rough, green to gray, puberulent to tomentulose, sometimes glaucous; mature bark dark gray to dark brown. Stipules thin, the bases and leafy segments sometimes semipersistent. Leaves alternate, evergreen to semideciduous at high elevations, evenly spaced, sometimes clustered on older branches; petioles 1–4 mm long. Leaf blades 9–21 mm long, 4–10 mm wide, usually broadly elliptic, oval, or orbicular, sometimes broadly obovate to oblong-ovate, flat, thin to somewhat leathery, three-veined from the base, sometimes one-veined; upper surfaces dull green, subglabrous to sparsely short-hairy, the hairs either straight or wavy, the veins appressed-puberulent; lower surfaces green to pale green, sometimes glaucous, glabrous to sparsely appressed-puberulent, the veins appressed-puberulent to strigulose; tips and bases obtuse to rounded; margins plane, entire to obscurely denticulate, with 14–33 minute, deciduous, conic glands when young. Inflorescences umbellate to subumbellate, in axils of 1- or 2-year-old branchlets, sometimes clustered, 10–13 mm long, sessile to subsessile; peduncles 1–5 mm long; peduncles and rachises puberulent. Pedicels 3–6 mm long, glabrous; sepals and petals five; perianth white, sometimes pink-tinged, disk white to greenish. Fruits 4–6 mm wide, lobed, viscid when young, dark brown to black; lobes smooth or weakly ridged near the middle; horns absent. Seeds 1.5–3 mm long, ovoid, brown. Flowering December–July; fruiting February–October; reproducing primarily from seeds, sometimes from basal shoots.

On rocky soils and outcrops derived from various geological substrates; ridges, steep slopes, and mesas; montane shrublands, open sites in pine or oak woodlands or conifer forests; 1,360–3,150 m (4,500–10,400 feet); from central Sonora east to Coahuila and Nuevo León, south to Jalisco, Puebla, and Hidalgo, Mexico.

Considerable variation in leaf shape, leaf margin, and leaf pubescence has resulted in recognition of as many as six taxa (Standley 1923). McMinn (1942) recognized two species, *Ceanothus buxifolius* and *C. depressus*. Fernández Nava (1996) and Fishbein et al. (1998) suggested that *C. depressus* may not be sufficiently distinct to warrant recognition as a species. Various combinations of broadly elliptic, ovate, or orbicular leaf blades with subglabrous to appressed-puberulent lower leaf surfaces can be seen

Ceanothus buxifolius

among specimens from throughout the range in Mexico. The names *C. pueblensis* and *C. ferox* have been applied to plants with orbicular to suborbicular leaf blades, the latter further distinguished by rough-surfaced fruits that appear to be viscid. Plants with hairs restricted almost entirely to the leaf blade veins, especially on the lower surfaces, have been referred to *C. durangoinus* and *C. huichagorare.* McMinn treated *C. ferox* as part of *C. buxifolius* but placed *C. durangoinus, C. huichagorare,* and *C. pueblensis* in *C. depressus.*

Some plants from higher elevations in northern Sonora and northern Chihuahua have broad leaves that are densely appressed-villous to tomentulose on both surfaces, and are treated here as *Ceanothus fendleri* var. *venosus.* The various combinations of leaf shape and amount of leaf pubescence in this complex appear to represent both broad and local patterns of intergradation. Their ecological and geographical distributions are not well understood and deserve critical study, especially in the field. The accompanying key provides the opportunity to separate the more distinctive forms but does not attempt to discriminate all taxa previously recognized.

Ceanothus buxifolius and *C. depressus*

1 Lower surfaces of leaf blades glabrous between the veins, sometimes with scattered appressed hairs between the veins . . . . *C. buxifolius*
1 Lower surfaces of leaf blades sparsely to moderately puberulent between the veins . . . . .
. . . .*C. depressus*

References. *Ceanothus buxifolius* Willdenow ex J. A. Schultes in J. Roemer & J. A. Schultes, *Systema Vegetabilium* 5: 300 (1819); *Colubrina buxifolia* (J. A. Schultes) Schlechtendal, *Linnaea* 15: 469 (1841); *C. ferox* Standley, *Contributions from the U.S. National Herbarium* 23: 723 (1923).
Ceanothus depressus Bentham, *Plantae Hartwegianae,* 8 (1839); *C. durangoinus* Loesener, *Repertorium Specierum Novarum Regni Vegetabilis* 8: 297 (1910); *C. huichagorare* Loesener, *idem* 8: 298 (1910); *C. pueblensis* Standley, *Contr. U.S. Natl. Herb.* 23: 723 (1923).

Ceanothus caeruleus Lagasca

azure ceanothus, chaquira, cuaicuastle, tlaxiste, sayolistle

Subgenus *Ceanothus.* Erect shrubs or small trees, 1–8 m tall; crown relatively open, usually obovoid; main branches erect to ascending or spreading; distal branchlets flexible, their internodes 19–32 mm long, smooth, gray to grayish brown, densely tomentulose; mature bark grayish brown. Stipules thin, deciduous. Leaves alternate, evergreen, evenly spaced; petioles 3–10(–20) mm long. Leaf blades 24–125 mm long, 10–65 mm wide, elliptic or ovate, sometimes lanceolate, flat, somewhat leathery, three-veined from the base; upper surfaces dark green, sparsely to densely puberulent or short-villous, sometimes becoming glabrous; lower surfaces tomentulose, rust-colored with age; tips obtuse to acute; bases rounded; margins plane, serrulate; teeth 24–75(–100) per leaf, with narrowly conic glands when young. Inflorescences usually in the upper axils of 1- or 2-year-old branchlets, sometimes terminal, racemose to paniculate, 30–85(–150) mm long; peduncles 5–31 mm long; peduncles and rachises tomentulose. Pedicels 5–7 mm long, usually puberulent but often becoming glabrous; sepals and petals five; perianth and disk blue to dark blue, sometimes pale blue or white. Fruits 4–5 mm wide, globose to somewhat lobed, somewhat viscid when young, dark brown to black; lobes smooth to weakly ridged or weakly horned near the middle. Seeds 1.5–2 mm long, subglobose to broadly ovoid, dark brown. Flowering and fruiting throughout most of the year, depending partly on elevation and latitude; reproducing primarily from seeds, sometimes from basal shoots.

On various geological substrates; open sites and clearings in oak woodlands, pine forests, mixed pine-oak forests, and cloud forests; 1,000–3,025 m (3,300–9,950 feet); widely distributed throughout the mountains of Mexico from Sonora east to Tamaulipas, south to Chiapas, and from Guatemala and Costa Rica south to Chiriquí province, Panama.

Ceanothus caeruleus is most closely related to *C. ochraceus*, with which it shares puberulent pedicels, densely short-villous inflorescence axes and peduncles, and tomentulose lower leaf surfaces that become rust-colored with age. *Ceanothus ochraceus* differs primarily in its shrubby habit, smaller leaves, and mostly white flowers. Some intergradation may occur, as evidenced by reports of bluish flowers in some plants of *C. ochraceus*. Further studies are needed to determine if the two taxa are best treated separately or as part of a single species. Raven and Axelrod (1978) suggested a relationship between *C. caeruleus* and *C. arboreus*, but the latter also appears related to *C. thyrsiflorus* and *C. oliganthus*.

References. *Ceanothus caeruleus* Lagasca, *Genera et Species Plantarum*, 11 (1816); *C. azureus* Desfontaines ex A. P. de Candolle, *Prodromus Systematis Naturalis Regni Vegetabilis* 2: 31 (1825), is based on *C. azureus* Desfontaines, *Tableau de l'École de Botanique*, 232 (1815), which was published without a description; *C. bicolor* Willdenow ex J. A. Schultes in J. Roemer & J. A. Schultes, *Systema Vegetabilium* 5: 300 (1819); *C. glandulosus*

Ceanothus caeruleus, branch and leaf detail ×½

Schlechtendal, *Linnaea* 15: 474 (1841); *C. candolleanus* Rose, *Contributions from the U.S. National Herbarium* 12: 283 (1909).

Ceanothus cordulatus A. Kellogg
mountain whitethorn, snowbush

Subgenus *Ceanothus*. Erect to spreading shrubs, 0.5–1.5 m tall; crown open to somewhat compact, hemispheric to mound-like, often flat-topped; main branches ascending to widely spreading; distal branchlets stiff, often becoming strongly spine-like, their internodes 6–16 mm long, smooth, strongly glaucous, sometimes puberulent; mature bark light gray to gray. Stipules thin, deciduous. Leaves alternate, evergreen, evenly spaced, sometimes clustered at nodes; petioles 2–8 mm long. Leaf blades 9–23 (–34) mm long, 6–18(–21) mm wide, elliptic to broadly ovate, flat, thin or somewhat leathery, three-veined from the base; upper surfaces light green to gray green, sparsely puberulent to glabrous, glaucous; lower surfaces pale green, glabrous to sparsely puberulent, sometimes tomentulose, the veins sparsely strigulose; tips obtuse to rounded; bases rounded; margins plane, entire, sometimes obscurely denticulate; teeth 18–30 per leaf, with subglobose to broadly conic glands when young. Inflorescences in upper axils of 1- or 2-year-old branchlets, subumbellate to racemose, 12–18 mm long, often densely clustered among short internodes and appearing paniculate

Ceanothus cordulatus, Yuba Gap, Sierra Nevada, California; also see page 142

(23–40 mm long), sessile or the peduncles 1–6 mm long; peduncles and rachises glabrous to sparsely puberulent. Pedicels 4–6 mm long, glabrous; sepals and petals five; perianth and disks white, sometimes pink. Fruits 3.5–5 mm wide, lobed, viscid when young, brown; lobes smooth to ridged above the middle; horns absent. Seeds 2–3 mm long, broadly ovoid, sometimes slightly compressed, dark brown. Flowering May–July; fruiting June–August; reproducing from seeds, and basal shoots following fires.

Ridges and slopes, on well-drained substrates of various geological substrates; montane chaparral and open sites in mixed evergreen and conifer forests; 450–3,150 m (1,450–10,400 feet); Coast and Cascade Ranges of southern Oregon, most mountain ranges of California (with the exception of the South Coast Range), the Charleston Mountains of western Nevada, and the Sierra Juárez and Sierra San Pedro Mártir, Baja California, Mexico.

Young plants have the principal stems radiating from the center, similar to the branching pattern of *Ceanothus lemmonii* and *C. parvifolius.* Plants from high elevations in the Cascade Range and Sierra Nevada are often less than 1 m tall, flat-topped, and have spine-like branchlets less than 25 mm long and leaves less than 12 mm long. Based on habit and leaf and stem morphology, close relatives include *C. incanus* and *C. leucodermis* (McMinn 1942). The three taxa appear to be geographically and ecologically isolated but are similar in having a low-growing habit with spreading branches, glaucous, spine-like branchlets, and entire to obscurely denticulate leaf margins. However, the inflorescences of *C. incanus* and *C. leucodermis* are evidently paniculate. In addition, *C. incanus* differs by having peduncles 10–18 mm long and conspicuously wrinkled fruit surfaces. *Ceanothus leucodermis* has peduncles 9–30 mm long and occurs at lower elevations than *C. cordulatus.*

McMinn (1942) reported naturally occurring hybrids between *Ceanothus cordulatus* and *C. diversifolius, C. integerrimus,* and *C. parvifolius.* Hybrids with *C. velutinus* var. *velutinus* were named *C. ×lorenzenii* (Jepson) McMinn; hybrids with *C. prostratus* were named *C. ×serrulatus* McMinn (McMinn 1942).

Reference. *Ceanothus cordulatus* A. Kellogg, *Proceedings of the California Academy of Sciences* 2: 124 (1861).

Ceanothus crassifolius Torrey

hoaryleaf ceanothus

Subgenus *Cerastes.* Erect shrubs, 1.5–4 m tall; crown open to dense, hemispheric to broadly obovoid; main branches ascending to spreading; distal branchlets stiff to somewhat flexible, their internodes 10–21 mm long, smooth, gray to brown,

Ceanothus cordulatus

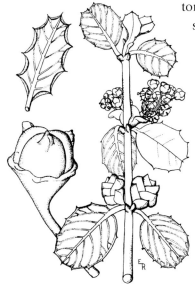

Ceanothus crassifolius, leaf detail ×1½

tomentulose; mature bark grayish brown. Stipules thick, persistent, 2.5–3 mm wide. Leaves opposite, evergreen, evenly spaced; petioles 2–5 mm long. Leaf blades 10–25(–40) mm long, 5–15(–22) mm wide, elliptic to broadly elliptic, sometimes obovate, flat, thick, stiff, one-veined; upper surfaces olive-green, sparsely tomentulose when young, soon glabrous and minutely papillose; lower surfaces pale to grayish green, densely white-tomentulose to sparsely appressed-tomentulose, sometimes appearing glabrous except for microscopic tomentulose patches between the secondary veins; tips and bases obtuse to rounded; margins thick to revolute, sometimes slightly wavy, dentate, rarely entire; teeth 8–19 per leaf, spinulose. Inflorescences terminal and in upper axils of 1- or 2-year-old branchlets, umbellate, 10–18 mm long, subsessile; peduncles 1–5 mm long; peduncles and rachises tomentulose. Pedicels 7–10 mm long, glabrous; sepals and petals five, white, disk dark to black. Fruits 5–9 mm wide, globose to weakly lobed, viscid when young, dark brown; lobes smooth, horned above the middle; horns 1–2 mm long, ascending to somewhat erect, smooth to somewhat wrinkled. Seeds 3–4 mm long, ellipsoid to ovoid, dark brown to black. Flowering January–April; fruiting April–July; reproducing entirely from seeds.

On various geological substrates; mostly in chaparral on coastal slopes, sometimes on slopes or ridges of interior mountains; 60–1,100 m (200–3,700 feet); from Santa Barbara County (Santa Ynez Mountains) east through the Transverse Ranges to San Bernardino County (San Bernardino Mountains), south through the Peninsular Ranges to San Diego County, California; in Mexico in northwestern Baja California. Two somewhat intergrading varieties can be recognized, and identified using the accompanying key.

Varieties of *Ceanothus crassifolius*

1 Leaf blade margins revolute and denticulate, the lower surfaces densely tomentose, the veins obscured by the hairs . . . . *C. crassifolius* var. *crassifolius*
1 Leaf blade margins thick to revolute and often entire, the lower surfaces sparsely to moderately tomentose, the veins evident . . . . *C. crassifolius* var. *planus*

Variety *planus* is restricted to the coastal slopes of the western Transverse Ranges of Santa Barbara, Ventura, and Los Angeles Counties, California, usually exclusive of variety *crassifolius*. Specimens previously identified as *Ceanothus crassifolius* from Guadalupe Island, Mexico, are more similar to *C. perplexans,* treated here as part of *C. vestitus.* The fruits of variety *planus* are somewhat wider (6–9 mm) than those of the typical variety (5–7 mm). Some plants with leaves intermediate with respect to dentation or hairiness in Santa Barbara and Ventura Counties suggest intergradation between the two extremes, but introgressive hybridization with *C. megacarpus* cannot be discounted as a contributing factor. McMinn (1942) reported variety *planus* from the San Jacinto Mountains of southern California, but such plants may also have resulted from hybridization between variety *crassifolius* and either *C. megacarpus* or *C. cuneatus. Ceanothus crassifolius* also hybridizes with *C. ophiochilus* (Boyd et al. 1991).

Closely related species include *Ceanothus megacarpus* and *C. verrucosus* (Howell 1940, McMinn 1942). The dark floral disks of *C. crassifolius* are shared in common only with *C. megacarpus* and *C. verrucosus. Ceanothus verrucosus* and *C. megacarpus* var. *megacarpus* differ by having alternate leaves. The opposite-leaved *C. megacarpus* var. *insularis* differs by having leaf blades with tapered bases and glabrous lower leaf blade surfaces, except for microscopically appressed-tomentulose patches between the ultimate veins.

References. *Ceanothus crassifolius* Torrey, *Reports of Explorations and Surveys, to Ascertain the Most Practicable and Economical Route for a Railroad from the Mississippi River to the Pacific Ocean* 4(5): 75 (1857); *C. verrucosus* Nuttall var. *crassifolius* (Torrey) K. Brandegee, *Proceedings of the California Academy of Sciences,* series 2, 4: 208 (1894).

Ceanothus crassifolius var. *planus* Abrams, *Bulletin of the New York Botanical Garden* 6: 415 (1910).

Ceanothus cuneatus Nuttall
buckbrush

Subgenus *Cerastes.* Erect shrubs, 1–3 m tall; crown open to somewhat dense, hemispheric to broadly obovoid, sometimes mound-like or flat-topped, rarely mat-like; main branches ascending to widely spreading; distal branchlets stiff to somewhat flexible, their internodes 5–21(–25) mm long, smooth, gray to grayish brown, appressed-puberulent to short-villous or tomentulose, sometimes glabrous; mature bark gray to grayish brown. Stipules thick, persistent, 1–2 mm wide. Leaves opposite, evergreen, evenly spaced or clustered at nodes, sessile or the petioles to 2 mm long. Leaf blades 5–25(–29) mm long, 4–15(–18) mm wide, oblanceolate to broadly elliptic or orbicular, flat or slightly folded, thick, stiff, one-veined; upper surfaces green, sparsely appressed-puberulent or strigulose to glabrous; lower surfaces pale to grayish green, appearing glabrous except for microscopic tomentulose patches between the secondary veins, the veins often sparsely strigulose; tips obtuse, rounded, or weakly notched; bases tapered to obtuse; margins plane, entire or dentate to denticulate with 3–13 spinulose teeth per leaf. Inflorescences in upper axils of 1- to 3-year-old branchlets, umbellate, subsessile, 6–18 mm long; peduncles 2–5 mm long; peduncles and rachises puberulent. Pedicels 4–10 mm long, glabrous; sepals and petals five; perianth and disks white, lavender, or pale blue, sometimes pink. Fruits 4.5–9 mm wide, weakly lobed, brown; lobes smooth, horned above the middle; horns 0.5–2 mm long, erect, smooth to somewhat wrinkled. Seeds 3–5 mm long, ellipsoid to oblong-ellipsoid, slightly compressed, dark brown to almost black. Flowering January–May; fruiting April–July; reproducing entirely from seeds.

Slopes, ridges, and marine terraces, on various substrates; chaparral and open sites or clearings in woodlands and forests; 15–1,815 m (50–6,000 feet); Coast and Cascade Ranges, from Benton and Linn Counties, Oregon, south to the Sierra Nevada, Coast, Transverse, and Peninsular Ranges of California, and the Sierra Juárez and Sierra San Pedro Mártir of Baja California, Mexico. Reports from Guadalupe Island, Mexico, are based on misidentifications of plants similar to *Ceanothus perplexans,* a form of *C. vestitus* as treated here. *Ceanothus cuneatus* vars. *fascicularis* and *rigidus* should be considered of special conservation concern because of their limited distribution and habitat loss.

Ceanothus cuneatus is one of the most widespread species in the California Floristic Province and often is an important element of chaparral, woodland, and forest communities throughout its range. A complex, often bewildering pattern of ecologi-

Ceanothus cuneatus, low-growing form on serpentinite, Scott Mountains, Siskiyou County, California

cal and geographical variation, especially in habit, branching, leaf morphology, and flower color, characterizes this species (McMinn 1942). Howell (1940) also brought attention to geographical variation in pubescence on young branchlets, which ranges from appressed-puberulent in Oregon and northern California to short-villous or somewhat tomentulose in southern California.

Ceanothus cuneatus var. *cuneatus* includes plants with white flowers and entire, oblanceolate to narrowly obovate leaves. Their shape typically ranges from hemi-spheric to obovoid, often with erect to ascending stems and rounded crowns. Such plants occur throughout the entire geographical range of the species and are generally found on flats and slopes of interior valleys and ranges in Oregon, California, and Baja California, Mexico. However, plants in the Klamath Mountains of northwestern California and southwestern Oregon are often less than 1 m tall, often mound-like and flat-topped, with spreading secondary branches, and have leaf blades that are 6–13 mm long and 2–5 mm wide. Such plants are almost indistinguishable from plants called *C. arcuatus*, which is discussed in greater detail under *C. fresnensis*. Nearly pros-trate forms with entire or denticulate leaves also have been reported (McMinn 1942). Leaf blades with either the upper side slightly convex (*C. cuneatus* var. *cuneatus*, *C. oblanceolatus*) or slightly concave (*C. submontanus*) also occur throughout the range of the species. Plants referable to *C. submontanus* are also unusual in that they often have fruits with dorsal, somewhat spreading horns similar to those of *C. megacarpus* and *C. vestitus*. Variety *dubius* represents another distinctive form with white flowers, restricted to the Santa Cruz Mountains. The leaf blades are 15–20 mm long, obovate to broadly elliptic, and usually have entire margins; the fruits are 4–6 mm wide. The habit, leaf shape, and leaf size are very similar to those of *C. ferrisiae*, which differs mainly by having spreading or curved branches, a higher frequency of leaves with denticulate margins, and larger fruits.

Lavender to blue flowers occur on short-statured plants with more compact or spreading habits, and often with rel-atively broad leaf blades. McMinn (1942) treated them as two species, *Ceanothus rigidus* and *C. ramulosus*, the latter with two varieties, *ramulosus* and *fascicularis*. Edward Lee Greene in his *Flora Franciscana* applied the name variety *ramulosus* to plants with lavender to bluish flowers and broadly elliptic to broadly obovate, sometimes orbicular leaves, and blades 6–19 mm long, with entire to few-toothed margins. The leaf tips on such plants vary from rounded to truncate or slightly notched. Such plants are

Ceanothus cuneatus var.
cuneatus, leaf details ×1 1/2

hemispheric to broadly obovoid and somewhat flat-topped, with relatively short, stiffly spreading, curved, or arched branches. Their distribution appears restricted to elevations less than 500 m (1,650 feet) in coastal mountains from Mendocino County south to the mountains north of San Francisco Bay, and disjunctly in coastal San Luis Obispo and Santa Barbara Counties, California (Hoover 1970). Somewhat rounded to flat-topped, intricately branched shrubs, less than 1.5 m tall, with bright blue to purplish flowers, were originally named *C. rigidus*. The leaf blades vary from suborbicular to broadly obovate, 6–11 mm long, and usually with three to nine teeth per leaf arrayed above the middle of the blade. This form is restricted to low elevations in the foothills of the northern Santa Lucia Range and elevated marine terraces near Monterey, California, but it also occurs locally in coastal San Luis Obispo County (Hoover 1970) and northwestern Santa Barbara County. The name *C. rigidus* var. *albus* has been applied to mound-like plants with toothed leaf blades and white flowers. Plants from coastal flats and slopes in western Santa Barbara and southwestern San Luis Obispo Counties have lavender to pale blue flowers and entire-margined, relatively small, oblanceolate leaves that are conspicuously clustered on short lateral shoots. Such plants were named variety *fascicularis*. However, leaves on the central shoots of variety *fascicularis* are usually broadly elliptic to suborbicular and thus similar in shape to those of variety *ramulosus*. Hoover brought attention to extensive intergradation among forms assignable to varieties *rigidus, fascicularis,* and *ramulosus* in coastal San Luis Obispo County.

Ceanothus cuneatus var. *ramulosus*, Chorro Creek, Santa Lucia Range, California

The geographical and ecological mosaic of overlapping variation in whole-plant architecture, branching patterns, pubescence, leaf morphology, and flower color has not been critically analyzed in the species as a whole. Recognition of two species, *Ceanothus cuneatus* and *C. rigidus* (including *C. ramulosus*), might be warranted if differences in branching pattern and leaf morphology are considered independently derived. The name *C. rigidus* would be applied to those plants with relatively dense, widely spreading, compact crowns and relatively broad leaf blades. The name *C. cuneatus* would be applied to those plants with relatively open crowns and oblanceolate to narrowly obovate leaf blades. Many populations are relatively uniform for particular combinations of these traits and can be assigned a particular name with ease. In other areas, however, especially in the central California Coast Ranges, intergradation apparently occurs among different forms and with other species, and the identity of some populations often is perplexing. The accompanying key provides the opportunity to separate the more distinctive forms but does not serve to distinguish many plants and populations that are intermediate in one or more of the diagnostic features.

Ceanothus cuneatus
var. *fascicularis*

Related species include *Ceanothus vestitus, C. megacarpus, C. ferrisiae,* and *C. roderickii. Ceanothus vestitus,* in the broad sense, appears to differ by consistently having young leaves with tomentulose or short curly hairs and fruits with spreading horns, often near the middle of the fruit. However, some plants treated as *C. vestitus* in the southern Sierra Nevada of California and elsewhere in Arizona and Nevada are difficult to separate because their horns or ridges are neither clearly spreading nor borne near the middle of the fruit. Some of these plants may represent evidence of hybridization with *C. cuneatus. Ceanothus megacarpus* var. *megacarpus* differs by its alternate leaves; the opposite-leaved variety *insularis* usually differs by the absence of horns on the fruits. *Ceanothus ferrisiae* is similar to *C. cuneatus* var. *dubius,* differing from it by having mostly denticulate leaves and slightly larger fruits. *Ceanothus roderickii* has bluish flowers, a somewhat prostrate habit, and clustered, erect to ascending leaves.

Howell (1939, 1940), McMinn (1942, 1944), Nobs (1963), and Roof (1973) collectively reported naturally occurring hybrids between *Ceanothus cuneatus* and at least eight other species, including plants referable to *C. fresnensis, C. gloriosus*

Ceanothus cuneatus
var. *rigidus*

(including *C. masonii*), *C. griseus, C. jepsonii, C. megacarpus, C. prostratus, C. pumilus,* and *C. vestitus* (including *C. perplexans*). Formally named hybrids putatively involving *C. cuneatus* as one parent include *C. ×connivens* E. L. Greene (with *C. prostratus* or *C. fresnensis*), *C. ×flexilis* E. L. Greene ex McMinn (with *C. prostratus*), *C. ×humboldtensis* J. B. Roof (with *C. pumilus*), and *C. ×veitchianus* Hooker (with *C. thyrsiflorus* var. *griseus*). The name *C. arcuatus* has been applied to hybrids between *C. cuneatus* and *C. fresnensis,* although it probably represents a taxon either distinct from either of the two species, or part of one of them at the varietal level (see *C. fresnensis* for further information).

Varieties of *Ceanothus cuneatus*

1 Most leaf blades oblanceolate to obovate, usually with their length 2 or more times their width 2

1 Most leaf blades broadly elliptic or broadly obovate to orbicular, their length usually less than 2 times their width, sometimes wider than long 3

2 Flowers white; umbels and peduncles 10–18 mm long . . . . *C. cuneatus* var. *cuneatus*

2 Flowers usually lavender to bluish; umbels and peduncles 6–11 mm long; restricted to coastal flats and slopes of northwestern Santa Barbara and southwestern San Luis Obispo Counties . . . . *C. cuneatus* var. *fascicularis*

3 Leaf blades 15–31(–40) mm long, 10–18(–24) mm wide, broadly oblanceolate to broadly elliptic; margins entire; petioles 2–3 mm long; plants with rounded crowns; flowers usually white; apparently restricted to the Santa Cruz Mountains . . . . *C. cuneatus* var. *dubius*

3 Leaf blades 5–21 mm long, 5–11 mm wide, broadly obovate to orbicular; margins sometimes denticulate with 3–9 teeth per leaf; petioles less than 1.5 mm long; plants with somewhat flat-topped crowns, often with short, rigidly spreading branches; flowers usually lavender to blue 4

4 Most leaves with 5–9 well-developed teeth; leaf blades 5–11 mm long, 5–8 mm wide; restricted to coastal flats and slopes of northern Monterey, southwestern San Luis Obispo, and northwestern Santa Barbara Counties . . . . *C. cuneatus* var. *rigidus*

4 Most leaves entire or with 1–5 teeth; leaf blades 9–21 mm long, 6–11 mm wide; coastal slopes of the southern North Coast Range north of San Francisco Bay and western Santa Barbara and southwestern San Luis Obispo Counties . . . . *C. cuneatus* var. *ramulosus*

References. *Ceanothus cuneatus* Nuttall in Torrey & A. Gray, *Flora of North America* 1: 267 (1838); *Rhamnus cuneatus* Hooker, *Flora Boreali-Americana* 1: 124 (1830); *C. cuneatus* α *rufescens* Hooker & Arnott, *Botany of Captain Beechey's Voyage, Supplement,* 329 (1838); *C. cuneatus* β *cinerascens* Hooker & Arnott, *idem* 329 (1838); *C. cuneatus* (Hooker) K. Brandegee, *Proceedings of the California Academy of Sciences,* series 2, 4: 204 (1894); *C. submontanus* Rose, *Contributions from the U.S. National Herbarium* 12: 284 (1909); *C. oblanceolatus* Davidson, *Bulletin of the Southern California Academy of Sciences* 20: 53 (1921); *C. cuneatus* (Hooker) Torrey & A. Gray var. *submontanus* (Rose) McMinn, *Ceanothus,* 241 (1942).

Many authors have used the name *Ceanothus cuneatus* "(Hooker) Nuttall," assuming that it was based on *Rhamnus cuneatus* Hooker. However, there are several reasons to suggest that the correct attribution is *C. cuneatus* Nuttall. In the preface of *A Flora of North America* (Torrey and Gray 1838), the authors stated, "To Mr. Nuttall we are indebted for a nearly complete suite of the plants collected during his recent journey across the Rocky Mountains to Oregon and California, accompanied with manuscript descriptions of the new genera and species; . . . ." On the original wrapper of the book, Torrey added, "The value of this flora will be greatly enhanced by the extensive contributions of Mr. Nuttall, who has communicated, for publication in this work, his notes and descriptions of plants." Throughout *Fl. N. Amer.*, the phrase "(Nutt. Mss.)" is always followed by a description in quotation marks, implying that Torrey and Gray used Nuttall's original descriptions. The name *C. cuneatus* on p. 267 is followed by "(Nutt. Mss.)": "branchlets pubescent; leaves fascicled . . . ." In contrast, new names authored by Torrey and Gray were simply stated with a colon separating the name and the description (e.g., *C. incanus:* branches short and very thick, . . .). Contemporaries of Torrey and Gray also acknowledged Nuttall as an author, including Hooker and Arnott, who either used "—Nutt. in Torr. et Gr." or "—Torr. et Gr." when citing names from *Fl. N. Amer.* Finally, the type of Nuttall's name is cited as "Dry gravelly islands and bars of the Wahlamet above the Falls."

In contrast, Hooker's *Rhamnus cuneatus* is based on a different specimen, collected from "North-West America, . . . near the sources of the Multomak River, in sandy soils, growing under the shade of Pinus Lambertiana. Douglas." It appears to be cited as a synonym of *Ceanothus cuneatus* by Torrey and Gray, who also stated, "Hooker describes the plants as ferrugineous, which is not the case in our specimens;" implying that Hooker's plant was different from Nuttall's.

In *The botany of Captain Beechey's Voyage,* Hooker and Arnott terminate their description of *Ceanothus cuneatus* with a somewhat ambiguous statement: "—α *rufescens* ; ramulis pubescenti—ferrugineis. —Rhamnus? cuneatus. Hook. Fl. Bor. Am. 1. P. 124. —Ceanothus macrocarpus. Nutt in Torr. et Gr. Fl. 1. P. 267. —β *cinerascens* ; ramulis cinereo—puberulis. —C. cuneatus. Nutt. in Torr. et Gr. Fl. 1. P. 167." This statement may be interpreted as referring to two different taxa, varieties *rufescens* and *cinerascens*; the symbols α and β were used by 19th century botanists to designate varieties within a species. Their recognition of two varieties is parallel to Torrey and Gray's observation of two different kinds of plants, with the name variety *rufescens* applicable to Hooker's *R. cuneatus* and Nuttall's *C. macrocarpus,* and variety *cinerascens* referable to Nuttall's *C. cuneatus.* However, Nuttall's *C. macrocarpus* belongs to *C. megacarpus,* which has alternate leaves. The proper disposition of varieties *rufescens* and *cinerascens* cannot be resolved without careful study of the type specimens, presumably in the Natural History Museum, London, which were collected by either David Douglas or John McLeod, an acquaintance of William Tolmie who provided Hooker and Arnott with specimens.

Ceanothus cuneatus Nuttall var. *ramulosus* E. L. Greene, *Flora Franciscana* 1: 86 (1891); *C. ramulosus* (E. L. Greene) McMinn, *Madroño* 5: 14 (1939).

Ceanothus cuneatus (Hooker) Torrey & A. Gray var. *dubius* J. T. Howell, *Leaflets of Western Botany* 3: 230 (1943).

Ceanothus cuneatus (Hooker) Nuttall var. *fascicularis* (McMinn) Hoover, *Leafl. W. Bot.* 10: 350 (1966), based on *C. ramulosus* (E. L. Greene) McMinn var. *fascicularis* McMinn, *Ceanothus,* 250 (1942).

Ceanothus cuneatus (Hooker) Nuttall var. *rigidus* (Nuttall) Hoover, *Leafl. W. Bot.* 10: 350 (1966), based on *C. rigidus* Nuttall in Torrey & A. Gray, *Fl. N. Amer.* 1: 268 (1838); *C. verrucosus*

Nuttall var. *rigidus* (Nuttall) K. Brandegee, *Proc. Calif. Acad. Sci.*, series 2, 4: 207 (1894); *C. rigidus* Nuttall var. *pallens* Sprague, *Bulletin of Miscellaneous Information, Kew* 1915: 380 (1915); *C. rigidus* Nuttall var. *albus* J. B. Roof, *Four Seasons* 2(3): 19 (1967).

Ceanothus cyaneus Eastwood

San Diego ceanothus, Lakeside ceanothus

Subgenus *Ceanothus*. Erect shrubs, 1–3 m tall; crown open to somewhat compact, hemispheric to obovoid; main branches ascending to spreading; distal branchlets flexible, their internodes 11–32 mm long, weakly angled, grayish green to green, puberulent, becoming glabrous, sometimes with small wart-like projections; mature bark gray to brown. Stipules thin, deciduous. Leaves alternate, evergreen, evenly spaced; petioles 2–6 mm long. Leaf blades 15–45 mm long, 7–20 mm wide, elliptic to broadly ovate, flat, somewhat leathery, three-veined from the base; upper surfaces dark green, glabrous; lower surfaces pale green, sparsely puberulent to glabrous, the veins puberulent; tips acute to obtuse; bases rounded; margins plane, denticulate to serrulate, rarely entire; teeth 23–58 per leaf, with conic glands when young. Inflorescences terminal on 1- or 2-year-old branchlets, paniculate, open, 35–190 mm long; peduncles 20–150 mm long; peduncles and rachises sparsely puberulent when young, becoming glabrous. Pedicels 5–7 mm long, glabrous; sepals and petals five; perianth and disks pale to deep blue. Fruits 3–5 mm wide, deeply lobed, viscid, brown to reddish brown; lobes smooth, sometimes faintly ridged above the middle; horns absent. Seeds about 2 mm long, broadly ovoid, sometimes slightly compressed, brown. Flowering April–June; fruiting May–July; reproducing primarily from seeds, rarely from basal shoots.

Ceanothus cyaneus

Rocky to gravelly soils derived from various substrates; ridges and slopes; chaparral; 45–510 m (150–1,670 feet); San Diego County, California, south to northern Baja California, Mexico. A species of special conservation concern because of its limited distribution and habitat loss.

Early 20th century collections (Rancho Santa Ana Botanic Garden) of *Ceanothus cyaneus* document occurrences in the eastern Santa Monica Mountains of Los Angeles County and in Redlands in the Santa Ana River Valley of San Bernardino County. However, they may also be attributable to early horticultural plantings.

McMinn (1942) suggested a relationship to *Ceanothus thyrsiflorus* based on their mutually shared angled branchlets and similarities in leaf morphology. *Ceanothus thyrsiflorus* differs by having more leathery leaves with prominent veins on the lower surfaces and much darker fruits. The large inflorescences and subglabrous leaves resemble those of *C. parryi,* which differs conspicuously by its partly revolute, softly tomentose leaf blades with weakly developed veins. Molecular analyses suggest relationships to *C. parvifolius* and *C. leucodermis* (Hardig et al. 2000). McMinn observed some plants in the foothills of the Palomar Mountains, California, that appeared intermediate between *C. cyaneus* and *C. leucodermis.* The name *C. divaricatus* var. *laetiflorus,* treated here as a synonym of *C. leucodermis,* may apply to such plants.

Reference. *Ceanothus cyaneus* Eastwood, *Proceedings of the California Academy of Sciences,* series 4, 16: 361 (1927).

Ceanothus dentatus Torrey & A. Gray
cropleaf ceanothus

Subgenus *Ceanothus.* Erect shrubs, 0.5–1.5 m tall; crown dense, intricately branched, often hemispheric to broadly obovoid; main branches ascending to spreading; distal branchlets flexible to somewhat stiff, their internodes 6–10 mm long, smooth, brown to grayish brown, densely puberulent or short-villous, sometimes glaucous; mature bark dark grayish brown to brown. Stipules thin, deciduous. Leaves alternate, evergreen, often clustered; petioles 1–2 mm long. Leaf blades 4–16 mm long, 2–8 mm wide, linear, oblong, or narrowly elliptic, convex above, concave below, somewhat leathery, one-veined; upper surfaces dark green, puberulent; lower surfaces pale green, densely short-villous to tomentulose, the veins appressed-puberulent; tips truncate or notched; bases rounded; margins plane to slightly wavy, revolute, denticulate; teeth 14–36 per leaf, with subglobose to broadly conic, persistent glands. Inflorescences in upper axils of 1- or 2-year-old branchlets, subumbellate to racemose, dense, globose to subglobose, 11–20(–40) mm long, the floral bracts somewhat persistent; peduncles 5–13 mm long; peduncles and rachises puberulent to short-villous. Pedicels 2.5–3.5 mm long, glabrous, sometimes puberulent and becoming glabrous; sepals and petals five; perianth and disk deep blue. Fruits 2.5–4 mm wide, globose to weakly lobed, viscid to slightly viscid when young, dark brown to black; lobes usually ridged above the middle; horns absent. Seeds 1.5–2 mm long, broadly ellipsoid to ovoid, black. Flowering March–June; fruiting May–July; reproducing entirely from seeds.

Sandy soils and recent marine terraces, sometimes on slopes; open sites in chaparral and closed-cone pine forests; 5–50 m (15–165 feet); southern foothills of the Santa Cruz Mountains south to the foothills of the northern Santa Lucia Range, California. A species of special conservation concern because of its limited distribution and habitat loss.

McMinn (1942) considered *Ceanothus dentatus* to be closely related to *C. papillosus.* Although *C. dentatus, C. papillosus,* and *C. hearstiorum,* the latter a prostrate plant, dif-

Ceanothus dentatus, leaf details ×2

Ceanothus dentatus near Seaside, Monterey County, California

fer with respect to habit, their inflorescences and leaf morphology are remarkably similar, an observation first made by Parry (1889). The absence of globose glands on the upper surface of leaves, densely branched habit, and relatively short internodes are the only traits serving to clearly separate *C. dentatus* from small-leaved, truncate-tipped forms of *C. papillosus*.

Hooker's *Ceanothus floribundus*, treated as a variety by McMinn (1942), was based on an illustration of cultivated plants grown in Europe. The name has been applied to wild plants with relatively large leaves and dense, subsessile inflorescences, but such plants do not appear to be ecologically or geographically distinct (Parry 1889). Hybrids between *C. dentatus* and *C. thyrsiflorus* var. *griseus* were named *C. ×lobbianus* Hooker (Parry 1889, Brandegee 1894, Trelease 1897, McMinn 1942).

References. *Ceanothus dentatus* Torrey & A. Gray, *Flora of North America* 1: 268 (1838); *C. papillosus* Torrey & A. Gray var. *dentatus* (Torrey & A. Gray) Parry, *Proceedings of the Davenport Academy of Sciences* 5: 170 (1889); *C. floribundus* Hooker, *Curtis's Botanical Magazine*, pl. 4806 (1864); *C. dentatus* subsp. *floribundus* (Hooker) Trelease, *Proceedings of the California Academy of Sciences*, series 2, 1: 112 (1888); *C. papillosus* var. *floribundus* (Hooker) Parry, *Proc. Davenport Acad. Sci.* 5: 170 (1889); *C. dentatus* var. *floribundus* (Hooker) Trelease in A. Gray, *Synoptical Flora of North America* 1: 415 (1897).

Ceanothus divergens Parry

Calistoga ceanothus

Subgenus *Cerastes*. Erect, spreading, or prostrate shrubs, 0.1–1.5 m tall; crown open to somewhat dense, hemispheric to mound-like, sometimes mat-like; main branches ascending to spreading, sometimes widely divergent, curved, or arched, sometimes decumbent in prostrate forms; distal branchlets somewhat flexible to stiff, their internodes 11–22 mm long, angled, brown to reddish brown, glabrous to sparsely puberulent, sometimes glaucous; mature bark grayish brown. Stipules thick, persistent, 1–2 mm wide. Leaves opposite, evergreen, evenly spaced, sometimes clustered at branchlet tips, sessile or subsessile; petioles less than 2 mm long. Leaf blades 10–19 mm long, 5–11 mm wide, elliptic to somewhat oblong or obovate, flat to more often with the upper surface somewhat convex, thick, stiff, one-veined; upper surfaces green, somewhat shiny, glabrous, rarely sparsely puberulent; lower surfaces grayish green, appearing glabrous except for microscopic tomentulose patches between the

Ceanothus divergens subsp. *divergens*, Franz Valley, Sonoma County, California

secondary veins, the veins sometimes short-villous or strigulose; tips sharply acute and spine-like or notched between adjacent teeth; bases obtuse to tapered; margins thick, sometimes wavy or slightly revolute, usually dentate above the middle; teeth (3–)5–11 per leaf, spinulose. Inflorescences in upper axils of 1- or 2-year-old branchlets, umbellate, 10–18 mm long, sessile to subsessile; peduncles 3–5 mm long; peduncles and rachises puberulent. Pedicels 9–12 mm long, glabrous; sepals and petals five; perianth and disks deep blue to purple. Fruits (4–)5–6 mm wide, globose to weakly lobed, dark brown; lobes smooth, ridged to horned above the middle; horns 1.5–2.5 mm long, erect, slender, smooth. Seeds 2.5–3 mm long, ellipsoid to ovoid, dark brown to black. Flowering February–April; fruiting March–June; reproducing entirely from seeds.

On volcanic or ultramafic substrates; chaparral and open sites in pine or oak woodlands; 110–1,300 m (360–4,300 feet); scattered localities in the Mayacmas, Napa, and Hood Mountain ranges and the mountains west of Alexander Valley in Lake, Mendocino, Napa, and Sonoma Counties, California. A species of special conservation concern because of its limited distribution and potential habitat loss.

Low-growing plants, less than 30 cm tall, with crowns mat- or mound-like, spreading to decumbent stems, and elliptic to ovate leaves have been treated as either a species (*Ceanothus confusus*; Howell 1939, McMinn 1942) or as *C. divergens* subsp. *confusus* (Rincon Ridge ceanothus). Erect plants with ascending to divergent branches and obovate to somewhat oblong leaves are treated as typical *C. divergens*. Nobs (1963)

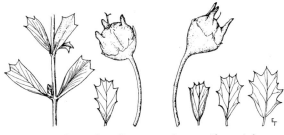

Ceanothus divergens subsp. confusus, left
(branch and leaf detail ×¾), and subsp.
divergens, right (leaves ×¾)

provided evidence of considerable over-lap in these traits between and within some populations. Prostrate, mat-like plants with three to seven teeth per leaf, which were named *C. prostratus* var. *occidentalis* by McMinn, are placed here, based partly on studies by Nobs and the possession of leaf blades with grayish lower surfaces. Plants belonging to *C. prostratus* var. *occidentalis* from the southern North Coast Range appear somewhat intermediate to *C. divergens* and typical *C. prostratus*, suggesting the influence of past hybridization and introgression. However, the occurrence of some plants similar to *C. prostratus* var. *occidentalis* in the northern Sierra Nevada and the southern Klamath Mountains indicates a more complex pattern of variation that deserves further study. Some plants from the northern Sierra Nevada strongly resemble plants referable to *C. ×connivens* E. L. Greene, a putative hybrid between *C. cuneatus* and either *C. prostratus* or *C. fresnensis*. Consequently, plants resembling *C. prostratus* var. *occidentalis* may be independently derived through hybridization involving at least one prostrate or low-growing species. Names at the subspecific level are used in this instance, only because names at the varietal level are not available. Most plants assignable to the three subspecies can be separated by using the accompanying key.

Subspecies of *Ceanothus divergens*

    1 Plants 0.4–1 m tall; most older branches ascending to somewhat erect; leaf blades with
      5–9(–11) teeth . . . . *C. divergens* subsp. *divergens*
    1 Plants usually less than 0.4 m tall; most older branches spreading or decumbent; leaf
      blades with 3–7(–9) teeth 2
    2 Plants somewhat mound- to mat-like, some branches spreading or decumbent, produc-
      ing roots at relatively remote nodes . . . . *C. divergens* subsp. *confusus*
    2 Plants strictly mat-like, branches spreading and rooting at multiple nodes . . . .
      . . . .*C. divergens* subsp. *occidentalis*

Ceanothus divergens is closely related to *C. purpureus*, *C. prostratus*, and *C. pumilus* (McMinn 1942). *Ceanothus purpureus*, an erect shrub, has 7–15 sharply spinulose teeth per leaf and stipules 2–3 mm wide. *Ceanothus prostratus* var. *prostratus* differs primarily by having fruits 6–9 mm wide. Some plants of *C. pumilus* cannot be easily separated from prostrate plants of *C. divergens*, especially plants referable to subspecies *occidentalis*. However, *C. pumilus* appears to differ consistently by having glaucous internodes and fruits with horns less than 1 mm long. Nobs (1963) suggested that populations referable to *C. divergens* (including *C. confusus*) may have arisen from a complex hybrid involving *C. prostratus, C. purpureus, C. gloriosus,* and *C. cuneatus* var. *ramulosus.* The erect habit and leaf morphology of *C. sonomensis* is similar to that of typical *C. divergens* and should not be discounted as a close relative. The influence of hybridization is also supported by molecular evidence (Hardig et al. 2000, 2002).

Even though *Ceanothus divergens* has a relatively restricted distribution, at least one population has been interpreted as consisting of hybrids, with plants resembling *C. gloriosus, C. cuneatus, C. sonomensis,* and both subspecies *confusus* and subspecies *divergens* (Howell 1940, Nobs 1963).

References. *Ceanothus divergens* Parry, *Proceedings of the Davenport Academy of Sciences* 5: 173 (1889); *C. prostratus* Bentham var. *divergens* (Parry) K. Brandegee, *Proceedings of the California Academy of Sciences,* series 2, 4: 210 (1894).

Ceanothus divergens subsp. *confusus* (J. T. Howell) Abrams, *Illustrated Flora of the Pacific States* 3: 78 (1951), based on *C. confusus* J. T. Howell, *Leaflets of Western Botany* 2: 160 (1939).

Ceanothus divergens subsp. *occidentalis* (McMinn) Abrams, *Ill. Fl. Pacific States* 3: 78 (1951), based on *C. prostratus* Bentham var. *occidentalis* McMinn, *Ceanothus,* 262 (1942).

Ceanothus diversifolius Kellogg

pine mat, trailing ceanothus

Subgenus *Ceanothus.* Shrubs usually less than 30 cm tall, rarely as tall as 50 cm; crown open to dense, mat- to mound-like; main branches widely spreading, rarely ascending; distal branchlets flexible, often erect, their internodes 6–15 mm long, smooth to slightly angled, green, sometimes red-tinged, short-villous; mature bark gray to grayish brown. Stipules thin, deciduous. Leaves alternate, evergreen, evenly spaced or clustered at nodes; petioles 3–11 mm long. Leaf blades 11–33(–45) mm long, 8–16(–25) mm wide, elliptic to obovate or ovate, flat, sometimes slightly wavy, somewhat leathery, one-veined, sometimes weakly three-veined from the base; upper surfaces pale to bluish green, short-villous, sometimes becoming glabrous; lower surfaces pale green, sparsely to moderately short-villous, the veins short-villous; tips acute to obtuse, sometimes rounded; bases obtuse to rounded; margins plane, serrulate to denticulate, sparsely villous; teeth 27–42 per leaf, with somewhat persistent, translucent, stipe-like to narrowly conic glands. Inflorescences in upper axils of 1- or 2-year-old branchlets, subumbellate to racemose, 12–20 mm long; peduncles 11–31 mm long; peduncles and rachises puberulent. Pedicels 5–7 mm long, glabrous, sometimes sparsely short-villous; sepals and petals five; perianth and disks blue to white. Fruits 4–5 mm wide, globose to weakly lobed, brown; lobes smooth, ridged above the middle; horns absent. Seeds 2.5–3 mm long, subglobose to ovoid, brown. Flowering April–June; fruiting July and August; reproducing primarily from seeds, sometimes by layering or basal shoots following fire.

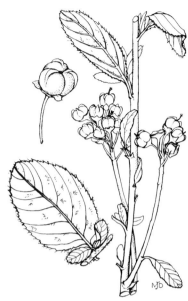

Ceanothus diversifolius

Ridges, flats, and talus on various geological substrates; 760–2,300 m (2,500–7,600 feet); open sites in mixed evergreen or conifer forest; North Coast Range from Mendocino County south to Lake County and the western slopes of the Cascade Range in California, and the Sierra Nevada from Butte and Plumas Counties south to Kern County.

Ceanothus diversifolius usually forms large mats to 2 m wide in open sites in conifer forests. The translucent, sometimes stipe-like glands on the leaf margins are apparently unique in the genus but are sometimes found on plants referable to *C. lemmonii*. McMinn (1942) suggested that *C. diversifolius* does not seem to be very closely related to any known species, but his treatment of it was juxtaposed with that of *C. lemmonii*, which shares somewhat similar patterns of leaf and fruit morphology. *Ceanothus lemmonii* differs primarily by its mound-like to hemispheric crowns, elliptic to oblong-elliptic, somewhat thicker leaves, more rigid stems, and conspicuously glaucous internodes. Inflorescences of *C. diversifolius* also appear shorter and have fewer flowers than those of *C. lemmonii*. Specimens of the two taxa are sometimes difficult to separate without knowledge of their habit, and some populations have intermediate leaf shapes and grayish green internodes, suggesting the influence of hybridization. McMinn reported hybrids with *C. cordulatus* in the Sierra Nevada.

References. *Ceanothus diversifolius* Kellogg, *Proceedings of the California Academy of Sciences* 1: 58 (1855); *C. decumbens* S. Watson, *Proceedings of the American Academy of Arts and Sciences* 10: 335 (1875).

Ceanothus fendleri A. Gray

Fendler ceanothus

Subgenus *Ceanothus*. Erect to spreading shrubs, 0.5–2(–2.5) m tall; crown somewhat open to compact, hemispheric to broadly obovoid, sometimes mound-like and flat-topped, often intricately branched; main branches broadly ascending to widely spreading; distal branchlets stiff, often becoming spine-like, their internodes (5–)8–12 mm long, usually smooth, green to grayish green, puberulent to tomentulose, becoming glaucous; mature bark dark gray to dark brown. Stipules thin, deciduous. Leaves alternate, evergreen to semideciduous at high elevations, evenly spaced, sometimes clustered on older branches; petioles 1–3 mm long. Leaf blades 9–21 mm long, 4–8 mm wide, usually elliptic-oblong to elliptic, sometimes oval or orbicular, flat, thin to somewhat leathery, three-veined from the base, rarely one-veined; upper surfaces dull green,

subglabrous or sparsely to densely short-hairy, the hairs
either straight or wavy, the veins appressed-puberulent;
lower surfaces green to pale green, sometimes glaucous,
sparsely appressed-puberulent to short-wavy-hairy, the veins
appressed-puberulent to strigulose; tips and bases obtuse to
rounded; margins plane, sometimes somewhat thickened,
entire, sometimes obscurely denticulate, with 14–33 minute,
deciduous, conic glands when young. Inflorescences umbellate to racemose, in axils of 1- to 3-year-old branchlets,
sometimes clustered, 10–13(–27) mm long, sessile to subsessile; peduncles 1–5 mm long; peduncles and rachises
puberulent. Pedicels 3–6 mm long, glabrous; sepals and
petals five; perianth white, sometimes pink-tinged, disk
white to greenish. Fruits 3.5–5 mm wide, lobed, viscid when
young, dark brown to black; lobes smooth, sometimes
weakly ridged near the middle; horns absent. Seeds 1.5–3
mm long, ovoid, brown. Flowering January–July; fruiting
March–October; reproducing primarily from seeds, sometimes from basal shoots.

Ceanothus fendleri var.
fendleri, above left and
right, and var. *venosus,*
below left and right

On rocky soils and outcrops derived from various geological substrates; ridges, steep slopes, and mesas; chapar-
ral, open sites in pine or oak woodlands or conifer forests; 1,360–2,650 m (4,500–
8,700 feet); from Arizona and southern Utah east to southern Wyoming, western Colorado, New Mexico, and southwestern Texas; in Mexico from northern Sonora east to
northern Chihuahua.

Ceanothus fendleri appears closely related to *C. buxifolius.* McMinn (1942) placed *C.
fendleri* close to *C. buxifolius, c. cordulatus,* and *C. depressus,* but Fishbein et al. (1998)
included *C. fendleri* as part of *C. depressus* (treated here as part of *C. buxifolius*).
Throughout most of its range, *C. fendleri* has entire leaf blades that are elliptic, with
their length at least twice their width, whereas *C. buxifolius* usually has broader leaves.
Plants with broadly elliptic to obovate, densely puberulent to tomentulose leaf blades
are assignable to *C. fendleri* var. *venosus* (including *C. endlichii*) and are found in southern Arizona east to southwestern Texas, south to Sonora and Chihuahua, Mexico.
These plants are more similar to *C. buxifolius* than to typical variety *fendleri,* having
more spine-like branches and relatively broad leaves, but McMinn considered them
part of *C. fendleri* (including *C. endlichii*). Such plants provide evidence of relatively
broad geographical and ecological intergradation with the less hairy *C. buxifolius.*
Other patterns of varying pubescence density, including variety *viridis* with glabrous
leaf surfaces and puberulent to subglabrous veins, occur sporadically throughout the

range in the Great Basin and Rocky Mountains, without a clear pattern of ecological or geographical distribution. Hybrids between typical *C. fendleri* and *C. herbaceus* in the eastern foothills of the Rocky Mountains have been named *C. ×subsericeus* Rydberg.

Varieties of *Ceanothus fendleri*

1 Leaf blades usually oblong-elliptic to elliptic . . . . *C. fendleri* var. *fendleri*
1 Leaf blades usually oval to broadly elliptic, broadly obovate, or orbicular . . . .
. . . .*C. fendleri* var. *venosus*

References. *Ceanothus fendleri* A. Gray, *Plantae Fendlerianae,* 29 (1849); *C. fendleri* var. *viridis* Trelease ex M. E. Jones, *Proceedings of the California Academy of Sciences,* series 2, 5: 629 (1895); *C. fendleri* var. *viridis* Trelease in A. Gray, *Synoptical Flora of North America* 1: 413 (1897). The name *C. fendleri* var. *viridis* A. Gray was first cited by Trelease (1888) but without a description. Jones published the name in 1895 with a description, typifying it with a collection from Utah (Lenz 1986). Consequently, Trelease's name, published with a description in 1897 and based on collections from Arizona, is a later, illegitimate homonym.
    Ceanothus fendleri var. *venosus* Trelease in A. Gray, *Syn. Fl. N. Amer.* 1: 413 (1897); *C. endlichii* Loesener, *Repertorium Specierum Novarum Regni Vegetabilis* 8: 298 (1910).

Ceanothus ferrisiae McMinn
coyote ceanothus, Ferris's ceanothus

Subgenus *Cerastes.* Erect shrubs, 1–2 m tall; crown open, hemispheric to broadly obovoid, sometimes flat-topped; main branches broadly ascending to spreading, the longer ones sometimes curved or arched; distal branchlets stiff, their internodes 9–15(–19) mm long, smooth, glaucous to grayish brown, puberulent, becoming glabrous; mature bark gray. Stipules thick, persistent, 1–2 mm wide. Leaves opposite, evergreen, evenly spaced or clustered near axils, sessile or petioles to 2 mm long. Leaf blades 11–22(–29) mm long, 7–16 mm wide, obovate to broadly elliptic, flat, thick, stiff, one-veined; upper surfaces dark green, glabrous; lower surfaces pale green, sparsely strigulose or appearing glabrous except for microscopic tomentulose patches between the secondary veins, the veins strigulose; tips rounded or weakly notched; bases tapered to rounded; margins plane, entire or dentate to denticulate; teeth none or 6–13 per leaf, spinulose. Inflorescences in upper axils of 1- or 2-year-old branchlets, umbellate to subumbellate, 12–15 mm long, subsessile; peduncles 1–6 mm long; peduncles and rachises puberulent. Pedicels 5–8 mm long,

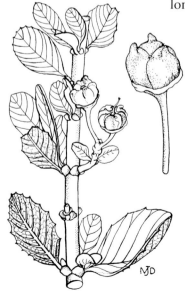
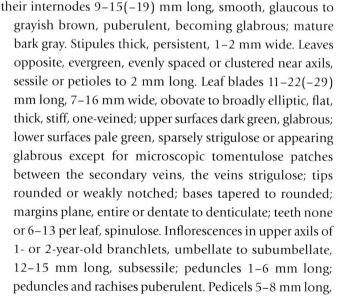

Ceanothus ferrisiae

glabrous; sepals and petals five; perianth and disks white to pale lavender. Fruits 6–9 mm wide, weakly lobed, brown; lobes horned above the middle; horns 1–2 mm long, erect, wrinkled. Seeds 4–5 mm long, ovoid to ellipsoid, slightly compressed, brown. Flowering January–May; fruiting March–July; reproducing entirely from seeds.

Primarily on ultramafic substrates; chaparral and pine or oak woodland; 120–320 m (400–1,100 feet); apparently restricted to the foothills of the Mount Hamilton Range northeast of Morgan Hill, Santa Clara County, California, but also reported from the adjacent Santa Cruz Mountains. A species of special conservation concern because of its limited distribution.

McMinn (1942) suggested relationships to several species, including *Ceanothus cuneatus, C. gloriosus, C. jepsonii,* and *C. megacarpus. Ceanothus ferrisiae* is very similar to and perhaps most closely related to *C. cuneatus* var. *dubius,* which occurs in the neighboring Santa Cruz Mountains. Some plants of variety *dubius* strongly resemble *C. ferrisiae* with regard to both habit and leaf morphology but apparently differ only by their occurrence on nonserpentinitic substrates and smaller fruits, which are 4–6 mm wide. The problem in discriminating between the two taxa is confounded by the presence of both entire and denticulate leaf margins on many plants of *C. ferrisiae.*

Reference. *Ceanothus ferrisiae* McMinn, *Madroño* 2: 89 (1933).

Ceanothus foliosus Parry

wavyleaf ceanothus

Subgenus *Ceanothus.* Erect shrubs, sometimes low growing, 0.5–3.5(–4) m tall; crown open to dense, hemispheric to broadly obovoid, sometimes mound- or mat-like; main branches ascending to spreading; distal branchlets flexible, their internodes 5–14 mm long, smooth, greenish to reddish green, sometimes glaucous, short-villous; mature bark brown. Stipules thin, deciduous. Leaves alternate, the smaller ones often clustered near the base of the lateral shoots, evergreen; petioles 1–3 mm long. Leaf blades 5–19 (–24) mm long, 4–10(–14) mm wide, elliptic to somewhat oblanceolate or oblong-elliptic, flat to more often wavy, sometimes folded (concave above), somewhat leathery, one-veined, sometimes weakly three-veined from the base; upper surfaces dark green, glabrous to sparsely puberulent; lower surfaces grayish green, short-villous to glabrous or slightly glaucous, the veins sparsely to densely short-villous; tips obtuse; bases obtuse to rounded; margins plane to somewhat revolute, entire to denticulate; teeth 31–42

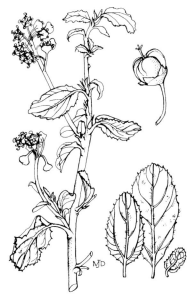

Ceanothus foliosus

Ceanothus foliosus var. *medius,* Cuesta Ridge, San Luis Obispo County, California

per leaf, with sessile to subsessile, globose to subglobose glands. Inflorescences in upper axils of 1- or 2-year-old branchlets, subumbellate to racemose, dense to somewhat open, 6–19(–27) mm long; peduncles 4–16(–24) mm long; peduncles and rachises short-villous. Pedicels 3–5 mm long, glabrous; sepals and petals five; perianth and disks pale to deep blue or purplish blue. Fruits 3–4 mm wide, globose to weakly lobed, slightly viscid when young, dark brown; lobes smooth to weakly ridged; horns absent. Seeds 2–3 mm long, ovoid, dark brown to almost black. Flowering March–June; fruiting May–July; reproducing from seeds, sometimes from basal shoots following fire.

Ridges and rocky slopes on soils derived from various substrates; chaparral and open sites or clearings in mixed evergreen, redwood, and conifer forests; 15–1,500 m (50–4,950 feet); outer Coast Ranges and Mount Hamilton Range of California, from Humboldt County south to San Luis Obispo County, and the Cuyamaca Mountains (1,200–1,500 m, 3,900–4,950 feet) of San Diego County. Variety *vineatus* (Vine Hill ceanothus), is considered to be of special conservation concern because of its very restricted distribution in Sonoma County. Three different varieties can be recognized, based primarily on leaf shape and size, and habit, as indicated in the accompanying key.

Varieties of *Ceanothus foliosus*

1 Plants mat- to mound-like, less than 1 m tall; both leaf surfaces glabrous except for the veins on the lower surface, the margins entire to only weakly denticulate . . . .*C. foliosus* var. *vineatus*

1 Plants erect, hemispheric to broadly obovoid, 1–3.5+ m tall; lower surfaces of leaf blades glabrous to densely short-villous, the margins glandular-denticulate 2

2 Lower surfaces of leaf blades glabrous to sparsely puberulent . . . . *C. foliosus* var. *foliosus*

2 Lower surfaces of leaf blades moderately to densely short-villous . . . *C. foliosus* var. *medius*

Ceanothus foliosus var. *foliosus* (wavyleaf ceanothus), an erect, often compact shrub as tall as 3.5 m, occurs below 1,100 m (3,700 feet) throughout the outer North Coast Range and Santa Cruz Mountains from Humboldt County south to Santa Clara County. Variety *medius* (La Cuesta ceanothus) is often less than 1.5–2 m tall and occurs in the Santa Lucia Range, the La Panza Range of San Luis Obispo County, and disjunctly in the Cuyamaca Mountains at 1,200–1,500 m (4,950 feet). Some populations in the Santa Cruz Mountains and the Santa Lucia and La Panza Ranges appear intermediate between varieties *foliosus* and *medius*. Populations from the Cuyamaca Mountains, previously named *C. austromontanus,* tend to have more densely puberulent lower leaf surfaces but cannot be distinguished otherwise from variety *medius* in the Santa Cruz Mountains and Santa Lucia Range.

McMinn (1942) suggested that *Ceanothus foliosus* is more closely related to *C. lemmonii* than to any other species, based partly on leaf shape, pubescence, and inflorescence morphology. The presence of globose to subglobose glands along the leaf margins in both taxa also provides evidence of a close relationship. *Ceanothus lemmonii* differs mainly by its relatively flat leaves, glaucous or pale branchlet internodes, and often stalked glands. Hybrids with *C. thyrsiflorus* var. *griseus* have been reported from near Salt Point in Sonoma County. McMinn reported naturally occurring hybrids with *C. thyrsiflorus* and *C. parryi*.

References. *Ceanothus foliosus* Parry, *Proceedings of the Davenport Academy of Sciences* 5: 172–173 (1889); *C. diversifolius* Kellogg var. *foliosus* (Parry) K. Brandegee, *Proceedings of the California Academy of Sciences*, series 2, 4: 201 (1894); *C. dentatus* Torrey & A. Gray var. *dickeyi* Fosberg, *American Midland Naturalist* 27: 256 (1942).

Ceanothus foliosus var. *medius* McMinn, *Ceanothus,* 222 (1942); *C. austromontanus* Abrams, *Bulletin of the New York Botanical Garden* 6: 412 (1910).

Ceanothus foliosus var. *vineatus* McMinn, *Ceanothus,* 221 (1942).

Ceanothus fresnensis Abrams

Fresno mat

Subgenus *Cerastes.* Prostrate shrubs, less than 1 m tall; crown dense, mat-like, to 3 m wide, or crown somewhat open and mound-like; main branches spreading and rooting at scattered nodes to weakly ascending and spreading, sometimes decumbent, the short terminal branches erect in prostrate forms; distal branchlets flexible to stiff, their internodes 4–12 mm long, smooth, brown to reddish brown to grayish brown, tomentulose, becoming glabrous; mature bark gray to grayish brown. Stipules thick, persistent, 1–1.5 mm wide. Leaves opposite, evergreen, evenly spaced or clustered on short, erect lateral shoots and somewhat spreading, subsessile; petioles 1–2 mm long. Leaf blades 4–12 mm long, 3–8 mm wide, elliptic to oblanceolate, flat, thick, stiff, one-veined; upper surfaces dull green, puberulent; lower surfaces pale green to somewhat glaucous, strigulose to minutely appressed-puberulent, sometimes appearing glabrous except for microscopic tomentulose patches between the secondary veins; tips rounded or notched; bases obtuse to rounded; margins plane, entire, sometimes denticulate near the tip. Inflorescences terminal or in upper axils of 1- or 2-year-old branchlets, umbellate, 9–16 mm long, sessile to subsessile; peduncles 1–4 mm long; peduncles and rachises puberulent. Pedicels 7–10 mm long, glabrous; sepals and petals five; perianth and disks blue, sometimes pale blue or white. Fruits 4–6 mm wide, subglobose to weakly lobed, brown to reddish brown; lobes smooth, horned above the middle; horns 1.5–2 mm long, slender, somewhat spreading to erect, smooth. Seeds 3–4 mm long, ellipsoid, slightly compressed, dark brown. Flowering May and June; fruiting July and August; reproducing primarily from seeds, sometimes from buried nodes.

Rocky, granitic soils of ridges and slopes; open sites in conifer forests; 970–2,300 m (3,200–7,600 feet); western slope of the Sierra Nevada from Nevada County south to Fresno County, California.

The prostrate, mat-like *Ceanothus fresnensis* forms large colonies in open sites of relatively dense conifer forests, often on steep slopes and along road cuts. Typical *C. fresnensis* has blue to pale blue flowers and appears restricted to granitic soils in the Sierra Nevada, from Tuolumne County south to Madera County. In contrast, mound-like plants with relatively open crowns, often as tall as 70 cm, are common in more open forests and on relatively thin soils or rock outcrops. Such plants often are the dominant shrub in the forest understory at elevations of 1,360–2,300 m (4,500–7,600 feet). The

Ceanothus fresnensis, Mariposa Grove, Yosemite National Park, California

name *C. arcuatus* has been applied to such plants, which Munz (1959) treated as a putative hybrid between *C. cuneatus* and *C. fresnensis*. Most plants referable to *C. arcuatus* also have distinctive spreading aerial branches, and white to pale blue flowers. The mature bark is often gray, and the fruits vary with respect to the prominence and location of their horns, which are often short or poorly developed. Although McMinn (1942) reported *C. arcuatus* from widely scattered localities in association with both *C. cuneatus* and *C. fresnensis* in the southern Sierra Nevada, similar plants elsewhere in the central and northern Sierra Nevada are perplexing because of the absence of one or both species. The problem is especially interesting because plants with a similar habit, leaf size and shape, and fruits are also widespread on ultramafic substrates in the Klamath Mountains of Siskiyou, Shasta, and Trinity Counties. Although these plants are tentatively treated as part of *C. cuneatus,* they are strikingly similar to plants referred to *C. arcuatus* in the Sierra Nevada and cannot be easily separated from them. The relationships of plants referable to *C. arcuatus* clearly need further study. The accompanying key provides a summary of the salient differences between the two forms.

Ceanothus fresnensis and C. arcuatus

1 Plants prostrate, less than 30 cm tall, crown mat-like, relatively dense, the spreading
  stems often rooting at scattered nodes; flowers blue to pale blue . . . . *C. fresnensis*
1 Plants semierect, 30–70 cm tall, crown mound-like, open, stems ascending to spreading,
  not rooting at nodes; flowers white to pale blue . . . . *C. arcuatus*

Ceanothus fresnensis, the form known as *C. arcuatus,* Chiquito Creek, Madera County, California

Howell (1940) suggested that *Ceanothus fresnensis* may have arisen as a hybrid between *C. prostratus* and *C. greggii* var. *vestitus* (treated here as *C. vestitus*). Flower color and the mat- to mound-like habit of *C. fresnensis* is similar to that of *C. pumilus*, but they differ significantly in their leaf and fruit morphology. Although McMinn (1942) treated *C. arcuatus* as a distinct species, he suggested that it was derived from hybrids between typical *C. fresnensis* and *C. cuneatus*. In most regional manuals, *C. arcuatus* has been treated as a hybrid, but its occurrence over a wide geographical range, often in the absence of both putative parents, suggests otherwise. Naturally occurring hybrids between *C. cuneatus* and either *C. fresnensis* or *C. prostratus* were named *C.* ×*connivens* and are difficult to distinguish from low-growing plants of *C. arcuatus*.

References. *Ceanothus fresnensis* Dudley ex Abrams, *Botanical Gazette* 53: 68 (1912); *C. rigidus* Nuttall var. *fresnensis* (Dudley ex Abrams) Jepson, *Manual of the Flowering Plants of California*, 623 (1925).

Ceanothus arcuatus McMinn, *Ceanothus*, 247–248 (1942).

Ceanothus gloriosus J. T. Howell

Point Reyes ceanothus

Subgenus *Cerastes*. Erect, spreading, or prostrate shrubs, 0.1–4 m tall; crown somewhat open to dense, broadly obovoid, sometimes mound- or mat-like; main branches ascending to widely spreading; distal branchlets flexible to somewhat stiff, their internodes 7–25(–35) mm long, smooth to angled distally, green to brown or purplish brown, short-villous or puberulent, becoming glabrous; mature bark brown. Stipules thick, persistent, 2.5–4.5 mm wide, often confluent. Leaves opposite, evergreen, evenly spaced, sometimes ascending or erect, subsessile; petioles 1–4 mm long. Leaf blades 7–43 mm long, 4–25 mm wide, broadly elliptic to broadly obovate, sometimes orbicular, flat to slightly wavy, thick, stiff, one-veined; upper surfaces dark green, glabrous, somewhat shiny; lower surfaces green, sparsely strigulose to glabrous except for microscopic tomentulose patches between the secondary veins; tips rounded to truncate or notched; bases tapered to somewhat rounded; margins plane, sometimes thickened, dentate; teeth 9–31 per leaf, spinulose. Inflorescences in upper axils of 1- to 3-year-old branchlets, umbellate to subumbellate, 8–16 mm long, sessile to subsessile; peduncles 1–5 mm long; peduncles and rachises puberulent, becoming glabrous. Pedicels 4–9 mm long, glabrous;

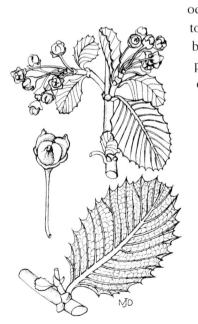

Ceanothus gloriosus var. *gloriosus*, leaf detail ×1½

sepals and petals five; perianth and disks deep blue to bluish purple. Fruits 4–6 mm wide, globose to weakly lobed, viscid to slightly viscid when young, dark brown to black; lobes smooth, sometimes weakly ridged, horned above the middle; horns erect, 1–2 mm long, smooth to slightly wrinkled. Seeds 3–3.5 mm long, ovoid, slightly compressed, dark brown. Flowering March–May; fruiting April–June; reproducing primarily from seeds.

Well-drained soils derived from various substrates on coastal bluffs, slopes, and ridges; chaparral, closed-cone pine forest; margins of mixed evergreen forest; 15–400 m (50–1,300 feet); coastal slopes of the outer North Coast Range of California from Mendocino County south to Marin County. Populations referable to *Ceanothus masonii* (Mason's ceanothus) and *C. gloriosus* var. *porrectus* (Mount Vision ceanothus) are taxa of special conservation concern, resulting from their highly restricted distributions.

Prostrate plants, usually less than 30 cm tall, which occur on consolidated sediments of coastal bluffs from Humboldt County south to Marin County are treated as variety *gloriosus* (Point Reyes ceanothus, glory mat). Erect shrubs, 1–4 m tall, with ascending to widely spreading, elongate branches, belong to variety *exaltatus* (Navarro ceanothus, glory bush). These plants occur on interior slopes of the North Coast Range from Humboldt County south to Marin County at elevations of 50–400 m (165–1,300 feet). Both varieties have relatively broad obovate or suborbicular leaf blades with 13–35 teeth per blade. However, plants in some populations from southern Humboldt County and northern Mendocino County vary from mound-like to broadly obovoid and cannot be easily separated into either one of the two varieties. Jepson (1936) and Howell (1937) considered *Ceanothus gloriosus* vars. *gloriosus* and *exaltatus* to be closely related to *C. purpureus*, which differs significantly by having somewhat wavy or folded leaf blades less than 15 mm wide and leaf margins with sharply spinulose teeth. Mound-like plants (30–40 cm high) with leaf blades 10–19 mm long and margins with 9–19 teeth were named variety *porrectus*.

The name *Ceanothus masonii* has been applied to erect shrubs restricted to ultramafic substrates on Bolinas Ridge, Marin County, which lies within the general geographical range of varieties *exaltatus* and *porrectus*. McMinn (1942) considered *C. masonii* to be closely related to *C. gloriosus*, especially variety *exaltatus*, which differs mainly by its more elongate, less rigid, and curved branches and somewhat larger leaves. Most leaf blades of *C. gloriosus* var. *exaltatus* are 13–43 mm long while those of *C. masonii* are 7–21 mm long. Nobs (1963) provided evidence showing considerable overlap in

Ceanothus gloriosus, the form known as C. masonii

leaf shape, number of marginal teeth, and young stipule morphology between *C. masonii* and *C. gloriosus*. The close similarity between *C. gloriosus* and *C. masonii* suggests that the latter is best treated as part of *C. gloriosus* rather than as a distinct species.

Variation within *Ceanothus gloriosus* has been attributed partly to hybridization. Complex hybrids involving *C. gloriosus* with *C. cuneatus, C. sonomensis,* and forms of *C. divergens* have been reported from the same population (Howell 1940, Nobs 1963). The typical forms referable to *C. gloriosus* and *C. masonii* may be separated by using the accompanying key.

Varieties of *Ceanothus gloriosus,* and *C. masonii*

1 Plants prostrate, mat- to mound-like, less than 0.5 m tall, the main branches spreading to weakly ascending 2
1 Plants erect, hemispheric to obovoid, 0.5–2(–3.5) m tall, the main branches ascending to erect 3
2 Most leaf blades broadly obovate to suborbicular, 23–31 mm long, 17–24 mm wide, with 13–31 teeth . . . . *C. gloriosus* var. *gloriosus*
2 Most leaf blades obovate, narrowly obovate, or oblong-obovate, 10–21 mm long, 5–15 mm wide, with 9–19 teeth . . . . *C. gloriosus* var. *porrectus*
3 Most leaf blades broadly obovate to suborbicular, sometimes oblong-obovate, 13–43 mm long, 17–22 mm wide, with 13–35 teeth; terminal branches somewhat equal and relatively short, diverging outward and somewhat rigid . . . . *C. gloriosus* var. *exaltatus*
3 Most leaf blades obovate to narrowly obovate, 7–21 mm long, 4–13 mm wide, with 9–17 teeth; terminal branches of variable length, ascending to spreading and somewhat flexible . . . . *C. masonii*

References. *Ceanothus gloriosus* J. T. Howell, *Leaflets of Western Botany* 2: 43 (1937); *C. rigidus* Nuttall var. *grandifolius* Torrey, *Reports of Explorations and Surveys, to Ascertain the Most Practicable and Economical Route for a Railroad from the Mississippi River to the Pacific Ocean* 4(5): 75 (1857); *C. prostratus* Bentham var. *grandifolius* (Torrey) Jepson, *Manual of the Flowering Plants of California,* 624 (1925).
Ceanothus gloriosus var. exaltatus J. T. Howell, Leafl. W. Bot. 2: 44 (1937).
Ceanothus masonii McMinn, Madroño 6: 171 (1942).
Ceanothus gloriosus var. porrectus J. T. Howell, Leafl. W. Bot. 4: 31 (1944).

Ceanothus hearstiorum Hoover & Roof
Hearst ceanothus

Subgenus *Ceanothus*. Prostrate shrubs, less than 30 cm tall; crown somewhat dense, mat- to mound-like, most branches widely spreading, sometimes prostrate; distal branchlets somewhat stiff, their internodes 8–14(–30) mm long, smooth to angled near the tips, green to reddish brown, densely puberulent or short-villous; mature bark dark gray or grayish brown. Stipules thin, deciduous. Leaves alternate, evergreen, evenly spaced to clustered, sessile to subsessile; petioles 1–2 mm long. Leaf blades 9–17 mm long, 2–5 mm wide, oblong to oblong-obovate, slightly convex above and concave below, leathery, one-veined; upper surfaces dark green, glabrous, sometimes sparsely short-villous, weakly papillose or with sessile to subsessile globose glands, the veins somewhat furrowed, sometimes strongly on short leaf blades; lower surfaces paler, densely tomentulose; tips truncate or notched; bases tapered to obtuse; margins revolute, entire or obscurely denticulate, with 23–31(–39) subglobose to broadly conic glands. Inflorescences in upper axils of 1- or 2-year-old branchlets, umbellate, rarely racemose, dense, 11–29(–110) mm long; peduncles 7–18(–40) mm long; peduncles and rachises puberulent to short-villous. Pedicels 3–5 mm long, glabrous; sepals and petals five; perianth and disks deep blue, rarely pale blue or white. Fruits 4–5 mm wide, globose to somewhat lobed, dark brown; lobes weakly ridged; horns absent. Seeds 2–3 mm long, broadly ellipsoid, slightly compressed, black. Flowering March and April; fruiting May and June; reproducing entirely from seeds.

Coastal bluffs and slopes on consolidated alluvial substrates; chaparral; 20–180 m (65–590 feet); coastal slopes of the Santa Lucia Range of northern San Luis Obispo County, California. A species of special conservation concern, resulting from a highly restricted distribution.

Based on overall morphology, *Ceanothus hearstiorum* is similar to *C. dentatus* and *C. papillosus*. *Ceanothus hearstiorum* differs primarily in its prostrate habit, which is retained in cultivation. The upper leaf surfaces of *C. dentatus* lack glands, and the marginal globose glands of both *C. dentatus* and *C. papillosus* are larger than those of *C. hearstiorum*. Some plants appear to be hybrids with *C. maritimus*, based on specimens in the California Polytechnic University at San Luis Obispo herbarium.

Reference. *Ceanothus hearstiorum* Hoover & Roof, *Four Seasons* 2(1): 4 (1966).

Ceanothus herbaceus Rafinesque
inland Jersey tea

Subgenus *Ceanothus*. Erect shrubs, 0.5–1 m tall; crown open, usually hemispheric; main branches ascending to spreading; distal branchlets flexible, their internodes 12–31 mm long, smooth, green, sometimes becoming red-tinged, appressed-puberulent to short-villous, often becoming glabrous; mature bark brown to grayish brown. Stipules thin, deciduous. Leaves alternate, deciduous; petioles 3–5(–10) mm long. Leaf blades (19–)35–74 mm long, 10–32 mm wide, narrowly elliptic to lanceolate, sometimes somewhat ovate, flat, thin to somewhat leathery, three-veined from the base; upper surfaces dull green, subglabrous or short-villous and becoming glabrous; lower surfaces dull green, often drying rusty brown, puberulent to short-villous, rarely glabrous except for the puberulent to short-villous veins; tips acute to obtuse; bases obtuse to rounded; margins plane, somewhat serrulate to crenate-serrate; teeth 37–71 per leaf, with minute conic glands when young. Inflorescences usually terminal, sometimes in uppermost axils of the current year's branchlets, usually hemispheric, 15–30 mm long; peduncles 26–48 mm long, often with a few reduced leaves near the base; peduncles and rachises puberulent to somewhat tomentulose. Pedicels 5–11 mm long, glabrous, sometimes puberulent; sepals and petals five; perianth white, disks dull white or greenish. Fruits 3–4.5 mm wide, subglobose to lobed, brown to dark brown; lobes smooth, sometimes weakly ridged near the middle; horns absent. Seeds subglobose to ovoid, 2–2.5 mm long, brown. Flowering March–August; fruiting July–September; reproducing from seeds, and basal shoots following fire or killing frosts.

Sandy to rocky soils derived from various geological substrates; shrublands, prairies, woodlands, and forest openings, 270–1,875 m (880–6,200 feet). In Canada from southeastern Manitoba east to Quebec; in the United States from Montana east to Massachusetts and Virginia, south through the front ranges of the Rocky Mountains to New Mexico, east to Arkansas and Louisiana; in Mexico in northern Coahuila.

Known widely in botanical and horticultural literature as *Ceanothus ovatus,* this species is correctly named *C. herbaceus* (Brizicky 1964). Plants with subglabrous to sparsely puberulent leaf blades occur throughout much of the species range east of the Mississippi River Valley. Although plants with puberulent leaves (variety *pubescens*) predominate in the western portion of the species' range, the extent of intergradation from a geographical perspective remains unclear.

Ceanothus herbaceus

Close relatives include *Ceanothus americanus* and *C. sanguineus* (McMinn 1942, Coile 1988), based on habit, the relatively large, deciduous, serrate to serrulate leaves, and overall fruit morphology. The two differ from *C. herbaceus* primarily by having racemose to paniculate, axillary inflorescences and broader leaves. Hybrids with *C. fendleri* var. *fendleri* in the eastern foothills of the Rocky Mountains have been named *C.* ×*subsericeus* Rydberg.

References. *Ceanothus herbaceus* Rafinesque, *Medical Repository,* series 2, 5: 360 (1808); *C. ovatus* Desfontaines, *Histoire des Arbres et des Arbrisseaux de la France* 2: 381 (1809); *C. ovalis* Bigelow, *Flora Bostoniensis,* ed. 2, 92 (1824); *C. ovalifolius* Wenderoth, *Schriften Gesellschaft Beförderung Gesammten Naturwissenschaften zu Marburg* 2: 247 (1830); *C. americanus* Linnaeus var. *herbaceus* (Rafinesque) Torrey & A. Gray, *Flora of North America* 1: 264 (1838); *C. ovatus* var. *pubescens* Torrey & A. Gray ex S. Watson, *Bibliographical Index to North American Botany,* 166

(1878); *C. pubescens* (Torrey & A. Gray ex S. Watson) Rydberg ex Small, *Flora of the Southeastern United States,* 751 & 1334 (1903); *C. ovatus* f. *pubescens* (Torrey & A. Gray ex S. Watson) Soper, *Rhodora* 43: 83 (1941); *C. herbaceus* var. *pubescens* (S. Watson) Shinners, *Field and Laboratory* 19: 33 (1951).

Based on Rafinesque's descriptions, at least two names without type specimens, often treated as synonyms of *C. americanus,* might also refer to *C. herbaceus: C. ellipticus* Rafinesque, *New Flora and Botany of North America* 3: 56 (1836), and *C. glandulosus* Rafinesque, *idem* 3: 57 (1836).

Ceanothus impressus Trelease

Santa Barbara ceanothus

Subgenus *Ceanothus.* Erect to somewhat spreading shrubs, sometimes arborescent, 0.5–2(–3) m tall; crown compact and dense to open, obovoid to hemispheric; main branches ascending to spreading; distal branchlets flexible to somewhat stiff, their internodes 10–14 mm long, smooth, brown, puberulent; mature bark brown or grayish brown. Stipules thin, deciduous. Leaves alternate, evergreen, somewhat clustered, subsessile; petioles 1–4 mm long. Leaf blades 7–18 mm long, 5–15 mm wide, elliptic to oblong or broadly ovate, convex above, concave below, somewhat leathery, one-veined; upper surfaces dark green, sparsely short-villous, the central and secondary veins deeply furrowed; lower surfaces pale green, veins densely short-villous; tips obtuse to rounded; bases rounded; margins thickened to revolute, obscurely denticulate to obscurely scalloped, with 11–29 glands per leaf when young; glands broadly conic, sometimes subglobose, deciduous. Inflorescences subumbellate to racemose, dense to open, 8–25 mm long; peduncles 5–11(–15) mm long, in upper axils of 1- or 2-year-old branchlets; rachises and peduncles puberulent. Pedicels 2–10 mm long, sparsely puberulent to glabrous; sepals and petals five; perianth and disks blue, sometimes deep lavender-blue. Fruits 3–4 mm wide, lobed, dark brown; lobes smooth or ridged; horns absent. Seeds 2–3 mm long, broadly ellipsoid to ovoid, black. Flowering February–April; fruiting April–July; reproducing entirely from seeds.

Sandy soils of coastal terraces and bluffs; chaparral and open sites in oak woodland; 10–100 m (30–330 feet); southwestern San Luis Obispo and western Santa Barbara Counties, California. A species of special conservation concern, resulting from a highly restricted distribution and loss of habitat, especially in the case of variety *nipomensis.*

Ceanothus impressus
var. *nipomensis*

The name *Ceanothus impressus* var. *nipomensis* (Nipomo ceanothus) was applied to shrubs as tall as 3 m with relatively open crowns and light green, somewhat flattened, slightly larger leaves with less prominently furrowed veins. It also has more open inflorescences, which are 15–25 mm long and with pedicels 6–10 mm long. Plants referable to variety *nipomensis* occur primarily on Nipomo Mesa and the eastern San Luis Range of southwestern San Luis Obispo County, less commonly in the Purissima Hills of northwestern Santa Barbara County. Variety *impressus* appears restricted to the bluffs and terraces of Burton Mesa in western Santa Barbara County. The leaves of plants assignable to variety *nipomensis* appear intermediate between variety *impressus* and *C. oliganthus,* suggesting that hybridization may be partly responsible for the patterns observed in the northern part of the geographical range (Hoover 1970). However, the habit and leaf morphology are retained in progenies grown from seed. Most plants assignable to the two varieties can be separated by using the accompanying key.

Varieties of *Ceanothus impressus*

1 Plants compact, hemispheric; leaf blades strongly convex above, concave below, the margins conspicuously revolute, the veins sunken in deep furrows . . . . *C. impressus* var. *impressus*
1 Plants relatively open, usually obovoid; leaf blades weakly convex above, the margins thick to weakly revolute, the veins not conspicuously furrowed . . . . *C. impressus* var. *nipomensis*

Both *Ceanothus oliganthus* and *C. dentatus* have been considered close relatives (McMinn 1942). The distinctively furrowed veins, especially in variety *impressus,* are apparently unique in the genus, although weakly furrowed leaf blades are found in *C. hearstiorum* and some populations of *C. lemmonii.* Naturally occurring hybrids between *C. impressus* and *C. thyrsiflorus* have been called *C. ×burtonensis.*

References. *Ceanothus impressus* Trelease, *Proceedings of the California Academy of Sciences,* series 2, 1: 112 (1888); *C. dentatus* Torrey & A. Gray var. *impressus* (Trelease) Trelease in A. Gray, *Synoptical Flora of North America* 1: 415 (1897).

Ceanothus impressus var. *nipomensis* McMinn, *Ceanothus,* 219 (1942).

Ceanothus incanus Nuttall
coast whitethorn

Subgenus *Ceanothus.* Erect shrubs, 1.5–4 m tall; crown somewhat open, broadly obovoid to somewhat hemispheric or mound-like; main branches spreading to erect; distal branchlets stiff, often becoming spine-like, sometimes mostly blunt-tipped, their internodes 10–21(–40) mm long, smooth, light gray, glaucous; mature bark light gray to grayish brown. Stipules thin, deciduous. Leaves alternate, evergreen; petioles

3–12 mm long. Leaf blades 19–42(–60) mm long, 10–30 (–35) mm wide, broadly elliptic to broadly ovate, flat, somewhat leathery, three-veined from the base; upper surfaces green to grayish green, glabrous, sometimes sparsely appressed-puberulent; lower surfaces light grayish green, appressed-puberulent; tips obtuse; bases rounded to subcordate; margins plane, entire, rarely denticulate, with 26–52 minute conic glands per leaf when young. Inflorescences usually in upper axils of 1- to 3-year-old branchlets, usually paniculate, sometimes racemose, 21–60 mm long; peduncles 10–18 mm long; peduncles and rachises puberulent. Pedicels 4–8 mm long, glabrous; sepals and petals five; perianth and disks white or cream. Fruits 4–6 mm wide, lobed, strongly viscid when young, brown to dark brown; lobes appearing strongly wrinkled when dry, ridged to weakly horned above the middle. Seeds 2.5–3 mm long, ovoid to subglobose, dark brown to black. Flowering April–June; fruiting June and July; reproducing from seeds, and from basal shoots following fire.

Ceanothus incanus

Ridges, slopes, and flats on various geological substrates; chaparral and open sites and clearings in conifer and mixed-evergreen forests; 60–1,030 m (200–3,400 feet); Santa Cruz Mountains, outer North Coast Range, and southern Klamath Mountains of California. Klein (1970) called attention to variation in number of spine-like versus blunt branchlets within and between populations. For those plants with mostly spine-like branchlets he applied the name forma *spinosissimus.* Because many populations apparently show considerable polymorphism, however, the spine-like form does not appear to warrant taxonomic recognition at a higher level. Plants with relatively narrow leaf blades having glabrous upper surfaces were named variety *minor.*

Closely related species include *Ceanothus cordulatus* and *C. leucodermis. Ceanothus cordulatus* differs by having umbellate to subumbellate inflorescences on peduncles less than 6 mm long. *Ceanothus leucodermis* usually has subglabrous rachises and leaf blades less than 10 mm wide. McMinn (1942) reported naturally occurring hybrids with *C. papillosus* and *C. thyrsiflorus.* Those with *C. thyrsiflorus* were named *C.* ×*vanrensselaeri* J. B. Roof. Specimens at the Humboldt State University herbarium suggest putative hybridization with *C. parryi* in Humboldt County.

References. *Ceanothus incanus* Nuttall in Torrey & A. Gray, *Flora of North America* 1: 265 (1838); *C. incanus* var. *minor* Hooker & Arnott, *Botany of Captain Beechey's Voyage, Supplement* 328 (1838); *C. incanus* f. *spinosissimus* F. K. Klein, *Four Seasons* 3(3): 21 (1970).

Ceanothus integerrimus Hooker & Arnott

deer brush

Subgenus *Ceanothus.* Erect shrubs, 1–4 m tall, sometimes arborescent; crown open, hemispheric to obovoid; main branches ascending to spreading, sometimes drooping; distal branchlets flexible, their internodes 15–32(–51) mm long, smooth, green to yellowish green, appressed-puberulent to tomentulose, often becoming glabrous with age; mature bark grayish brown. Stipules thin, deciduous. Leaves alternate, deciduous but some persisting longer than others; petioles 3–12 mm long. Leaf blades (15–) 21–53(–75) mm long, 5–40(–45) mm wide, elliptic to oblong-elliptic or ovate, flat, thin to somewhat leathery, one- or three-veined from the base, the two lateral veins as long as or shorter than the central vein; upper surfaces somewhat shiny green, glabrous to puberulent; lower surfaces dull green, glabrous to sparsely puberulent, the veins often puberulent; tips acute to obtuse; bases rounded; margins plane, entire. Inflorescences terminal or in axils of 1- or 2-year-old branchlets, paniculate, rarely racemose, 35–180 mm long; peduncles 21–75 mm long; peduncles and rachises puberulent to short-villous. Pedicels 4–9 mm long, glabrous; sepals and petals five; perianth and disks white to blue. Fruits 4–6.5 mm wide, globose to somewhat lobed, viscid when young, brown; lobes smooth, sometimes with a weakly developed dorsal ridge or bulge; horns absent. Seeds 2–3 mm long, ovoid to broadly ovoid, slightly compressed,

Ceanothus integerrimus var. *macrothyrsus,* Chiquito Creek, Sierra Nevada, Madera County, California; also see page 132

brown. Flowering May–July; fruiting July and August; reproducing from seeds, and from basal shoots following fire.

Slopes, ridges, and flats on various substrates; clearings and open sites in chaparral and conifer and mixed-evergreen forests; 140–2,570 m (460–8,500 feet); Cascade and Coast Ranges of southwestern Washington and Oregon south through the Coast Ranges, Sierra Nevada, Transverse Ranges, and northern Peninsular Ranges of California, east to the mountains of Arizona and southwestern New Mexico.

Leaf blades can have a single prominent midvein with several pairs of lateral veins, or three prominent veins, the lowest pair often extending beyond the midpoint of the blade. One-veined leaf blades are elliptic to oblong-elliptic, 18–35 mm long, 7–10 mm wide, and are found on plants from only a few localities in the southern Santa Cruz Mountains and the northern Santa Lucia Range of California. These plants belong to variety *integerrimus* (Parry 1889, Jepson 1936, McMinn 1942). The relationships and status of variety *integerrimus* need careful study because its restricted distribution suggests that it may be of special conservation concern. In contrast, three-veined leaves with broadly elliptic, lanceolate, or ovate blades 25–75 mm long are found throughout the entire range of the species, and to them several names have been applied. Jepson discussed the anatomical, ecological, and geographical differences between the two forms, the putative relationship to *Ceanothus palmeri*, and considered the problem "the most interesting in *Ceanothus* which is at once historical and ecological."

Several regional forms with three-veined leaves have been treated as taxonomic varieties, but they do not merit recognition based on geographical or ecological distribution. Plants with white corollas and elliptic to narrowly ovate, mostly glabrous leaf blades were named variety *californicus* and are widespread throughout California in the Coast Range north of San Francisco Bay, the Cascade Range, and the Sierra Nevada. Plants with white to blue corollas, elliptic, lanceolate, or ovate leaf blades, with the upper surfaces glabrous and the lower surfaces glabrous to pubescent, were named variety *macrothyrsus.* This form is common from northwestern California northward to Washington, but plants with subglabrous upper surfaces also occur in Arizona and New Mexico. Plants with similar blade shapes but with white corollas and both leaf surfaces pubescent were named variety *puberulus.* Such plants can be found throughout most of the geographical range of the species. Coile (1988) was unable to detect distinct patterns of variation coincident either with

Ceanothus integerrimus,
leaf details ×½ (lower
left, var. *macrothyrsus;*
right, var. *integerrimus*)

the named varieties or with geographical distribution, although upper leaf surface pubescence tended to be denser in populations throughout the southern part of the geographical range.

Two varieties are recognized, based on a combination of leaf shape, size, and venation, with variety *macrothyrsus* being the earliest available name at the varietal level for the three-veined form (Greuter et al. 2000, Article 11.4). Most plants assignable to the two varieties can be separated by using the accompanying key.

Varieties of *Ceanothus integerrimus*

1 Leaf blades with a single prominent vein from the base, the blades elliptic to somewhat oblong-elliptic . . . . *C. integerrimus* var. *integerrimus*

1 Leaf blades with 3 prominent veins from the base, the lateral ones extending to or beyond the midpoint of the blade, the blades ovate, sometimes elliptic . . . .*C. integerrimus* var. *macrothyrsus*

McMinn (1942) implicitly suggested relationships with both *Ceanothus palmeri* (treated here as part of *C. spinosus*) and *C. parvifolius*. The former is more closely related to *C. spinosus*, based on leaf longevity, thickness, and fruit morphology, but its leaves are somewhat similar in shape to those of *C. integerrimus* var. *integerrimus*. *Ceanothus parvifolius* is similar in leaf shape, leaf venation, and fruit morphology to small-leaved forms of *C. integerrimus* var. *macrothyrsus* but differs by its low-growing habit and radial branching pattern. In contrast, putatively closer relationships to *C. americanus*, *C. sanguineus*, and *C. herbaceus* were discussed by Coile (1988).

Hybrids with *Ceanothus cordulatus*, *C. lemmonii*, *C. papillosus*, and *C. tomentosus* var. *tomentosus* have been reported (McMinn 1942, Thomas 1961). Hybrids with *C. oliganthus* occur in the Santa Lucia Range of Monterey County, California, based on specimens at the Rancho Santa Ana Botanic Garden herbarium.

References. *Ceanothus integerrimus* Hooker & Arnott, *Botany of Captain Beechey's Voyage*, Supplement 329 (1838); *C. andersonii* Parry, *Proceedings of the Davenport Academy of Sciences* 5: 172 (1889).

Ceanothus integerrimus var. *macrothyrsus* (Torrey) G. T. Benson, *Contributions of the Dudley Herbarium* 2: 121 (1930); *C. thyrsiflorus* Eschscholtz var. *macrothyrsus* Torrey, *Botany of the Wilkes Expedition*, 263 (1874); *C. macrothyrsus* (Torrey) E. L. Greene, *Leaflets of Botanical Observation and Criticism* 1: 68 (1904); *C. californicus* Kellogg, *Proceedings of the California Academy of Sciences* 1: 54 (1855); *C. nevadensis* Kellogg, *idem* 2: 152 (1863); *C. mogollonicus* E. L. Greene, *Leafl. Bot. Observ. Crit.* 1: 67 (1904); *C. myrianthus* E. L. Greene, *idem* 1: 67 (1904); *C. peduncularis* E. L. Greene, *idem* 1: 67 (1904; this name is based on a collection from Mount Hood, Oregon, and is not the same as that of Jepson 1925); *C. integerrimus* var. *puberulus* (E. L. Greene) Abrams, *Bulletin of the New York Botanical Garden* 6: 409 (1910), based on *C. puberulus* E. L. Greene, *Leafl. Bot. Observ. Crit.* 1: 66 (1904); *C. integerrimus* var. *peduncularis* Jepson, *Manual of the Flowering Plants of California*, 620 (1925; this name is based on a collection by Jepson from Shasta Springs, California, and is not the same as that of Greene 1904); *C. integerrimus* var. *californicus* (Kellogg) G. T. Benson, *Contr. Dudley Herb.* 2: 120 (1930); *C. integerrimus* var. *mogollonicus* (E. L. Greene) McMinn, *Ceanothus,* 183 (1942).

Ceanothus jepsonii E. L. Greene

musk brush, Jepson's ceanothus

Subgenus *Cerastes.* Erect shrubs, 0.5–1 m tall; crown somewhat dense, usually broadly obovoid, sometimes hemispheric or flat-topped; main branches ascending to widely spreading; distal branchlets stiff, their internodes 6–20 mm long, smooth or slightly angled, reddish brown, becoming grayish, appressed-puberulent, glabrous with age; mature bark gray to grayish brown. Stipules thick, persistent, 1.5–2 mm wide. Leaves opposite, evergreen, evenly spaced, somewhat curved and deflexed, subsessile or petioles to 2 mm long. Leaf blades 10–20 mm long, 5–12 mm wide, elliptic to oblong, almost flat to concave above and convex below, often wavy, thick, stiff, one-veined; upper surfaces light green to yellow-green, glabrous; lower surfaces pale yellowish green, appearing glabrous except for microscopic tomentulose patches between the secondary veins; tips sharply acute or rounded; bases rounded; margins thick or slightly revolute, dentate; teeth 7–11 per leaf, sharply spinulose. Inflorescences in upper axils of 1- or 2-year-old branchlets, umbellate, 10–15 mm long, sessile to subsessile; peduncles 3–10 mm long; peduncles and rachises puberulent. Pedicels 4–8 mm long, glabrous; sepals and petals six, sometimes eight; perianth blue to white, sometimes violet, the disks often darker. Fruits 5–7 mm wide, globose to weakly lobed, dark brown; lobes weakly ridged, horned above the middle; horns 1–3 mm long, erect, conspicuously wrinkled. Seeds about 4 mm long, ellipsoid, slightly compressed, dark brown to black. Flowering March and April; fruiting May and June; reproducing entirely from seeds.

Slopes and ridges; on ultramafic substrates; chaparral and open sites in oak and pine woodland; 60–880 m (200–2,900 feet); southern North Coast Range of California from Mendocino and Tehama Counties south to Marin and Napa Counties.

Plants with deep blue or bluish violet flowers occur in the outer North Coast Range. Plants with white flowers were named variety *albiflorus* and occur in the eastern portion of the species' range. The relatively narrow distribution of each variety suggests that the species is a candidate for special conservation concern. Nobs (1963) brought attention to the almost universal occurrence of six sepals and six petals

Ceanothus jepsonii

in the flowers of *Ceanothus jepsonii*, a unique trait in the genus. *Ceanothus jepsonii* also may have the largest flowers, judging from comparisons of flower diameters with other species. It is probably closely related to *C. purpureus*, with which it shares a similar habit and wavy, sharply dentate leaves. However, *C. purpureus* differs by having five sepals and five petals, leaves with green to dark green upper surfaces, and fruits 4–5 mm wide.

Putative hybrids with *Ceanothus cuneatus* and *C. prostratus* were reported by McMinn (1942) and Nobs (1963). The number of perianth parts in such hybrids is variable, ranging from five to seven in flowers on the same plant.

References. *Ceanothus jepsonii* E. L. Greene, *Manual of the Botany of the Region of San Francisco Bay*, 78 (1894).

Ceanothus jepsonii var. *albiflorus* J. T. Howell, *Leaflets of Western Botany* 3: 231 (1943).

Ceanothus lemmonii Parry
Lemmon's ceanothus

Subgenus *Ceanothus.* Spreading, sometimes erect shrubs, 0.5–1 m tall; crown open to somewhat dense, mound-like to hemispheric, often flat-topped; main branches ascending to spreading; distal branchlets stiff to somewhat flexible, their internodes 9–15 mm long, smooth, pale grayish green, often glaucous and light gray, sparsely short-villous; mature bark gray. Stipules thin, deciduous. Leaves alternate, evergreen; petioles 3–6 mm long. Leaf blades 12–33 mm long, 6–14 mm wide, elliptic to oblong-elliptic, flat, somewhat leathery, one- to inconspicuously three-veined from the base; upper surfaces green, appressed-puberulent, glabrous with age, the major veins sometimes weakly furrowed; lower surfaces pale green, densely short-villous, especially on the veins; tips acute to obtuse; bases tapered to rounded; margins plane, denticulate to serrulate; teeth 34–45 per leaf, with stalked or subsessile, subglobose glands when young. Inflorescences in upper axils of 1- or 2-year-old branchlets, subumbellate to racemose, dense to somewhat open, 15–65 mm long; peduncles 10–27 mm long; peduncles and rachises puberulent. Pedicels 5–7 mm long, glabrous; sepals and petals five; perianth and disks pale to

Ceanothus lemmonii, Trinity Mountains, northern California

deep blue. Fruits 3–4 mm wide, weakly lobed, brown; lobes smooth, ridged above the middle; horns absent. Seeds 2.5–3 mm long, broadly ellipsoid to ovoid, weakly compressed, dark brown to black. Flowering April and May; fruiting June–August; reproducing primarily from seeds.

Slopes and flats on gravelly or rocky soils derived from igneous and metamorphic substrates; chaparral and open sites in conifer forests and oak and pine woodlands; 180–1,300 m (590–4,300 feet); inner North Coast Range from Humboldt and Trinity Counties south to Lake County, and the western slope of the southern Cascade Range and Sierra Nevada, from Shasta County south to El Dorado County, California.

Young plants have the principal stems radiating from the center, similar to the branching pattern of *Ceanothus parvifolius*. Overall similarities in leaf morphology and flower color suggest close relationships to *C. foliosus, C. oliganthus,* and *C. tomentosus* (McMinn 1942). *Ceanothus lemmonii* sometimes is difficult to distinguish from *C. diversifolius,* a prostrate plant

Ceanothus lemmonii

with obovate to ovate leaf blades and leaf margins with translucent, stipe-like to narrowly conic marginal glands when young. Some low-growing plants that are intermediate for these traits are difficult to assign to either species and may represent hybrids. McMinn reported plants intermediate to *C. foliosus* and *C. oliganthus* var. *sorediatus* in the inner North Coast Range, and putative hybrids with *C. integerrimus* in the Sierra Nevada foothills.

Reference. *Ceanothus lemmonii* Parry, *Proceedings of the Davenport Academy of Sciences* 5: 192 (1889).

Ceanothus leucodermis E. L. Greene

chaparral whitethorn

Subgenus *Ceanothus.* Erect or somewhat spreading shrubs, 1.5–4 m tall; crown somewhat open to dense, obovate to broadly obovoid, often somewhat flat-topped; main branches widely spreading to ascending; distal branchlets stiff, mostly becoming spine-like, their internodes 10–17 mm long, smooth, light gray, sometimes weakly puberulent to tomentulose, becoming glabrous and glaucous; mature bark smooth, light gray or grayish green. Stipules thin, deciduous. Leaves alternate, evergreen, evenly spaced, sometimes clustered; petioles 5–7 mm long. Leaf blades 12–30 mm long, 5–15 mm wide, broadly elliptic to ovate, flat, somewhat leathery, three-veined from the base; upper surfaces pale green, somewhat glaucous; lower surfaces usually glaucous, glabrous, sometimes puberulent; tips acute to obtuse; bases rounded to subcor-

Ceanothus leucodermis codominating in chaparral, Sespe River, Ventura County, California

date; margins plane, usually entire, often with 16–20 minute conic glands when young, sometimes obscurely denticulate or serrulate. Inflorescences racemose to paniculate, dense to open, 25–120 mm long; peduncles 9–30 mm long, in upper axils of 1- to 3-year-old branchlets; rachises and peduncles glabrous. Pedicels 4–9 mm long, glabrous; sepals and petals five; perianth and disks white to pale blue, sometimes lavender-blue. Fruits 3–5 mm wide, globose, viscid when young, brown, smooth to weakly wrinkled; ridges and horns absent. Seeds 2.5–3 mm long, ovoid, slightly compressed, dark brown. Flowering April–June; fruiting June–August; reproducing from seeds, and from basal shoots following fire.

Slopes and ridges, on various geological substrates; chaparral and open sites in conifer and oak woodlands or forests; 270–1,810 m (880–6,000 feet); South Coast Range, western slopes of the Sierra Nevada, and coastal mountains of southern California, south to the Sierra San Pedro Mártir, Baja California, Mexico.

Some plants have been confused with *Ceanothus cordulatus*, which differs mainly by its shorter, often flat-topped stature, densely clustered, sessile to short-peduncled inflorescences, and occurrence at higher elevations. Overall similarities in habit, spine-like branches, leaf morphology, and inflorescence architecture suggest relationships to *C. cordulatus* and *C. incanus* (McMinn 1942). However, molecular analyses suggest relationships to *C. cyaneus* and *C. parvifolius* (Hardig et al. 2000).

In 19th century literature, *Ceanothus leucodermis* was confused with *C. divaricatus,* now considered a synonym of *C. oliganthus* (Jepson 1936, McMinn 1942). Local and geographical variation for obscurely toothed leaves and sparsely puberulent lower leaf surfaces, especially on the veins, may be the result of introgressive hybridization with *C. oliganthus.* Such intermediates occur in the Santa Ynez Mountains of Santa Barbara County, and hybrids with *C. oliganthus* occur in the San Gabriel Mountains of Los Angeles County.

Ceanothus leucodermis

References. *Ceanothus leucodermis* E. L. Greene, *Kew Bulletin* 1895: 15 (1895); *C. divaricatus* Nuttall var. *grosse-serratus* Torrey, *Reports of Explorations and Surveys, to Ascertain the Most Practicable and Economical Route for a Railroad from the Mississippi River to the Pacific Ocean* 4(5): 75 (1857); *C. divaricatus* var. *eglandulosus* Torrey, *idem* 4(5): 75 (1857); *C. eglandulosus* (Torrey) Trelease, *Proceedings of the California Academy of Sciences,* series 2, 1: 110 (1888); *C. divaricatus* var. *laetiflorus* Jepson, *Manual of the Flowering Plants of California,* 620 (1925; based on a collection from the foothills of the Palomar Mountains, this name may apply to putative hybrids or hybrid derivatives involving *C. cyaneus* and *C. leucodermis*).

Ceanothus maritimus Hoover

maritime ceanothus

Subgenus *Cerastes.* Prostrate plants, less than 50 cm tall; crown dense, mat-like, sometimes mound-like; main branches spreading, sometimes ascending or curved, sometimes rooting at remote nodes; distal branchlets stiff, their internodes 6–14 mm long, smooth, reddish brown, becoming grayish brown, tomentulose; mature bark gray to grayish brown. Stipules thick, persistent, 1–1.5 mm wide. Leaves opposite, evergreen, evenly spaced; petioles 1–2 mm long. Leaf blades 8–16(–21) mm long, 4–11(–15) mm wide, obovate to oblong-obovate, flat to slightly folded lengthwise, thick, stiff, one-veined; upper surfaces green, somewhat shiny, glabrous; lower surfaces densely tomentulose; tips notched, truncate, or sometimes obtuse or acute; bases tapered; margins thick to somewhat revolute, usually entire, sometimes with three to five spinulose teeth above the middle. Inflorescence in upper axils of 1- or 2-year-old branchlets, umbellate, 8–12 mm long, sessile or the peduncles 1–6 mm long; rachises and peduncles tomentulose. Pedicels 7–9 mm long, glabrous; sepals and petals five; perianth and disks blue to light blue. Fruits globose to weakly lobed, brown, 5–8 mm wide; lobes smooth, often horned above the middle; horns 1–2 mm long, erect, slightly wrinkled. Seeds 3.5–4 mm long, ellipsoid, somewhat compressed, dark brown to black. Flowering February–May; fruiting April–June; reproducing entirely from seeds.

Coastal bluffs and slopes on alluvial substrates; open sites in grassland or coastal chaparral; 10–60 m (30–200 feet); coastal foothills of the Santa Lucia Range, western San Luis Obispo County, California. A species of special conservation concern because of its narrow distribution and potential habitat loss.

Hoover, in his description of the species, speculated that *Ceanothus maritimus* may have arisen as a hybrid between *C. crassifolius* and plants similar to *C. gloriosus*. With the exception of leaf pubescence, however, *C. maritimus* also may be considered closely related to *C. cuneatus*, based on similarities in leaf shape and fruit morphology. Some plants may be hybrids with *C. hearstiorum*, based on specimens at the California Polytechnic University at San Luis Obispo herbarium.

Reference. *Ceanothus maritimus* Hoover, *Leaflets of Western Botany* 7: 111 (1953).

Ceanothus martinii M. E. Jones

Utah mountain lilac, Martin's ceanothus

Subgenus *Ceanothus*. Erect shrubs, 0.2–1.5 m tall; crown open to somewhat dense, hemispheric to broadly obovoid, sometimes windswept and mound-like, sometimes flat-topped; main branches ascending to spreading; distal branchlets flexible to somewhat stiff, their internodes 7–18(–23) mm long, smooth, green to grayish green, glaucous and puberulent, often becoming glabrous with age; mature bark grayish brown. Stipules thin, deciduous. Leaves alternate, deciduous to semideciduous, evenly spaced to clustered; petioles 3–7 mm long. Leaf blades 13–23(–31) mm long, 9–21 mm wide, broadly elliptic to orbicular, flat, thin to somewhat leathery, three-veined from the base; upper surfaces green, glabrous to sparsely appressed-puberulent; lower surfaces green, glabrous, the veins sometimes appressed-puberulent or strigulose; tips obtuse to rounded; bases rounded; margins plane, entire or obscurely serrulate above the middle, with 23–41 minute conic glands when young. Inflorescences subumbellate to racemose, open to somewhat dense, 15–30 mm long; peduncles 5–14 mm long, usually in upper axils of 1- or 2-year-old branchlets; rachises and peduncles sparsely puberulent to glabrous. Pedicels 3–7 mm long, glabrous; sepals and petals five; perianth and disks white. Fruits 4–5 mm wide, globose to lobed, slightly viscid when young, brown; lobes smooth to somewhat wrinkled, ridged to short-horned above the middle; horns less than 1 mm long, smooth. Seeds 2–3.5 mm long, ovoid, dark brown. Flowering May–July; fruiting July and August; reproducing primarily from seeds.

Ceanothus martinii

Ridges and slopes on rocky soils and outcrops derived from various substrates; shrublands, pine-oak or pine-juniper woodlands, and open sites in conifer forests; 1,810–3,200 m (6,000–10,500 feet); mountains and plateaus from central Nevada, Utah, and northwestern Arizona east to southwestern Wyoming and northwestern Colorado.

McMinn (1942) suggested a relationship to *Ceanothus integerrimus*, but Coile (1988) showed a close relationship to both *C. microphyllus* and *C. parvifolius*, based on the assumption that deciduousness was a shared derived trait. The leaf shape of *C. martinii* is remarkably similar to *C.* ×*lorenzenii* (Jepson) McMinn, a naturally occurring hybrid between *C. cordulatus* and *C. velutinus* var. *velutinus* (McMinn 1942), and to small-leaved forms of *C. velutinus*.

References. *Ceanothus martinii* M. E. Jones, *Contributions to Western Botany* 8: 41 (1898); *C. utahensis* Eastwood, *Proceedings of the California Academy of Sciences*, series 4, 16: 363 (1927).

Ceanothus megacarpus Nuttall

big-pod ceanothus

Subgenus *Cerastes.* Erect shrubs, 1.5–6 m tall; crown open to somewhat dense, hemispheric to broadly obovoid; main branches erect to spreading; distal branchlets stiff to slightly flexible, their internodes 7–15 mm long, smooth, gray to grayish brown, tomentulose to appressed-puberulent, becoming glabrous; mature bark gray to grayish brown. Stipules thick, persistent, 1–2 mm wide. Leaves alternate or opposite, sometimes on the same plant, evergreen, usually evenly spaced; petioles 1–4 mm long. Leaf blades 8–25(–34) mm long, 5–12 mm wide, obovate to broadly elliptic, flat to slightly convex above, thick, stiff, one-veined; upper surfaces dull green, glabrous; lower surfaces pale dull green, appearing glabrous except for microscopic tomentulose patches between the secondary veins, the veins minutely strigulose or appressed-puberulent; tips usually truncate or slightly notched; bases tapered; margins plane, thick to slightly revolute, usually entire, sometimes remotely denticulate with three to five spinulose teeth per leaf. Inflorescences terminal or in upper axils of 1- or 2-year-old branchlets, umbellate, 8–19 mm long, subsessile; peduncles 2–4 mm long; peduncles and rachises puberulent. Pedicels 6–9 mm long, glabrous; sepals and petals five; perianth white, disks often black. Fruits 7–12 mm wide, globose to weakly lobed, viscid when young, brown; lobes smooth to slightly

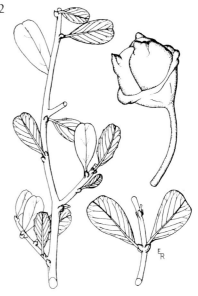

Ceanothus megacarpus var. *megacarpus*, left, and var. *insularis*, lower right leaf details ×½

wrinkled, slightly ridged and horned above the middle; horns less than 1 mm long, smooth, sometimes absent (see page 148). Seeds 4–5 mm long, suborbicular in outline, slightly compressed, brown to dark brown. Flowering December–March; fruiting April–July; reproducing entirely from seeds.

Slopes, ridges, and flats on rocky or gravelly soils derived from various geological substrates; chaparral; 30–850 m (100–2,800 feet); coastal slopes of the western Transverse Ranges and outer Peninsular Ranges, from Santa Barbara County south to San Diego County, California, and most of the California Channel Islands (except San Nicolas and Santa Barbara Islands). Most plants assignable to the two varieties can be separated by using the accompanying key.

Varieties of *Ceanothus megacarpus*

1 Leaves mostly alternate; fruits usually with prominent lateral ridges or dorsal horns . . . . .
. . . .*C. megacarpus* var. *megacarpus*
1 Leaves mostly opposite; fruits usually smooth or with weakly developed dorsal horns . . . .
. . . .*C. megacarpus* var. *insularis*

Ceanothus insularis was described by Alice Eastwood as having an opposite or closely alternate leaf arrangement and smooth fruit surfaces. Although McMinn first treated such plants as a variety (1939), he later (1942) considered them as a distinct species. However, fruits with weakly developed horns can be found in mainland populations with uniformly alternate leaves. Prominent dorsal ridges or horns can be found on plants with opposite leaves. Several authors have brought attention to plants with intermediate traits in the Santa Ynez Mountains of mainland Santa Barbara County and on San Clemente, Santa Catalina, and Santa Cruz Islands (McMinn 1942, Raven 1963, Thorne 1967, Junak et al. 1993). There appear to be no other differences between the two taxa; thus it seems reasonable to treat them as part of a single species.

Plants of *Ceanothus megacarpus* with relatively long flowering branches were named by McMinn as variety *pendulus*, but plants with varying stem lengths are common throughout the northern range of the species, including variety *insularis*. The trait appears related to the plant size and also occurs in large plants of *C. cuneatus*. The frequently dark to almost black floral disks of *C. megacarpus* are apparently shared in common only with *C. crassifolius* and *C. verrucosus*. *Ceanothus megacarpus* is closely related to *C. cuneatus, C. crassifolius,* and *C. verrucosus* (Howell 1940, McMinn 1942). *Ceanothus cuneatus* differs by having erect horns borne above the middle. *Ceanothus crassifolius* can usually be distinguished by its thick to revolute leaf margins and tomentulose leaf blades. *Ceanothus verrucosus* differs primarily by its more prominently notched or truncate leaf tips and shorter leaf blades (5–14 mm long).

Hybridization with *Ceanothus cuneatus* was implied by McMinn (1942), based on his observations of intermediate forms in the western Santa Ynez Mountains of California.

References. *Ceanothus megacarpus* Nuttall, *North American Sylva* 2: 46 (1846; Nuttall provided this name when he realized that his earlier name, *C. macrocarpus* Nuttall in Torrey & A. Gray, *Flora of North America* 1: 267 (1838), was preceded by the name *C. macrocarpus* Cavanilles, which is now considered a species of *Colubrina*); *C. cuneatus* Nuttall var. *macrocarpus* (Nuttall) K. Brandegee, *Proceedings of the California Academy of Sciences,* series 2, 4: 205 (1894); *C. megacarpus* var. *pendulus* McMinn, *Ceanothus,* 230 (1942).

Ceanothus megacarpus var. *insularis* (Eastwood) Munz, *Bulletin of the Southern California Academy of Sciences* 31: 68 (1932), based on *C. insularis* Eastwood, *Proc. Calif. Acad. Sci.,* series 4, 16: 362 (1927); *C. megacarpus* subsp. *insularis* (Eastwood) Raven, *Aliso* 5: 329 (1963).

Ceanothus microphyllus Michaux

sandflat ceanothus, thymeleaf ceanothus

Subgenus *Ceanothus.* Erect, diffusely branched shrubs, less than 70 cm tall, with several erect to ascending stems from the base; crown open, somewhat hemispheric to obovoid; distal branchlets flexible, their internodes 3–9(–12) mm long, smooth to angled, green to yellowish green, gray-puberulent, becoming glabrous; mature bark grayish brown. Stipules thin, deciduous. Leaves alternate, usually deciduous, evenly spaced and in axillary clusters; petioles less than 1 mm long. Leaf blades 2–6(–11) mm long, 1.5–4(–6) mm wide, elliptic to narrowly obovate, flat, thin, three-veined from the base, the lateral veins absent or minute and obscure; upper surfaces green, glabrous; lower surfaces pale green, the veins glabrous to sparsely puberulent or strigulose; tips rounded to obtuse; bases tapered; margins plane, entire, sometimes remotely denticulate with five to nine teeth and minute conic glands when young. Inflorescences terminal on the tips of the current year's or 1-year-old branchlets, umbellate to subumbellate, sometimes racemose, 5–19(–25) mm long; peduncles 5–41 mm long, sometimes leafy below the middle; peduncles and rachises glabrous. Pedicels 4–8 mm long, glabrous; sepals and petals five; perianth and disks white. Fruits 3–4.5 mm wide, weakly lobed, dark brown; lobes smooth, ridges and horns absent. Seeds 1–1.5 mm long, broadly ovoid to somewhat globose, brown to dark reddish brown. Flowering March–June; fruiting May–July; reproducing from seeds, and from basal shoots following fire.

Ceanothus microphyllus

Sandy soils and barrens, flats; open sites and clearings in pine forests, oak woodlands, and shrublands; 3–135 m (10–440 feet) from southern Alabama and Georgia south to Florida.

Ceanothus microphyllus is notable in having the smallest leaves in the genus. Leaf venation is often reduced to only three, often faint veins, without apparent secondary veins. McMinn (1942) treated *C. serpyllifolius* as a distinct species, based on its slightly larger leaves, but variation in leaf size appears continuous between the two forms. The name *C. serpyllifolius* has been applied to small-leaved plants of *C. americanus* var. *intermedius,* of which some may be hybrids between the two species. Coile (1988) suggested close relationships to *C. martinii* and *C. parvifolius,* but affinities to *C. americanus* and *C. herbaceus* should not be discounted.

References. *Ceanothus microphyllus* Michaux, *Flora Boreali-Americana* 1: 154 (1803); *C. serpyllifolius* Nuttall, *Genera of North American Plants* 1: 154 (1818); *C. microphyllus* var. *serpyllifolius* (Nuttall) Alph. Wood, *Class-Book of Botany,* 291 (1861).

Ceanothus ochraceus Suessenguth

ochre-leaf ceanothus

Subgenus *Ceanothus.* Erect shrubs, 0.5–2 m tall; crown relatively open, mound-like to hemispheric, sometimes flat-topped; main branches erect to ascending; distal branchlets flexible, their internodes 15–24 mm long, smooth, brown, tomentulose, often becoming glabrous; mature bark dark gray or grayish brown. Stipules thin, deciduous. Leaves alternate, evergreen, evenly spaced; petioles 2–3 mm long. Leaf blades 8–17 mm long, 3–7 mm wide, elliptic, flat, somewhat leathery, usually one-veined, sometimes three-veined from the base, the basal pair of veins then extending halfway to the leaf tip; upper surfaces green, short-villous, sometimes sparsely tomentulose; lower surfaces white-tomentulose but becoming rust-colored with age; tips obtuse;

Ceanothus ochraceus

bases obtuse to rounded; margins plane, sometimes thick and becoming revolute near the base, entire to serrulate; teeth 9–29 per leaf, with narrowly conic glands when young. Inflorescences in upper axils of 1- or 2-year-old branchlets, subumbellate to racemose, sometimes paniculate, 11–32 mm long; peduncles 8–36 mm long; peduncles and rachises short-villous to tomentulose. Pedicels 5–7 mm long, puberulent, sometimes becoming glabrous; sepals and petals five; perianth and disks white, sometimes bluish or pink-tinged. Fruits 3–4 mm wide, globose to weakly lobed, somewhat viscid when young, dark brown to black; lobes smooth to weakly ridged; horns absent. Seeds 1.5–2 mm long, subglobose to broadly ovoid, brown. Flowering July and August (to October); fruiting August–November; reproducing primarily from seeds, sometimes from basal shoots.

Rocky or well-drained soils derived from various substrates; open sites in oak-pine woodlands and forests; 1,790–2,670 m (5,900–8,800 feet); mountains of Sonora, Chihuahua, and Durango south to Michoacán, Puebla, Vera Cruz, and Oaxaca, Mexico; reproducing primarily from seeds.

Ceanothus ochraceus is closely related to *C. caeruleus*, which differs primarily by its larger leaves, larger inflorescences, and deep blue flowers (McMinn 1942). Further studies are needed to determine if the two taxa are best treated separately or as part of a single species.

References. *Ceanothus ochracea* Suessenguth, *Repertorium Specierum Novarum Regni Vegetabilis* 49: 11 (1940; Suessenguth's use of the feminine *ochracea* was incorrect); *C. azureus* Desfontaines var. *parvifolius* S. Watson, *Proceedings of the American Academy of Arts and Sciences* 23: 270 (1888); *C. parvifolius* (S. Watson) Rose, *Contributions from the U.S. National Herbarium* 12: 284 (1909; this name is an illegitimate, later homonym because it is preceded by *C. parvifolius* Trelease 1888).

Ceanothus oliganthus Nuttall

hairy ceanothus

Subgenus *Ceanothus.* Erect shrubs, often arborescent, 1.5–3.5 m tall; crown open to somewhat dense, obovoid; main branches erect to ascending; distal branchlets somewhat flexible to rigid but not spine-like, their internodes 7–19 mm long, smooth to rough, grayish green to reddish brown, densely to moderately short-villous; mature bark brown or grayish brown. Stipules thin, deciduous. Leaves alternate, evergreen, evenly spaced; petioles 3–7 mm long. Leaf blades 11–30 mm long, 8–25 mm wide, ovate to elliptic, flat, somewhat leathery, three-veined from the base; upper surfaces dark green, almost glabrous to sparsely short-villous, the veins often more densely short-villous; lower surfaces pale green, sometimes glaucous, sparsely to densely short-villous, especially on the veins; tips acute to obtuse; bases rounded to subcordate; margins plane, denticulate; teeth 19–71 per leaf, usually with broadly conic to subglobose glands. Inflorescences terminal or in upper axils of 1- or 2-year-old branchlets, racemose, sometimes umbel-like, 13–35 mm long; peduncles 5–17 mm long; peduncles and rachises puberulent to short-villous. Pedicels 4–11 mm long, glabrous; sepals and petals five; perianth and disks pale to dark or purplish blue, rarely white. Fruits 4–7 mm wide, weakly to deeply lobed, slightly viscid when young, brown to dark brown; lobes smooth, sometimes somewhat wrinkled, ridged at or slightly above the middle or with a dorsal, glandular bulge; horns absent. Seeds 2.5–3 mm long, subglobose to broadly ovoid, brown to dark brown. Flowering February–June; fruiting May–August; reproducing primarily from seeds, sometimes from basal shoots in variety *sorediatus* (Jim brush).

Rocky slopes, ridges, and flats on substrates derived from various substrates; chaparral, mixed evergreen forest, oak woodland, and open sites in pine forest; 160–1,900 m (520–6,300 feet); Coast Ranges, western Transverse Ranges, and Peninsular Ranges of California south to the Sierra Juárez, Baja California, and Volcán las Tres Vírgenes, Baja California Sur (León de la Luz et al. 1995). Most plants assignable to the three varieties can be separated by using the accompanying key.

Varieties of *Ceanothus oliganthus*

1 Ovaries and young fruits puberulent, the hairs deciduous with age; mature fruit often appearing wrinkled; Palomar Mountain and Cuyamaca and Laguna Mountains of southern California and the mountains of Baja California, Mexico . . . *C. oliganthus* var. *orcuttii*
1 Ovaries and young fruits glabrous; mature fruits usually smooth except sometimes with a dorsal glandular ridge or bulge; Coast Ranges, Transverse Ranges, and northern Peninsular Ranges of California 2
2 Branchlet internodes and upper surfaces of leaf blades puberulent to short-villous . . . . . .
. . . .*C. oliganthus* var. *oliganthus*
2 Branchlet internodes and upper surfaces of leaf blades subglabrous to sparsely puberulent . . . . *C. oliganthus* var. *sorediatus*

Although McMinn (1942) treated varieties *oliganthus* and *sorediatus* as separate species, Hoover (1966, 1970) drew attention to substantial overlapping variation between the two forms throughout the range of the species, including the southern North Coast Range, Santa Cruz Mountains, and southern Santa Lucia Range. Intergradation between the two forms in the Santa Ynez Mountains may have led to the recognition of *Ceanothus hirsutus* and *C. divaricatus* (McMinn 1942), although the latter may also be attributable to hybrids involving *C. leucodermis.* Populations of *C. oliganthus* in this region also tend to have a higher frequency of glaucous lower leaf surfaces and somewhat short and rigid lateral branches, traits that may have been inherited from *C. leucodermis* or *C. incanus,* depending on geographical distribution. Plants with pubescent ovaries are referable to variety *orcuttii* and occur on Palomar Mountain and in the Santa Ana, Cuyamaca, and Laguna Mountains of southern California, south to the Sierra Juárez of Baja California. Pubescent ovaries do not occur elsewhere in *Ceanothus.* Some plants in the Santa Ana Mountains cannot be clearly assigned to either *C. tomentosus* or *C. oliganthus* and are presumably hybrids.

According to McMinn (1942), putatively related taxa include *Cea-*

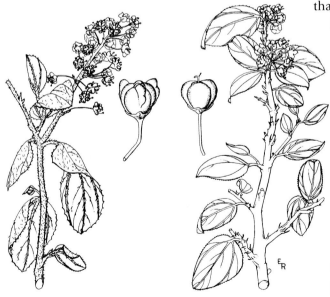

Ceanothus oliganthus var. *oliganthus,* left, and var. *sorediatus,* right

nothus tomentosus, C. lemmonii, and *C. impressus* var. *nipomensis. Ceanothus tomentosus* appears to be the closest relative, differing primarily by having tomentulose lower leaf blades, but it is sometimes difficult to separate some populations from variety *sorediatus* in southern California. *Ceanothus lemmonii* differs conspicuously by its low-growing (less than 1 m tall), often flat-topped habit and glaucous internodes. *Ceanothus impressus* var. *nipomensis* differs primarily by having upper leaf surfaces with furrows coincident with the primary and secondary veins.

McMinn (1942) reported naturally occurring hybrids with *Ceanothus tomentosus* and *C. thyrsiflorus.* Putative hybrids with *C. leucodermis* in the San Gabriel Mountains and with *C. integerrimus* in the Santa Lucia Range are documented by specimens at the Rancho Santa Ana Botanic Garden herbarium.

References. *Ceanothus oliganthus* Nuttall in Torrey & A. Gray, *Flora of North America* 1: 266 (1838); *C. hirsutus* Nuttall, *idem* 1: 266 (1838); *C. divaricatus* Nuttall, *idem* 1: 266–267 (1838); *C. oliganthus* Nuttall var. *hirsutus* (Nuttall) K. Brandegee, *Proceedings of the California Academy of Sciences,* series 2, 4: 197 (1894).

Ceanothus oliganthus var. *orcuttii* (Parry) Jepson, *Flora of California* 2: 473 (1936), based on *C. orcuttii* Parry, *Proceedings of the Davenport Academy of Sciences* 5: 194 (1889); *C. hirsutus* Nuttall var. *orcuttii* (Parry) Trelease in A. Gray, *Synoptical Flora of North America* 1: 414 (1897).

Ceanothus oliganthus var. *sorediatus* (Hooker & Arnott) Hoover, *Leaflets of Western Botany* 10: 349 (1966), based on *C. sorediatus* Hooker & Arnott, *Botany of Captain Beechey's Voyage,* Supplement 328 (1838); *C. intricatus* Parry, *Proc. Davenport Acad. Sci.* 5: 168 (1889).

Ceanothus ophiochilus S. Boyd, T. Ross & L. Arnseth

Vail Lake ceanothus

Subgenus *Cerastes.* Erect shrubs, 1–2 m tall; crown open, hemispheric to broadly obovoid, sometimes flat-topped; main branches ascending to widely spreading; distal branchlets somewhat flexible to stiff, their internodes 3–11 mm long, smooth to slightly angled near the tips when young, reddish brown to gray, glabrous; mature bark gray. Stipules thick, persistent, 1–1.5 mm wide. Leaves opposite, evergreen, evenly spaced, sometimes clustered on older branches; petioles less than 1 mm long. Leaf blades 3–7 mm long, 1.5–3 mm wide, narrowly oblanceolate to narrowly obovate, thick, stiff, often folded lengthwise and concave above, obscurely one-veined; upper surfaces pale to yellowish green, glabrous, often slightly folded, concave above and convex below; lower surfaces yellowish green, appearing glabrous except for microscopic tomentulose patches between the secondary veins; tips toothed, obtuse, or rounded; bases tapered; margins plane, usually entire, rarely with a few,

Ceanothus ophiochilus,
leaf detail ×2

obscure, spinulose teeth. Inflorescences terminal or in upper axils of 1- or 2-year-old branchlets, 6–11 mm long, subumbellate, sessile to subsessile; peduncles 1–4 mm long; peduncles and rachises glabrous to sparsely puberulent. Pedicels 3–5 mm long, glabrous; sepals and petals five; perianth and disks pale blue to pink-tinged. Fruits 3–3.5 mm wide, globose, brown, smooth, sometimes with minute horns. Seeds about 2 mm wide, broadly ellipsoid to ovoid, weakly compressed, dark brown. Flowering March and April; fruiting June and July; reproducing entirely from seeds.

Outcrops and rocky soils derived from igneous (pyroxenite) substrates; chaparral; west of Vail Lake and at 600–640 m (2,000–2,100 feet) on northern slopes of Agua Tibia Mountain, southern Riverside County, California. A species of special conservation concern because of its limited distribution, potential habitat loss, and hybridization with *Ceanothus crassifolius*.

Ceanothus ophiochilus is one of the most geographically restricted and rarest species in the genus. Boyd et al. (1991) suggested a relationship to *C. greggii* vars. *vestitus* and *perplexans* (both referred to here as part of *C. vestitus*). The color of the leaves is similar to those in typical *C. perplexans*, but the leaf shape approaches that of the smallest leaves in typical *C. vestitus*, both forms differing by the presence of tomentulose or short-curly hairs on their leaf surfaces, at least when young. A relationship to *C. bolensis*, based on overall leaf morphology, should not be discounted. *Ceanothus ophiochilus* hybridizes with *C. crassifolius* (Boyd et al. 1991).

Reference. *Ceanothus ophiochilus* S. Boyd, T. Ross & L. Arnseth, *Phytologia* 70: 29 (1991).

Ceanothus otayensis McMinn
Otay Mountain ceanothus

Ceanothus otayensis

Subgenus *Cerastes*. Erect shrubs, 1–2 m tall; crown open to somewhat dense, hemispheric to obovoid; main branches erect to ascending; distal branchlets stiff, their internodes 5–16 mm long, smooth, grayish, tomentulose; mature bark gray to grayish brown. Stipules thick, persistent, 2–3 mm wide, often confluent on young branches. Leaves opposite, evergreen, evenly spaced, sessile or petioles 1–2 mm long. Leaf blades 6–12 mm long, 4–10 mm wide, broadly elliptic to obovate, flat to somewhat wavy, thick, stiff, one-veined; upper surfaces dull green, minutely papillose, glabrous to sparsely puberulent; lower surfaces white- to brown-tomentulose when young, becoming glabrous except for microscopic tomentulose patches between the secondary veins; tips truncate, notched, or sharply toothed; bases tapered to obtuse; margins plane, thick to revolute, entire to sharply dentate above the middle; teeth three to five per leaf, these often clustered near the tip, spinu-lose. Inflorescences terminal or in upper axils of 1- or 2-year-old branchlets, umbellate, 6–16 mm long, sessile to subsessile; peduncles 1–4 mm long; rachises and peduncles puberulent to tomentulose. Pedicels 6–8 mm long, puberulent; sepals and petals five; perianth and disks light to deep blue. Fruits 4–6 mm wide, subglobose to weakly lobed, brown, smooth, ridges absent, sometimes weakly horned. Seeds 2.5–3 mm long, broadly ellipsoid to ovoid, weakly compressed, black. Flowering January–April; fruiting June–August; reproducing entirely from seeds.

Rocky slopes, often on volcanic or metamorphic substrates; chaparral, 510–1,100 m (1,670–3,700 feet). Otay and San Miguel Mountains, southern San Diego County, California. A species of special conservation concern because of its limited distribution and potential habitat loss.

Ceanothus otayensis was described as a hybrid by McMinn, who suggested that it is intermediate to *C. crassifolius* and *C. greggii* (plants from California treated here as *C. vestitus*). However, neither of the parental species occurs with the species (Boyd and Keeley 2003). Variation in populations of *C. otayensis* appears relatively uniform, and plants grown from seed do not differ from maternal plants. Its closest relatives appear to be *C. bolensis* and *C. vestitus,* with which it shares short internodes and prominent stipules.

Reference. *Ceanothus ×otayensis* McMinn, *Ceanothus,* 273 (1942).

Ceanothus papillosus Torrey & A. Gray
wartleaf ceanothus, Tranquillon Mountain ceanothus, Rowe ceanothus

Subgenus *Ceanothus.* Erect shrubs, 1–3.5 m tall; crown open, hemispheric to broadly obovoid, sometimes flat-topped; main branches ascending to widely spreading; distal branchlets somewhat flexible to stiff, their internodes 15–28 mm long, smooth, dark green or purplish green, densely tomentose; mature bark grayish brown. Stipules thin, deciduous to somewhat persistent. Leaves alternate, evergreen, evenly spaced, sometimes clustered; petioles 1–3 mm long. Leaf blades (8–)11–50 mm long, (2–)4–12 mm wide, linear to oblong, sometimes narrowly elliptic, convex above, concave below, one-veined, leathery; upper surfaces green, glabrous, sparsely pubescent, viscid, with sessile to short-stalked globose glands; lower surfaces pale green, densely short-villous to tomentulose, especially on the veins; tips obtuse to truncate or notched; bases rounded;

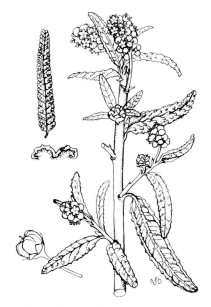

Ceanothus papillosus,
leaf details ×3

margins revolute, obscurely denticulate; teeth 17–31 per leaf, often tipped with short-stalked globose glands. Inflorescences terminal or in upper axils of 1- or 2-year-old branchlets, racemose, dense, 10–50 mm long; peduncles 10–35 mm long; peduncles and rachises densely short-villous. Pedicels 3–7 mm long, usually glabrous, sometimes puberulent; sepals and petals five; perianth and disks deep blue or purplish blue. Fruits 2–3 mm wide, lobed, somewhat viscid, dark brown to black; lobes smooth, weakly ridged; horns absent. Seeds about 2 mm long, broadly ellipsoid to ovoid, black. Flowering March–May; fruiting May–July; reproducing primarily from seeds.

Slopes and ridges on rocky soils derived from various geological substrates; chaparral and open sites in mixed evergreen and redwood forests; 25–1,510 m (65–5,000 feet); South Coast Range from San Francisco south to the western Transverse Ranges and Santa Ana Mountains of California, and Cerro Bola, northern Baja California, Mexico.

Most regional and local floras (e.g., Abrams 1951, Munz 1959, Schmidt 1993, Matthews 1997) have separated *Ceanothus papillosus* into two varieties (*papillosus* versus *roweanus*) on the presence of obtuse versus truncate or notched leaf tips. Obtuse tips are usually correlated with relatively broad, oblong leaves, and truncate to notched tips with shorter, narrowly oblong or linear leaves. However, McMinn originally described variety *roweanus* as different from the typical form by its more compact, spreading habit, having "branches arched and in somewhat horizontal sprays," without reference to leaf apices. In his *Illustrated Manual of California Shrubs*, McMinn also added that specimens "gathered throughout the range of the species show this character" (i.e., linear leaves with truncate apices), implying that the leaf apex is not a reliable diagnostic trait. However, he inexplicably later expanded the description (1942), using the phrases "apices usually not retuse" versus "apices usually truncate to retuse" (i.e., not notched versus notched) to separate variety *papillosus* from variety *roweanus.* Some plants from throughout the range of the species in the South Coast Range and western Transverse Ranges have oblong leaves with obtuse tips borne on shoots produced early in the season, followed by narrower shorter leaves with truncate to notched tips borne later in the season. On other plants, both obtuse, truncate to notched, and intermediate leaf blade tips can be found on the same branch. Thus variety *roweanus,* in the original sense of McMinn, should be applied only to low-growing, relatively compact plants less than 1.5 m tall and without reference to differences in leaf morphology. This form appears restricted to coastal slopes in the western Santa Ynez Mountains of California.

Prostrate plants less than 30 cm tall, with leaves 6–12 mm long and truncate to somewhat notched tips, were considered by McMinn (1942) as part of *Ceanothus papillosus* var. *roweanus* but were later recognized as *C. hearstiorum* by Hoover and Roof (1966). *Ceanothus dentatus* also appears to be a close relative, although it lacks glands on the upper surface of the leaf blades.

Hybrids between *Ceanothus papillosus* and *C. thyrsiflorus* var. *thyrsiflorus* occur in the Santa Cruz Mountains and were named *C. ×regius* (Jepson) McMinn. Some advanced-generation derivatives of *C. ×regius*, with weakly papillose leaf surfaces and narrowly elliptic leaves, have been confused with variety *papillosus*. McMinn (1942) reported hybrids with *C. integerrimus* and *C. oliganthus* in the Santa Cruz Mountains. Hybrids between *C. papillosus* and *C. oliganthus* also occur in the eastern Santa Ynez Mountains of Ventura County, based on specimens at the Santa Barbara Botanic Garden herbarium, and are probably the source of 'Wheeler Canyon'.

References. *Ceanothus papillosus* Torrey & A. Gray, *Flora of North America* 1: 268 (1838); *C. dentatus* Torrey & A. Gray var. *papillosus* (Torrey & A. Gray) K. Brandegee, *Proceedings of the California Academy of Sciences*, series 2, 4: 203 (1894).

Ceanothus papillosus var. *roweanus* McMinn, *Madroño* 5: 13 (1939); *C. papillosus* subsp. *roweanus* (McMinn) Munz, *Flora of Southern California*, 735 (1974).

Ceanothus parryi Trelease

Parry's ceanothus

Subgenus *Ceanothus*. Erect shrubs, 2–6 m tall; crown somewhat open, hemispheric to obovoid; main branches ascending to spreading; distal branchlets flexible, their internodes 10–22 mm long, smooth to sometimes angled, grayish green to brown, often loosely white-tomentose when young, becoming glabrous; mature bark dark grayish brown to brown. Stipules thin, deciduous. Leaves alternate, evergreen, evenly spaced, sometimes clustered at the upper nodes; petioles 1–5 mm long. Leaf blades 12–33(–50) mm long, 5–15(–20) mm wide, elliptic to somewhat oblong, sometimes narrowly ovate, flat, thin to somewhat leathery, usually three-veined from the base, sometimes appearing one-veined, the lower lateral veins obscured by the revolute margins; upper surfaces dark green, glabrous; lower surfaces dull or pale green, villous to loosely tomentulose or cobwebby, especially when young, becoming subglabrous; tips obtuse; bases rounded; margins revolute, sometimes entire above the middle, obscurely denticulate with 21–36 teeth per leaf and minute conic glands when young. Inflorescences racemose to paniculate, dense to somewhat open, 32–72 mm long; peduncles 35–74 mm long, somewhat leafy, terminal or in upper axils of 1- or 2-year-old branchlets; rachises and peduncles puberulent to short-villous or tomentulose. Pedicels 4–9 mm long, glabrous; sepals and petals five; perianth and disks deep blue. Fruits 2–3 mm wide, lobed, brown; lobes smooth,

Ceanothus parryi

ridges and horns absent. Seeds 1.5–2 mm long, subglobose to broadly ovoid, dark brown. Flowering April and May; fruiting June and July; reproducing primarily from seeds, sometimes from basal shoots.

Rocky slopes and flats on soils derived from various substrates; chaparral and open sites or clearings in mixed evergreen and redwood forest; 30–760 m (100–2,500 feet); outer Coast Ranges in California from Humboldt County south to Napa County, and in west-central Oregon in Lane and Benton Counties.

Similarity in habit, somewhat angled branchlets, and leaf and fruit morphology suggest a relationship to *Ceanothus thyrsiflorus* (McMinn 1942), which differs by its greenish, glabrous to sparsely puberulent branchlets, darker, thicker leaves, and puberulent to short-villous lower leaf surfaces, which bear prominent veins. *Ceanothus parryi* also resembles *C. cyaneus*, which differs primarily by its subglabrous lower leaf surfaces and the absence of revolute leaf margins. McMinn reported naturally occurring hybrids with *C. foliosus* and *C. thyrsiflorus*, and putative hybrids with *C. incanus* are represented by specimens at the Humboldt State University herbarium.

References. *Ceanothus parryi* Trelease, *Proceedings of the California Academy of Sciences,* series 2, 1: 109 (1888); *C. integerrimus* var. *parryi* (Trelease) K. Brandegee, *idem,* series 2, 4: 183 (1894).

Ceanothus parvifolius Trelease
littleleaf ceanothus

Subgenus *Ceanothus.* Spreading shrubs, usually less than 1.5 m tall; crown relatively open, broadly ovate to mound-like and somewhat flat-topped; main branches weakly

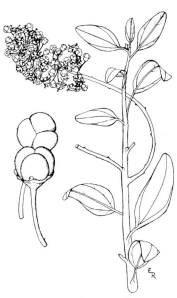

Ceanothus parvifolius

ascending to widely spreading; distal branchlets flexible, their internodes 5–19 mm long, smooth, green, sometimes reddish, tomentulose, often becoming glabrous with age; mature bark reddish brown to brown. Stipules thin, deciduous. Leaves alternate, deciduous, evenly spaced, sometimes clustered at the upper nodes; petioles 1.5–4 mm long. Leaf blades 8–21 mm long, 4–11 mm wide, elliptic to narrowly elliptic, flat, somewhat leathery, three-veined from the base; upper surfaces shiny, green, glabrous; lower surfaces pale green, glabrous, the veins sometimes strigulose; tips and bases obtuse to rounded; margins plane, entire, sometimes denticulate near the tip and with conic glands when very young. Inflorescences in upper axils of 1- to 3-year-old branchlets, often erect, racemose to paniculate, open to somewhat dense, 19–38 mm long; peduncles 25–51 mm long; peduncles and rachises glabrous. Pedicels 4–9 mm long, glabrous; sepals and petals five; perianth and disks pale to deep blue. Fruits 3.5–5 mm wide, globose to weakly lobed, somewhat viscid when young, brown to dark brown; lobes smooth, ridges and horns absent. Seeds 2.5–3 mm long, ovoid to orbicular in outline, slightly compressed, brown. Flowering May–July; fruiting July and August; reproducing from seeds, and from basal shoots following fire.

Ridges, slopes, and flats on soils derived from igneous or metamorphic substrates; open sites in conifer forests; 1,360–2,210 m (4,500–7,300 feet); western slope of the Sierra Nevada, from Plumas County south to Tulare County, California.

Ceanothus parvifolius near Dutch Oven Creek, Sierra Nevada, Madera County, California

Ceanothus parvifolius displays an interesting branching pattern with the main branches ascending and often radiating from a vertical central axis. This branching pattern can also be seen in relatively young plants of *C. cordulatus, C. lemmonii,* and *C. leucodermis.* Molecular analyses suggest relationships to *C. cyaneus* and *C. leucodermis* (Hardig et al. 2000). Coile (1988) suggested relationships with *C. martinii* and *C. microphyllus,* but overall morphology suggests that *C. parvifolius* may also be closely related to *C. integerrimus* (McMinn 1942), which differs by its erect stature and larger leaves and fruits.

References. *Ceanothus parvifolius* Trelease, *Proceedings of the California Academy of Sciences,* series 2, 1: 110 (1888); *C. integerrimus* Hooker & Arnott var. *parviflorus* S. Watson, *Proceedings of the American Academy of Arts and Sciences* 10: 334 (1875). Watson's use of the epithet *parviflorus* may have been a typographical error because his diagnostic description referred to its smaller leaves as compared to *C. integerrimus* without mention of flower size (*parviflorus,* "small flowers," versus *parvifolius,* "small leaves"). Brewer and Watson (1876) used the name variety *parvifolius* in referring to the same taxon but without any explanation for the change in spelling. Trelease treated *C. parvifolius* as a species and erroneously cited Watson's original name as "*C. integerrimus,* var. ×*parvifolius.*" Regardless of the disparity between Watson's or Brewer and Watson's names, one may also consider Trelease's use of *parvifolius* as a new name at the species level.

Ceanothus pauciflorus de Candolle
woolly ceanothus, Gregg's ceanothus

Subgenus *Cerastes.* Erect shrubs, sometimes arborescent, 0.2–3 m tall; crown somewhat open to dense, hemispheric to broadly obovoid, sometimes flat-topped, some-

Ceanothus pauciflorus

times intricately branched; main branches ascending to widely spreading; distal branchlets flexible to stiff, their internodes 5–15(–20) mm long, smooth, glaucous, gray to grayish brown or almost white, curly-puberulent to tomentulose, becoming glabrous; mature bark gray to grayish brown. Stipules thick, persistent, 1–3 mm wide. Leaves opposite, evergreen, evenly spaced, sometimes clustered at the branch tips; petioles 1–3 mm long, puberulent to tomentulose, sometimes becoming glabrous. Leaf blades 5–14(–19) mm long, 3–14(–19) mm wide, oblanceolate to elliptic or broadly obovate, somewhat flat to convex above to folded lengthwise or concave above, sometimes flat, thick, stiff, one-veined; upper surfaces green to grayish green, sometimes yellowish green, appressed-puberulent or curly-puberulent when young, becoming glabrous; lower surfaces pale to grayish green, densely white- or brown-tomentulose or curly-puberulent, veins often strigulose; tips acute to obtuse, sometimes rounded or weakly truncate; bases tapered to obtuse or rounded; margins plane, thick to weakly revolute, entire, sometimes remotely denticulate near the base or unevenly denticulate with three to six weakly spinulose teeth. Inflorescences terminal or in upper axils of 1- to 3-year-old branchlets, umbellate to subumbellate, 5–14 mm long; peduncles 2–5 mm long; peduncles and rachises puberulent to tomentulose. Pedicels 3–8 mm long, glabrous, sometimes puberulent; sepals and petals five; perianth and disks white, sometimes bluish or pink-tinged. Fruits 3.5–6 mm wide, globose to weakly lobed, brown; lobes smooth, sometimes faintly ridged or weakly horned near the middle; horns somewhat erect to spreading, 0.5–2 mm long, smooth to slightly wrinkled. Seeds 2.5–4 mm wide, ellipsoid to broadly ovoid, slightly compressed, dark brown to black. Flowering February–June; fruiting April–August; reproducing entirely from seeds.

Rocky slopes, ridges, and outcrops derived from various geological substrates; desert and montane shrublands, and open sites in woodlands or forests, 900–2,200 m (2,960–7,200 feet); apparently in southwestern Texas and at widely scattered localities in Mexico from Sonora, Chihuahua, Coahuila, and Nuevo León south to Tamaulipas and San Luis Potosí.

Although Johnston (1974) suggested that the name *Ceanothus pauciflorus* could not be satisfactorily applied to any known species, McVaugh (1998) presented a convincing discussion that this name should be used for plants previously referred to as *C. greggii*. Asa Gray based his description of *C. greggii* on specimens with elliptic leaves 5–8 mm long and with persistently tomentulose lower leaf surfaces. The leaf blades are convex above and usually have entire, thick to revolute margins, although some plants have remotely denticulate leaves. Marcus Jones's description of *C. greggii* var. *lanuginosus* was based on specimens with slightly longer leaves (6–11 mm) but with the same shape, margin, and pubescence. However, McMinn (1942) recognized *C. lanuginosus* as a distinct species, even though its leaf morphology overlaps in size and shape with that of typical *C. greggii*. Both forms have somewhat convex upper leaf surfaces and thickened to revolute leaf margins. Plants with the features of typical *C. lanuginosus* are apparently restricted to Sonora, Chihuahua, Coahuila, and Nuevo León south to Tamaulipas and San Luis Potosí, Mexico. Some plants from several sites in the same region, with remotely denticulate leaf margins, appear to match the original description and type of *C. pauciflorus*. Plants with grayish green leaves, leaf blades somewhat folded lengthwise or concave above, and entire to remotely toothed, elliptic to obovate blades have been treated as either *C. vestitus* or *C. greggii* var. *vestitus*. The pubescence on both surfaces of the leaf blades varies from short-tomentulose to moderately curly-puberulent, especially when young, and with strigulose veins on the lower surfaces. Such plants provide evidence for intergradation between *C. pauciflorus* and *C. vestitus*, especially in northern Mexico.

McMinn (1942) considered *Ceanothus cuneatus* the closest relative, but Howell (1940), who treated *C. greggii, C. perplexans,* and *C. vestitus* as distinct species, suggested relationships to *C. crassifolius, C. megacarpus,* and *C. verrucosus*. Howell also correctly suggested that plants referable to typical *C. greggii* are probably restricted to Mexico. Lower leaf surfaces in typical *C. pauciflorus* are similar to those of *C. crassifolius,* but the pubescence of *C. cuneatus, C. megacarpus,* and *C. verrucosus,* when present, is generally composed of relatively straight, often appressed hairs.

References. *Ceanothus pauciflorus* Sessé & Moçiño ex A. P. de Candolle, *Prodromus Systematis Naturalis Regni Vegetabilis* 2: 33 (1825); *C. greggii* A. Gray, *Plantae Wrightianae* 2: 228 (1853); *C. verrucosus* Nuttall var. *greggii* (A. Gray) K. Brandegee, *Proceedings of the California Academy of Sciences,* series 2, 4: 208 (1894); *C. greggii* var. *lanuginosus* M. E. Jones, *idem,* series 2, 5: 629 (1895); *C. lanuginosus* (M. E. Jones) Rose, *Contributions from the U.S. National Herbarium* 12: 284 (1909).

Ceanothus pinetorum Coville

Kern Plateau ceanothus, Coville's ceanothus

Subgenus *Cerastes.* Erect to semierect shrubs, 0.2–1.5 m tall, to 2 m across; crown dense, mat- to mound-like; main branches weakly ascending to spreading, sometimes curved, sometimes rooting at some nodes near the base; distal branchlets stiff, their internodes 12–25 mm long, smooth, reddish brown, becoming gray and somewhat glaucous, glabrous to sparsely puberulent; mature bark brown to grayish brown or glaucous. Stipules thick, persistent, 1–2 mm wide, often confluent. Leaves opposite, evergreen, evenly spaced or clustered at nodes; petioles 1–3 mm long. Leaf blades 10–19 mm long, 8–17 mm wide, broadly elliptic or orbicular, flat to some what folded (concave above), thick, stiff, one-veined; upper surfaces green, glabrous; lower surfaces pale green, appearing glabrous except for microscopic tomentulose patches between the

Ceanothus pinetorum, Trinity Mountains, northern California

secondary veins, the veins sometimes sparsely strigulose; tips rounded; bases rounded; margins plane to slightly revolute, denticulate to dentate; teeth 9–15 per leaf, weakly spinulose. Inflorescences terminal or in upper axils of 1- or 2-year-old branchlets, umbellate, sessile to subsessile, 12–21 mm long; peduncles 1–5 mm long; peduncles and rachises sparsely puberulent. Pedicels 5–8 mm long, glabrous; sepals and petals five; perianth and disks blue to pale blue or bluish lavender. Fruits 6–9 mm wide, globose to weakly lobed, brown to dark brown; lobes smooth to slightly wrinkled, slightly ridged, horned above the middle; horns erect, 1–2 mm long, sometimes weakly developed, wrinkled. Seeds 3–4.5 mm long, broadly ovoid, dorsally convex, dark brown. Flowering May and June; fruiting June and July; reproducing primarily from seeds.

Rocky to gravelly soils primarily derived from granitic substrates, sometimes ultramafic substrates, slopes and flats, open sites in conifer forest; 1,630–2,570 m (5,400–8,500 feet); Greenhorn Mountains and Kern Plateau of the southern Sierra Nevada, Tulare and Kern Counties, and in the southern Trinity Mountains of Trinity and Shasta Counties, California.

McMinn (1942) stated that *Ceanothus pinetorum* "does not seem to be very closely related to any other species" but pointed out that stipule size and some fruit and leaf traits resemble those of *C. jepsonii*. Howell (1940) suggested that *C. pinetorum* is more closely related to *C. prostratus* than to *C. jepsonii,* and Jepson (1936) suggested a relationship to *C. greggii* var. *perplexans* (i.e., *C. vestitus* as it is treated here). The differences in number of perianth parts, flower size, and weakly developed teeth exclude *C. jepsonii* as a close relative. The strigulose hairs of the leaf surfaces are like those of *C. cuneatus* and *C. prostratus* rather than the short-curly hairs in some forms of *C. vestitus*, including plants referable to *C. perplexans*. Plants from the southern Trinity Mountains, where it reportedly intergrades with *C. prostratus*, often have fruits with weakly developed horns.

References. *Ceanothus pinetorum* Coville, *Contributions from the U.S. National Herbarium* 4: 80 (1893); *C. prostratus* Bentham var. *pinetorum* (Coville) K. Brandegee, *Proceedings of the California Academy of Sciences*, series 2, 4: 211 (1894).

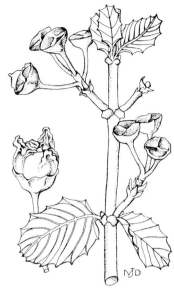

Ceanothus pinetorum

Ceanothus prostratus Bentham
mahala mat

Subgenus *Cerastes*. Prostrate, mat-like, sometimes mound-like shrubs, usually less than 30 cm tall but often 1–2.5 m wide; crown dense to somewhat open; main branches spreading, rooting at the nodes, sometimes ascending; distal branchlets flexible to somewhat stiff, their internodes 5–18 mm long, smooth, reddish brown, puberulent to glabrous; mature bark grayish brown. Stipules thick, persistent, 1–2 mm wide. Leaves opposite, evergreen, evenly spaced; petioles 1–3 mm long. Leaf blades 9–30 mm long, 5–16 mm wide, elliptic to obovate, flat, thick, stiff, one-veined; upper surfaces dark green, glabrous; lower surfaces pale green, appearing glabrous except for microscopic tomentulose patches between the secondary veins, veins strigulose; tips rounded; bases tapered; margins plane, sometimes thickened, usually dentate to serrate or serrulate above the upper two-thirds of the blades; teeth three to nine per leaf, spinulose. Inflorescences terminal or in upper axils of 1- or 2-year-old branchlets, sometimes erect, umbellate, 5–17 mm long, subsessile peduncles 4–11 mm long; peduncles and rachises sparsely puberulent. Pedicels 7–14 mm long, glabrous; sepals and petals five; perianth and disks blue or bluish lavender, rarely white. Fruits 6–9 mm wide, globose to weakly lobed, dark brown; lobes smooth to slightly wrinkled, weakly ridged, horned above the middle; horns 1–2 mm long, erect, conspicuously wrinkled. Seeds 3.5–4 mm long, broadly ovoid, slightly compressed. Flowering April–June; fruiting June–August; reproducing from seeds, sometimes from basal shoots following fire, or by layering.

Rocky or gravelly soils usually derived from igneous or metamorphic substrates; slopes and flats, open sites in conifer forest; 790–2,720 m (2,600–9,000 feet). Cascade

Range, Klamath Mountains, and the Sierra Nevada, from Yakima County, Washington, and Adams County, Idaho, south to Alpine County, California, and Carson City, Nevada.

Plants with relatively large, prominently denticulate leaves with six to nine teeth have been called variety *laxus*. Plants with white flowers in western Nevada were named forma *albiflorus*. McMinn (1942) considered several low-growing species as close relatives, including *Ceanothus pinetorum, C. pumilus,* and *C. divergens. Ceanothus pinetorum* differs by its broadly elliptic to orbicular leaf blades, relatively weakly toothed leaf margins, and spreading, aerial stems. *Ceanothus pumilus* differs primarily by its glaucous internodes, smaller leaves, and smaller fruits. McMinn's *C. prostratus* var. *occidentalis,* treated here as part of *C. divergens,* differs from typical *C. prostratus* by its smaller and narrower leaf blades with margins sharply toothed at or above the middle, and fruits 4–5 mm wide.

Plants from a single population in the Sierra Nevada near Lake Tahoe were named *Ceanothus serrulatus* McMinn, which is now considered to be a hybrid, *C. prostratus* × *C. cordulatus.* McMinn (1942) reported hybrids between *C. prostratus* and *C. velutinus* from several localities in the southern Cascade Range and northern Sierra Nevada, including them under the name *C.* ×*rugosus* E. L. Greene. Hybrids with *C. cuneatus* were named *C.* ×*flexilis* E. L. Greene ex McMinn, and putative hybrids with *C. cuneatus* or *C. vestitus, C.* ×*bakeri* E. L. Greene ex McMinn.

Ceanothus prostratus

Ceanothus prostratus, Scott Mountains, Siskiyou County, California

References. *Ceanothus prostratus* Bentham, *Plantae Hartwegianae*, 302 (1849); *C. prostratus* var. *laxus* Jepson, *Manual of the Flowering Plants of California*, 624 (1925); *C. prostratus* f. *albiflorus* J. T. Howell, *Mentzelia* 1: 7 (1975).

Ceanothus pumilus E. L. Greene
Siskiyou mat, Siskiyou ceanothus

Subgenus *Cerastes*. Prostrate shrubs, mat- to mound-like and flat-topped, less than 50 cm tall but often 1–2 m wide; crown dense to somewhat open, sometimes intricately branched; main branches spreading, sometimes rooting at remote nodes; distal branchlets flexible to somewhat stiff, their internodes 5–11 mm long, smooth, reddish brown, puberulent to tomentulose; mature bark grayish brown. Stipules thick, persistent, 0.5–1 mm wide. Leaves opposite, evergreen, evenly spaced; petioles 1–2 mm long. Leaf blades 5–14 mm long, 3–5 mm wide, oblanceolate to oblong, flat to slightly folded lengthwise and concave above, thick, stiff, one-veined; upper surfaces green, glabrous; lower surfaces pale green, appearing glabrous except for microscopic tomentulose patches between the secondary veins, the veins sparsely strigulose to glabrous; tips truncate, sometimes acute and toothed; bases tapered; margins plane, thickened, usually dentate above the middle; teeth (three to) five to seven per leaf, spinulose. Inflorescences in upper axils of 1- or 2-year-old branchlets, umbellate, 9–13 mm long, sessile to subsessile; peduncles 1–5 mm long; peduncles and rachises puberulent. Pedicels 5–7 mm long, glabrous; sepals and petals five; perianth and disks blue to lavender or pale blue. Fruits 4–6 mm wide, globose to weakly lobed, somewhat viscid when young, brown; lobes smooth to slightly wrinkled, weakly ridged, horned above the middle; horns erect, less than 1 mm long, smooth to slightly wrinkled. Seeds 3.5–4 mm long, broadly ovoid, slightly compressed. Flowering April–June; fruiting June–August; reproducing primarily from seeds.

Rocky ultramafic substrates; slopes, summits, and ridges; chaparral and open sites in conifer forests; 140–2,240 m (460–7,400 feet); Klamath Mountains from Curry and Josephine Counties, Oregon, south to the Coast Range of Mendocino County, California.

Trelease (1897) considered *Ceanothus pumilus* to be a hybrid, *C. cuneatus* × *C. prostratus,* and Jepson (1936) and McMinn (1942) suggested that it might be part of *C. prostratus.* Recent hybridity seems unlikely, given its broad distribution and almost exclusive occurrence on ultramafic substrates, on which *C. prostratus* does not appear to occur. In general, *C. prostratus* differs from *C. pumilus* by less intri-

Ceanothus pumilus

cate branching, larger stipules, larger leaves, and larger fruits. Low-growing forms of *C. cuneatus* have entire leaves and white flowers. In the Klamath Mountains, *C. pumilus* may be confused with low-growing forms of *C. cuneatus,* which differs primarily in having entire leaf margins, obtuse to rounded leaf tips, and white flowers.

McMinn (1942) reported hybrids with *Ceanothus cuneatus* in southwestern Oregon; hybridization between *C. cuneatus* and *C. pumilus* in the North Coast Range of California is documented by specimens at the Humboldt State University herbarium. Hybrids with *C. cuneatus* were named *C. ×humboldtensis* J. B. Roof.

References. *Ceanothus pumilus* E. L. Greene, *Erythea* 1: 149 (1893); *C. prostratus* Bentham var. *profugus* Jepson, *Flora of California* 2: 479 (1936).

Ceanothus purpureus Jepson
hollyleaf ceanothus, Napa ceanothus

Subgenus *Cerastes.* Erect shrubs, 0.5–1.5 m tall; crown somewhat open, sometimes flat-topped or sprawling, broadly obovoid; main branches weakly ascending to spreading; distal branchlets stiff, their internodes 7–10 mm long, angled, reddish brown, glabrous, sometimes glaucous; mature bark gray to brown. Stipules thick, persistent, 2–3.5 mm wide, sometimes confluent. Leaves opposite, evergreen, evenly spaced, sessile or petioles 1–2 mm long. Leaf blades 12–21 mm long, 7–14 mm wide, broadly elliptic to broadly obovate, wavy to slightly folded and concave above, thick, stiff, one-veined; upper surfaces dark green, glabrous, somewhat shiny; lower surfaces pale green, appearing glabrous except for microscopic tomentulose patches between

the secondary veins, the veins appressed-puberulent or strigulose; tips rounded or sharply acute; bases obtuse to tapered; margins dentate to serrate; teeth 7–15 per leaf, sharply spinulose. Inflorescences terminal or in upper axils of 1- or 2-year-old branchlets, umbellate, 11–17 mm long, sessile to subsessile; peduncles 2–5 mm long; peduncles and rachises puberulent. Pedicels 5–9 mm long, glabrous; sepals and petals five; perianth and disks deep blue to purple. Fruits 4–5 mm wide, globose to weakly lobed, brown to dark brown; lobes smooth, ridges absent, horned above the middle; horns erect, slender, 1–2 mm long, somewhat wrinkled. Seeds 2.5–3 mm long, ellipsoid to ovoid, dark brown. Flowering February–April; fruiting April–June; reproducing entirely from seeds.

Ridges and slopes on rocky soils and outcrops derived primarily from volcanic substrates; open sites in chaparral and woodlands; 145–425 m (475–1,400 feet); Vaca Moun-

Ceanothus purpureus, fruit detail ×2½

tains of Napa and northern Solano Counties, California. A species of special conservation concern because of its limited distribution and potential habitat loss.

McMinn (1942) considered *Ceanothus purpureus* to be closely related to *C. divergens* and *C. sonomensis. Ceanothus purpureus* may be considered part of a closely related complex involving the latter two species and plants referred to as *C. prostratus* var. *occidentalis* (Nobs 1963). *Ceanothus divergens* differs by having marginal teeth usually restricted to above the middle of the leaf blade, and *C. sonomensis* differs from both by its sessile, smaller leaf blades (5–11 mm long, 2–5 mm wide). *Ceanothus purpureus* sometimes has been confused with *C. jepsonii;* both species have similar life forms and leaf morphology. *Ceanothus jepsonii* differs in having six to eight petals, deflexed leaves, and larger fruits (5–7 mm wide) with conspicuously wrinkled horns.

References. *Ceanothus purpureus* Jepson, *Flora of Western Middle California,* 258 (1901); C. *jepsonii* E. L. Greene var. *purpureus* (Jepson) Jepson, *Manual of the Flowering Plants of California,* 624 (1925).

Ceanothus roderickii W. Knight

Pine Hill ceanothus, Roderick's ceanothus

Subgenus *Cerastes.* Prostrate, mat- or mound-like shrubs, less than 50 cm tall; crown somewhat dense to open; main branches spreading, sometimes curved or arched, sometimes rooting at remote nodes; distal branchlets somewhat flexible to stiff, their internodes 7–11 mm long, smooth, brown to grayish brown, puberulent, becoming glabrous and somewhat glaucous; mature bark gray to gray-brown. Stipules thick, persistent, about 1 mm wide. Leaves opposite, evergreen, evenly spaced, or clustered on short lateral shoots and ascending; petioles 1–2 mm long. Leaf blades 4–11 mm long, 2–5 mm wide, somewhat elliptic to oblanceolate, flat to folded lengthwise, thick, stiff, one-veined; upper surfaces green, glabrous to sparsely puberulent; lower surfaces pale green, sparsely strigulose or appearing glabrous except for microscopic tomentulose patches between the secondary veins, the veins sparsely strigulose; tips obtuse to slightly notched; bases obtuse to tapered; margins plane, entire or denticulate above the mid-

Ceanothus roderickii, Sierra Nevada foothills, El Dorado County, California

Ceanothus roderickii

dle; teeth three to five per leaf, spinulose. Inflorescences terminal or in upper axils of 1- or 2-year-old branchlets, often erect, umbellate, 5–11 mm long, subsessile; peduncles 1–3 mm long; peduncles and rachises puberulent. Pedicels 3–6 mm long, glabrous; sepals and petals five; perianth white to pale blue, disks slightly darker than the petals. Fruits 4–5 mm wide, globose to weakly lobed, brown; lobes smooth to slightly wrinkled, sometimes slightly ridged or minutely horned above the middle. Seeds about 3 mm long, ellipsoid to ovoid, slightly compressed, brown. Flowering April–June; fruiting June and July; reproducing entirely from seeds.

Rocky soils and outcrops, on substrates derived primarily from gabbroic igneous rocks, sometimes on ultramafic substrates, chaparral and woodlands; 260–630 m (850–2,070 feet); Sierra Nevada foothills of El Dorado County, California. A species of special conservation concern because of its limited distribution and potential habitat loss.

Ceanothus roderickii appears closely related to and might be considered part of *C. cuneatus.* Bluish flowers and life forms with prostrate branches occur in the latter species, but such forms are known only from the Coast Ranges and Klamath Mountains of California. Leaf blade morphology is similar to that of *C. cuneatus* var. *cuneatus,* but their clustered arrangement on short ascending lateral shoots appears distinctive. A close relationship to variety *cuneatus* is also supported by molecular evidence (Hardig et al. 2000).

Reference. *Ceanothus roderickii* W. Knight, *Four Seasons* 2(3): 23 (1968).

Ceanothus sanguineus Pursh

redstem ceanothus, Oregon tea-tree, northern buckbrush

Subgenus *Ceanothus*. Erect shrubs, 1–3 m tall; crown open, hemispheric to broadly obovoid; distal branchlets flexible, their internodes 25–45 mm long, smooth, green, sometimes becoming reddish brown, puberulent, becoming glabrous; mature bark reddish or purplish brown. Stipules thin, deciduous. Leaves alternate, deciduous, evenly spaced; petioles 5–18(–25) mm long. Leaf blades 25–68 mm long, 20–45 mm wide, ovate to broadly elliptic, flat, thin, three-veined from the base; upper surfaces dull to somewhat shiny, green, glabrous; lower surfaces dull pale green, sparsely puberulent to glabrous, the veins glabrous to sparsely puberulent or short-villous; tips obtuse to rounded; bases rounded to subcordate; margins plane, serrulate; teeth 50–100+ per leaf, with conic glands when young. Inflorescences usually in upper axils of previous year's branchlets, racemose to paniculate, open, 28–79(–110) mm long; peduncles 10–43(–73) mm long; peduncles and rachises glabrous to sparsely puberulent.

Pedicels 6–11 mm long, glabrous; perianth white, sometimes pink-tinged, the disks cream. Fruits 3–4.5 mm wide, brown to dark brown, globose to weakly lobed, viscid when young, brown; lobes smooth to weakly ridged at the middle; horns absent. Seeds subglobose to ovoid, 2–2.5 mm long, brown to reddish brown. Flowering April–July; fruiting June–August; reproducing from seeds, and sometimes from basal shoots following fire.

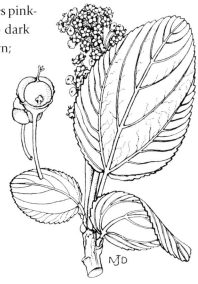

Sandy to rocky soils; forest openings and margins, prairies, and abandoned clearings, 30–1,360 m (100–4,500 feet); southern British Columbia, Canada; in the United States from Washington east to western Montana, south through Oregon and Idaho to northwestern California, disjunct in northern Michigan.

Related species include *Ceanothus americanus* and *C. herbaceus* (McMinn 1942, Coile 1988), based on habit, the relatively large, deciduous, serrate to serrulate leaves,

Ceanothus sanguineus

and overall fruit morphology. Both species have inflorescences borne terminally or in the upper axils of the current year's branches. *Ceanothus americanus* usually has peduncles longer than the inflorescences, and *C. herbaceus* differs by its narrowly elliptic to lanceolate leaves and hemispheric inflorescences. McMinn reported putative hybrids with *C. velutinus*, based on specimens from British Columbia.

References. *Ceanothus sanguineus* Pursh, *Flora Americae Septentrionalis,* 167 (1814); *C. oreganus* Nuttall in Torrey & A. Gray, *Flora of North America* 1: 265 (1838).

Ceanothus sonomensis J. T. Howell

Sonoma ceanothus

Subgenus *Cerastes.* Erect shrubs, 0.5–1.5 m tall; crown somewhat open, obovoid; main branches ascending to spreading; distal branchlets stiff, their internodes 8–18 mm long, smooth, gray to grayish brown, glabrous; mature bark gray to grayish brown. Stipules thick, persistent, 1–1.5 mm wide. Leaves opposite, evergreen, evenly spaced or clustered at nodes, sessile; petioles less than 1 mm long. Leaf blades 5–11 mm long, 2–5 mm wide, broadly obovate, usually flat, sometimes slightly wavy to slightly folded (concave above), thick, stiff, one-veined; upper surfaces dark green, glabrous, somewhat shiny; lower surfaces pale grayish green, appearing glabrous except for microscopic tomentulose patches between the secondary veins, the veins sparsely strigulose to appressed-puberulent, becoming glabrous; tips somewhat truncate to notched, sometimes acute; bases obtuse to tapered; margins plane, thickened, dentate; teeth three to seven per leaf, spinulose. Inflorescences terminal or in upper axils of 1- or 2-

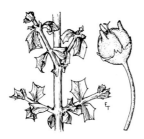

Ceanothus sonomensis

year-old branchlets, umbellate, 8–12 mm long, sessile to subsessile; peduncles 1–2 mm long; peduncles and rachises puberulent. Pedicels 4–7 mm long, glabrous; sepals and petals five; perianth and disks blue to lavender. Fruits 4–5 mm wide, globose to weakly lobed, brown to dark brown; lobes smooth, ridges absent, horned above the middle; horns 2–3 mm long, slender, erect, smooth to slightly wrinkled. Seeds about 3 mm long, ellipsoid to somewhat oblong-ellipsoid, slightly compressed, black. Flowering March and April; fruiting April–June; reproducing entirely from seeds.

Summits, ridges, and slopes on rocky soils derived primarily from volcanic substrates; chaparral; 140–620 m (460–2,050 feet); mountains between the Napa and Sonoma Valleys, Napa and Sonoma Counties, California. A species of special conservation concern because of its very restricted distribution.

Howell (1939) considered *Ceanothus confusus* (a prostrate plant treated here as a variety of *C. divergens*) and *C. divergens* to be close relatives, although McMinn (1942) suggested a relationship to *C. cuneatus*. Though there are some similarities to *C. cuneatus* with respect to habit and leaf shape, *C. cuneatus* differs primarily by having more rigid branchlets, short-petiolate leaves, and fruits with shorter, more wrinkled horns. *Ceanothus divergens* differs primarily by its elliptic to relatively narrowly obovate leaf blades, 10–19 mm long, and brown to reddish brown internodes. Erect forms of *C. divergens* often have relatively long, sometimes curved or arched stems, while those of *C. sonomensis* are erect or ascending and relatively rigid and straight.

Reference. *Ceanothus sonomensis* J. T. Howell, *Leaflets of Western Botany* 2: 162–163 (1939).

Ceanothus spinosus Nuttall
green-bark ceanothus

Subgenus *Ceanothus*. Erect shrubs, sometimes arborescent, 2–6 m tall; crown open, broadly obovate to hemispheric; main branches ascending to spreading; distal branchlets stiff to somewhat flexible, sometimes becoming spine-like, often mostly blunt-tipped, their internodes 9–19 mm long, smooth to somewhat angled, green to yellowish green, glabrous to sparsely puberulent, often becoming glabrous with age; mature bark grayish green or gray. Stipules thin, deciduous. Leaves alternate, evergreen to semideciduous, some leaves more persistent than others, evenly spaced; petioles 2–7 mm long. Leaf blades 11–30(–41) mm long, 9–20 mm wide, elliptic to elliptic-oblong, flat, somewhat leathery, one-veined; upper surfaces green, shiny, glabrous, darker than the lower surface when dry, often somewhat purplish; lower surfaces pale green, glabrous to slightly glaucous, the veins sometimes appressed-puberulent or strigulose; tips acute to obtuse, sometimes slightly notched; bases rounded to obtuse;

margins plane, entire, sometimes serrulate on rapidly growing shoots, glands apparently absent, even on young leaves. Inflorescences terminal or in upper axils of 1- or 2-year old branchlets, racemose to paniculate, open to somewhat dense, 30–150 mm long; peduncles 15–70 mm long; peduncles and rachises glabrous or sparsely puberulent near the base. Pedicels 5–8 mm long, glabrous; sepals and petals five; perianth and disks blue to pale blue or almost white. Fruits 4–9 mm in diameter, globose to weakly lobed, dark brown, viscid when young, smooth or lobes with a dorsal glandular ridge or bulge; horns absent. Seeds 2.5–3 mm long, subglobose to broadly ovoid, dark brown. Flowering January–June; fruiting June–August; reproducing from seeds, and from basal shoots following fire.

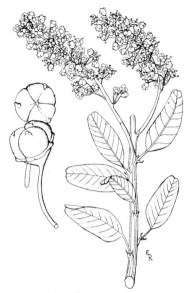

Ceanothus spinosus var. *spinosus*, branch detail ×³⁄₄

Slopes and flats on soils derived from various geological substrates; open sites in chaparral, oak woodlands, and conifer forests; 60–1,800 m (200–5,900 feet); Sierra Nevada foothills of Amador and Eldorado Counties, California, inner South Coast Range (San Benito County), coastal hills and Transverse Ranges from San Luis Obispo County east to Los Angeles County, and the Peninsular Ranges of southern California, south to the foothills of the Sierra Juárez, Baja California, Mexico.

Well-developed branchlets in *Ceanothus spinosus* var. *spinosus* are often blunt rather than spine-like; there also appears to be substantial variation within and between populations with respect to the proportion of spine-like branchlets, a situation similar to that in *C. incanus*. *Ceanothus palmeri* (Palmer's ceanothus) has been recognized as a closely related species, distinguished by absence of spine-like branches, the presence of dorsal ridges or bulges on fruit surfaces, white flowers, and fruit size (Jepson 1925, McMinn 1942, Abrams 1951, Munz 1959, Schmidt 1993). However, there appears to be considerable variation in most of these traits throughout the range of both taxa. Typical populations of *C. palmeri* lack spine-like branches, have white flowers and relatively large mature fruits with smooth surfaces, and generally occur at elevations above 1,000 m (3,300 feet). Most populations of *C. spinosus* occur below 1,000 m,

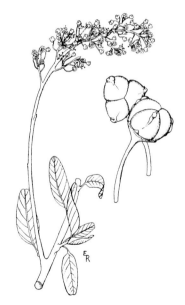

Ceanothus spinosus var. *palmeri*, branch detail ×¹⁄₂

usually have bluish flowers, and have slightly smaller fruits that lack a glandular ridge or bulge. A majority of terminal branches are often blunt rather than spine-like. However, some plants bear pale blue or bluish white flowers, which produce fruits as much as 8 mm in diameter with weakly developed ridges or bulges on the dorsal surface. Leaves of *C. palmeri* appear lighter in color than those of *C. spinosus*, especially when dry. The upper surfaces of dried leaves of *C. spinosus* are somewhat shiny and dark reddish purple, while those of *C. palmeri* remain dull green. Overall, the differences between the two taxa and apparent intergradation do not appear sufficient to warrant separation of them as species, and they are treated here as two intergrading varieties, discriminated in the accompanying key.

Varieties of *Ceanothus spinosus*

1 Upper surfaces of dry leaf blades dull green, slightly darker than the lower surfaces; perianth white, sometimes pale blue; fruits somewhat triangular in cross section, often with a dorsal glandular ridge or bulge . . . . *C. spinosus* var. *palmeri*
1 Upper surfaces of dry leaf blades reddish purple, somewhat shiny, much darker than the lower surfaces; perianth blue to pale blue; fruits circular in cross section, often smooth
. . . . *C. spinosus* var. *spinosus*

Variety *palmeri* (see photograph on page 130) bears a strong resemblance to *Ceanothus integerrimus* var. *integerrimus* and sometimes has been misidentified as such (McMinn 1942). However, the latter nearly always has thinner, completely deciduous leaves, which sometimes bear a basal pair of lateral veins that slightly exceed the length of those above. Regardless, the relationship between *C. spinosus* var. *palmeri* and *C. integerrimus* var. *integerrimus* clearly deserves more careful study. The disjunct occurrence of plants assignable to variety *palmeri* in the foothills of the western Sierra Nevada is of considerable floristic interest (Jepson 1936), as are plants in San Benito County. *Ceanothus spinosus*, including variety *palmeri*, is notably absent from the San Bernardino Mountains of California, unlike other widespread species such as *C. integerrimus*, *C. leucodermis*, and *C. oliganthus*.

References. *Ceanothus spinosus* Nuttall in Torrey & A. Gray, *Flora of North America* 1: 267 (1838).

Ceanothus spinosus var. *palmeri* (Trelease) K. Brandegee, *Proceedings of the California Academy Sciences*, series 2, 4: 185 (1894), emended by Jepson (1925), based on *C. palmeri* Trelease, *idem*, series 2, 1: 109 (1888). Both Jepson (1925) and McMinn (1942) rejected Brandegee's circumscription of variety *palmeri* because she confused it with plants referable to *C. divaricatus* and *C. eglandulosus*, whose types and original descriptions belong to *C. oliganthus* and *C. leucodermis*, respectively. However, Jepson's comments may be considered as emending the original combination by Brandegee (Greuter et al. 2000, Article 47).

Ceanothus thyrsiflorus Eschscholtz
blueblossom

Subgenus *Ceanothus*. Erect, spreading, or prostrate shrubs, sometimes arborescent, 0.5–6 m tall; crown open to compact, oblanceolate to obovoid, sometimes mound-like and flat-topped or mat-like with prostrate stems; main branches ascending to spreading; distal branchlets flexible to somewhat stiff, their internodes 12–30 mm long, angled near the tips, green, glabrous to sparsely puberulent; mature bark gray to grayish brown. Stipules thin, deciduous. Leaves alternate, evergreen, evenly spaced; petioles 3–9 mm long. Leaf blades 10–39 mm long, 6–25 mm wide, narrowly to broadly elliptic or ovate, flat, somewhat leathery, three-veined from the base; upper surfaces dark green, glabrous; lower surfaces pale green, sparsely to moderately puberulent or short-villous, the veins often more puberulent than the surfaces between the veins, sometimes strigulose; tips obtuse; bases obtuse to rounded; margins plane to slightly revolute, weakly denticulate or serrulate with 23–48 teeth per leaf, tipped with broadly conic to subglobose glands when young. Inflorescences terminal or in upper axils of 1- or 2-year-old branchlets, racemose to paniculate, open to somewhat dense, 15–53(–75) mm long; peduncles 12–33 mm long; peduncles and rachises sparsely puberulent to glabrous. Pedicels 5–8 mm long, glabrous; sepals and petals five; perianth and disks deep violet-blue to blue, rarely white. Fruits 2.5–4 mm wide, lobed, viscid when young, dark brown to black; lobes smooth, ridges and horns absent. Seeds 1.5–2 mm long, subglobose to ovoid, dark brown to black. Flowering March–June; fruiting June–August; reproducing from seeds, from basal shoots following fire, and sometimes by layering.

Slopes, ridges, and flats on sandy or rocky soils derived from various geological substrates; coastal chaparral and open sites in mixed-evergreen woodlands or coastal conifer forests; 15–600 m (50–2,000 feet); outer Coast Ranges from Coos County, Oregon, south to near Point Conception, Santa Barbara County, California, with a disjunct population near the coastal town of Eréndira, northwestern Baja California, Mexico.

Based on specimens from throughout the geographic range, the distinction between plants with subglabrous leaf surfaces and plane margins (variety *thyrsiflorus*) versus puberulent leaf surfaces and revolute margins (variety *griseus*) is not as clear as implied by McMinn, who first treated them as varieties (1939), later (1942) as distinct

Ceanothus thyrsiflorus
var. *thyrsiflorus*

Ceanothus thyrsiflorus
var. griseus

species. Some plants bearing incompletely revolute leaf margins have subglabrous leaf surfaces, and some with revolute leaf surfaces appear subglabrous between the veins. Plants referable to variety *thyrsiflorus* tend to have narrower leaves than those referable to variety *griseus*. Plants clearly assignable to variety *thyrsiflorus* tend to occur at higher elevations (up to 600 m, 2,000 feet), while plants with short-villous leaf surfaces (variety *griseus*, Carmel ceanothus) are apparently limited to coastal bluffs and slopes below 200 m (660 feet). The two varieties can be separated by using the accompanying key.

Tree-like, shrub, and prostrate growth forms are found in both varieties. Low-growing or prostrate plants with subglabrous lower leaf surfaces, puberulent veins, and plane leaf margins were previously called *Ceanothus thyrsiflorus* var. *repens* (creeping blueblossom). Such plants appear to be restricted to coastal bluffs at widely scattered localities in Mendocino, Marin, and Monterey Counties, California. Plants with a similar growth form, but with puberulent to short-villous lower leaf surfaces, are referable to what has been called *C. griseus* var. *horizontalis*. Such plants are apparently restricted to coastal bluffs between Hurricane Point and Yankee Point in northern Monterey County. The cultivars derived from these plants retain their distinctive life form under cultivation and are highly desirable horticulturally. However, the existence of intermediate forms, which range from prostrate to mound-like in both varieties under natural conditions, provides sufficient evidence for not recognizing the prostrate entities as distinct taxa.

Jepson (1936) and McMinn (1939) applied the name *Ceanothus thyrsiflorus* var. *chandleri* to plants from the Pajaro Hills, Monterey County, with elliptic leaf blades 12–19 mm long and 6–9 mm wide. However, such plants also occur throughout the range of the species, including the coastal slope of the western Santa Ynez Mountains in Santa Barbara County, California, and coastal Baja California, Mexico.

Ceanothus thyrsiflorus (including variety *griseus*) is similar to and is presumed to be related to *C. parryi*, which differs primarily in having elliptic to elliptic-oblong leaf blades, villous to loosely tomentulose lower leaf surfaces, at least when young, and relatively open inflorescences. The two species are sometimes difficult to distinguish, especially when they hybridize. Naturally occurring hybrids between *C. thyrsiflorus* var. *griseus* and *C. dentatus* were named *C. ×lobbianus* Hooker, and those between variety *griseus* and *C. cuneatus* var. *rigidus* were named *C. ×veitchianus* Hooker. Naturally occurring hybrids between *C. thyrsiflorus* and *C. impressus* have been called *C. ×burto-*

nensis. McMinn (1942) also reported naturally occurring hybrids between *C. thyrsiflorus* and *C. foliosus,* and *C. oliganthus* (as *C. sorediatus*). Hybrids between variety *thyrsiflorus* and *C. papillosus* were named *C. ×regius* (Jepson) McMinn, those between *C. thyrsiflorus* and *C. incanus* were named *C. ×vanrensselaeri* J. B. Roof, and those with *C. velutinus* var. *hookeri* were named *C. ×mendocinensis* McMinn.

Varieties of *Ceanothus thyrsiflorus*

1 Leaf margins mostly plane throughout their length; lower surfaces of leaves subglabrous to sparsely short-villous between the veins . . . . *C. thyrsiflorus* var. *thyrsiflorus*
1 Leaf margins mostly revolute throughout their length; lower surfaces of leaves moderately to sometimes densely short-villous or short-tomentulose between the veins . . . .*C. thyrsiflorus* var. *griseus*

References. *Ceanothus thyrsiflorus* Eschscholtz, *Memoirs de l'Académie Impériale des Sciences de St. Pétersbourg, avec l'Histoire de l'Académie* 10: 285 (1826); *C. thyrsiflorus* var. *chandleri* Jepson, *Manual of the Flowering Plants of California,* 619 (1925); *C. thyrsiflorus* var. *repens* McMinn, *Ceanothus,* 212 (1942).

Ceanothus thyrsiflorus var. *griseus* Trelease in A. Gray, *Synoptical Flora of North America* 1: 415 (1897); *C. griseus* (Trelease) McMinn, *Ceanothus,* 210 (1942); *C. griseus* var. *horizontalis* McMinn, *idem,* 210 (1942).

Ceanothus tomentosus Parry

woollyleaf ceanothus

Subgenus *Ceanothus.* Erect shrubs, sometimes arborescent, 1–3 m tall; crown open, hemispheric to obovoid, rarely low growing and mound-like; main branches ascending to spreading; distal branchlets somewhat flexible, their internodes 9–20 mm long, smooth, white tomentulose when young, becoming glabrous, brown; mature bark gray to reddish brown. Stipules thin, deciduous. Leaves alternate, evergreen, evenly spaced; petioles 1–3 mm long. Leaf blades 10–15 mm long, 5–11 mm wide, elliptic to broadly ovate, flat, somewhat leathery, usually three-veined from the base, sometimes one-veined; upper surfaces dark green, moderately short-villous to puberulent, often becoming glabrous; lower surfaces densely to moderately white-tomentulose, the veins puberulent to tomentulose, sometimes obscured by the tomentum; tips obtuse to rounded; bases rounded; margins plane, denticulate to serrulate; teeth 39–61 per leaf,

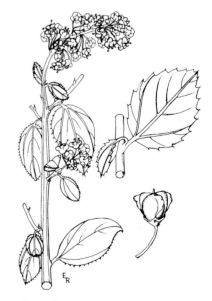

Ceanothus tomentosus

with conic glands when young. Inflorescences terminal or in upper axils of 1- or 2-year-old branchlets, umbellate to racemose, dense to somewhat open, 15–35 mm long; peduncles 5–17 mm long; peduncles and rachises puberulent to tomentulose. Pedicels 4–7 mm long, glabrous; sepals and petals five; perianth and disks deep violet-blue to very pale blue or white. Fruits 3–5 mm wide, lobed, viscid, brown to dark brown; lobes smooth, sometimes slightly ridged above the middle; horns absent. Seeds 1.5–2 mm long, subglobose to broadly ovoid, slightly compressed, dark brown. Flowering February–May; fruiting April–June; reproducing from seeds, and from basal shoots following fire.

Rocky soils derived from various geological substrates; chaparral, woodlands, and open sites in pine forests; 45–2,060 m (150–6,800 feet); western slope of the Sierra Nevada, from Nevada County south to Mariposa County, and the eastern Transverse and Peninsular Ranges from San Bernardino County, California, south to the Sierra Juárez and Sierra San Pedro Mártir, Baja California, Mexico. Most plants assignable to the two varieties can be separated by using the accompanying key.

Varieties of *Ceanothus tomentosus*

1 Lower surfaces of leaf blades uniformly and densely tomentulose, the veins usually obscure . . . . *C. tomentosus* var. *tomentosus*
1 Lower surfaces of leaf blades moderately tomentulose, the veins usually evident and often appearing less pubescent than the surfaces . . . . *C. tomentosus* var. *olivaceus*

Variety *tomentosus* occurs almost exclusively on the western slope of the Sierra Nevada, but some plants in southern California have leaves with densely tomentulose lower surfaces. Low-growing mound-like plants referable to this variety are known only from nutrient-poor soils near Ione, Amador County. Plants with moderately tomentulose lower leaf surfaces, with the veins usually evident, are referable to variety *olivaceus,* which occurs primarily in the mountains of southern California and northern Baja California, Mexico. The two varieties have also been separated by differences in their leaf margins (serrulate with deciduous glands in variety *tomentosus* versus denticulate with somewhat persistent glands in variety *olivaceus*), but no clear geographical pattern is evident. Some plants in the Santa Ana Mountains of California referable to variety *olivaceus* appear to be intermediate to either *Ceanothus oliganthus* var. *sorediatus* or var. *orcuttii.* Plants with moderately tomentulose lower leaf surfaces and puberulent ovaries suggest hybridization with *C. oliganthus* var. *orcuttii,* but other plants with glabrous ovaries appear intermediate to *C. oliganthus* var. *sorediatus.*

Ceanothus tomentosus is most closely related to *C. oliganthus,* with which it shares similar patterns of leaf morphology and flower color (McMinn 1942). *Ceanothus oliganthus* usually differs by having young leaf blades with glabrous to sparsely puberulent upper surfaces. However, the differences often become obscured with age. The marginal teeth of *C. oliganthus*, especially on young leaves, are often broadly conic to subglobose.

McMinn (1942) reported naturally occurring hybrids between *Ceanothus tomentosus* var. *tomentosus* and *C. integerrimus*, and hybrids between *C. tomentosus* var. *olivaceus* and *C. oliganthus* var. *sorediatus*.

References. *Ceanothus tomentosus* Parry, *Proceedings of the Davenport Academy of Sciences* 5: 190 (1889); *C. azureus* Kellogg, *Proceedings of the California Academy of Sciences* 1: 55 (1855; the name is illegitimate because it was preceded by the name *C. azureus* Desfontaines ex A. P. de Candolle, *Prodromus Systematis Naturalis Regni Vegetabilis* 2: 31 (1825), which is a synonym of *C. caeruleus*); *C. oliganthus* Nuttall var. *tomentosus* (Parry) K. Brandegee, *Proc. Calif. Acad. Sci.*, series 2, 4: 198 (1894).

Ceanothus tomentosus var. *olivaceus* Jepson, *Manual of the Flowering Plants of California*, 621 (1925); *C. tomentosus* subsp. *olivaceus* (Jepson) Munz, *Flora of Southern California*, 737 (1974).

Ceanothus velutinus Hooker

snow brush, mountain balm, sticky laurel, tobacco brush, varnish-leaf ceanothus
Subgenus *Ceanothus*. Erect shrubs, 0.5–6 m tall, often in dense thickets, sometimes arborescent; crown open to compact, hemispheric or broadly obovoid, sometimes flat-topped; distal branchlets flexible, their internodes 9–23 mm long, smooth, greenish to reddish brown, subglabrous to sparsely tomentulose; mature bark gray to gray-

Ceanothus velutinus var. *velutinus* near Yuba Gap, Sierra Nevada, California

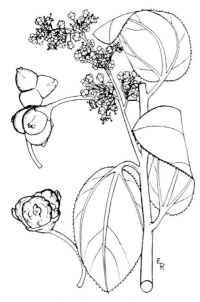

Ceanothus velutinus

ish brown. Stipules thin, deciduous. Leaves alternate, evergreen, with a distinctive pungent or spicy odor when crushed; petioles 9–32 mm long. Leaf blades 33–81 mm long, 21–53 mm wide, broadly elliptic to ovate, flat, leathery, three-veined from the base; upper surfaces shiny dark green, strongly viscid and often appearing resinous or glossy, glabrous; lower surfaces pale green or grayish green, viscid or sometimes appearing glabrous except for microscopic tomentulose patches between the ultimate veins, the veins glabrous to sparsely puberulent or strigulose; tips rounded to obtuse; bases rounded to subcordate; margins plane, obscurely denticulate; teeth 93–163 per leaf, tipped with conic glands when young. Inflorescences terminal or in upper axils of 1-year-old branchlets, paniculate, open to somewhat dense, 30–81 mm long; peduncles 15–45 mm long; peduncles and rachises sparsely puberulent. Pedicels 10–13 mm long, glabrous; sepals and petals five; perianth and disks white or cream. Fruits 3.5–5 mm wide, lobed, viscid, brown to dark brown; lobes smooth to slightly wrinkled, sometimes weakly ridged above the middle; horns absent. Seeds ovoid, 2–3 mm long, brown to dark brown. Flowering March–June (to August); fruiting July and August; reproducing from seeds, and from basal shoots following fire.

Rocky soils derived from various geological substrates, ridges and slopes, chaparral and montane shrublands, open sites in conifer forests; 15–3,400 m (50–11,200 feet); mountains of southern British Columbia and southwestern Alberta in Canada, and in the United States from Washington east to the Black Hills of South Dakota, south to central California, Nevada, Utah, and Colorado. Two weakly defined varieties can be recognized, and discriminated by using the accompanying key.

Varieties of *Ceanothus velutinus*

1 Lower surfaces of leaves with puberulent veins; plants often hemispheric . . . .
. . . .*C. velutinus* var. *velutinus*
1 Lower surfaces of leaves with glabrous to sparsely puberulent veins; plants often
obovoid, sometimes arborescent . . . . *C. velutinus* var. *hookeri*

Plants of variety *hookeri* are apparently restricted to coastal mountains from southern British Columbia (including Vancouver Island), Canada, south to northwestern California. *Ceanothus velutinus* is often a common and dominant member of the shrub understory in open conifer forests and montane chaparral throughout the western United States, sometimes forming dense stands.

The combination of strongly viscid leaf blades and viscid fruits are particularly noteworthy as diagnostic traits. Although McMinn (1942) suggested that *Ceanothus velutinus* "does not seem to be very closely related to other living species," its leaf shape and pubescence are similar to that of several species, including *C. incanus* and *C. martinii*. Naturally occurring hybrids between *C. velutinus* and *C. prostratus* were named *C. ×rugosus* E. L. Greene. Those between variety *velutinus* and *C. cordulatus* from the Sierra Nevada were named *C. ×lorenzenii* (Jepson) McMinn, and those between variety *hookeri* and *C. thyrsiflorus* were named *C. ×mendocinensis* McMinn.

References. *Ceanothus velutinus* Douglas ex Hooker, *Flora Boreali-Americana* 1: 125 (1830); *C. hirsutus* Nuttall var. *glaber* S. Watson ex S. Watson, *Proceedings of the American Academy of Arts and Sciences* 10: 336 (1875; this name was first used by Watson (1871) without a description in the *United States Geological Exploration of the Fortieth Parallel* 5: 51); *C. glaber* S. Watson ex Trelease in A. Gray, *Synoptical Flora of North America* 1(1) 412 (1897).

Ceanothus velutinus var. *hookeri* M. C. Johnston, *Leaflets of Western Botany* 10: 64 (1963); *C. laevigatus* Douglas ex Hooker, *Fl. Bor.-Amer.* 1: 125 (1830); *C. velutinus* var. *laevigatus* (Douglas ex Hooker) Torrey & A. Gray, *Flora of North America* 1(Supplement): 686 (1840); *C. velutinus* subsp. *laevigatus* (Douglas ex Hooker) E. Murray, *Kalmia* 13: 4 (1983). Johnston provided the name variety *hookeri* for plants referred to as variety *laevigatus* because the basionym *C. laevigatus* Douglas ex Hooker was preceded by the validly published *C. laevigatus* A. P. de Candolle (1825). The disposition of the latter name remains unclear, although Johnston (1964) suggested that it probably belongs to a species of *Rhamnus*.

Ceanothus verrucosus Nuttall

wart-stemmed ceanothus, barranca brush

Subgenus *Cerastes*. Erect shrubs, 1–3 m tall; crown open to dense, hemispheric to broadly obovoid, sometimes flat-topped; main branches ascending to spreading; distal branchlets stiff, their internodes 4–12 mm long, smooth, dark grayish brown, short-villous to somewhat tomentulose; mature bark dark gray to grayish brown. Stipules thick, persistent, 2.5–3 mm wide. Leaves alternate, evergreen, evenly spaced, sometimes clustered at nodes; petioles 1–3 mm long. Leaf blades 5–14 mm long, 3–10 mm wide, broadly obovate to somewhat deltate or suborbicular, flat to concave above, thick, stiff, one-veined; upper surfaces green, glabrous; lower surfaces pale green, sparsely strigulose or appearing glabrous except for microscopic tomentulose patches between the secondary veins, the veins sparsely puberulent to strigulose; tips truncate to notched, sometimes obtuse; bases tapered to rounded; margins plane, entire to obscurely denticulate above the middle; teeth 9–16 per leaf, spinulose. Inflorescences in upper axils of 1- or 2-year-old branchlets, umbellate, 9–14 mm long, subsessile; peduncles 2–4 mm long; peduncles and rachises puberulent. Pedicels 4–7 mm long, glabrous; sepals and petals five; perianth white, disks usually black. Fruits 4–6 mm wide, globose to weakly lobed, viscid when young, brown; lobes smooth or weakly ridged to minutely horned near the middle. Seeds 2.5–3 mm long, ellipsoid, dark brown to black. Flowering January–April; fruiting April–June; reproducing entirely from seeds.

On rocky or sandy soils of slopes, ridges, and coastal terraces; chaparral and coastal pine woodlands; 20–785 m (65–2,580 feet). Coastal San Diego County, California, south to the foothills of the Sierra San Pedro Mártir and on Cedros Island, Baja California, Mexico. A species of special conservation concern because of its limited distribution and historic loss of habitat.

Ceanothus verrucosus is unusual in subgenus *Cerastes* in having alternate leaves, a condition shared only with *C. megacarpus* var. *megacarpus,* to which it appears closely related. *Ceanothus megacarpus* differs by having narrower, obovate to elliptic, entire-margined leaf blades and fruits 7–12 mm wide. McMinn (1942) also suggested relationships to *C. cuneatus,* especially varieties *ramulosus* and *rigidus,* based primarily on leaf shape.

References. *Ceanothus verrucosus* Nuttall in Torrey & A. Gray, *Flora of North America* 1: 267–268 (1838); *C. rigidus* Torrey, *Report on the United States and Mexican Boundary Survey,* 2: pl. 9 ("1859," i.e., 1858; Torrey's name is illegitimate because the name *C. rigidus* Nuttall, a synonym of *C. cuneatus,* was published in 1838 and has priority).

Ceanothus vestitus E. L. Greene
cupleaf ceanothus, Mojave ceanothus

Subgenus *Cerastes.* Erect shrubs, sometimes arborescent, 0.2–3 m tall; crown somewhat open, hemispheric to broadly obovoid, sometimes flat-topped, somewhat intricately branched; main branches ascending to widely spreading; distal branchlets relatively stiff, their internodes 5–15(–20) mm long, smooth, glaucous, gray to grayish brown or almost white, curly-puberulent to sparsely tomentulose, becoming glabrous; mature bark gray to grayish brown. Stipules thick, persistent, 1–2 mm wide. Leaves opposite, evergreen, evenly spaced, sometimes clustered at the branch tips; petioles 1–3 mm long, puberulent to tomentulose, sometimes becoming glabrous. Leaf blades 5–14(–19) mm long, 3–14(–19) mm wide, oblanceolate to elliptic or broadly obovate, somewhat flat to convex above to folded lengthwise or concave above, sometimes flat, thick, stiff, one-veined; upper surfaces green to grayish green, sometimes yellowish green, appressed-puberulent or sparsely tomentulose to curly-puberulent when young, becoming glabrous; lower surfaces pale to grayish green, curly-puberulent, sometimes appearing glabrous except for microscopic tomentulose patches between the secondary veins, veins often strigulose; tips acute to obtuse, sometimes rounded or weakly truncate; bases tapered to obtuse or rounded; margins plane, thick, entire, sometimes denticulate with three to seven spinulose teeth. Inflorescences terminal or in upper axils of 1- to 3-year-old branchlets, umbellate to subumbellate, 5–14 mm long; peduncles 2–5 mm long; peduncles and rachises puberulent to tomentulose. Pedicels 3–8 mm long, glabrous or sometimes puberulent; sepals and petals five; perianth and disks white, sometimes bluish or pink-tinged. Fruits 3.5–5 mm wide, globose to weakly lobed, brown; lobes smooth, sometimes faintly ridged or weakly horned near the middle; horns somewhat erect to spreading, 0.5–2 mm long, smooth to slightly wrinkled. Seeds 2.5–4 mm wide, ellipsoid to broadly ovoid, slightly compressed, dark brown to black. Flowering February–May; fruiting April–August; reproducing entirely from seeds.

Rocky slopes, ridges, and outcrops derived from various geological substrates; desert and montane shrublands, and open sites in woodlands or forests, 900–2,330 m (2,960–7,700 feet); interior slopes of mountains bordering the southern San Joaquin Valley (Los Angeles, Santa Barbara, and Ventura Counties), the eastern slopes of the Cascade Range and eastern Sierra Nevada of California, desert slopes of the Transverse and Peninsular Ranges, the higher mountains of the Mojave Desert, eastward through the mountains of central Nevada, through southern Utah and northern Arizona, to southwestern New Mexico and southwestern Texas; widely scattered in northern Mexico from Sonora to Chihuahua, and the mountains of Baja California, Mexico.

Plants referable to *Ceanothus vestitus* often have folded or cupped (concave above) leaf blades that are glabrous or have curly-puberulent hairs. This species has been interpreted as part of *C. greggii* (included here as part of *C. pauciflorus*), which is characterized by plants with convex or flat upper leaf surfaces, tomentulose lower leaf surfaces, and thick to revolute margins. These two taxa may be closely related and may intergrade in the mountains of northern Mexico. Plants with broadly elliptic to orbicular, denticulate, yellowish green leaves have been called *C. perplexans* or *C. greggii* var. *perplexans* (including *C. goldmanii*), which occurs on the desert slopes of the San Bernardino Mountains in California south through the eastern Peninsular Ranges of California and Baja California, Mexico. Specimens from Guadalupe Island, Mexico, previously referred to *C. cuneatus* and *C. crassifolius* (McMinn 1942, Moran 1996), are more similar to typical *C. perplexans* in all respects except for their entire leaf margins. Some plants in the southern Sierra Nevada and the mountains bordering the western Mojave Desert have remotely or unevenly denticulate, obovate, sometimes orbicular leaf blades. McMinn (1942) and Howell (1940) suggested that they may represent the result of hybridization between

Ceanothus vestitus

Ceanothus vestitus, the form known as *C. perplexans*

typical *C. vestitus* and typical *C. perplexans.* Plants from Arizona, with broadly obovate to orbicular leaves and entire leaf margins, were named *C. greggii* var. *orbicularis.* Low-growing plants, less than 50 cm tall, with blue flowers from southwestern Utah were named *C. greggii* var. *franklinii.* Plants referable to *C. oblanceolatus* from Baja California have been considered part of *C. cuneatus* (Standley 1923, McMinn 1942), but the fruits and leaf pubescence might be considered intermediate to *C. vestitus.*

The name *Ceanothus australis* has been applied to plants with elliptic to obovate leaves that are glabrous at maturity and that have relatively short internodes and prominent, dark stipules. Such plants occur at widely scattered localities in the mountains of Hidalgo, Oaxaca, Coahuila, and Puebla, Mexico, at 1,600–2,300 m (5,300–7,600 feet). The leaf blades are often flat and have moderately thickened, entire margins. However, Standley (1923) and McMinn (1942) inexplicably treated *C. australis* as a synonym of *C. greggii* without any discussion. Based on the original descriptions of both *C. australis* and *C. vestitus,* treatment as two species might be warranted, but other specimens from the same region and elsewhere in northern Mexico are intermediate in leaf, internode, and stipule morphology. Some specimens have leaves with intermediate densities of short curly hairs, suggesting intergradation between the two forms.

Variation within and between populations of *Ceanothus vestitus* as treated here suggests a geographically broad pattern of intergradation among relatively distinct forms varying in leaf shape, size, and pubescence. However, this wide array of habits, leaf forms, and other traits has not been carefully examined and clearly deserves further attention. The accompanying key provides the opportunity to separate the more distinct forms but does not serve to distinguish those plants that are intermediate for one or more traits.

Ceanothus vestitus and relatives

1 Internodes 3–11 mm long, usually shorter than the leaves; stipules often confluent; lower surface of mature leaf blades glabrous except for minute patches of tomentulose hairs between the ultimate veins on the lower leaf surfaces . . . . *C. australis*

1 Internodes 5–20 mm long, usually longer than the leaves; stipules not usually confluent; lower surface of mature leaf blades sparsely or appressed-puberulent, sometimes becoming glabrous 2

2 Leaf blades broadly obovate to orbicular, usually flat, the margins with 5–11 weakly
  spinulose teeth, sometimes entire, the surfaces yellowish green; Peninsular Ranges
  of California south to the Sierra San Borja, Baja California Sur, and Guadalupe Island,
  Mexico . . . . *C. perplexans*
2 Leaf blades mostly elliptic to oblanceolate or obovate, often folded lengthwise or
  concave above, the margins entire to few-toothed, the surfaces grayish green 3
3 Plants with compact, mound-like crowns; plants less than 0.5 m tall; flowers blue to pale
  blue . . . . *C. greggii* var. *franklinii*
3 Plants with relatively open, hemispheric to obovoid crowns; plants 0.5–3 m tall; –flowers
  white to pale blue . . . . *C. vestitus*

McMinn (1942) considered *Ceanothus cuneatus* the closest relative, but Howell
(1940), who treated *C. greggii, C. vestitus,* and *C. perplexans* as distinct species, suggested relationships to *C. crassifolius, C. megacarpus ,* and *C. verrucosus.* Lower leaf surfaces of *C. crassifolius* are tomentulose, and the pubescence of *C. cuneatus, C. megacarpus,* and *C. verrucosus,* when present, is generally composed of relatively straight, often
appressed hairs. The leaf blade pubescence in typical *C. vestitus* can be described as
curly-puberulent, at least on young leaves. Relationships between plants referable to
C. vestitus and both *C. bolensis* and *C. otayensis,* based on leaf morphology and pubescence, have also been suggested (Boyd and Keeley 2003).

Both McMinn (1942) and Howell (1940) discussed putative hybridization between
Ceanothus vestitus (as *C. greggii*) and *C. cuneatus* in the southern Sierra Nevada of California. Variation in leaf shape and the number of marginal teeth on plants from the
San Bernardino Mountains and Peninsular Ranges of California suggest intergradation
between forms assignable to *C. vestitus* and *C. perplexans.*

References. *Ceanothus vestitus* E. L. Greene, *Pittonia* 2: 101 (1890); *C. greggii* A. Gray var.
vestitus (E. L. Greene) McMinn, *Illustrated Manual of California Shrubs,* 312 (1939); *C. greggii*
var. *orbicularis* E. H. Kelso, *Rhodora* 39: 151 (1951); *C. greggii* subsp. *vestitus* (E. L. Greene) R. F.
Thorne, *Aliso* 10: 163 (1981).

Ceanothus perplexans Trelease in A. Gray, *Synoptical Flora of North America* 1: 417 (1897); *C.
goldmanii* Rose, *Contributions from the U.S. National Herbarium* 12: 284 (1909); *C. greggii* var. *perplexans* (Trelease) Jepson, *Manual of the Flowering Plants of California,* 623 (1925); *C. greggii*
subsp. *perplexans* (Trelease) R. M. Beauchamp, *Phytologia* 59: 440 (1986).

Ceanothus australis Rose, *Contr. U.S. Natl. Herb.* 12: 283 (1909).

Ceanothus greggii var. *franklinii* Welsh, *Rhodora* 95: 413 (1993); *C. greggii* subsp. *franklinii*
(Welsh) Kartesz & Gandhi, *Phytologia* 78: 11 (1995).

Other Ceanothus Names

The following list includes the names of species and artificial or naturally occurring hybrids that are not otherwise fully treated in Part 2. Some of these names were originally for species of *Ceanothus* but are now considered names that should be applied to plants in other genera. The list also includes names of subgenera and sections, for groups of species below the taxonomic level of genus. Names applied to fossils are not included. Some names in *Ceanothus* were originally published with the specific epithets treated as feminine. This resulted from the practice of 18th and 19th century taxonomists to treat classical generic names of arborescent plants (e.g., *Fagus, Pinus,* and *Quercus*) as feminine, even though they ended with the usually nominative masculine *-us* (Stearn 1992). However, the name *Ceanothus* was established as masculine by Linnaeus through his use of the names *C. americanus, C. asiaticus,* and *C. africanus.* Consequently, epithets with feminine declensions (e.g., *americana, durangoina,* and *ochracea*) were used incorrectly. However, such names are not necessarily considered illegitimate and can be corrected without formal publication (Greuter et al. 2000). Names used as the basis for a transfer to another genus or lower taxonomic level are referred to as basionyms. Some names are considered illegitimate because their publication did not fulfill the rules of the *International Code of Botanical Nomenclature.* For example, names that are the same as those validly published earlier in the literature are referred to as later homonyms and are usually considered illegitimate. Other names were applied to horticultural selections or cultivars, which are treated separately from scientific botanical names and which follow somewhat different rules (Brickell et al. 2004). In some cases we were unable to correctly determine the proper disposition of a name that was published in early literature, especially those that may have been applied to horticultural forms or specimens of horticultural origin, or those that were not described using a type specimen.

Names of Subgenera and Sections

Subgenus *Ceanothus.* Subgenus *Ceanothus* was established when Weberbauer (1895) treated the unranked name *Cerastes* S. Watson as a subgenus. *Ceanothus americanus* Linnaeus is considered the type species because the other two species named by Linnaeus, *C. africanus* and *C. asiaticus,* are placed in *Noltea* and *Colubrina,* respectively.

Subgenus *Cerastes* (S. Watson) Weberbauer in Engler & Prantl, *Natürlichen Pflanzenfamilien* 3(5): 414 (1895). This name is based on the unranked name *Cerastes* S. Watson, *Proceedings of the American Academy of Arts and Sciences* 10: 338 (1875). Watson circumscribed the group to include five species with opposite leaves and horned fruits: *Ceanothus crassifolius* Torrey, *C. cuneatus* Nuttall, *C. greggii* A. Gray, *C. rigidus* Nuttall, and *C. prostratus* Bentham.

Section *Americani* (Parry) Weberbauer in Engler & Prantl, *Nat. Pflanzenfam.* 3(5): 413 (1895) (as part of subgenus *Euceanothus*). Based on the unranked "Group" *Americanus* Parry, *Proceedings of the Davenport Academy of Sciences* 5: 168 (1889). Weberbauer circumscribed this section to include *C. americanus* L., *C. ovatus* Desfontaines, *C. sanguineus* Pursh, *C. orcuttii* Parry, *C. decumbens* S. Watson, *C. lemmonii* Parry, and *C. azureus* Desfontaines. The name is superfluous because it includes the type of the genus, and *Ceanothus* must be used for all subdivisions that include the type of the genus (Greuter et al. 2000, Article 22).

Section *Cerastes* (S. Watson) Parry, *Proc. Davenport Acad. Sci.* 5: 173 (1889). Parry's name is based on the unranked name *Cerastes* S. Watson, *Proc. Amer. Acad. Arts and Sciences* 10: 338 (1875).

Section *Euceanothus* A. P. de Candolle, *Prodromus Systematis Naturalis Regni Vegetabilis* 2: 31 (1825). Section *Euceanothus* was erected to include 10 species, all of which are members of subgenus *Ceanothus*. The name *Euceanothus* is superfluous because *Ceanothus* must be used for all subdivisions that include the type of the genus. In addition, the use of the prefix *Eu-* is not permitted for the subdivision of a genus (Greuter et al. 2000, Articles 22 and 21.3, respectively).

Section *Euceanothus* Parry, *Proc. Davenport Acad. Sci.* 5: 167–168 (1889). Parry did not cite de Candolle's earlier name. The name may be considered a later homonym of section *Euceanothus* A. P. de Candolle and also is superfluous for the same reasons given for section *Euceanothus* A. P. de Candolle.

Section *Incani* (Parry) Weberbauer in Engler & Prantl, *Nat. Pflanzenfam.* 3(5): 413 (1895) (as part of subgenus *Euceanothus*). Based on the unranked "Group" *Incanus* Parry, *Proc. Davenport Acad. Sci.* 5: 168 (1889). Weberbauer circumscribed this section to include *C. incanus* Torrey & A. Gray, *C. cordulatus* Kellogg, *C. divaricatus* Nuttall, *C. intricatus* Parry, *C. fendleri* A. Gray, and *C. depressus* Bentham.

Section *Integerrimi* (Parry) Weberbauer in Engler & Prantl, *Nat. Pflanzenfam.* 3(5): 414 (1895) (as part of subgenus *Euceanothus*). Based on the unranked "Group" *Integerrimus* Parry, *Proc. Davenport Acad. Sci.* 5: 171 (1889). Weberbauer circumscribed this section to include *C. integerrimus* Hooker & Arnott (including *C. parvifolius* Trelease and *C. palmeri* Trelease as synonyms), *C. andersonii* Parry, and *C. spinosus* Nuttall.

Section *Microphylli* (Parry) Weberbauer in Engler & Prantl, *Nat. Pflanzenfam.* 3(5): 414 (1895) (as part of subgenus *Euceanothus*). Based on the unranked "Group" *Microphyllus* Parry, *Proc. Davenport Acad. Sci.* 5: 172 (1889). Weberbauer circumscribed this section to include *C. microphyllus* Michaux, *C. serpyllifolius* Nuttall, and *C. foliosus* Parry.

Section *Pomaderroides* A. P. de Candolle, *Prodr.* 2: 32 (1825). This section included four species, *C. globulosus* Labillardière, *C. spathulatus* Labillardière, *C. capsularis* G. Forster, and *C. wendlandianus* J. A. Schultes, each of which belong in other genera, including *Colubrina, Pomaderris, Spyridium,* and *Trymalium*.

Section *Rigidi* (Parry) Weberbauer in Engler & Prantl, *Nat. Pflanzenfam.* 3(5): 414 (1895) (as the only section of subgenus *Cerastes*). Based on the unranked "Group" *Rigidus* Parry, *Proc. Davenport Acad. Sci.* 5: 173 (1889). Weberbauer circumscribed this section to include *Ceanothus rigidus* Nuttall, *C. crassifolius* Torrey, *C. prostratus* Bentham, *C. divergens* Parry, *C. cuneatus* Nuttall, *C. greggii* A. Gray, *C. megacarpus* Nuttall, and *C. verrucosus* Nuttall.

Section *Sarcomphaloides* A. P. de Candolle, *Prodr.* 2: 32 (1825). De Candolle included one species, *C. africanus,* which is the basionym of *Noltea africana* (Linnaeus) Endlicher and the type species of *Noltea.*

Section *Scutia* A. P. de Candolle, *Prodr.* 2: 29 (1825). De Candolle erected section *Scutia* to include 20 tropical species of which all are now treated as members of such genera as *Colubrina, Krugiodendron, Scutia, Ventilago,* and *Ziziphus.* None of them is currently considered as belonging to *Ceanothus.*

Section *Sorediati* (Parry) Weberbauer in Engler & Prantl, *Nat. Pflanzenfam.* 3(5): 414 (1895) (as part of subgenus *Euceanothus*). Based on the unranked "Group" *Sorediatus* Parry, *Proc. Davenport Acad. Sci.* 5: 169 (1889). Weberbauer circumscribed this section to include *C. hirsutus* Nuttall, *C. tomentosus* Parry (including *C. azureus* Kellogg as a synonym), *C. sorediatus* Hooker & Arnott, *C. arboreus* E. L. Greene, and *C. velutinus* Douglas ex Hooker.

Section *Thyrsiflori* (Parry) Weberbauer in Engler & Prantl, *Nat. Pflanzenfam.* 3(5): 414 (1895) (as part of subgenus *Euceanothus*). Based on the unranked "Group" *Thyrsiflorus* Parry, *Proc. Davenport Acad. Sci.* 5: 169–170 (1889). Weberbauer circumscribed this section to include *C. thyrsiflorus* Eschscholtz, *C.* ×*lobbianus* Hooker, *C.* ×*veitchianus* Hooker, *C. parryi* Trelease, *C. papillosus* Torrey & A. Gray, *C. dentatus* Torrey & A. Gray, and *C. impressus* Trelease.

Names of Ceanothus Hybrids and of Species in Other Genera

C. africanus Linnaeus, *Species Plantarum* 1: 196 (1753), is the basionym of *Noltea africana* (Linnaeus) Endlicher (Mabberley 1984).

C. alamani A. P. de Candolle, *Prodr.* 2: 31 (1825), is a synonym of *Colubrina macrocarpa* Cavanilles (Johnston 1971).

C. arborescens Miller, *Gardeners Dictionary,* ed. 8, 3 (1768), is the basionym of *Colubrina arborescens* (Miller) Sargent (Johnston 1971, Fernández Nava 1986).

C. ×*arnoldii* Dippel, *Handbuch der Laubholzkunde* 2: 536 (1892); *C.* ×*arnouldii* Koehne, *Deutsche Dendrologie* 396 (1893). These names were attributed to putative artificial hybrids, *C. americanus* × *C. caeruleus* (Van Rensselaer 1942). The earliest available name for this hybrid is *C.* ×*delilianus* Spach.

C. asiaticus Linnaeus, *Species Plantarum* 1: 196 (1753), is the basionym of *Colubrina asiatica* (Linnaeus) Brongniart (Johnston 1971).

C. atropurpureus Rafinesque, *New Flora and Botany of North America* 3: 56 (1836), was published with a brief description but without citation of a type specimen. However, the name is illegitimate because Rafinesque considered its application doubtful, suggesting that it also might be a member of *Bumelia* or *Ilex.*

C. axillaris Carrière, *Revue Horticole*, 87 (1876), was apparently applied to a horticultural selection of *C. caeruleus.*

C. azureus Desfontaines ex Paxton, *Magazine of Botany* 2: 74 (1835), is a later homonym of *C. azureus* Desfontaines ex A. P. de Candolle, *Prodr.* 2: 31 (1825). Both names are synonyms of *C. caeruleus.*

C. ×bakeri E. L. Greene ex McMinn, *Ceanothus,* 276 (1942), was applied to putative hybrids between *C. prostratus* and either *C. cuneatus* or *C. vestitus* from Kings Canyon, Ormsby County (now Carson City), Nevada (McMinn 1942). The name was originally published as *C. bakeri* (E. L. Greene) Baker, *Western American Plants* 1: 16 (1902), which is illegitimate because it was published without a description. Greene's *C. bakeri* appeared on herbarium specimens but was never published; McMinn provided a diagnosis and cited a type specimen.

C. baumannianus E. Spach, *Histoire Naturelle des Végétaux* 2: 460 (1834), may be a horticultural name for a selection of *C. ovatus,* treated here as *C. herbaceus.*

C. bertinii Carrière, *Rev. Hort.*, 440 (1872), appears to be a horticultural name for a cultivar of *C. caeruleus.*

C. bicolor Rafinesque, *New Fl. Bot. N. Amer.* 3: 57 (1856), is a later homonym of *C. bicolor* J. A. Schultes, a synonym of *C. caeruleus* Lagasca. Rafinesque considered his *C. bicolor* a relative of *C. thyrsiflorus.*

C. burkwoodii is a horticultural name anonymously published in *Gardeners' Chronicle,* series 3, 89: 438, and 90: 366 (1931), and apparently was applied to a complex horticultural hybrid involving either *C. ×delilianus* or *C. ×delilianus* 'Indigo' (Rehder 1940, Van Rensselaer 1942, Huxley et al. 1992). However, the parentage remains unclear.

C. ×burtonensis Van Rensselaer, *Ceanothus,* 46 (1942), is a horticultural name without a formal description or designation of a type, applied to a naturally occurring hybrid, *C. impressus* × *C. thyrsiflorus.*

C. capensis (Thunberg) A. P. de Candolle, *Prodr.* 2: 30 (1825), is a synonym of *Scutia myrtina* (N. L. Burman) Kurz (Johnston 1974).

C. capsularis G. Forster, *Florulae Insularum Australium Prodromus,* 18 (1876), is a synonym of *Colubrina asiatica* (Linnaeus) Brongniart (Johnston 1971).

C. celtidifolius Chamisso & Schlechtendal, *Linnaea* 5: 602 (1830), is the basionym of *Colubrina celtidifolia* (Chamisso & Schlechtendal) Schlechtendal (Johnston 1971, Fernández Nava 1986).

C. chloroxylon (Linnaeus) Nees, *Systema Laurinarum,* 660 (1836), is a synonym of *Ziziphus chloroxylon* (Linnaeus) Oliver (Johnston 1964).

C. circumscissus (Linnaeus fil.) Gaertner, *De Fructibus et Seminibus Plantarum* 2: 110 (1791), is a synonym of *Scutia myrtina* (N. L. Burman) Kurz (Johnston 1974).

C. circumscissus var. *pauciflorus* A. P. de Candolle, *Prodr.* 2: 30 (1825), is a synonym of *Scutia myrtina* (N. L. Burman) Kurz (Johnston 1974).

C. collinus Douglas ex Knight & West, *Floral Cabinet and Magazine of Exotic Botany* 1: pl. 13 (1837–1840), was apparently applied to a horticultural selection of *C. oliganthus* var. *sorediatus,* grown from seeds collected by David Douglas.

C. ×*connivens* E. L. Greene, *Pittonia* 2: 16 (1889), was applied to a naturally occurring hybrid, *C. cuneatus* × (*C. fresnensis* or *C. prostratus*) (McMinn 1942).

C. colubrinus (Jacquin) Lamarck, *Encyclopédie Méthodique* 2: 90 (1793), is a synonym of *Colubrina arborescens* (Johnston 1971).

C. cubensis (Jacquin) Lamarck, *Encycl. Méthod.* 2: 90 (1793), is a synonym of *Colubrina cubensis* (Jacquin) Brongniart (Johnston 1971).

C. ×*cyam* Lenz, *Aliso* 3: 53 (1954), is an artificial hybrid, *C. cyaneus* × *C. americanus.*

C. ×*delilianus* Spach, *Hist. Nat. Vég.* 2: 459 (1834), is a horticultural selection of an artificial hybrid, *C. caeruleus* × *C. americanus* (Huxley et al. 1992). Synonyms include *C.* ×*arnoldii* Dippel, *C.* ×*arnouldii* Koehne, and apparently *C. hybridus* K. H. E. Koch. Other informal horticultural names that have been applied to this hybrid include *C. versaillensis* and *C. azureus* (Rehder 1940).

C. dillenianus K. H. E. Koch, *Dendrologie* 1: 620 (1869), apparently is either the name for a horticultural selection of *C. americanus* or an artificial hybrid involving *C. americanus* as one parent.

C. discolor Ventenat, *Jardin de la Malmaison* 2: pl. 58 (1804), may be a synonym of *Pomaderris elliptica* Labillardière (Suessenguth 1953).

C. divergens Poeppig ex Endlicher, *Genera Plantarum,* 1,099 (1840), is an illegitimate name, based on an unpublished manuscript, and referred to *Ochetophila* by Endlicher without a description or citation of specimens. *Ochetophila* included species now placed in either *Discaria* or *Sageretia.*

C. elegans Lemaire, *Illustration Horticole* 7: 268 (1860), was apparently applied to a horticultural selection of *C. thyrsiflorus.*

C. elongatus Salisbury, *Prodromus Stirpium in Horto,* 140 (1796), may be a synonym of *Noltea africana* (Suessenguth 1953).

C. exaltatus Van Rensselaer, *Ceanothus,* 30 (1942), is a horticultural name, without a formal description or designation of a type, applied to a selection of *C. gloriosus* var. *exaltatus.*

C. excelsus (Fenzl) Steudel, *Nomenclator Botanicus,* ed. 2, 1: 313 (1840), is a synonym of *Alphitonia excelsa* (Fenzl) Bentham (Mabberley 1997).

C. ferreus (Vahl) A. P. de Candolle, *Prodr.* 2: 30 (1825), is a synonym of *Krugiodendron ferreum* (Vahl) Urban (Johnston 1962, Fernández Nava 1996).

C. ferrugineus Wendland ex Steudel, *Nomencl. Bot.*, ed. 2, 1: 313 (1840), is an illegitimate name, published without a description, but treated as a synonym of *Pomaderris lanigera* Sims (Suessenguth 1953).

C. ×flexilis E. L. Greene ex McMinn, *Ceanothus*, 274 (1942), is a naturally occurring hybrid, *C. cuneatus × C. prostratus*, known from widely separated localities in the Klamath Mountains, the southern Cascade Range, and the northern Sierra Nevada of California.

C. fontanesianus Spach, *Hist. Nat. Vég.* 2: 460 (1834), was apparently applied to a horticultural selection of *C. ovatus*, treated here as *C. herbaceus*.

C. glaber Spach, *Hist. Nat. Vég.* 2: 459 (1834), was apparently applied to a horticultural selection of a plant originally obtained from North America and grown in Europe, but its identity remains unknown.

C. globulosus Labillardière, *Novae Hollandiae Plantarum Specimen* 1: 61 (1805), is the basionym of *Cryptandra globulosa* (Labillardière) F. Mueller, *Pomaderris globulosa* (Labillardière) G. Don, *Trymalium globulosum* (Labillardière) Fenzl, and *Spyridium globulosum* (Labillardière) Bentham (Chapman 1991, Rye 1996).

C. grandiflorus Dippel, *Handb. Laubholzk.* 2: 536 (1892), was apparently applied to a horticultural selection of *C. ovatus*, treated here as *C. herbaceus*.

C. grandis Douglas ex Hooker, *Flora Boreali-Americana* 1: 125 (1830), is an illegitimate name, published without a description, and listed by a Hooker as a synonym of *C. laevigatus* Hooker (*C. velutinus* var. *hookeri* M. C. Johnston).

C. granulosus Ruiz López & Pavón, *Flora Peruviana et Chilensis* 3: 5, pl. 228 (1802), is the basionym of *Rhamnus granulosa* (Ruiz López & Pavón) M. C. Johnston (Johnston and Johnston 1978).

C. guadalupae (A. P. de Candolle) Steudel, *Nomencl. Bot.*, ed. 2, 1: 313 (1840), is apparently based on *C. laevigatus* (Vahl) A. P. de Candolle var. *guadalupae* A. P. de Candolle. The type was collected on Guadalupe in the West Indies and thus is unlikely to be a *Ceanothus*.

C. guineensis A. P. de Candolle, *Prodr.* 2: 30 (1825), is the basionym of *Dichapetalum guineense* (A. P. de Candolle) Keay (Johnston 1971).

C. hartwegii Heynhold, *Nomenclator Botanicus Hortensis* 2: 128 (1840), is an illegitimate name, apparently published without a description, and applied to a horticultural selection of an unknown species.

C. ×humboldtensis J. B. Roof, *Four Seasons* 4(3): 21 (1973), is a naturally occurring hybrid, *C. pumilus × C. cuneatus* var. *ramulosus*.

C. hybridus K. H. E. Koch, *Dendrologie* 1: 620 (1869), was apparently applied to an artificial hybrid involving *C. americanus* and *C. caeruleus*.

C. hypericoides L'Héritier ex A. P. de Candolle, *Prodr.* 2: 32 (1825), is illegitimate because de Candolle treated the name as a synonym of *C. microphyllus*.

C. infestus Humboldt, Bonpland & Kunth, *Nova Genera et Species* 7: 61 (1825), is the basionym of *Adolphia infesta* (H.B.K.) Meissner (Fernández Nava 1986).

C. intermedius Hooker, *Fl. Bor.-Amer.* 1: 124 (1830), published without a description, is a later homonym of *C. intermedius* Pursh and apparently referable to *C. herbaceus* Rafinesque.

C. intermedius Koehne, *Deut. Dendrol.*, 396 (1893), was apparently applied to a horticultural selection of unknown origin but probably referable to what is now called *C. americanus* var. *intermedius* (Pursh) Trelease. The name is a later homonym of *C. intermedius* Pursh, a synonym of *C. americanus* var. *americanus.*

C. laevigatus (Vahl) A. P. de Candolle, *Prodr.* 2: 30 (1825), was apparently based on *Rhamnus laevigatus* Vahl, *Symbolae Botanicae* 3: 41 (1794). However, Johnston (1964) concluded that the description and type are ambiguous, and its disposition remains unclear. The type was collected on Saint Croix in the West Indies and thus unlikely to be a *Ceanothus.*

C. laevigatus (Vahl) A. P. de Candolle var. *guadalupae* A. P. de Candolle, *Prodr.* 2: 30 (1825). The type was collected on Guadalupe in the West Indies and thus is unlikely to be a *Ceanothus.*

C. laevigatus T. J. Howell, *Flora of Northwest America*, 114 (1898), a later homonym, was apparently published without reference to the earlier name, *C. laevigatus* Douglas ex Hooker, a synonym of *C. velutinus* var. *hookeri.*

C. lancifolius Moench, *Methodus Plantas Horti*, 651 (1794), was apparently applied to a horticultural selection of *Noltea africana* (Linnaeus) Endlicher.

C. laniger Andrews, *Botanist's Repository* 9: pl. 569 (1809), is the basionym of *Pomaderris lanigera* (Andrews) Sims and *Pomatoderris lanigera* (Andrews) Schultes (Chapman 1991).

C. leschenaultii A. P. de Candolle, *Prodr.* 2: 31 (1825). Johnston (1971) concluded that this name is not applicable to a member of Rhamnaceae, but its taxonomic disposition remains unresolved. The type, attributed to Leschenault, was collected in Ceylon and thus is unlikely to be a *Ceanothus.*

C. ×lobbianus Hooker, *Curtis's Botanical Magazine*, pl. 4,811 (1864), was described as a species, but Parry (1889) considered it a putative hybrid between *C. thyrsiflorus* and an unknown species. Brandegee (1894) and Trelease (1894) suggested that the hybrid involved *C. dentatus* × *C. thyrsiflorus*. The original illustration of *C. ×lobbianus* is similar to naturally occurring hybrids, *C. dentatus* × *C. thyrsiflorus* var. *griseus,* from the Del Monte Forest near Monterey, based on specimens at the California Academy of Sciences herbarium. Synonyms include *C. dentatus* Torrey & A. Gray subsp. *lobbianus* (Hooker) Trelease, *Proc. Calif. Acad. Sci.*, ser. 2, 1: 112 (1888), and *C. dentatus* Torrey & A. Gray var. *lobbianus* (Hooker) Jepson, *Manual of the Flowering Plants of California*, 618 (1925).

C. ×*lorenzenii* (Jepson) McMinn, *Ceanothus,* 267 (1942), is a naturally occurring hybrid, *C. cordulatus* × *C. velutinus* var. *velutinus,* and is known from widely separated localities in the Klamath Mountains, the southern Cascade Range, and the Sierra Nevada of California. The name is based on *C. velutinus* Douglas ex Hooker var. *lorenzenii* Jepson, *Man. Fl. Pl. Calif.,* 619 (1925).

C. macrocarpus Cavanilles, *Icones et Descriptiones Plantarum* 3: 38 (1795), is the basionym of *Colubrina macrocarpa* (Cavanilles) G. Don (Johnston 1971, Fernández Nava 1996).

C. macrocarpus A. P. de Candolle, *Prodr.* 2: 32–33 (1825), was apparently published as a synonym of *C. mocinianus* A. P. de Candolle but with a clear indication by de Candolle that it was not the same as *C. macrocarpus* Cavanilles. Regardless, it is a later homonym of *C. macrocarpus* Cavanilles, a synonym of *C. megacarpus.*

C. macrocarpus Steudel, *Nomencl. Bot.,* ed. 2, 1: 313 (1840), is a later homonym of *C. macrocarpus* Cavanilles.

C. macrophyllus Dippel, *Handb. Laubholzk.* 2: 533 (1892), is apparently a horticultural name for a selection of *C. americanus.*

C. ×*mendocinensis* McMinn, *Ceanothus,* 266 (1942), is a naturally occurring hybrid, *C. thyrsiflorus* × *C. velutinus* var. *hookeri.*

C. milleri Tausch, *Flora* 21(Beiblatt): 79 (1838), was published without citation of a specimen, although reference was made to a North American origin. The disposition of this name remains unresolved.

C. mocinianus A. P. de Candolle, *Prodr.* 2: 32 (1825). Johnston (1971) suggested that the description and type are ambiguous and could not be clearly assigned. The name may be considered illegitimate, however, because de Candolle included his *C. macrocarpus* as a synonym.

C. mollissimus Torrey in J. C. Frémont, *Report of an Exploration of the Country Lying Between the Missouri River and the Rocky Mountains,* 84 (1843), was published without a description, but the specimen referred to by Torrey belongs to *C. herbaceus* (Welsh 1998).

C. multiflorus Dippel, *Handb. Laubholzk.* 2: 533 (1892), was apparently applied to a horticultural selection of *C. americanus.*

C. mysticinus (Aiton) A. P. de Candolle, *Prodr.* 2: 31 (1825), is a synonym of *Helinus mystacinus* (Aiton) E. Meyer ex Steudel (Johnston 1971).

C. napalensis Wallich in Roxburgh, *Flora Indica* 2: 375 (1825), is the basionym of *Rhamnus napalensis* (Wallich) Wallich ex Lawson (Johnston 1971).

C. neumannii Tausch, *Flora* 21: 738 (1838), was published without citation of a specimen, although reference was made to a North American origin. The disposition of this name remains unresolved.

C. nitidus Torrey. Brewer and Watson, *Botany of California* 1: 103 (1880), attributed this name to Torrey as having been published in the *Reports of Explorations and Surveys, to Ascertain the Most Practicable and Economical Route for a Railroad from the Mississippi*

River to the Pacific Ocean 4(5): 75 (1857) and cited it as a synonym of *C. sorediatus*. The name does not appear in the latter publication, however, and McMinn (1942) inexplicably treated it as a synonym of *C. tomentosus*.

C. ×*pallidus* Koehne, *Deut. Dendrol.,* 396 (1893), is a horticultural name for an artificial hybrid, *C.* ×*delilianus* × *C. ovatus,* treated here as *C. herbaceus* (Rehder 1940, Van Rensselaer 1942).

C. paniculatus Roth, *Novae Plantarum Species,* 154 (1821), is a synonym of *Celastrus paniculatus* Willdenow (Hou 1955).

C. procumbens K. H. E. Koch, *Dendrologie* 1: 620 (1869), apparently is a horticultural name for a selection of *C. americanus* or an artificial hybrid involving *C. americanus* as one parent.

C. pubescens Ruiz López & Pavón, *Fl. Peruv. Chil.* 3: 6, pl. 228 (1802), is a synonym of *Rhamnus sphaerosperma* (Johnston and Johnston 1978).

C. pubiflorus A. P. de Candolle, *Prodr.* 2: 30 (1825), may be a synonym of *Ventilago oblongifolia* (Johnston 1971).

C. pulchellus Delile ex E. Spach, *Hist. Nat. Vég.* 2: 459 (1834), is apparently a horticultural name and a synonym of *C.* ×*delilianus* (Suessenguth 1953).

C. radicans was apparently published without an author, description, or citation of a specimen in the *Hand-list of Trees and Shrubs Grown in the Royal Botanic Gardens,* part 1 (1894).

C. reclinatus L'Héritier, *Sertum Anglicum,* 6 (1789), is a synonym of *Colubrina elliptica* (Swartz) Brizicky & Stern (Johnston 1971, Fernández Nava 1996).

C. reclinatus Steudel, *Nomencl. Bot.,* ed. 2, 1: 313 (1840), was apparently published without a description or citation of a type specimen, and also is a later homonym of *C. reclinatus* L'Héritier.

C. ×*regius* (Jepson) McMinn, *Ceanothus,* 268 (1942), is a naturally occurring hybrid, *C. papillosus* × *C. thyrsiflorus* var. *thyrsiflorus,* in the Santa Cruz Mountains of California and is based on *C. papillosus* Torrey & A. Gray var. *regius* Jepson, *Man. Fl. Pl. Calif.,* 618 (1925).

C. riparius Poeppig ex Endlicher, *Gen. Pl.,* 1,099 (1840), is an illegitimate name, based on an unpublished manuscript, and referred to *Ochetophila* without a description and without citation of specimens. *Ochetophila* included species now placed in either *Discaria* or *Sageretia.*

C. ×*roseus* Koehne, *Deut. Dendrol.,* 395 (1893), is apparently a horticultural name for an artificial hybrid, *C.* ×*delilianus* × *C. ovatus* (Van Rensselaer 1942), and thus is similar to *C.* ×*pallidus* Koehne.

C. roweanus Van Rensselaer, *Ceanothus,* 83 (1942), is a horticultural name, without a formal recombination at the species level, applied to a selection made from a natural population of *C. papillosus* var. *roweanus.*

C. ×*rugosus* E. L. Greene, *Flora Franciscana* 1: 88 (1891), is a naturally occurring hybrid, *C. prostratus* × *C. velutinus,* from the Cascade Range and Sierra Nevada of California (McMinn 1942).

C. sarcomphalus (Linnaeus) A. P. de Candolle, *Prodr.* 2: 30 (1825), is a synonym of *Ziziphus sarcomphalus* (Linnaeus) M. C. Johnston (Johnston 1963).

C. scandens D. Dietrich, *Synopsis Plantarum* 1: 812 (1839), is a synonym of *Noltea africana* (Linnaeus) Endlicher (Mabberley 1984).

C. ×*serrulatus* McMinn, *Madroño* 2: 89 (1933), is a naturally occurring hybrid, *C. cordulatus* × *C. prostratus* (McMinn 1942).

C. spathulatus Labillardière, *Nov. Holl. Pl.* 1: 60 (1805), is the basionym of *Pomaderris spathulata* (Labillardière) G. Don and *Trymalium spathulatus* (Labillardière) Ostenfeld (Chapman 1991, Rye 1996).

C. sphaerocarpus A. P. de Candolle, *Prodr.* 2: 30 (1825), is an illegitimate name, apparently based on *Rhamnus sphaerosperma* Swartz (Johnston and Johnston 1978).

C. ×*subsericeus* Rydberg, *Bulletin of the Torrey Botanical Club* 31: 564 (1904), is apparently a naturally occurring hybrid, *C. fendleri* var. *fendleri* × *C. ovatus,* treated here as *C. herbaceus.*

C. tardivus Lavallée, *Arboretum Segrezianum,* 51 (1877), is a horticultural name published without a description, referring to a species of unknown origin.

C. triflorus (Brongniart ex Sweet) Steudel, *Nomencl. Bot.,* ed. 2, 1: 313 (1840), is a synonym of *Colubrina triflora* (Brongniart) ex Sweet (Johnston 1971).

C. triqueter Wallich in Roxburgh, *Fl. Ind.* 2: 376 (1824), is the basionym of *Rhamnus triquetra* (Wallich) Wallich (Suessenguth 1953).

C. ×*vanrensselaeri* J. B. Roof, *Four Seasons* 2(3): 17 (1967), is a naturally occurring hybrid, *C. incanus* × *C. thyrsiflorus.*

C. ×*veitchianus* Hooker, *Curtis's Bot. Mag.* 85: pl. 5,127 (1859), is a naturally occurring hybrid, *C. cuneatus* var. *rigidus* × *C. thyrsiflorus* var. *griseus* (Trelease 1897, McMinn 1944).

C. venosus Royle, *Illustrations of the Botany of the Himalayan Mountains,* 169 (1835), is apparently based on a specimen from the Himalaya. Although its disposition is unknown, it is unlikely to be a *Ceanothus.*

C. wendlandianus J. A. Schultes in J. Roemer & J. A. Schultes, *Systema Vegetabilium* 5: 299 (1819), is the basionym of *Pomaderris wendlandiana* (Schultes) G. Don and *Trymalium wendlandianum* (Schultes) Sweet (Chapman 1991).

C. wightianus Heyne in Wallich, *List of Dried Specimens of Plants (Wallich's Catalogue),* number 4,264 (1831), was published without a description, based on a specimen collected in India. It may be the same species as *Rhamnus wightii* Wight & Arnott, *Prodromus Florae Peninsulae Indiae Orientalis,* 164 (1839).

C. zeylandicus Roth, *Nov. Pl. Sp.,* 153 (1821), is a synonym of *Scutia myrtina* (N. L. Burman) Kurz (Johnston 1974).

Conversion Tables

Elevations are given in both feet and meters throughout. Here, equivalents are provided for the other metric measurements used in Part 2 and the nonmetric measurements used in Part 1.

INCH	MM		CM	CM OR INCHES	INCHES		M	M OR FEET	FEET
1/8	3.2		2.5	1	0.4		0.3	1	3.3
1/6	4.2		5	2	0.8		0.6	2	6.6
1/4	6.4		8	3	1.2		0.9	3	9.8
1/3	8.5		10	4	1.6		1.2	4	13
3/8	9.5		13	5	2.0		1.5	5	16
1/2	12		15	6	2.4		1.8	6	20
3/4	19		18	7	2.8		2.1	7	23
1	25		20	8	3.1		2.4	8	26
			23	9	3.5		2.7	9	30
			25	10	4		3	10	33
			51	20	8		6	20	66
			76	30	12		9	30	98
			100	40	16		12	40	130
			130	50	20		15	50	160
			150	60	24		18	60	200
			180	70	28		21	70	230
			200	80	32		24	80	260
			230	90	35		27	90	300
			250	100	40		30	100	330

Glossary

appressed hairs that are pressed against the surface, thus appearing parallel to the surface

axillary attached at the junction of the leaf and stem (node)

cismontane in California, meaning west of the Sierra Nevada and Peninsular Range

deltate shape of an equilateral triangle

dentate leaf margin with relatively large teeth pointing outward, not toward the tip

denticulate leaf margin with relatively small teeth pointed outward, not toward the tip

disk in *Ceanothus,* a fleshy, plate-like structure located at the base of the ovary

glaucous appearing white or pale gray because of a waxy surface

globose shape of a globe or sphere

internode segment of the stem between two nodes (junctions of the leaf and the stem)

lanceolate leaf blade longer than wide, widest below the middle

midvein central vein of a leaf blade, extending from the petiole to the tip

oblanceolate leaf blade longer than wide, widest above the middle

obovate leaf blade with the outline of an egg, widest above the middle

obovoid three-dimensional shape with the shape of an egg, widest above the middle

ovate leaf blade with the outline of an egg, widest below the middle

ovoid three-dimensional shape with the outline of an egg, widest below the middle

paniculate in *Ceanothus,* of an inflorescence with multiple series of branches bearing terminal, umbellate clusters of flowers

papillose surface with globose multicellular hairs or projections

perianth structure composed of the calyx (sepals) and the corolla (petals)

petiolate petioles at least 2 mm long

phylogenetic (adverb, **phylogenetically**) referring to patterns of evolutionary descent

puberulent small, short, straight, erect hairs

pyrene in *Ceanothus,* a fleshy unit of the fruit enclosing a seed with hard walls

racemose in *Ceanothus,* of an inflorescence with a set of branches each bearing terminal, umbellate clusters of flowers

reflexed bent backward or downward along the stem

retuse leaf tip that appears notched

serrulate leaf margin with relatively small teeth pointing toward the tip

sessile without a stalk or petiole

spinulose leaf margin with small, sharply pointed teeth

strigulose short, straight, appressed hairs

subcordate weakly heart-shaped leaf base

subg. abbreviation for the taxonomic rank of subgenus

subglabrous surface with only a few scattered hairs

subglobose three-dimensional shape that appears almost round in outline

suborbicular leaf shape that appears almost round in outline

subsessile in *Ceanothus*, pedicels or peduncles less than 1 mm long, thus appearing almost sessile

subsp. (plural, **subspp.**) abbreviation for the taxonomic rank of subspecies

subumbellate flowers with pedicels of equal length but with some attached at slightly different levels near the tip of the solitary peduncle

taxon (plural, **taxa**) naturally occurring group of organisms given a botanical name

tomentum (adjective, **tomentose**) densely entangled, white hairs

transmontane in California, meaning east of the Sierra Nevada and Peninsular Range

var. (plural, **vars.**) abbreviation for the taxonomic rank of variety

veinlet terminal vein in the leaf blade

Bibliography

Abrams, L. 1951. *Illustrated Flora of the Pacific States,* vol. 3. Stanford, California: University Press.

Baker, D. D., and B. C. Mullin. 1994. Diversity of *Frankia* nodule endophytes of the actinorhizal shrub *Ceanothus* as assessed by RFLP patterns from single nodule lobes. *Soil Biology and Biochemistry* 26: 547–567.

Barbour, M. G., and J. Major. 1977. *Terrestrial Vegetation of California.* New York: Wiley.

Bean, W. J. 1936. *Trees and Shrubs Hardy in the British Isles.* London: John Murray.

Boyd, S., T. S. Ross, and L. Arnseth. 1991. *Ceanothus ophiochilus* (Rhamnaceae): A distinctive, narrowly endemic species from Riverside County, California. *Phytologia* 70: 28–41.

Brandegee, K. 1894. Studies in *Ceanothus. Proceedings of the California Academy of Sciences,* series 2, 4: 173–222.

Brickell, C. D., et al., editors. 2004. International Code of Nomenclature for Cultivated Plants. *Acta Horticulturae* 647: 1–123.

Brizicky, G. K. 1964. A further note on *Ceanothus herbaceus* versus *C. ovatus. Journal of the Arnold Arboretum* 45: 471–473.

Chapman, A. D. 1991. *Australian Plant Name Index,* vol. 1, A–C. Canberra: Australian Government Publishing Service.

Coile, N. C. 1988. Taxonomic Studies on the Deciduous Species of *Ceanothus* L. (Rhamnaceae). Ph.D. dissertation, University of Georgia, Athens.

Conard, S. G., A. E. Jaramillo, K. Cromack Jr., and S. Rose. 1985. The role of the genus *Ceanothus* in western forest ecosystems. *General Technical Report* PNW-182. Portland, Oregon: U.S. Department of Agriculture Forest Service, Pacific Northwest Forest and Range Experiment Station.

Conrad, C. E., and W. C. Oechel. 1982. Proceedings of the symposium on dynamics and management of Mediterranean-type ecosystems. *General Technical Report* PSW-58. Berkeley, California: U.S. Department of Agriculture Forest Service, Pacific Southwest Forest and Range Experiment Station.

Correll, D. S., and M. C. Johnston. 1970. *Manual of the Vascular Plants of Texas.* Renner: Texas Research Foundation.

Delwiche, C. C., P. J. Zinke, and C. M. Johnson. 1965. Nitrogen fixation by *Ceanothus.* *Plant Pathology* 40: 1045–1047.

Di Castri, F., and H. A. Mooney. 1973. *Mediterranean Type Ecosystems.* London: Chapman and Hall.

Dreistadt, S. H., J. K. Clark, and M. L. Flint. 1994. *Pests of Landscape Trees and Shrubs, an Integrated Pest Management Guide.* Berkeley: University of California Press.

Emery, D. 1988. *Seed Propagation of Native California Plants.* Santa Barbara, California: Santa Barbara Botanic Garden.

Evans, R. A., H. H. Biswell, and D. E. Palmquist. 1987. Seed dispersal in *Ceanothus cuneatus* and *C. leucodermis* in a Sierran oak-woodland savanna. *Madroño* 34: 283–293.

Everett, P. C. 1957. *A Summary of the Culture of California Plants at the Rancho Santa Ana Botanic Garden, 1927–1950.* Claremont, California: Rancho Santa Ana Botanic Garden.

Fernald, M. L. 1950. *Gray's Manual of Botany,* ed. 8. New York: American Book Company.

Fernández Nava, R. 1986. Rhamnaceae. In A. Gómez-Pompa, editor, *Flora de Veracruz* 50: 1–63. Xalapa, Veracruz, Mexico: Instituto Nacional de Investigaciones Sobre Recursos Bióticos.

Fernández Nava, R. 1996. Rhamnaceae. In J. Rzedowski and G. C. Rzedowski, editors, *Flora del Bajío y de Regiones Adyacentes* 43: 1–69. Pátzcuaro, Michoacán, Mexico: Instituto de Ecología.

Fishbein, M., R. K. Wilson, D. Yetman, P. Jenkins, and P. S. Martin. 1998. Annotated list of Río Mayo vascular plants. In P. S. Martin, D. Yetman, M. Fishbein, P. Jenkins, T. R. van Devender, and R. K. Wilson, editors, *Gentry's Río Mayo Plants,* pp. 167–522. Tucson: University of Arizona Press.

Gleason, H. A., and A. Cronquist. 1991. *Manual of Vascular Plants of Northeastern United States and Adjacent Canada,* ed. 2. Bronx: New York Botanical Garden.

González Elizondo, M., S. González Elizondo, and Y. Herrera Arrieta. 1991. Flora de Durango. *Listados Florísticos de México* 9. México: Instituto de Biología, Universidad Nacional Autónoma de México.

Greuter, W., et al., editors. 2000. International Code of Botanical Nomenclature. *Regnum Vegetabile* 138: 1–474.

Hanes, T. L. 1971. Succession after fire in the chaparral of southern California. *Ecological Monographs* 41: 27–52.

Hannan, L. 1974. An intersectional hybrid in *Ceanothus. Madroño* 22: 402.

Hardig, T. M., P. S. Soltis, and D. E. Soltis. 2000. Diversification of the North American shrub genus *Ceanothus* (Rhamnaceae): Conflicting phylogenies from nuclear ribosomal DNA and chloroplast DNA. *American Journal of Botany* 87: 108–123.

Hardig, T. M., P. S. Soltis, D. E. Soltis, and R. B. Hudson. 2002. Morphological and molecular analysis of putative hybrid speciation in *Ceanothus* (Rhamnaceae). *Systematic Botany* 27: 734–746.

Hillier, J., and A. Coombert, editors. 2002. *The Hillier Manual of Trees and Shrubs,* ed. 7. Trowbridge, England: Redwood Books.

Hoover, R. F. 1966. Miscellaneous new names for California plants. *Leaflets of Western Botany* 10: 337–350.

Hoover, R. F. 1970. *The Vascular Plants of San Luis Obispo County, California.* Berkeley: University of California Press.

Hoover, R. F., and J. B. Roof. 1966. Two new shrubs from San Luis Obispo County, California. *Four Seasons* 2(1): 2–5.

Hou, D. 1955. A revision of the genus *Celastrus. Annals of the Missouri Botanical Garden* 42: 215–302.

Howell, J. T. 1937. New Californian plants. *Leaflets of Western Botany* 2: 42–45.

Howell, J. T. 1939. Studies in *Ceanothus* 1. *Leaflets of Western Botany* 2: 159–165.

Howell, J. T. 1940. Studies in *Ceanothus* 3–5. *Leaflets of Western Botany* 2: 228–240, 259–262, 285–289.

Huxley, A., M. Griffiths, and M. Levy, editors. 1992. *The New Royal Horticultural Society Dictionary of Gardening.* London: Macmillan.

James, S. 1984. Lignotubers and burls—Their structure, function, and ecological significance in Mediterranean ecosystems. *Botanical Review* 50: 225–266.

Jeong, S.-C., A. Liston, and D. D. Myrold. 1997. Molecular phylogeny of the genus *Ceanothus* (Rhamnaceae) using *rbc*L and *ndh*F sequences. *Theoretical and Applied Genetics* 94: 852–857.

Jepson, W. L. 1925. *Manual of the Flowering Plants of California.* Berkeley: Associated Students Store, University of California.

Jepson, W. L. 1936. *A Flora of California,* vol. 2, Capparidaceae to Cornaceae. Berkeley: Associated Students Store, University of California.

Johnston, M. C. 1962. Revision of *Condalia* including *Microrhamnus* (Rhamnaceae). *Brittonia* 14: 332–368.

Johnston, M. C. 1963. The species of *Ziziphus* indigenous to United States and Mexico. *American Journal of Botany* 50: 1020–1027.

Johnston, M. C. 1964. The fourteen species of *Ziziphus* including *Sarcomphalus* (Rhamnaceae) indigenous to the West Indies. *American Journal of Botany* 51: 1113–1118.

Johnston, M. C. 1971. Revision of *Colubrina* (Rhamnaceae). *Brittonia* 23: 2–53.

Johnston, M. C. 1974. Revision of *Scutia* (Rhamnaceae). *Bulletin of the Torrey Botanical Club* 101: 64–72.

Johnston, M. C., and L. A. Johnston. 1978. *Rhamnus. Flora Neotropica* 20: 1–96.

Junak, S., T. Ayers, R. Scott, D. Wilken, and D. Young. 1993. *A Flora of Santa Cruz Island.* Santa Barbara, California: Santa Barbara Botanic Garden.

Keeley, J. E. 1975. Longevity of nonsprouting *Ceanothus. American Midland Naturalist* 93: 504–507.

Keeley, J. E. 1987. Role of fire in seed germination of woody taxa in California chaparral. *Ecology* 68: 434–443.

Keeley, J. E. 1991. Seed germination and life history syndromes in the California chaparral. *Botanical Review* 57: 81–116.

Klein, F. 1970. Chemotaxonomic evidence for a new form of *Ceanothus incanus* Nutt. in Torrey and A. Gray. *Four Seasons* 3(3): 19–22.

Kruckeberg, A. R. 1982. *Gardening with Native Plants of the Pacific Northwest.* Seattle: University of Washington Press.

Kruckeberg, A. R. 1984. California serpentines: Flora, vegetation, geology, soils, and management problems. *University of California Publications in Botany* 78: 1–180.

Lenz, L. W. 1986. *Marcus E. Jones: Western Geologist, Mining Engineer & Botanist.* Claremont, California: Rancho Santa Ana Botanic Garden.

León de la Luz, J. L., R. del Carmen Coria Benet, and J. Cansino. 1995. Reserva de la Biósfera El Vizcaíno, Baja California Sur. *Listados Florísticos de México* 11. México: Instituto de Biología, Universidad Nacional Autónoma de México.

Lindley, J. 1840. *Ceanothus pallidus. Edwards's Botanical Register* 26: pl. 20.

Lucas, N. 1996. *National Collection of Ceanothus Cultivars.* Wimborne, England: Knoll Gardens and Nursery.

Mabberley, D. J. 1984. Pallas's buckthorn and two and half centuries of neglected binomials. *Taxon* 33: 435.

Mabberley, D. J. 1997. *The Plant-Book,* ed. 2. Cambridge: Cambridge University Press.

McMinn, H. E. 1939. *An Illustrated Manual of California Shrubs.* Berkeley: University of California Press.

McMinn, H. E. 1942. A systematic study of the genus *Ceanothus.* In M. Van Rensselaer and H. E. McMinn, *Ceanothus,* part 2, pp. 131–303. Santa Barbara, California: Santa Barbara Botanic Garden.

McMinn, H. E. 1944. The importance of field hybrids in determining species in the genus *Ceanothus. Proceedings of the California Academy of Sciences,* series 4, 25: 323–356.

McVaugh, R. 1998. Botanical results of the Sessé and Moçiño expedition (1787–1803). 6. Reports and records from western Mexico, 1790–1792. *Boletín del Instituto de Botánica* 6: 1–178.

Matthews, M. A. 1997. *An Illustrated Field Key to the Flowering Plants of Monterey County.* Sacramento: California Native Plant Society.

Medan, D., and C. Schirarend. 2004. Rhamnaceae. In K. Kubitzki, editor, *The Families and Genera of Vascular Plants,* vol. 6, Celastrales, Oxalidales, Rosales, Cornales, Ericales, pp. 320–339. Berlin: Springer-Verlag.

Mills, J. N., and J. Kummerow. 1989. Herbivores, seed predators, and chaparral succession. In S. Keeley, The California chaparral, paradigms reexamined, pp. 50–55. *Natural History Museum of Los Angeles Science Series* 34: 1–171.

Mooney, H. E., and C. E. Conrad, editors. 1977. Proceedings of the symposium on the environmental consequences of fire and fuel management in Mediterranean ecosystems. *General Technical Report* WO-3. U.S. Department of Agriculture Forest Service.

Moran, R. 1996. The flora of Guadalupe Island, Mexico. *Memoirs of the California Academy of Sciences* 19: 1–190.

Munz, P. A. 1959. *A California Flora.* Berkeley: University of California Press.

Nobs, M. A. 1963. Experimental studies on species relationships in *Ceanothus. Publication* 623. Washington D.C.: Carnegie Institution of Washington.

Parry, C. C. 1889. *Ceanothus,* L. A synoptical list, comprising thirty-three species, with notes and descriptions. *Proceedings of the Davenport Academy of Sciences* 5: 162–174.

Quick, C. R., and A. S. Quick. 1961. Germination of *Ceanothus* seeds. *Madroño* 16: 23–30.

Raven, P. H. 1963. A flora of San Clemente Island. *Aliso* 5: 289–347.

Raven, P. H., and D. I. Axelrod. 1978. Origin and relationships of the California flora. *University of California Publications in Botany* 72: 1–134.

Rehder, A. 1940. *Manual of Cultivated Trees and Shrubs.* New York: Macmillan.

Richardson, J. E., M. F. Fay, Q. C. B. Cronk, and M. W. Chase. 2000a. A revision of the tribal classification of Rhamnaceae. *Kew Bulletin* 55: 311–340.

Richardson, J. E., M. F. Fay, Q. C. B. Cronk, D. Bowman, and M. W. Chase. 2000b. A phylogenetic analysis of Rhamnaceae using *rbc*L and *trn*L-F plastid DNA sequences. *American Journal of Botany* 87: 1309–1324.

Roderick, W. 1991. My life among the clones. *Four Seasons* 9(1): 18–23.

Roof, J. B. 1973. An odd *Ceanothus* in Humboldt County, California. *Four Seasons* 4(3): 18–22.

Rowntree, L. 1939. *Flowering Shrubs of California.* Stanford: Stanford University Press.

Rye, B. L. 1996. A synopsis of the genera *Pomaderris, Siegfriedia, Spyridium* and *Trymalium* (Rhamnaceae) in Western Australia. *Nuytsia* 11: 109–131.

Schlesinger, W. H., J. T. Gray, D. S. Gill, and B. E. Mahall. 1982. *Ceanothus megacarpus* chaparral: A synthesis of ecosystem processes during development and annual growth. *Botanical Review* 48: 71–117.

Schmidt, C. L. 1993. *Ceanothus.* In J. Hickman, editor, *The Jepson Manual: Higher Plants of California,* pp. 932–938. Berkeley: University of California Press.

Schmidt, M. G. 1980. *Growing California Native Plants.* Berkeley: University of California Press.

Schwintzer, C. R., and Tjepkema, J. D., editors. 1990. *The Biology of Frankia and Actinorhizal Plants.* San Diego: Academic Press.

Smith, M. N. 1979. *Ceanothus* of California: A gardener's guide. *Pacific Horticulture* 40(2): 37–45, 40(3): 36–43.

Smith, M. N. 1999. *A Guide to Ornamental Plants for Coastal California.* Watsonville: Suncrest Nurseries.

Standley, P. C. 1923. Trees and shrubs of Mexico. *Contributions from the U.S. National Herbarium* 23: 1–848.

Stearn, W. T. 1992. *Botanical Latin,* ed. 4. Newton Abbot, England: David & Charles, and Portland, Oregon: Timber Press.

Steyermark, J. A. 1963. *Flora of Missouri.* Ames: Iowa State University Press.

Suessenguth, K. 1953. Rhamnaceae. In A. Engler and K. Prantl, editors, *Die Natürlichen Pflanzenfamilien,* ed. 2, vol. 20d, pp. 7–173. Berlin: Duncker und Humblot.

Thomas, J. H. 1961. *Flora of the Santa Cruz Mountains of California.* Stanford: Stanford University Press.

Thorne, R. F. 1967. A flora of Santa Catalina Island, California. *Aliso* 6: 1–77.

Torrey, J., and A. Gray. 1838. *A Flora of North America,* vol. 1(2), pp. 185–360. New York: Wiley & Putnam.

Trelease, W. 1888. Synoptical list of North American species of *Ceanothus. Proceedings of the California Academy of Sciences,* series 2, 1: 106–118.

Trelease, W. 1897. *Ceanothus.* In A. Gray, *Synoptical Flora of North America,* vol. 1(1), pp. 409–417. New York: Ivison, Blakeman, Taylor, and Company.

Van Rensselaer, M. 1942. *Ceanothus* for gardens, parks, and roadsides. In M. Van Rensselaer and H. E. McMinn, *Ceanothus,* part 1, pp. xvi–xvii, 1–128. Santa Barbara, California: Santa Barbara Botanic Garden.

Van Rensselaer, M. 1952. *Ceanothus* 'Julia Phelps'. *Plant Cultural Data Sheets.* San Martin, California: Saratoga Horticultural Research Foundation.

Villareal Quintanilla, J. 2001. Flora de Coahuila. *Listados Florísticos de México* 23. México: Instituto de Biología, Universidad Nacional Autónoma de México.

Weberbauer, A. 1895. Rhamnaceae. In A. Engler and K. Prantl, editors, *Die Natürlichen Pflanzenfamilien,* part 3, vol. 5, pp. 393–427. Leipzig: W. Engelmann.

Welsh, S. L. 1998. John Charles Frémont, botanical explorer. *Monographs in Systematic Botany from the Missouri Botanical Garden* 66: 1–450. Saint Louis.

Index